Number 3 Manual
(combined with)
Motorcycle & Scooter Manual
1950 - 1969

dealing with the servicing

and maintenance of

MAGNETOS
IGNITION GENERATORS
ALTERNATORS–SWITCHES

THE **WIPAC** GROUP

BUCKINGHAM   BUCKS   ENGLAND

INTRODUCTION

Welcome to the world of digital publishing ~ the book you now hold in your hand was printed using the latest state of the art digital technology. The advent of print-on-demand has forever changed the publishing process, never has information been so accessible and it is our hope that this book serves your informational needs for years to come. If this is your first exposure to digital publishing, we hope that you are pleased with the results. Many more titles of interest to the classic automobile and motorcycle enthusiast, collector and restorer are available via our website at www.VelocePress.com. We hope that you find this title as interesting as we do.

NOTE FROM THE PUBLISHER

The information presented is true and complete to the best of our knowledge. All recommendations are made without any guarantees on the part of the author or the publisher, who also disclaim all liability incurred with the use of this information.

TRADEMARKS

We recognize that some words, model names and designations, for example, mentioned herein are the property of the trademark holder. We use them for identification purposes only. This is not an official publication.

INFORMATION ON THE USE OF THIS PUBLICATION

This manual is an invaluable resource for those interested in performing their own maintenance. However, in today's information age we are constantly subject to changes in common practice, new technology, availability of improved materials and increased awareness of chemical toxicity. As such, it is advised that the user consult with an experienced professional prior to undertaking any procedure described herein. While every care has been taken to ensure correctness of information, it is obviously not possible to guarantee complete freedom from errors or omissions or to accept liability arising from such errors or omissions. Therefore, any individual that uses the information contained within, or elects to perform or participate in do-it-yourself repairs or modifications acknowledges that there is a risk factor involved and that the publisher or its associates cannot be held responsible for personal injury or property damage resulting from the use of the information or the outcome of such procedures.

WARNING!

One final word of advice, this publication is intended to be used as a reference guide, and when in doubt the reader should consult with a qualified technician.

CONTENTS

SPARE PARTS PRICE LIST   PAGE

Published September 1969   5-12

SERVICE INSTRUCTIONS

Magneto	Series 90	14-15
Ignition Generator	Series 55 MK8	16-17
Ignition Generator	Series 72 MK1	18-19
Ignition Generator	Series 73 MK1	20-21

SPECIFICATIONS - APPLICATION LIST
SERVICE INSTRUCTIONS & SPARE PARTS LIST

Alternators	Series 114 – 124 – 167 & 125	22-25
Testing Instructions	Series 114 MK1	26-27
Ignition Generators	Series 55 & 73	28-33

SERVICE INSTRUCTIONS WITH ILLUSTRATED PARTS LIST

Ignition Generator	IG 1555	34-35
Ignition Generator	IG 1586	36-37
Ignition Generator	IG 1649	38-39
Ignition Generator	IG 1688	40-41
Ignition Generator	IG 1741	42-43

LIGHTING EQUIPMENT (For A.J.S. see Matchless)

In alphabetic order by manufacturer/model   44-79

WIRING DIAGRAMS

Index to wiring diagrams   80

*SERVICE BULLETINS   158-180

*TECHNICAL DATA SHEETS   181-194

SERVICE TOOLS   195

*IMPORTANT: As the Service Bulletins and Technical Data Sheets were issued at different times from the balance of the manual the reader is encouraged to check both of those sections for additional information pertaining to various model updates and modifications.

Motor Cycles and Scooters

Abbreviated

Spare Parts Price List

**ALTERNATOR UNITS · IGNITION GENERATORS
HEADLAMPS · REAR LAMPS and RECTIFIERS**

ASP2 9/69/1/8

Manufacturers	Model and Year	Lighting Output	Flywheel Magneto and Alternator Unit	Price	Stator Plate Unit	Price	Flywheel Rotor Unit	Price	Breaker Point Set	Price	Condenser Set	Price	Ignition Coil Set	Price
A.J.S.	MODEL 14, 250 c.c. May 58 to Sept. 59	DC 6 volt	G1521	217/6	*S0602	115/6	*S0221	120/-	S2312	13/-	S0226	11/-	S0793	37/6
	Oct. 59 to Dec. 64	DC 6 volt	G1521	217/6	*S0602	115/6	*S0221	120/-	S2312	13/-	S0226	11/-	S0793	37/6
	MODEL 14CSR, 250 c.c. SAPPHIRE NINETY March 65	DC 6 volt	G1521	217/6	*S0602	115/6	*S0221	120/-	S2312	13/-	S0226	11/-	S0793	37/6
	MODEL 8, 350 c.c. Sept. 59 to Dec. 64	DC 6 volt	G1521	217/6	*S0602	115/6	*S0221	120/-	S2312	13/-	S0226	11/-	S0793	37/6
	MODEL 14S, 250 c.c. SPORTS Oct. 60 to Dec. 62	DC 6 volt	G1521	217/6	*S0602	115/6	*S0221	120/-	S2312	13/-	S0226	11/-	S0793	37/6
ARIEL	PIXIE 50 c.c. A.C. LIGHTING March 63 to Aug. 65	6 volt 21 watt	IG1688	212/9	S3404	100/-	S3382	120/-	S3440	12/6	S2847	10/6	S2846	30/-
B.S.A.	BANTAM D1, 125 c.c. A.C. LIGHTING Nov. 48 to Oct. 63	6 volt 30 watt	*IG1452	272/6	*S1226	150/-	*S1239	150/-	S1233	11/3	S1231	12/6	S0206	35/-
	BANTAM D1 and BANTAM MAJOR D3 A.C. LIGHTING (Fitted with Stop Light Set) Feb. 58 to Sept. 59	6 volt 30 watts	*IG1452	272/6	*S1226	150/-	*S1239	150/-	S1233	11/3	S1231	12/6	S0206	35/-
	BANTAM-MAJOR D3, 150 c.c. A.C. LIGHTING Oct. 53 to Sept. 58	6 volt 30 watt	*IG1452	272/6	*S1226	150/-	*S1239	150/-	S1233	11/3	S1231	12/6	S0206	35/-
	BANTAM D1, 125 c.c. D.C. LIGHTING June 50 to Aug. 55	DC 6 volt	*IG1450	272/6	*S1225	150/-	*S1239	150/-	S1233	11/3	S1231	12/6	S0206	35/-
	From Sept. 55	DC 6 volt	*IG1450	272/6	*S1225	150/-	*S1239	150/-	S1233	11/3	S1231	12/6	S0206	35/-
	BANTAM-MAJOR D3, 150 c.c. D.C. LIGHTING Oct. 53 to Aug. 54	D.C. 6 volt	*IG1450	272/6	*S1225	150/-	*S1239	150/-	S1233	11/3	S1231	12/6	S0206	35/-
	Sept. 54 to Aug. 55	D.C. 6 volt	*IG1450	272/6	*S1225	150/-	*S1239	150/-	S1233	11/3	S1231	12/6	S0206	35/-
	Sept. 55 to Sept. 58	D.C. 6 volt	*IG1450	272/6	*S1225	150/-	*S1239	150/-	S1233	11/3	S1231	12/6	S0206	35/-
	BANTAM SUPER D5, 175 c.c. A.C. LIGHTING Sept. 57 to Sept. 58	6 volt 30 watt	*IG1452	272/6	*S1226	150/-	*S1239	150/-	S1233	11/3	S1231	12/6	S0206	35/-
	BANTAM SUPER D5, 175 c.c. D.C. LIGHTING Sept. 57 to Sept. 58	DC 6 volt	*IG1450	272/6	*S1225	150/-	*S1239	150/-	S1233	11/3	S1231	12/6	S0206	35/-
	BANTAM SUPER D7, 175 c.c. A.C./D.C. LIGHTING Oct. 58 to Sept. 63	AC/DC	*IG1552	272/6	*S0824	200/-	*S1239	150/-	S1233	11/3	S1231	12/6	S0206	35/-
	BANTAM SUPER D7, 175 c.c. A.C. LIGHTING Oct. 58 to June 66	6 volt 30 watt	*IG1452	272/6	*S1226	150/-	*S1239	150/-	S1233	11/3	S1231	12/6	S0206	35/-
	BANTAM D7, A.C. LIGHTING (TRICKLE CHARGE WITH COIL IGNITION) Oct. 63 to June 66	A.C./D.C.	*IG1704	272/6	*S3540	135/-	*S1239	150/-	S1233	11/3	S1231	12/6	S0793	37/6
	D10 AND D14 SILVER BANTAM AND D10 AND D14 SUPREME FULL D.C. COIL IGNITION July 66 to Dec. 68	DC 6 volt	G1767	217/6	*S4186	136/6	S4063	120/-	S0584	13/-	S2767	12/6	S0769	37/6
	D10 AND D14 SPORTS Sept. 66 to Dec. 68 D10 AND D14 BUSHMAN Jan. 67 to Dec. 68 FULL D.C. LIGHTS AND IGNITION	DC 6 volt	G1767	217/6	*S4186	136/6	S4063	120/-	S0584	13/-	S2767	12/6	S0769	37/6
	D10 AND D14 BUSHMAN PASTORAL E.T. IGNITION A.C. LIGHTING April 67 to Dec. 68	6 volt 30 watt	G1778	217/6	*S4183	136/6	S4063	120/-	S0584	13/-	S2767	12/6		
	D14 BUSHMAN PASTORAL E.T. IGNITION, A.C. LIGHTING ENGINE/FRAME No. D14C, 5543 Jan. 68 to Dec. 68	6 volt 30 watt	G1792	217/6	*S4221	140/-	S4063	120/-	S0584	13/-	S2767	12/6		
	BUSHMAN, 175 c.c. E.T. IGNITION, A.C. LIGHTING From 1969.	6 volt 30 watt	G1792	217/6	*S4221	140/-	S4063	120/-	S0584	13/-	S2767	12/6		
	BANTAM 175 c.c. FULL D.C. From 1969	DC 6 volt	G1767	217/6	*S4186	136/6	S4063	120/-	S0584	13/-	S2767	12/6	S0769	37/6

ASPL. 9/69/2/8 *THESE UNITS AND SETS ARE AVAILABLE UNDER THE WIPAC B.4. EXCHANGE SERVICE. SEE SEPARATE LIST.

L.T. Coils Set		Headlamp Unit (less Harness)		Harness (Main)		Reflector and Lens Set		Rim		Switch (Ignition)		Switch (Lights)		Main Bulb Holder		Rear Lamp		Rectifier		Flywheel Extractor	
	Price		Price		Price		Price		Price		Price		Price		Price		Price		Price		Price
		S0777	130/-	S2616	75/-	S0507	15/6	S0066	13/6	S0782	16/-	S0781	16/-	S0768	5/-	S3704	19/6	S2642	55/-		
		S2615	135/-	S2616	75/-	S2612	25/-	S2617	16/6	S0782	16/-	S0781	16/-	S0768	5/-	S3704	19/6	S2642	55/-		
		S2615	135/-	S2616	75/-	S2612	25/-	S2617	16/6	S0782	16/-	S0781	16/-	S0768	5/-	S3704	19/6	S2642	55/-		
		S2615	135/-	S2616	75/-	S2612	25/-	S2617	16/6	S0782	16/-	S0781	16/-	S0768	5/-	S3704	19/6	S2642	55/-		
		S2615	135/-	S2616	75/-	S2612	25/-	S2617	16/6	S0782	16/-	S0781	16/-	S0768	5/-	S3704	19/6	S2642	55/-		
S2844	20/-	S3491	59/6	S3494	25/-	S3492	22/6					S0837	16/-	S0768	5/-	S0213	13/6			S0282	8/-
S1235	29/6			S2388	31/-	S0886	18/3	S0889	14/6			S0781	16/-	S2345	7/6	S3737	19/6			S1256	10/-
S1235	29/6			S2388	31/-	S0886	18/3	S0889	14/6			S0781	16/-	S2345	7/6	S3611	19/6			S1256	10/-
S1235	29/6			S2388	31/-	S0886	18/3	S0889	14/6			S0781	16/-	S2345	7/6	S3737	19/6			S1256	10/-
S1234	40/-	S0900	85/-	S0573	32/6	S0507	15/6	S0889	14/6			S0781	16/-	S0768	5/-	S3611	19/6	S2642	55/-	S1256	10/-
S1234	40/-	S0900	85/-	S2534	45/-	S0507	15/6	S0889	14/6			S0781	16/-	S0768	5/-	S3611	19/6	S2642	55/-	S1256	10/-
S1234	40/-	S0900	85/-	S0573	32/6	S0507	15/6	S0889	14/6			S0781	16/-	S0768	5/-	S0213	13/6	S2642	55/-	S1256	10/-
S1234	40/-	S0900	85/-	S0573	32/6	S0507	15/6	S0889	14/6			S0781	16/-	S0768	5/-	S3611	19/6	S2642	55/-	S1256	10/-
S1234	40/-	S0900	85/-	S2363	47/6	S0507	15/6	S0889	14/6			S0781	16/-	S0768	5/-	S3611	19/6	S2642	55/-	S1256	10/-
S1235	29/6			S2388	31/-	S0886	18/3	S0889	14/6			S0781	16/-	S2345	7/6	S3737	19/6			S1256	10/6
S1234	40/-	S0900	85/-	S2363	47/6	S0507	15/6	S0889	14/6			S0781	16/-	S0768	5/-	S3611	19/6	S2642	55/-	S1256	10/-
S0826	40/-	S0891	52/6	S3347	37/6	S0507	15/6	S0873	14/-			S0781	16/-	S0768	5/-	S3611	19/6	S1044	26/-	S1256	10/-
S1235	29/6	S0856	55/-	S3348	37/6	S0507	15/6	S0873	14/6			S0781	16/-	S0768	5/-	S3737	19/6			S1256	10/-
S1235	29/6	S0891	52/6	S3538	55/-	S0507	15/6	S0873	14/-	S0782	16/-	S0781	16/-	S0768	5/-	S3611	19/6	S1044	26/-	S1256	10/-
		S4067	55/-	S4069	50/-	S0507	15/6	S0873	14/-	S0782	16/-	S0781	16/-	S0768	5/-	S3611	19/6	S2642	55/-		
		S4187	140/-	S4069	50/-	S4087	22/-	S0066	13/6	S0782	16/-	S0781	16/-	S0768	5/-			S2642	55/-		
		S4178	134/6	S4179	55/-	S0875	15/6	S0066	13/6			S0781	16/-	S0768	5/-	S3611	19/6				
		S4187	140/-	S4179	55/-	S0875	15/6	S0066	13/6			S0781	16/-	S0768	5/-	S3611	19/6				
		S4178	134/6	S4220	52/6	S0875	15/6	S0066	13/6			S0781	16/-	S0768	5/-	S3611	19/6				
		S4288	110/-	S4069	50/-	S4087	22/-	S0066	13/6	S0782	16/-	S0781	16/-	S0768	5/-	S3611	19/6	S2642	55/-		

ASPL. 9/69/3/8

Manufacturers	Model and Year	Lighting Output	Flywheel Magneto and Alternator Unit	Price	Stator Plate Unit	Price	Flywheel Rotor Unit	Price	Breaker Point Set	Price	Condenser Set	Price	Ignition Coil Set	Price
B.S.A. (Contd.)	BEAGLE 75 c.c. LIGHTWEIGHT MOTOR CYCLE, A.C. LIGHTING March 63 to Aug. 65	6 volt 21 watt	IG1688	212/9	S3404	100/-	S3382	120/-	S3440	12/6	S2847	10/6	S2846	30/-
	BEAGLE 75 c.c. LIGHTWEIGHT MOTOR CYCLE, A.C. LIGHTING FITTED WITH STOP LAMP March 63 to Aug. 65	6 volt 21 watt	IG1715	212/9	S3643	100/-	S3382	120/-	S3440	12/6	S2847	10/6	S2846	30/-
	SUNBEAM SCOOTER, 175 c.c. A.C./D.C. LIGHTING Oct. 58 to Sept. 63	A.C./D.C.	IG1555	253/-	S1045	175/-	S1071	160/-	S0577	12/6	S1051	10/9	S1046	30/-
	SUNBEAM SCOOTER, 175 c.c. D.C. COIL IGNITION Oct. 63 to Aug. 65	DC 6 volt	IG1676	333/6	S3548	140/-	S3547	117/6	S0577	12/6	S3550	11/6	S0769	37/6
COTTON	CONTANZA (TWIN) Dec. 55	DC 6 volt	IG1358	317/6	S0363	190/-	S1265	200/-	S1233	11/3	S0364	17/6	S0365	55/-
EXCELSIOR	TALISMAN, 250 c.c. TWIN Oct. 52 to Dec. 54	DC 6 volt	IG1358	317/6	S0363	190/-	S1265	200/-	S1233	11/3	S0364	17/6	S0365	55/-
FRANCIS-BARNETT	CRUISER 80, 250 c.c. Aug. 56 to April 63	DC 6 volt	G1585	217/6	S0217	115/6	S0221	120/-	S2312	13/-	S0226	11/-	S0793	37/6
	CRUISER 84, 250 c.c. May 59 to Sept. 62	DC 6 volt	G1585	217/6	S0127	115/6	S0221	120/-	S2312	13/-	S0226	11/-	S0793	37/6
	FALCON 87, 200 c.c. Aug. 59	DC 6 volt	G1585	217/6	S0217	115/6	S0221	120/-	S2312	13/-	S0226	11/-	S0793	37/6
	PLOVER 86, 150 c.c. A.C. LIGHTING April 59 to Sept. 59	6 volt 30 watt	IG1586	253/-	S0152	123/6	S1032	200/-	S1178	13/6	S0051	10/9	S1046	30/-
	Oct. 59 to Sept. 60	6 volt 30 watt	IG1586	253/-	S1052	123/6	S1032	200/-	S1178	13/6	S0051	10/9	S1046	30/-
	PLOVER 86, 150 c.c. A.C./D.C. (TRICKLE CHARGE) April 59 to Sept. 60	A.C./D.C.	IG1586	253/-	S1052	123/6	S1032	200/-	S1178	13/6	S0051	10/9	S1046	30/-
	FULMAR 88, 150 c.c. A.C. LIGHTING Oct. 61 to Aug. 65	6 volt 30 watt	IG1586	253/-	S1052	123/6	S1032	200/-	S1178	13/6	S0051	10/9	S1046	30/-
	FULMAR 88, 150 c.c. A.C./D.C. (TRICKLE CHARGE) Oct. 61 to Aug. 65	A.C./D.C.	IG1586	253/-	S1052	123/6	S1032	200/-	S1178	13/6	S0051	10/9	S1046	30/-
	FULMAR 90 SPORTS, 150 c.c. A.C. LIGHTING Oct. 62 to Aug. 65	6 volt 30 watt	IG1586	253/-	S1052	123/6	S1032	200/-	S1178	13/6	S0051	10/9	S1046	30/-
	FULMAR 90 SPORTS, 150 c.c. (A.C./D.C. TRICKLE CHARGE) Oct. 62 to Aug. 65	A.C./D.C.	IG1586	253/-	S1052	123/6	S1032	200/-	S1178	13/6	S0051	10/9	S1046	30/-
	MODEL 96, 150 c.c. A.C. LIGHTING Jan. 65	6 volt 30 watt	IG1586	253/-	S1052	123/6	S1032	200/-	S1178	13/6	S0051	10/9	S1046	30/-
GREEVES	FLEETWING Nov. 54	DC 6 volt	IG1358	317/6	S0363	190/-	S1265	200/-	S1233	11/3	S0364	17/6	S0365	55/-
	FLEETMASTER Nov. 54	DC 6 volt	IG1358	317/6	S0363	190/-	S1265	200/-	S1233	11/3	S0364	17/6	S0365	55/-
JAMES	CAPTAIN, 200 c.c. MODEL, L20 Aug. 59 to Sept. 62	DC 6 volt	G1585	217/6	S0217	115/6	S0221	120/-	S2312	13/-	S0226	11/-	S0793	37/6
	Oct. 62	DC 6 volt	G1585	217/6	S0217	115/6	S0221	120/-	S2312	13/-	S0226	11/-	S0793	37/6
	COMMODORE, 250 c.c. MODEL, L. 25 Aug. 55 to July 63	DC 6 volt	G1585	217/6	S0217	115/6	S0221	120/-	S2312	13/-	S0226	11/-	S0793	37/6
	FLYING CADET, 150 c.c. MODEL, L.15, A.C. LIGHTING April 59 to Sept. 59	6 volt 30 watt	IG1586	253/-	S1052	123/6	S1032	200/-	S1178	13/6	S0051	10/9	S1046	30/-
	Oct. 59 to Sept. 63	6 volt 30 watt	IG1586	253/-	S1052	123/6	S1032	200/-	S1178	13/6	S0051	10/9	S1046	30/-
	FLYING CADET, 150 c.c. MODEL L.15, A.C./D.C. LIGHTING April 59 to Sept. 63	A.C./D.C.	IG1586	253/-	S1052	123/6	S1032	200/-	S1178	13/6	S0051	10/9	S1046	30/-

* THESE UNITS ARE AVAILABLE UNDER THE WIPAC B4 EXCHANGE SERVICE. SEE SEPARATE LIST.

L.T. Coils Set	Price	Headlamp Unit (less Harness)	Price	Harness (Main)	Price	Reflector and Lens Set	Price	Rim	Price	Switch (Ignition)	Price	Switch (Lights)	Price	Main Bulb Holder	Price	Rear Lamp	Price	Rectifier	Price	Flywheel Extractor	Price
S2844	20/-	S3484	70/-	S3485	40/-	S3489	20/-	S0349	13/6	S3490	6/-	S0907	16/-			S0213	13/6			S0282	8/-
S3644	20/-	S3636	99/9	S3638	30/-	S3640	18/-	S0349	13/6	S3490	6/-	S0907	16/-							S0282	8/-
S1048	45/-	S0867	45/-	S0869	50/6	S0507	15/6	S0889	14/6			S0781	16/-	S0768	5/-	S3611	19/6	S1044	26/-		
Use *S3548		S0867	45/-	S3544	67/6	S0507	15/6	S0889	14/6	S0782	16/-	S0781	16/-	S0768	5/-	S3611	19/6	S1044	26/-		
S0367	40/-	S0900	85/-	S2363	47/6	S0507	15/6	S0889	14/6			S0781	16/-	S0768	5/-	S3611	19/6	S2642	55/-	S1256	10/-
S0367	40/-																	S2642	55/-	S1256	10/-
		S0902	115/-	S0903	70/-	S0507	15/6	S0066	13/6	S0782	16/-	S0781	16/-	S0768	5/-			S2642	55/-		
		S0902	115/-	S0903	70/-	S0507	15/6	S0066	13/6	S0782	16/-	S0781	16/-	S0768	5/-			S2642	55/-		
		S0902	115/-	S1081	72/6	S0507	15/6	S0066	13/6	S0782	16/-	S0781	16/-	S0768	5/-			S2642	55/-		
S1053	46/-	S1057	120/-	S0924	33/3	S0507	15/6	S0066	13/6			S0781	16/-	S0768	5/-	S3704	19/6				
S1053	46/-	S1127	120/-	S0924	33/3	S0507	15/6	S0066	13/6			S0781	16/-	S0768	5/-	S3704	19/6				
S1053	46/-	S1057	120/-	S1058	30/-	S0507	15/6	S0066	13/6			S0781	16/-	S0768	5/-	S3704	19/6	S1044	26/-		
S1053	46/-	S1127	120/-	S2870	52/6	S0507	15/6	S0066	13/6			S0781	16/-	S0768	5/-	S3704	19/6				
S1053	46/-	S1057	120/-	S2871	57/6	S0507	15/6	S0066	13/6			S0781	16/-	S0768	5/-	S3704	19/6	S2856	17/6		
S1053	46/-	S1127	120/-	S2870	52/6	S0507	15/6	S0066	13/6			S0781	16/-	S0768	5/-	S3704	19/6				
S1053	46/-	S1057	120/-	S2871	57/6	S0507	15/6	S0066	13/6			S0781	16/-	S0768	5/-	S3704	19/6	S2856	17/6		
S1053	46/-	S1127	120/-	S2870	52/6	S0507	15/6	S0066	13/6			S0781	16/-	S0768	5/-	S3704	19/6				
S0367	40/-																	S2642	55/-	S1256	10/-
S0367	40/-																	S2642	55/-	S1256	10/-
		S0777	130/-	S3413	75/-	S0507	15/6	S0066	13/6	S0782	16/-	S0781	16/-	S0768	5/-	S3704	19/6	S2642	55/-		
		S3412	118/-	S3413	75/-	S0507	15/6	S0066	13/6	S0782	16/-	S0781	16/-	S0768	5/-	S3704	19/6	S2642	55/-		
		S0777	130/-	S0901	76/3	S0507	15/6	S0066	13/6	S0782	16/-	S0781	16/-	S0768	5/-	S3704	19/6	S2642	55/-		
S1053	46/-	S1057	120/-	S0924	33/3	S0507	15/6	S0066	13/6			S0781	16/-	S0768	5/-	S3704	19/6				
S1053	46/-	S1127	120/-	S0924	33/3	S0507	15/6	S0066	13/6			S0781	16/-	S0768	5/-	S3704	19/6				
S1053	46/-	S1057	120/-	S1058	30/-	S0507	15/6	S0066	13/6			S0781	16/-	S0768	5/-	S3704	19/6	S1044	26/-		

ASPL. 9/69/5/8

Manufacturers	Model and Year	Lighting Output	Flywheel Magneto and Alternator Unit	Price	Stator Plate Unit	Price	Flywheel Rotor Unit	Price	Breaker Point Set	Price	Condenser Set	Price	Ignition Coil Set	Price
JAMES (CONT'D.)	CADET M15, 150 c.c. A.C. LIGHTING Oct. 61 to Sept. 62	6 volt 30 watt	*IG1586	253/-	*S1052	123/6	*S1032	200/-	S1178	13/6	S0051	10/9	S1046	30/-
	Oct. 62 to Dec. 64	6 volt 30 watt	*IG1586	253/-	*S1052	123/6	*S1032	200/-	S1178	13/6	S0051	10/9	S1046	30/-
	CADET M15, 150 c.c. A.C./D.C. LIGHTING Oct. 62 to Dec. 64	A.C./D.C.	*IG1586	253/-	*S1052	123/6	*S1032	200/-	S1178	13/6	S0051	10/9	S1046	30/-
	MODEL M16, 150 c.c. A.C. LIGHTING Jan. 65	6 volt 30 watt	*IG1586	253/-	*S1052	123/6	*S1032	200/-	S1178	13/6	S0051	10/9	S1046	30/-
	MODEL M16, 150 c.c. A.C./D.C. LIGHTING Jan. 65	A.C./D.C.	*IG1586	253/-	*S1052	123/6	*S1032	200/-	S1178	13/6	S0051	10/9	S1046	30/-
MATCHLESS	MODEL G2, 250 c.c. July 58 to Sept. 59	DC 6 volt	G1521	217/6	*S0602	115/6	*S0221	120/-	S2312	13/-	S0226	11/-	S0793	37/6
	MODEL G2, 250 c.c. AND G5, 350 c.c. Oct. 59 to Dec. 64	DC 6 volt	G1521	217/6	*S0602	115/6	*S0221	120/-	S2312	13/-	S0226	11/-	S0793	37/6
	MODEL G2 CSR, 250 c.c. March 65	DC 6 volt	G1521	217/6	*S0602	115/6	*S0221	120/-	S2312	13/-	S0226	11/-	S0793	37/6
NORMAN	MODEL 250 c.c. T.S. TWIN Nov. 54	DC 6 volt	IG1358	317/6	S0363	190/-	S1265	200/-	S1233	11/3	S0364	17/6	S0365	55/-
NORTON	JUBILEE 250 c.c. Nov. 58 to Aug. 60	DC 6 volt	G1450	217/6	*S0733	115/6	S0734	120/-	S0584	13/-	S0761	10/9	S0793	37/6
	Sept. 60 to Sept. 62	DC 6 volt	G1685	217/6	*S3536	115/6	S0734	120/-	S0584	13/-	S2767	12/6	S0793	37/6
	Oct. 62	DC 6 volt	G1685	217/6	*S3536	115/6	S0734	120/-	S0584	13/-	S2767	12/6	S0793	37/6
	NAVIGATOR 350 c.c. Sept. 60 to Sept. 62	DC 6 volt	G1685	217/6	*S3536	115/6	S0734	120/-	S0584	13/-	S2767	12/6	S0793	37/6
	Oct. 62 to Sept. 64	DC 6 volt	G1685	217/6	*S3536	115/6	S0734	120/-	S0584	13/-	S2767	12/6	S0793	37/6
	Oct. 64	DC 6 volt	G1685	217/6	*S3536	115/6	S0734	120/-	S0584	13/-	S2767	12/6	S0793	37/6
	ELECTRA 400 c.c. TWIN 12v. SELF STARTER Feb. 63 to Sept. 64	DC 12 volt	G1697	217/6	*S3419	115/6	S0734	120/-	S0584	13/-	S2767	12/6	S0793	37/6
	ELECTRA 400 AND E.S.B. 400 c.c. 12v. SELF STARTER Oct. 64	DC 12 volt	G1697	217/6	*S3419	115/6	S0734	120/-	S0584	13/-	S2767	12/6	S0793	37/6
RALEIGH	RALEIGH MOPED MODELS RM8 AND RM9 (STATE MODEL ON ORDER) May 64													
TANDON	SUPREME AND VISCOUNT Nov. 54	DC 6 volt	IG1358	317/6	S0363	190/-	S1265	200/-	S1233	11/3	S0364	17/6	S0365	55/-
TRIUMPH	TIGRESS SCOOTER T.S.1. 175 c.c. A.C./D.C. LIGHTING Oct. 58 to Sept. 63	A.C./D.C.	IG1555	253/-	S1045	175/-	S1071	160/-	S0577	12/6	S1051	12/6	S1046	30/-
	TIGRESS SCOOTER 175 c.c. D.C. COIL IGNITION Oct. 63 to Aug. 65	DC 6 volt	*IG1676	333/6	*S3548	140/-	*S3547	117/-	S0577	12/6	S3550	11/6	S0769	37/6
	TINA 100 c.c. SCOOTER A.C. LIGHTING March 62	6 volt 21.6 watt	*IG1649	212/9	*S3663	100/-	*S2729	130/-	S3440	12/6	S2847	10/6	S2846	30/-
	MODEL T10 AUTOMATIC 100 c.c. SCOOTER A.C. LIGHTING April 65	6 volt 21.6 watt	*IG1741	258/9	*S3851	100/-	*S2729	130/-	S3853	10/6	S2847	10/6		
	SUPER CUB T20 FULL D.C. COIL IGNITION Jan. 67	DC 6 volt	G1731	217/6	*S4186	136/6	S0221	120/-					S0769	37/6

ASPL 9/69/6/8   * THESE UNITS AND SETS ARE AVAILABLE UNDER THE WIPAC B4 EXCHANGE SERVICE. SEE SEPARATE LIST.

L.T. Coils Set	Price	Headlamp Unit (less Harness)	Price	Harness (Main)	Price	Reflector and Lens Set	Price	Rim	Price	Switch (Ignition)	Price	Switch (Lights)	Price	Main Bulb Holder	Price	Rear Lamp	Price	Rectifier	Price	Flywheel Extractor	Price
S1053	46/-	S1057	120/-	S2901	33/9	S0507	15/6	S0066	13/6			S0781	16/-	S0768	5/-	S3704	19/6				
S1053	46/-	S1127	120/-	S2870	52/6	S0507	15/6	S0066	13/6			S0781	16/-	S0768	5/-	S3704	19/6				
S1053	46/-	S1057	120/-	S2871	57/6	S0507	15/6	S0066	13/6			S0781	16/-	S0768	5/-	S3704	19/6	S1044	26/-		
S1053	46/-	S1127	120/-	S2870	52/6	S0507	15/6	S0066	13/6			S0781	16/-	S0768	5/-	S3704	19/6				
S1053	46/-	S1057	120/-	S2871	57/6	S0507	15/6	S0066	13/6			S0781	16/-	S0768	5/-	S3704	19/6	S1044	26/-		
		S0777	130/-	S2616	75/-	S0507	15/6	S0066	16/-	S0782	16/-	S0781	16/-	S0768	5/-	S3704	19/6	S2642	55/-		
		S2615	135/-	S2616	75/-	S2612	25/-	S2617	16/6	S0782	16/-	S0781	16/-	S0768	5/-	S3704	19/6	S2642	55/-		
		S2615	135/-	S2616	75/-	S2612	25/-	S2617	16/6	S0782	16/-	S0781	16/-	S0768	5/-	S3704	19/6	S2642	55/-		
S0367	40/-																	S2642	55/-	S1256	10/-
		S1084	115/-	S2610	70/-	S0507	15/6	S0529	13/6	S0782	16/-	S0781	16/-	S0768	5/-			S2642	55/-		
		S2615	135/-	S2610	70/-	S2612	25/-	S2617	16/6	S0782	16/-	S0781	16/-	S0768	5/-			S2642	55/-		
		S3334	140/-	S2610	70/-	S2612	25/-	S2617	16/6	S3297	22/6	S0781	16/-	S0768	5/-			S2642	55/-		
		S2615	135/-	S2610	70/-	S2612	25/-	S2617	16/6	S0782	16/-	S0781	16/-	S0768	5/-			S2642	55/-		
		S3334	140/-	S2610	70/-	S2612	25/-	S2617	16/6	S3297	22/6	S0781	16/-	S0768	5/-			S2642	55/-		
		S3819	132/6	S2610	70/-	S2612	25/-	S2617	16/6	S3297	22/6	S0781	16/-	S0768	5/-			S2642	55/-		
		S3428	135/-	S3429	75/-	S2612	25/-	S2617	16/6	S3297	22/6	S0781	16/-	S0768	5/-			S2642	55/-		
		S3799	136/6	S3429	75/-	S2612	25/-	S2617	16/6	S3297	22/6	S0781	16/-	S0768	5/-			S2642	55/-		
		† S3688	58/-	S3691	33/6	S3690	15/-					S3692	17/6	Part of Harness		S3835	11/-				
S0367	40/-																	S2642	55/-	S1256	10/-
S1048	45/-	S0867	45/-	S0869	50/6	S0507	15/6	S0889	14/6			S0781	16/-	S0768	5/-	S3611	19/6	S1044	26/-		
Use *S3548		S0867	45/-	S3544	67/6	S0507	15/6	S0889	14/6			S0781	16/-	S0768	5/-	S3611	19/6	S1044	26/-		
S2844	20/-	S2906	45/-	S2878	40/-	S2909	20/-	S0349	13/6			S0781	16/-			S3102	13/6				
S4007	20/-	S2906	45/-	S3855	45/-	S2909	20/-	S0349	13/6			S0781	16/-			S3952	14/6				
		S4187	140/-	S4188	70/-	S4087	22/-	S0066	13/6	S0782	16/-	S0781	16/-	S0768	5/-	S3611	19/6				

† INCLUDES HARNESS

The home of the Wipac Group

Manufacturers of the World's finest vehicle accessories

Magnetos * Alternators * Battery Chargers

* Filters * * Switches *

Ignition Coils * Mobilite * Lamps

THE WIPAC GROUP OF COMPANIES LIMITED
Buckingham   **England**
Telephone: Buckingham 3031   Telegrams: Wicomagsco Buckingham

NOTES

WIPAC SERIES Ninety MAGNETO

COMPLETE SERVICE INSTRUCTIONS

The WIPAC "Series NINETY" magneto is a flywheel Ignition Generator, approximately 4 ins. in diameter and weighing about 30 ozs. yet capable of producing 9,000 volts at 350 r.p.m. It is suitable for engines up to 100 c.c. When employed to produce a current for ignition only the type number of the magneto is prefixed with the letter I. Thus: I.1263. When employed to give ignition and lighting currents, the letters IG prefix the type number. Thus: IG.1184.

THE PARTS OF A WIPAC "NINETY" MAGNETO

There are only two main parts in this type of magneto. One is the flywheel and the other is the stator plate. The flywheel contains permanent magnets but due to its design and construction a "Keeper Ring" is NOT necessary when removing it from the stator plate. (This feature applies to all WIPAC built magnetos.)

The stator plate contains a laminated core with ignition coil (and a smaller coil for lighting if it is an "IG" unit), condenser and contact breaker set. The cam which operates the contact breaker set is attached to the engine crankshaft.

The stator plate is held stationary in relation to the engine whilst the flywheel revolves around it.

The magneto is highly efficient and requires very little attention in normal use. It is designed to give a powerful and stable spark over a very wide range of speeds. A spark performance of 9,000 volts at 350 r.p.m. rising to 12,000 volts at 6,000 r.p.m. is obtained, with a large enough air gap maintained between the flywheel and stator to ensure a trouble-free system. Frequent adjustment of the contacts is unnecessary and a fair tolerance for the accuracy of their setting has been allowed for.

"Ninety" magnetos fitted with a lighting coil will give an exceptional and reliable light at low speed without flicker yet will not seriously overload the bulbs if the engine runs at extremely high speeds. Two standard lighting coils are employed, either a 7.8 watt output or a 9 watt output, depending on the Engine Manufacturer's specification.

Flywheels are also made in two types. Finned or Plain. The finned type is employed with a cowl to give the engine extra cooling air and is usually fitted to stationary industrial engines. The plain flywheel has large slots in its face so that the contact breaker points can be adjusted without removing the flywheel. These flywheels are drilled and tapped around the boss for attaching a flywheel extractor tool which is made and supplied by WIPAC.

RUNNING MAINTENANCE

Occasionally

Check the contact points for cleanliness. (It is impossible to lay down a definite time for doing this as conditions will vary, e.g. the "points" will need watching more during a long spell of muddy weather.)

If dirty, clean by inserting a piece of tissue paper between the contacts and withdrawing, while in the closed position. Do not allow the engine to run with oil or petrol on the contacts or they will burn and turn black. If this has happened, polish with extra fine emery cloth.

Every 5,000 miles

1. Check contact points for gap setting. If adjustment is necessary see "Adjustment of Breaker Points" below.
2. Re-lubricate the cam oil pad. To do this, slide the pad out from its holder and squeeze and work into it a Summer grade of motor transmission grease. Do not use oil.
3. Check the plug lead for chafing and see that the terminal at the spark plug end of the lead is gripping tightly.

GENERAL MAINTENANCE

Checking magneto for spark

If the engine fails to start and there is indication that the magneto is at fault:—

A. Disconnect H.T. lead from the spark plug and hold it about $\frac{3}{16}''$ away from some unpainted portion of the frame or engine. Rotate the engine and a spark should jump this gap.
B. If no spark is visible:—
   1. Check H.T. lead for continuity.
   2. Make sure there are no metallic particles inside the unit.

Series 90 Stator Plate with H.T. and Lighting Coils

Series 90 Stator Plate with H.T. Coil only

 *George says* "SERIES 90" MAGNETOS ARE FITTED TO MOST MAKES OF CYCLE POWER UNITS

Series 90 Flywheel with Fins

Series 90 Plain Flywheel
The Slots allow easy adjustment of "Points"

3. Check contact breaker points for correct gap setting and see that the breaker arm is free to move. See that the breaker points are clean. If burnt and badly pitted this will indicate a faulty condenser (renew), or magneto run with dirt between the points. (Renew " points " if they are in this condition.)
Check breaker point adjustment screws for tightness.
4. Make sure the nut securing the flywheel is tight and that there is no free play of the flywheel.
5. By removing the flywheel examine the internal leads for breaks and see they are all properly secured. Make sure covered leads are not chafed and earthing.
6. If the insulation of the H.T. coil has broken down it will show signs of charring on the outside but it is unlikely that this will happen in normal use.

(*Note: The ignition coil can only be tested with a high voltage A.C. voltmeter.*)

H.T. coil
Removal. First remove the laminated core complete, then take off the coil. The core is held to the stator plate on three studs. If a lighting coil is fitted as well, see that the thin wire from it is not wrenched when removing the core. The H.T. coil will slide off the core pole after straightening up the brass tab seen at the top. Sometimes a fibre wedge may be found between the coil and core but this is only used to ensure a tight fit and may not be necessary if another coil is refitted. Due to their individual manufacture, coil sizes vary slightly.

Replacement. The small brass tab protruding from the side of the coil must face towards the flywheel being at the corner nearest to the felt, cam lubricating pad. The two leads should come out from under the coil when it is on with the short lead nearest the stator plate. This short lead is attached to the core stud for earthing. The long lead is attached to the breaker arm spring block together with the condenser lead. Bend the leads so that they do not foul the flywheel or cam. It is most important to refit the red plastic band round the coil and H.T. lead attachment and to see that it is in good condition.

Lighting coil
Removal. This is the smaller coil and can be removed without dismantling the core. First, remove the terminal from the stator plate. Straighten the brass tab of the core and slide the coil off.

Replacement. Replace in the same manner. Bend the brass tab back over the coil after fitting to secure tight fit.

Condenser
A weak or faulty condenser can be detected by badly burnt and pitted contacts or a continuous, *intense blue* spark across the contacts when running. A very small white spark across the points when running is normal.

Removal. Release the condenser lead from the breaker arm spring nylon block. Take out the clamp screw seen near the top of the condenser and ease the condenser out. The bottom clamp is attached to the stator plate only. Replace in the same manner.

Flywheel
This unit is robustly constructed and it is unlikely that any faults will ever develop. They are scientifically balanced before leaving the factory and made of a rust-proof metal. Attachment of the flywheel to the crankshaft is by taper shaft and key, locked with nut and shakeproof washer. The magnets cast into the rim of the wheel are made of a special alloy and will not de-magnetize in normal use. A keeper ring is not necessary when dismantling.

Removal. Extractor tools are made and supplied by WIPAC and should be used when removing the flywheel to save damage to engine parts.

First, remove the flywheel nut and lock washer. Screw back the main bolt of the extractor to its fullest travel, then screw the smaller bolts into the flywheel. Continue tightening the main bolt until the flywheel is freed. It is important to use the small bolts supplied as they are designed to fit without causing internal damage.

When replacing the flywheel make sure metalized dust or small steel items have not been attracted onto the magnets. Clean the flywheel inside and outside.

The finned-type flywheel must be removed to check the contact breaker points as there are no slots.

The contact setting is cast on each type of SERIES " NINETY " flywheel.

Flywheel extractors
Two types are available as there are two classes of flywheel. One wheel has three holes drilled and tapped for an extractor and the other has four holes. The THREE-hole extractor is Part No. 00586, price 5s. 0d. The FOUR-hole extractor is Part No. 00494, price 5s. 0d.

Contact breaker points
Gap adjustment. Turn the engine over until the breaker points are fully open.

Test with feeler gauge between " points ". The correct setting is cast on the flywheel but most " NINETY " magnetos should be 0.018".

If the " points " require adjustment two screw heads will be seen beside them. Slacken the large screw and carefully turn the small screw, which is eccentric, until the correct gap is obtained. Tighten large screw.

Removal. The complete contact set may be removed by taking out the large-headed screw mentioned above and undoing the two leads in the nylon block.

It is essential for the best performance to use only WIPAC spare parts and where possible the name WIPAC is stamped or cast on the parts. All " SERIES NINETY " magnetos are guaranteed for six months from date of purchase and should any fault develop within this time, return it complete to a WIPAC agent or send it direct to the WIPAC GROUP.

THE WIPAC GROUP — BLETCHLEY — ENGLAND
TELEPHONE: BLETCHLEY 320　　TELEGRAMS: WICOMAGSCO BLETCHLEY

Ref. S90/1.

SERVICE INSTRUCTIONS

FOR THE WIPAC SERIES 55 MK 8

FLYWHEEL IGNITION GENERATOR

RUNNING MAINTENANCE

The magneto requires very little maintenance and if the following notes are observed the life of the machine should prove trouble free.

Check and if necessary re-adjust the contacts once every 5,000 miles. (See Service Instructions.)

Occasionally clean the contacts by inserting a dry smooth piece of paper between them and withdrawing while the contacts are in the closed position. Do not allow the engine to run with oil or petrol on the contacts or they will start to burn and blacken, and if they do, lightly polish with a piece of smooth emery cloth.

After every 5,000 miles it is necessary to re-lubricate the cam oil pad. This is done by removing the pad and squeezing and working into it a Summer grade of motor transmission grease which will very closely resemble that used at the factory. Do not use ordinary grease.

Do not run with a faulty or damaged high-tension lead and occasionally clean away mud and dirt from around the H.T. insulator.

If the magneto requires any attention beyond the replacement of contact points and condenser, it is recommended that the complete machine should be sent to us or to an authorised Wico service station. The following information is given for the benefit of those unable to do so :—

GENERAL MAINTENANCE

Checking the Magneto for Spark

If the engine fails to start and there is an indication of the magneto causing trouble, the spark can be checked by holding the H.T. lead $\frac{3}{16}$" away from a point on the frame. When the engine is kicked over in the usual way, a spark should jump this gap. If no spark is visible, see that the H.T. lead is in good condition and examine the contact breaker.

Make sure there are no metallic particles inside the housing, and that the contacts are perfectly clean, and the contact breaker gap is correct to the recommended setting.

If the contacts are found to be in a burnt or badly pitted condition, a faulty condenser is indicated. If the contact breaker appears to be in order, the stator plate may be removed from the engine complete with coils. To do this, the following procedure should be adopted :—

Unscrew the two cover securing screws and remove the cover, unscrew the cam screw and withdraw the cam free of the shaft. The small cam key in some instances may leave its keyway, so care should be taken to make sure of this point when taking the cam from the shaft. Next remove the three stator plate securing screws. The stator can now be withdrawn clear of the engine.

The leads of the ignition coil should be examined to ensure that there is no break in the wiring. One lead will be found to be joined to a tab which is clamped underneath one of the nuts which anchor the stator coil assembly to the stator housing. If this is in order, check the sleeved lead of the primary ignition coil which is connected to the front of the insulated post, which also carries the condenser lead and contact breaker return spring.

The screw which locks the insulated post in position will be found underneath the low tension coil on the right-hand side looking at the inside of the stator housing when in its upright position.

There is, however, no need to remove this screw for any of the investigations recommended in these instructions. The second screw lying at a larger radius and appearing over the top of the coil is the earthing screw for the No. 2 terminal on the front of the machine.

If the leads joined to the insulated post are in order and firmly clamped and the tags not earthing in any way, the ignition coil should be in working order. Should it be necessary to completely remove the stator plate entirely, the low and high tension leads should be freed from the insulated terminal boards on the front of the unit and the plugs respectively, the former by the loosening off of the grub screws and withdrawing the low tension leads which are coloured through the rubber insulator. The stator plate assembly should then be entirely free of the engine.

In the unlikely event of the H.T. insulation of the coil breaking down, provided this is not internal, it should be possible to detect signs of charring on the binding tape of the coil. If the absence of spark is due to tracking, track burns may be visible on the insulator gasket.

Replacement of Ignition Coil

The removal of the stator coil assembly is effected by first disconnecting the ignition lead from the coil, then freeing the white, red and green low tension leads from the terminals marked 3, 1 and 4 respectively, and unscrewing the two clamp nuts. The live lead of the primary winding of the ignition coil must then be disconnected from the insulated post by removing the securing screw. The stator coil assembly may then be gently eased off the two stator plate studs.

In order to slide the ignition coil from the iron limb, it is necessary to straighten the small brass tab which will be found on the side of the coil which faces the stator housing. If the coil is grasped firmly in one hand with the fingers under the insulator gasket and on either side of the core, it may be quite easily pulled off.

THE WIPAC GROUP — BUCKINGHAM BUCKS

SERVICE INSTRUCTIONS

To refit the ignition coil proceed as follows :—

(a) Hold the coil in the left hand with the brass contact pointing away from the line of vision and the lead wires projecting downwards from the underside, and drop the leads through the rectangular hole in the insulating gasket, the extended end of which must point in the same direction as the coil tab.

(b) With the other hand, push the coil core through the coil, making sure that the brass locking tab rivetted to the iron is on the same side as the coil contact. Drive the fibre wedge provided in between the core and the coil, on the same side as the locking tab and bend over the tab.

(c) Replace the stator coil assembly in position on the stator plate and before pushing right down on the studs, bring the sleeved low tension lead of the ignition coil inside the base of the right-hand stator core stud. This keeps the lead clear of the flywheel rotor. Pass the low tension leads through to the front of the unit. Note also that none of the coil leads become clamped in between the stator and the housing.

(d) Press the core down firmly and tighten down the two clamp nuts anchoring the ignition coil earth lead tab underneath the left-hand nut.

(e) Reconnect the sleeved ignition coil lead to the insulated post together with the condenser lead tab and the contact breaker return spring. Firmly screw home the securing screw.

(f) Reconnect the ignition lead to the H.T. terminal of the ignition coil, and reconnect the low tension leads to the appropriate terminals as follows :—

The white lead to No. 3, green to No. 4 and red lead to No. 1 terminal on the front of the unit.

(g) Make sure that all tabs are clean and all clamped connections are tight.

IMPORTANT: Bend all stray loops of wire to behind the radius of the stator to ensure they do not foul the rim of the flywheel rotor.

Removal of Condenser

To replace the condenser, remove the condenser terminal nut and free the condenser lead. Unscrew the condenser bracket fixing screw and withdraw the condenser.

Adjustment and Replacement of Breaker Points

The only adjustable part of the magneto is the breaker plate which provides for the setting of the breaker points. To set these points proceed as follows :—

Turn the engine over until the breaker points are fully open and insert the feeler gauge. Slacken off the locking screw which is to be found immediately above the points, and if the gauge is tight, adjust the fixed contact plate, by means of a suitable screwdriver engaged in the recess provided, in an anti-clockwise direction until the correct setting of 0.015" is obtained. Tighten up the fixed contact plate locking screw. The breaker point setting should only be adjusted in the manner described and at no time should the fixed contact platform be bent to provide adjustment. The moving contact is integral with the breaker arm. If the points need replacement it is recommended that both fixed and moving points be replaced at the same time.

When assembling the moulded breaker arm to the magneto it is necessary to lightly prime the pivot pin with oil or soft grease, and an occasional priming throughout its life will be found to be advantageous.

Care must be taken to put in the correct number of thin spacing washers behind the breaker arm in order to bring the contacts in line with one another. The free end of the contact breaker spring is then anchored to the insulated terminal post with a screw and shakeproof washer. The condenser and primary ignition coil sleeved lead is secured by the same screw and washer. Place one of the spacing washers over the pivot on the outer side of the breaker arm and insert the spring clip in its groove.

The Low Tension Coils

These coils are robust in character and are most unlikely to develop fault. In the event of a fault developing in the coil group, the removal more so than the replacement, of the coil or coils may not be an easy operation, and it is likely that further damage to the windings will occur during the removal process. It is advisable before any steps are taken to remove the low tension coils, that the coils be thoroughly checked and proved beyond doubt to be at fault. The coils are secured to the iron core by means of a varnish adherent assisted by a fibre wedge. Paper formers are used, so damage to the windings can occur when being taken off.

In view of this, it is strongly recommended that should a fault occur in the low tension coil group, that application be made for a coil group replacement already secured to the iron core.

The ignition coil can be removed from the stator assembly as previously described and replaced on the new stator core and coil group replacement. Having completed the coil assembly, proceed as instructed under paragraph " Replacement of Ignition Coil."

Care should be taken to see that the wire connections face toward the front of the machine when assembling the stator coil assembly into the housing.

Any wire loops or wires that could come into contact with the flywheel rotor should be pushed back clear to prevent any fouling or electrical breakdown.

Finally, when connecting the low tension leads of the frame wiring to the magneto generator, make sure that the white, red and green leads are placed on the machine terminals already carrying that colour of lead. This is part of a colour coding scheme, the complete scheme of which is given with the wiring diagram.

The Flywheel Rotor

The robust construction of the flywheel rotor reduces the possibility of any faults on this unit to a minimum. The three powerful magnet inserts are cast in the rim of the rotor and it is not possible to demagnetise them by ordinary usage. No keepers are necessary when the magneto housing and stator are removed. The boss of the flywheel rotor is located on the crankshaft by a keyed taper and locked by a nut and shakeproof washer. It is unnecessary to remove the rotor unless at any time the engine has to be dismantled. A thread cut on the outside of the rotor boss enables it to be removed by the use of a special extractor. When replacing, the rotor must be perfectly clean inside and out.

THE WIPAC GROUP — BUCKINGHAM BUCKS

SERVICE INSTRUCTIONS

FOR THE WIPAC SERIES 72 MK I

FLYWHEEL IGNITION GENERATOR

RUNNING MAINTENANCE

The magneto requires very little maintenance and if the following notes are observed the life of the machine should prove trouble free.

Check and if necessary re-adjust the contacts once every 5,000 miles. (See Service Instructions.)

Occasionally clean the contacts by inserting a dry smooth piece of paper between them and withdrawing while the contacts are in the closed position. Do not allow the engine to run with oil or petrol on the contacts or they will start to burn and blacken, and if they do, lightly polish with a piece of smooth emery cloth.

After every 5,000 miles it is necessary to re-lubricate the cam oil pad. This is done by removing the pad and squeezing and working into it a Summer grade of motor transmission grease which will very closely resemble that used at the factory. Do not use ordinary grease.

Do not run with a faulty or damaged high-tension lead and occasionally clean away mud and dirt from around the H.T. insulator.

If the magneto requires any attention beyond the replacement of contact points and condenser, it is recommended that the complete machine should be sent to us or to an authorised Wico service station. The following information is given for the benefit of those unable to do so :—

GENERAL MAINTENANCE

Checking the Magneto for Spark

If the engine fails to start and there is an indication of the magneto causing trouble, the spark can be checked by holding the H.T. lead $\frac{3}{16}$" away from a point on the frame. When the engine is kicked over in the usual way, a spark should jump this gap. If no spark is visible, see that the H.T. lead is in good condition and examine the contact breaker. Make sure there are no metallic particles inside the housing and that the contacts are perfectly clean, and the gap is correct to the recommended setting. If the contacts are found to be in a burnt or badly pitted condition, a faulty condenser is indicated. If the contact breaker appears to be in order, the flywheel rotor may be removed from the engine by means of the captive extractor nut, allowing full examination of the stator assembly. The leads of the ignition coil should be examined to ensure that there is no break in the wiring. One lead will be found to be joined to a tab which is held secure by one of the four main core screws which anchor the stator to the stator housing. If this is in order check the other end of the primary ignition coil which is connected to the insulated post together with the condenser lead, the insulated post thus forming part of the contact breaker assembly.

If both these leads are connected and the tabs are not earthing on the stator plate or core, the ignition coil should be in working order. In the unlikely event of the H.T. insulation of the secondary coil breaking down, it may be possible to detect signs of charring on the binding tape of the coil. Should, however, the breakdown be internal, then these symptoms will not be present.

Replacement of Ignition Coil.

To remove the coil, the stator assembly should be removed from the crankcase, thus allowing maximum freedom for the operations involved. Take off the H.T. insulator moulding by unscrewing the two fixing nuts, and free the live primary lead from the insulated post fitted to the fixed contact breaker plate.

Remove the two stator securing screws on either side of the ignition coil core, and if necessary just slacken off the remaining two stator securing screws. It is now possible to ease the ignition coil core clear of the two " Tee " shaped laminated stacks. There is no need to entirely remove the two stator securing screws which are remote from the coil, enough clearance being obtained if the foregoing instructions are carried out.

Four dowel pins are used to locate the iron circuit, so that when the four stator securing screws are re-tightened down, the positioning of these stacks should not have altered, assuring the correct air gaps on each of the six stator poles. This point should be carefully noted when reassembling the stator.

To refit the ignition coil proceed as follows :—

Assemble the ignition coil core to the coil, care being taken to see that the positioning of the coil H.T. terminal and coil core is in correct relation to mating parts. Now gently push the ignition coil core into its seating, and re-insert the securing screws on either side of the ignition coil. If the coil core is difficult to push right home, then a few taps on either end of the core should be sufficient to push the core completely home. Finally,

THE WIPAC GROUP — BUCKINGHAM BUCKS

SERVICE INSTRUCTIONS

tighten up all four stator screws, care being taken to see that the ignition coil primary earth tab, and the lighting coil earth tab, are secured by the two screws holding down the right-hand stator stack as observed when removing the flywheel rotor, and are clear of the rotor. Replace the high tension insulator moulding making sure that it is possible to observe the high tension terminal contact at the bottom of the ignition cable lead in. Replace the nuts and lock-washers and tighten firmly down.

Any wire loops or wires that could come into contact with the flywheel rotor should be pushed back behind the radius of the stator to prevent fouling and electrical breakdown.

Replace the live primary ignition lead and the condenser lead on the insulated post which also carries the contact breaker return spring and tighten up the nut, making sure that the terminal tabs do not come into contact with any earth point. Make sure that all tabs are clean and all clamped connections are tight.

Removal of Flywheel Rotor

Only in the case of absolute necessity should the flywheel rotor be removed. Use a suitable spanner to undo the centre extracting nut.

Turn the nut in an anti-clockwise direction firmly holding the rotor until the rotor is felt to give from the taper then continue to turn the nut until the rotor is free of the shaft.

Removal of Condenser

Remove rotor as described above. Slacken off the nut of the insulated post, thus freeing the condenser lead. Unscrew condenser case fixing screw and withdraw condenser.

When reassembling, firmly re-tighten nut and screw, and make sure that the condenser lead is pushed back clear of the rotor.

Adjustment and replacement of Breaker Points

The only adjustable part of the magneto is the breaker plate which provides for the setting of the breaker points.

To set these points proceed as follows :—

Turn the engine over until the points are fully open, and insert the feeler gauge. Slacken off the locking screw which is to be found immediately above the points and if the gauge is tight, adjust the fixed contact plate by means of a suitable screwdriver engaged in the recess provided, in an anti-clockwise direction until the correct setting of 0.020" is obtained. Tighten up the locking screw. The breaker point setting should be adjusted in the manner described, and at no time should the fixed contact platform be bent to provide adjustment.

The moving contact is integral with the breaker arm. If the points need replacement, it is recommended that both fixed and moving contacts be replaced at the same time.

Before assembling the breaker arm to the pivot pin, smear the pin with oil or soft grease. An occasional smear of oil on the exposed end of the pivot pin will allow sufficient ingress of lubricant to prevent the parts running dry.

The contact breaker return spring is slotted to allow easy assembly of the moving contact assembly. Care should be taken to note that when fitting a new contact breaker, the insulating washers of the insulated post assembly are correctly placed, otherwise the primary winding will be permanently earthed. Tighten up the fixing nut, pushing the condenser lead behind the radius of the stator poles.

The Lighting Coils

These coils are of robust construction, and are therefore unlikely to develop faults under normal conditions of use. The coils are secured to the iron core by means of a varnish adherent, and are therefore not readily removed. In addition, the construction of the stator is such that the iron core must be taken off the stator plate before the coil can be removed from the core.

In order to be sure of sound assembly of coil to core, and to avoid damage to the paper former, the replacement lighting coil is supplied complete with core. Ample lead lengths are supplied for the necessary cross connecting, the coils being in series.

When fitting a new coil and core assembly, proceed as follows :—

Remove the stator securing screws of the coil core affected, and gently ease the core up to bring the dowel pins clear of the back plate. Refit the dowel pins to the new core and connect the new coil in circuit, care being taken to note that the finishes of the coils are connected together, and well insulated all connections.

Lower the core back into position and firmly screw home the stator securing screws. If difficulty is experienced in locating the core, slacken off the securing screws of the opposite core, when the replacement core will readily find its seating. Tighten up all four stator screws, seeing that the earth tabs of the lighting coils and ignition primary winding are in place and free of the flywheel rotor.

Bend all stray loops of wire and leads that can come into contact with the rotor, well clear behind the radius of the stator.

The Flywheel Rotor

The robust construction of the rotor reduces the possibility of any faults on this unit to a minimum. The three powerful magnet inserts are cast in the rim of the wheel and it is not possible to demagnetise them by ordinary usage. No keepers are necessary when the rotor is removed from the stator.

The boss of the flywheel rotor which carries the cam, is located on the crankshaft by a keyed taper and locked by the captive extractor nut of the rotor.

It is unnecessary to remove the flywheel unless at any time the engine has to be dismantled, or a fault develops in the magneto itself. No timing is necessary, the cam being keyed to the rotor boss. Contact setting is done through the ports provided in the rotor. When replacing, the rotor must be perfectly clean inside and out.

THE WIPAC GROUP — BUCKINGHAM BUCKS

Ref. B.91.R.

SERVICE INSTRUCTIONS

FOR THE WIPAC SERIES 73 MK I

FLYWHEEL IGNITION GENERATOR

RUNNING MAINTENANCE

The magneto requires very little maintenance and if the following notes are observed the life of the machine should prove trouble free.

Check and if necessary re-adjust the contacts once every 5,000 miles. (See Service Instructions.)

Occasionally clean the contacts by inserting a dry smooth piece of paper between them and withdrawing while the contacts are in the closed position. Do not allow the engine to run with oil or petrol on the contacts or they will start to burn and blacken, and if they do, lightly polish with a piece of smooth emery cloth.

After every 5,000 miles it is necessary to re-lubricate the cam oil pad. This is done by removing the pad and squeezing and working into it a Summer grade of motor transmission grease which will very closely resemble that used at the factory. Do not use ordinary grease.

Do not run with a faulty or damaged high-tension lead and occasionally clean away mud and dirt from around the H.T. insulator.

If the magneto requires any attention beyond the replacement of contact points and condenser, it is recommended that the complete machine should be sent to us or to an authorised Wico service station. The following information is given for the benefit of those unable to do so :—

GENERAL MAINTENANCE

Checking the Magneto for spark

If the engine fails to start and there is an indication of the magneto causing trouble, the spark can be checked by holding one of the H.T. leads $\frac{3}{16}$" away from a point on the frame. When the engine is kicked over in the usual way, a spark should jump this gap. If no spark is visible, see that the H.T. leads are in good condition and that the fixing of the leads in the distributor block is secure, and examine the contact breaker. Make sure there are no metallic particles inside the housing and that the contacts are perfectly clean, and the contact breaker gap is correct to the recommended setting. If the contacts are found to be in a burnt or badly pitted condition, a faulty condenser is indicated. If the contact breaker appears to be in order, the stator plate may be removed from the engines complete with coils. To do this, the cam and distributor rotor should first be withdrawn by unscrewing the large headed retaining screw, then the three stator plate securing screws removed, allowing the stator plate assembly to be withdrawn clear of the engine casting. Should it be necessary to completely remove the stator plate entirely, the low and high tension leads should be freed from the distributor moulding and the plugs respectively, the former by the loosening off of the grub screws and drawing the low tension leads which are coloured through the rubber insulator. The stator plate assembly should then be entirely free of the engine.

The leads of the ignition coil should be examined to ensure that there is no break in the wiring. One lead will be found to be joined to a tab which is clamped underneath one of the nuts which anchor the stator to the stator housing. If this is in order, check the other end of the primary ignition coil which is connected to the condenser terminal.

The screw which locks the insulated post in position will be found underneath the low tension coil on the right-hand side looking at the inside of the stator housing when in its upright position. There is, however, no need to remove this screw for any of the investigations recommended in these instructions.

The condenser lead is held by a screw on the front of the insulated post. If the primary live lead is secured firmly to the condenser terminal and the condenser lead also secured to the front of the insulated terminal post, and both tags are not earthing in any way, the ignition coil should be in working order.

In the unlikely event of the H.T. insulation of the secondary coil breaking down, provided this is not internal, it should be possible to detect signs of charring on the binding tape of the coil. If absence of spark is due to tracking, track burns may be visible on the distributor moulding.

Replacement of Coil

The removal of the stator coil assembly is effected by first unsoldering the ignition lead from the coil, then freeing the white, red and green low tension leads from the distributor block moulding and unscrewing the two clamp nuts. The live lead of the primary ignition coil must then be disconnected from the condenser by the removal of the condenser nut. The stator coil assembly may then be gently eased off the two stator studs.

In order to slide the coil from the iron limb, it is necessary to straighten the small brass tab which will be found on the side of the coil which faces the stator housing. If the coil is grasped firmly in one hand with the fingers under the insulator gasket and on either side of the core, it may be quite easily pulled off.

To refit the ignition coil proceed as follows :—

(a) Hold the coil in the left hand with the brass contact pointing away from the line of vision and the lead wires projecting downwards from the underside, and drop the leads through the rectangular hole in the insulating gasket, the extended end of which must point in the same direction as the coil tab.

(b) With the other hand, push the coil core through the coil making sure that the brass locking tab rivetted to the iron is on the same side as the coil

---

THE WIPAC GROUP — BLETCHLEY ENGLAND

Ref. B.102.R.

SERVICE INSTRUCTIONS

contact. Drive the fibre wedge provided, in between the core and the coil on the same side as the locking tab and bend over the tab.

(c) Connect up the sleeved lead to the condenser via hole No. 5 in the distributor moulding, and firmly tighten up the condenser nut.

(d) Screw down the stator assembly anchoring the ignition coil earth lead under one of the clamp nuts.

(e) Make sure that all tabs are clean and all clamped connections are tight, and before lowering the stator see that none of the coil leads become clamped in between the stator and the housing.

IMPORTANT: Bend all stray loops of wire to behind the radius of the stator assembly and screw down the condenser lead to the insulated post so that the lead passes under the contact breaker return spring to ensure that it does not foul the rim of the distributor rotor. Other wires in the near vicinity of the distributor rotor of flywheel rotor should always be pushed back clear to prevent any fouling.

Removal of Condenser

To replace the condenser, remove condenser nut and free the condenser and primary coil leads. Unscrew condenser fixing screw and withdraw the condenser.

When replacing, make sure that leads to the condenser are clear of the flywheel rotor and that the condenser itself is clear of the distributor rotor.

Adjustment and replacement of Breaker Points

The only adjustable part of the magneto is the breaker plate which provides for the setting of the breaker points. To set these points proceed as follows:—

Turn the engine over until the breaker points are fully open and insert the feeler gauge. Slacken off the locking screw which is to be found immediately above the points and if the gauge is tight, adjust the fixed contact plate, by means of a suitable screwdriver engaged in the recess provided, in an anti-clockwise direction until the correct setting of 0.015" is obtained. Tighten up the adjusting screw.

The breaker point setting should only be adjusted in the manner described and at no time should the fixed contact platform be bent to provide adjustment.

The moving contact is integral with the breaker arm. If the points need replacement it is recommended that both fixed and moving points be replaced at the same time.

When assembling the moulded breaker arm to the magneto, it is necessary to lightly prime the pivot pin with oil or soft grease, and an occasional priming throughout its life will be found to be advantageous. Care must be taken to put in the correct number of thin spacing washers behind the breaker arm, in order to bring the contacts in line with one another. The end of the contact breaker spring is then anchored to the terminal post with a screw and shakeproof washer. Care should be taken to see that the condenser lead is secured by the same screw. Place one of the spacing washers over the pivot on the outer side of the breaker arm and insert the spring clip in its groove.

The Low Tension Coils

These coils are robust in character and are most unlikely to develop faults.

In the event of a fault developing in the coil group, the removal, more so than the replacement, of the coil or coils may not be an easy operation, and it is likely that further damage to the windings will occur during the removal process. It is advisable, before any steps are taken to remove the low tension coils, that the coils be thoroughly checked and proved without doubt to be at fault. The coils are secured to the iron core by means of a varnish adherent assisted by a fibre wedge. Paper formers are used, so damage to the winding can occur when being taken off.

In view of this, it is strongly recommended that should a fault occur in the low tension coil group, that application be made for a coil group replacement already secured to the iron core.

The ignition coil can be removed from the stator assembly as previously described and replaced on the new stator core and coil group replacement.

Having completed the stator coil assembly proceed as follows when building up the complete stator.

Care should be taken to see that the wire connections face toward the front of the machine when assembling the starter coil assembly into the housing. Connect up the low tension leads to the distributor block securing the leads to the grub screw terminals as follows. The white lead to terminal No. 2, the green lead to terminal No. 4, and the red lead to terminal No. 3.

Tighten down the two stator assembly securing nuts, but before doing so, see that the earth lead tab of the ignition coil primary winding is placed over the stator stud on the left, looking on the inside of the stator, and that the live ignition coil primary lead is taken back to the condenser. All nuts should be firmly tightened down. Any wire loops or wires that could come into contact with either the flywheel rotor or distributor rotor should be pushed back clear to prevent any fouling or electrical breakdown.

Finally, when connecting the low tension leads of the frame wiring to the magneto generator, make sure that the white, red and green leads are placed on the machine terminals already carrying that colour of lead.

This is part of a colour coding scheme, the complete scheme of which is given with the wiring diagram.

The Flywheel

The robust construction of the flywheel reduces the possibility of any faults on this unit to a minimum. The three powerful magnet inserts are cast in the rim of the wheel and it is not possible to demagnetise them by ordinary usage. No keepers are necessary when magneto housing and stator are removed. The boss of the flywheel is located on the crankshaft by a keyed taper and locked by a nut and shakeproof washer. It is unnecessary to remove the flywheel unless at any time the engine has to be dismantled. A thread cut on the outside of the flywheel boss enables the wheel to be removed by use of a special extractor. When replacing, the flywheel must be perfectly clean inside and outside.

Running Instructions (See Excelsior Handbook)

Instructions as to care and the disconnecting of the generator input to the rectifier if the battery has been removed apply equally well with the Wipac Unit. We, however, specify an alternative to disconnecting the generator supply, if so desired. If the battery is removed, connect the negative and Positive leads together forming a short circuit on the rectifier. The short circuit current of the generator is controlled, the maximum being very close to maximum full load current.

THE WIPAC GROUP — BLETCHLEY ENGLAND

Ref. B.102.R.

SERIES 114, 124, 167, 125
SPECIFICATIONS

ALTERNATOR EQUIPMENT
(INCLUDING DISTRIBUTOR UNITS, IGNITION COILS AND RECTIFIERS)
SPARE PARTS LIST

GENERAL ILLUSTRATIONS

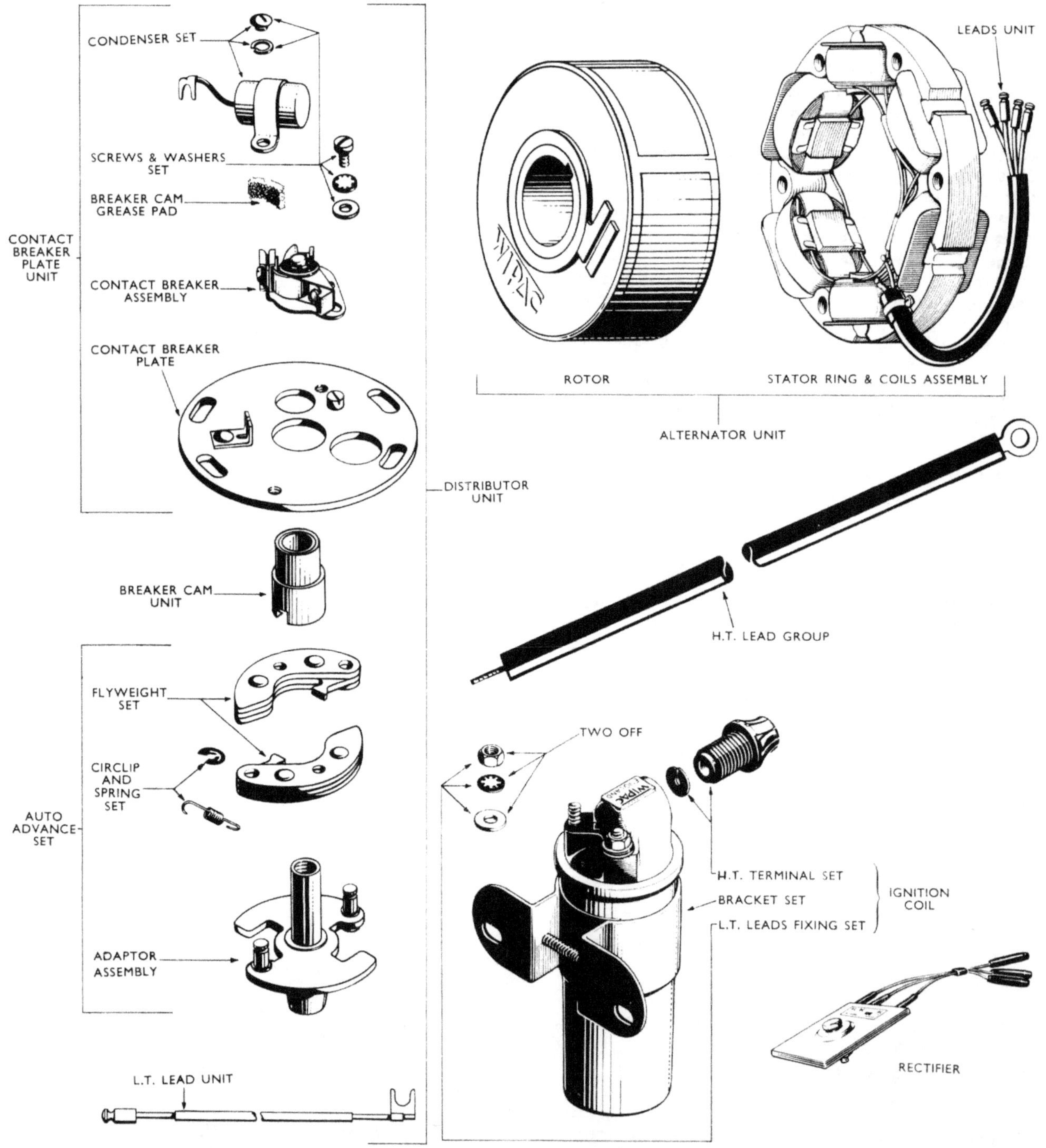

CONTACT BREAKER PLATE UNIT:
- CONDENSER SET
- SCREWS & WASHERS SET
- BREAKER CAM GREASE PAD
- CONTACT BREAKER ASSEMBLY
- CONTACT BREAKER PLATE

DISTRIBUTOR UNIT
- BREAKER CAM UNIT

AUTO ADVANCE SET:
- FLYWEIGHT SET
- CIRCLIP AND SPRING SET
- ADAPTOR ASSEMBLY

L.T. LEAD UNIT

ALTERNATOR UNIT:
- ROTOR
- STATOR RING & COILS ASSEMBLY
- LEADS UNIT

H.T. LEAD GROUP

IGNITION COIL:
- TWO OFF
- H.T. TERMINAL SET
- BRACKET SET
- L.T. LEADS FIXING SET

RECTIFIER

THE WIPAC GROUP — BUCKINGHAM — BUCKS — ENGLAND
TELEPHONE: BUCKINGHAM 3031   TELEGRAMS: WICOMAGSCO BUCKINGHAM

ISSUED 4/69   REF. AA/1/4

SPECIFICATIONS

MAIN-COMPONENTS

Equipment Specification Number	Alternator Unit	Distributor Unit	Ignition Coil	Rectifier	H.T. Lead Group
GA1476	G1585	S1024	S0793	S2642	S0992
GA1542	G1540	S0758	S0793	S2642	S0812
GA1597	G1585	S1024	S0793	S2642	S0992
GA1598	G1585	S1024	S0793	S2642	S0992
GA1640	G1685	S2630	S0793	S2642	S0812
GA1641	G1521	S1141	S0793	S2642	S0991
GA1684	G1685	S2630	S0793	S2642	S0812
GA1691	G1585	S1024	S0793	S2642	S0992
GA1695	G1697	S2630	S0810	S2642	S0812
GA1734	G1685	S2630	S0793	S2642	S0812
GA1748	G1521	S3881	S0793	S2642	S0991
GA1769	G1767	S4060	S0769	S2642	S0773
GA1772	G1767	S4060	S0769	S2642	S0773
GA1776	G1778	S4060			
GA1779	G1781		S0769	S2642	S0773
GA1790	G1792	S4060			
GA1804	G1767	S4060	S0769	S2642	S0773
GA1806	G1792	S4060			

APPLICATION LIST

MANUFACTURER	Part of Equipment Specification No. (Ignition)	EQUIPMENT DETAILS	YEAR
A.J.S.	GA1641	Model 14 250 c.c. O.H.V.	May 1958 to Dec 1964
	GA1641	Model 14S 250 c.c. O.H.V. Sports	Oct. 1960 to Dec 1962
	GA1641	Model 8 350 c.c.	Sept. 1959 to Dec 1964
	GA1748	Model 14 C.S.R. 250 c.c. Sapphire Ninety	March 1965
	GA1675	Model 14 250 c.c. and 8 350 c.c. (Special)	Oct. 1960 to Dec. 1964
B.S.A.	GA1769	D.10 and D.14 Models 175 c.c. Supreme and Silver Bantam (Full D.C. Coil Ignition)	July 1966 to Feb. 1969
	GA1772	D.10 and D.14 Models 175 c.c. Bantam Sports and Bushman (Full D.C. Lights and Ignition)	Sept. 1966 to Feb. 1969
	GA1776	D.10 and D.14 Models 175 c.c Bushman Pastoral (E.T. Ignition A.C. Lights)	April 1967 to Feb. 1969
	GA1804	Bantam 175 c.c. (Full D.C.)	1969 Models
	GA1806	Bushman 175 c.c. (E.T. Ignition A.C. Lights)	1969 Models
FRANCIS-BARNETT	GA1476	Cruiser 80 250 c.c.	Aug. 1956 to Sept. 1963
	GA1476	Cruiser 84 250 c.c.	May 1959 to Sept. 1962
	GA1598	Falcon 87 200 c.c.	Aug. 1959
JAMES	GA1597	Captain 200 c.c. L.20 (A.M.C. Engine)	Oct. 1959 to Sept. 1962
	GA1691	Captain 200 c.c. L.20 (A.M.C. Engine)	Oct. 1962
	GA1475	Commodore 250 c.c. L.25	Aug. 1959 to July 1963
MATCHLESS	GA1641	Model G2 250 c.c.	July 1958 to Dec. 1963
	GA1748	Model G2 250 c.c.	March 1965
	GA1641	Model G5 350 c.c.	Oct. 1959 to Dec. 1964
NORTON	GA1542	Jubilee 250 c.c. Twin	Nov. 1958 to Aug. 1960
	GA1640	Jubilee 250 c.c. Twin and Navigator 350 c.c. Twin	Sept. 1960 to Sept. 1963
	GA1684	Jubilee 250 c.c. Twin and Navigator 350 c.c. Twin	Sept. 1963 to Sept. 1964
	GA1734	Navigator 350 c.c. Twin	Oct. 1964
	GA1695	Electra 400 c.c. Twin and E.S.B. 400 Twin	Feb. 1963
TRIUMPH	GA1779	Super Cub T.20 Full D.C. Coil Ignition	Jan. 1967

Each component on this list is made up of several parts and these are shewn, on separate lists, headed SUB-COMPONENTS.
For Prices refer to Master Price List.

RE:- OBSOLETE SPECIFICATIONS. SEE NOTE ON PAGE AA3/4

THE WIPAC GROUP — BUCKINGHAM — BUCKS — ENGLAND

REF. AA/2/4

SERVICE INSTRUCTIONS

OBSOLETE ALTERNATOR UNITS

It has been found necessary to obsolete certain alternator unit specifications. It is therefore recommended, when attention is required, that the user returns the alternator unit to our Service Department at Buckingham where every endeavour will be made to carry out a complete repair.

REMOVAL OF ALTERNATOR

When the stator ring with its coils is removed for inspection or replacement the visible soldered connections should be checked to make sure none are touching each other, nor touching " earth ". Before replacement ensure that the pole surfaces are free from metallic dust and that the main cable is clear from the chain. See also note on " magnetic rotor ".

MAGNETIC ROTOR UNIT

This is a 6-pole unit and can be removed or stored indefinitely without loss of magnetism. When being replaced care should be taken to make sure that the shaft key-way position is correct as there are variations.

Check the outside diameter because these also vary, and they must be used with their corresponding stator ring to maintain the common air-gap of approximately .007".

DISTRIBUTOR UNIT

This comprises the contact set and condenser, and where used the automatic advance unit and cam. The contact set is designed to be replaced as complete unit and not intended to have the replacement of either fixed or moving contact separately. The only attention needed to the condenser is a periodic check of the tightness of both its electrical connections—live and earth.

The advance unit should be checked for freedom of movement, and oil applied sparingly to the bearing surfaces.

Oil should not be applied to the cam lubricating pad. The pad should be removed and a quantity of high melting point grease worked into it.

BREAKER POINT SETTING

The contact gap should be maintained at the figure specified in the vehicle manufacturer's instruction book. This is particularly important on Sports machines using A.C. feed for ignition. A difference of as little as .002 can have an appreciable effect on performance.

THE WIPAC GROUP — BUCKINGHAM — BUCKS — ENGLAND

REF. AA/3/4

SPARE PARTS LIST

SUB-COMPONENTS

ALTERNATOR UNITS

DESCRIPTION OF PARTS	These Columns are headed by the Part Numbers of complete units, which include all the Parts shown beneath them.							
Alternator Unit	G1521	G1540	G1585	G1685	G1697	G1767	G1778	G1781	G1792
Stator Ring and Coils Assembly	S0602	S0733	S0217	S3536	S3419	S4186	S4183	S4186	S4221
Rotor	S0221	S0734	S0221	S0734	S0734	S4063	S4063	S0221	S4063
Leads Unit (includes Clip and Screws)	S0603	S0735	S0220	S3537	S3423	S4065	S4184	S4065	S4222

DISTRIBUTOR UNITS

DESCRIPTION OF PARTS	These Columns are headed by the Part Numbers of complete units, which include all the Parts shown beneath them.					
Distributor Unit	S0758	S1024	S1141	S2630	S3881	S4060
Contact Breaker Plate Unit	S0759	S0224	S2330	S2631	S2330	S4059
Contact Breaker Plate Only	S0760	S0225	S2313	S2634	S2313	S2634
Condenser Set	S0761	S0226	S0226	S2767	S0226	S2767
Contact Breaker Assembly	*S0584	S2312	S2312	*S0584	S2312	S0584
Cam Unit	S0762	S0223	S2725	S2632	S1119	S4058
Auto-Advance Unit	S0765		S1143	S2636	S1143	
Adaptor Assembly	S0763		S0608	S2637	S0608	
Flyweight Set	S0764		S0002	S0764	S0002	
Screw and Washer Set	S0767	S0227	S2387	S0767	S2387	S0054
Circlip and Spring Set	S0683		S1142	S0683	S1142	
Cam Grease Pad	S1994	S1994	S1994	S1994	S1994	S4061
Contact Breaker Plate (Adjustable)				S2635		

IGNITION COILS

DESCRIPTION OF PARTS	These Columns are headed by the Part Numbers of complete units, which include all the Parts shown beneath them.		
Ignition Coil	S0769	S0793	S0810
H.T. Terminal Set	S0772	S0795	S0795
L.T. Lead Fixing Set	S0813	S0813	S0813
Bracket Set	S0771	S0771	S0771

RECTIFIER UNITS

DESCRIPTION OF PARTS	These Columns are headed by the Part Numbers of complete units
Rectifier Unit	S2642

H.T. LEAD GROUPS

DESCRIPTION OF PARTS	These Columns are headed by the Part Numbers of complete units			
H.T. Lead Group	S0773	S0812	S0991	S0992

* 2 Sets Required

The appropriate equipment to which these parts are fitted can be found by referring the Part No. in heavy type, to sheets headed **Main Components**

For Prices refer to Master Price List.

THE WIPAC GROUP — BUCKINGHAM — BUCKS — ENGLAND

REF. AA/4/4

WIPAC MARK I ALTERNATOR EQUIPMENT

TESTING INSTRUCTIONS

The Series 114 Alternator consists of a six pole Stator ring 5" in diameter with six coils and a six pole permanent magnet Rotor. There are four main leads coloured White, Light Green, Yellow and Orange. Two coils on opposite poles are connected in parallel to White and Light Green, the other four coils are connected in parallel to Yellow and Orange. The output from these coils is A.C., converted to D.C. by means of a bridge-connected metal rectifier. The output of the alternator is controlled through the switch on the headlamp and connects two or six coils according to its position.

EMERGENCY STARTING

The Emergency Position is mainly intended for starting when the battery is flat. (This position is marked "EMG" on the Ignition switch). The engine will have power enough to drive in this position if it is necessary but the speed will be slow (approximately 30 m.p.h.) and continuous driving like this is not advisable. If the battery has been completely removed the negative battery terminal from the harness must be earthed to the machine before starting on "EMG" to avoid damage to the rectifier.

When the Ignition switch is in the emergency position, four of six Alternator coils are connected to the primary winding of the Ignition coil. (Yellow lead is earthed, Orange lead connected to the Ignition coil). The other two Alternator coils will continue to charge the battery at a rate between .5 to 1.5 amps.

TESTING

Testing of component parts can be carried out if the following instruments are available:

- 0-12 D.C. Volt Meter
- 0-15 A.C. Volt Meter
- 1 ohm resistance (capable of carrying 8 amps.)
- 10-0-10 D.C. ammeter.

High grade moving coil instruments must be used and accurate. The 1 ohm resistor must also be accurate otherwise correct readings cannot be obtained. ENGINE SPEED when testing should be in the region of 2,500 r.p.m. Tests should not be attempted at speeds below 2,000 r.p.m. A few revs. above or below 2,500 will not affect the readings of an alternator in good condition.

ROTOR DEMAGNETISED

Although the WIPAC Rotor is robustly built and holding a very high magnetic charge it can become demagnetized if the machine is run with battery connections reversed or if the Rectifier breaks down. A demagnetized rotor should be returned to WIPAC for satisfactory remagnetization.

TEST 1

Connections	Switch Position	Meter Reading
D.C. Output Check. Engine speed over 2,000 r.p.m. Connect ammeter 10-0-10 amps. in series with battery. If battery voltage reading is less than 5.5 volts connect to a fully charged battery.	Off	½—2 amps.
	L	½—1 amp.
	H	¼—1 amp.

Diagram 1

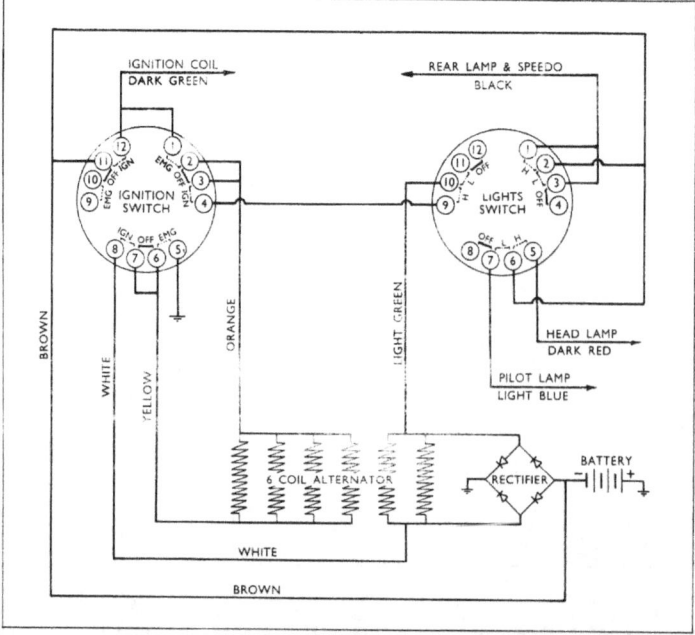

 THIS EQUIPMENT IS FITTED TO THE 1954-55 MODELS OF THE ARIEL "COLT" L.H. AND B.S.A. C.10.L.

ALTERNATOR TEST INSTRUCTIONS

FAULT LOCATION

SYMPTOMS	CHECK
All bulbs burning out when engine is accelerated	1. Battery connections faulty. 2. Battery EARTH to machine faulty. 3. Rectifier connections faulty. 4. Snap connectors faulty between Rectifier and Battery. 5. Battery in bad condition.
No charge reading	1. Carry out TEST 1. 2. If still no charge reading after Test 1, carry out TEST 2 with *chaincase in position*. Should a voltage reading be obtained at C2, D2, E2, or F2, in TEST 2 it indicates that one or more of the ALTERNATOR coils are shorting to EARTH and the chaincase may be the cause of this. Retest with *chaincase removed*. 3. If above tests show no faults check Rectifier. See TEST 3.
Will not start on " EMG " nor " IGN "	1. Connect Ammeter in the Dark Green lead from Battery to Ignition Coil—Switch to " IGN "—With contact breaker points closed the reading should be 3.5 AMPS. if Battery voltage is not less than 6 volts. If this test is in order proceed to check:— 2. Contact breaker setting. (Should be .015"). 3. Contacts for dirt. 4. Condenser. 5. Connections and wiring.
Will not start on " EMG " O.K. on " IGN "	1. Voltage across YELLOW & ORANGE (SEE TEST 2). 2. Connections and wiring. 3. Engine timing.
Will not start on " IGN " O.K. on " EMG "	1. Battery. 2. Connectors and wiring.

TEST 2

Procedure	Connections	Meter Reading	Conclusions
Alternator Check Engine Speed over 2,000 r.p.m. Connect A.C. voltmeter in parallel with 1 ohm resistor across corresponding pairs of alternator leads.	(A) Yellow—Orange (B) White—Light Green (C) Yellow—Machine Earth (D) Orange—Machine Earth (E) White—Machine Earth (F) Light Green—Machine Earth	5·5 to 6·5 3·8 to 4·8 Nil Nil Nil Nil	Alternator O.K.
	(A2) Yellow—Orange or (B2) White—Light Green	Nil	Check Soldered connections to coils.
	(C2) Yellow—Machine (Earth) (D2) Orange—Machine (Earth) (E2) White—Machine (Earth) (F2) Light Green—Machine (Earth)	Any Reading Here	One or more coils shorted to earth. Stator and coil group faulty. Replace.
	(A3) Yellow—Orange and (B3) White—Light Green	Under 5·5 Under 3·8	Rotor faulty. Replace.
	(A4) Yellow—Orange and (B4) White—Light Green or (A5) Yellow—Orange and (B5) White—Light Green	5·5 to 6·5 Under 3·8 Under 5·5 3·8 to 4·8	One or more coils open circuit. Stator & coil group faulty. Replace.

TEST 3

Procedure	Battery Connections	Bulb Connections	Conclusions
Rectifier Check. Connect a 6 volt battery in series with a 6v. 3w. bulb across the rectifier terminals (See diagram 3)	Positive—Light Green Positive—White Positive—Brown Positive—Brown	Earthed Earthed Green White	Bulb lights Rectifier O.K. Bulb does not light. Rectifier faulty replace.
Reverse battery connections. (See diagram 3)	Negative—Light Green Negative—White Negative—Brown Negative—Brown	Earthed Earthed Green White	Bulb does not light. Rectifier O.K. Bulb lights Rectifier faulty replace.

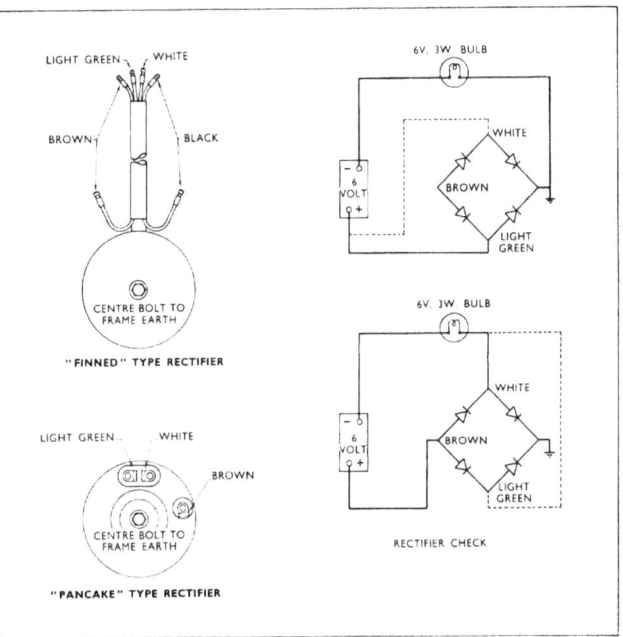

Diagram 3

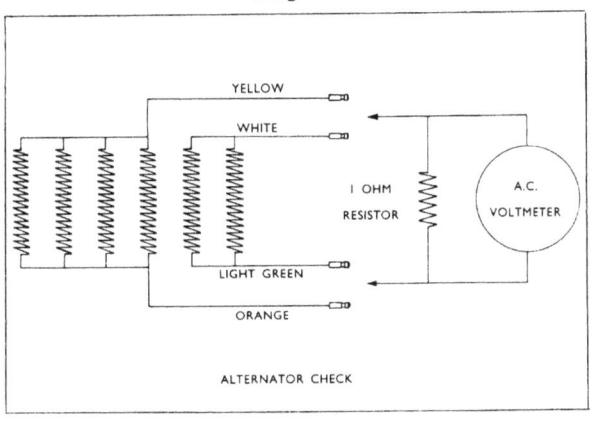

Diagram 2

THE WIPAC GROUP — BLETCHLEY — ENGLAND
TELEPHONE: BLETCHLEY 320   TELEGRAMS: WICOMAGSCO BLETCHLEY

Ref. A.E.I.

| SERIES 55 & 73 SPECIFICATIONS |  | IGNITION GENERATOR SPARE PARTS LIST |

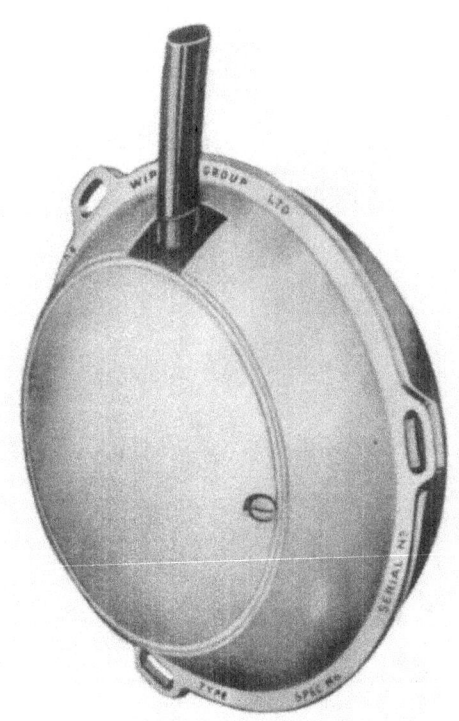

THE WIPAC GROUP — BUCKINGHAM — BUCKS — ENGLAND
TELEPHONE: BUCKINGHAM 3031 · TELEGRAMS: WICOMAGSCO BUCKINGHAM

REF. BA1/6

GENERAL ILLUSTRATION

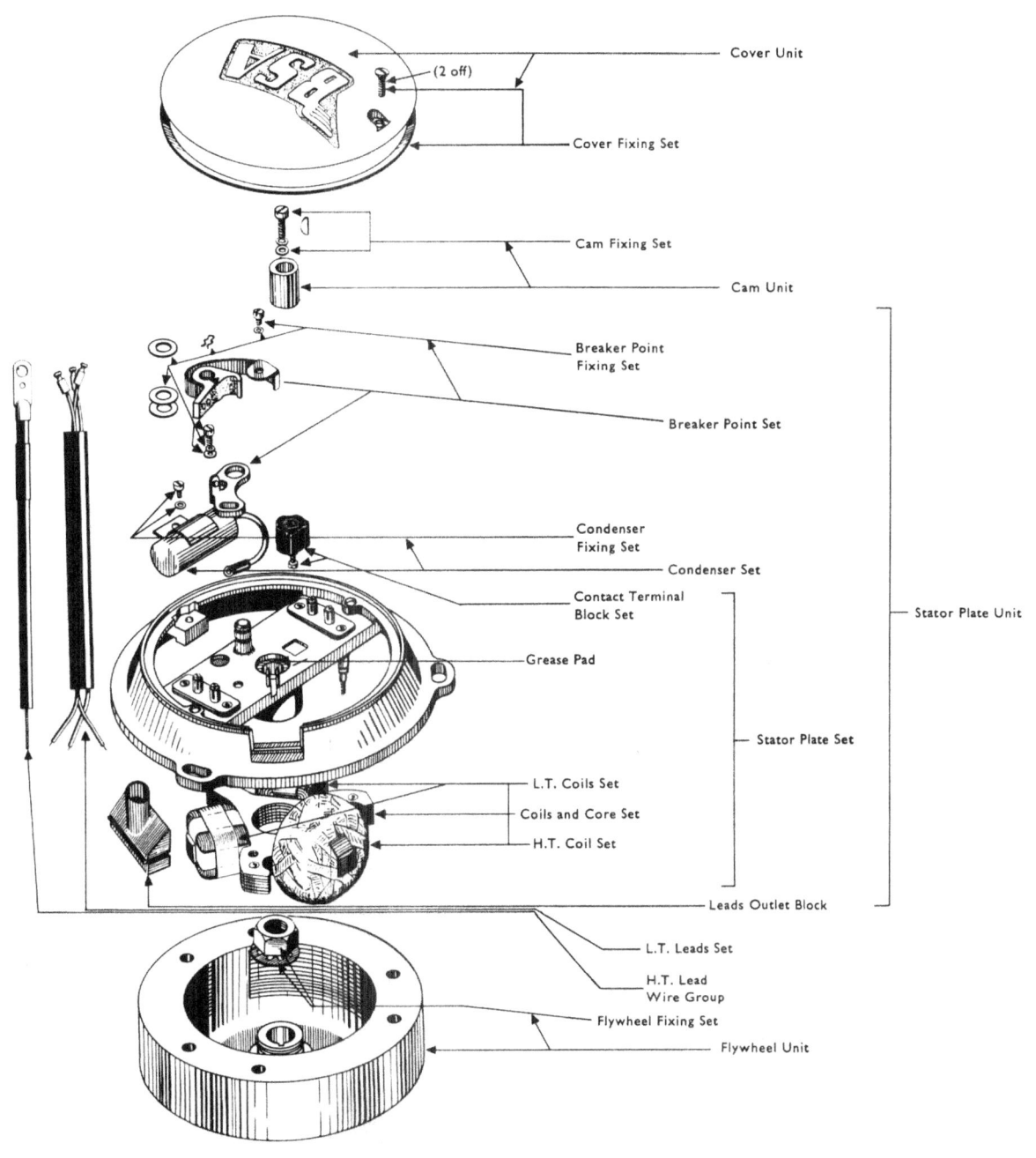

THE WIPAC GROUP — BUCKINGHAM — BUCKS — ENGLAND

REF. BA 2/6

GENERAL ILLUSTRATION

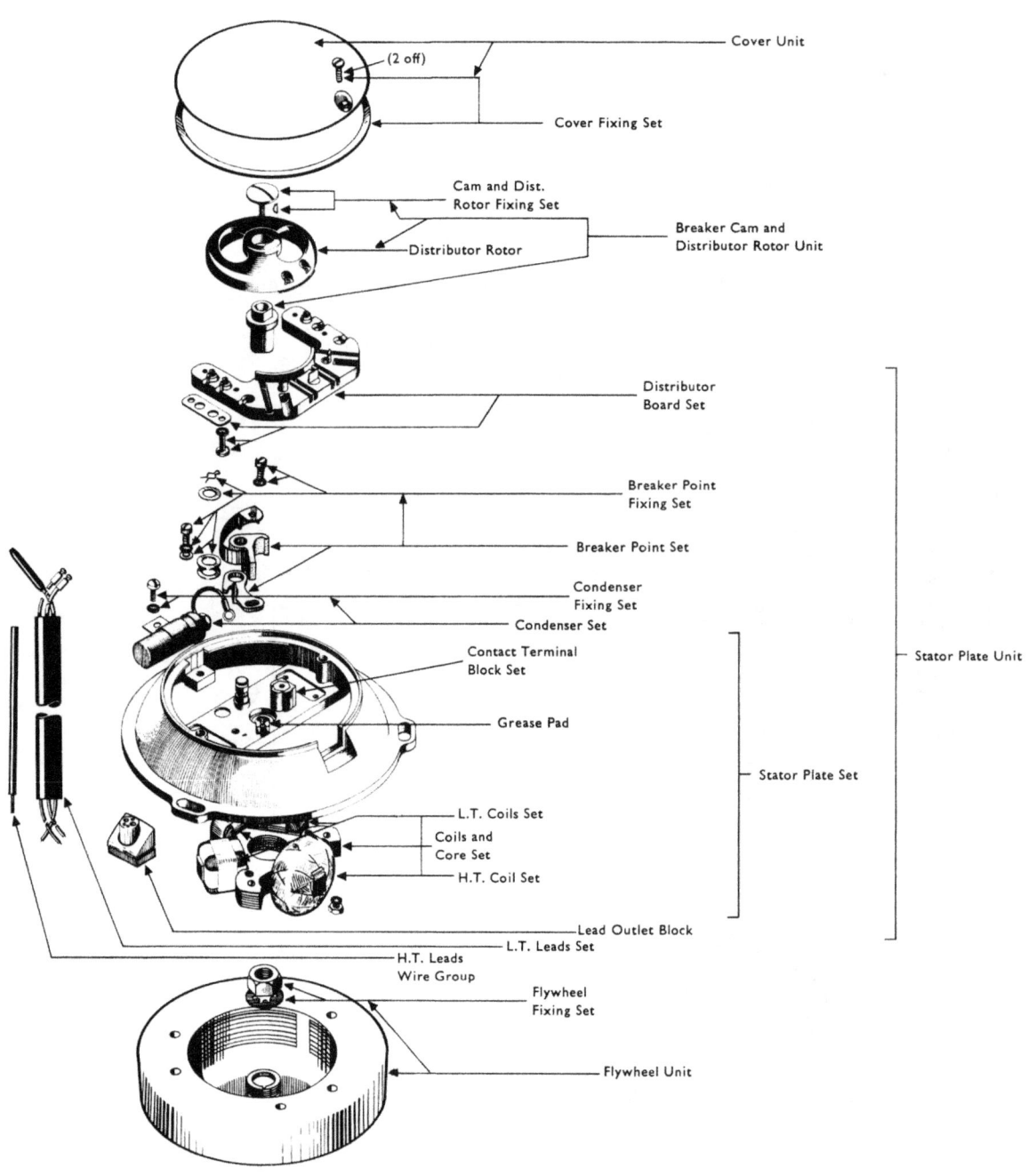

THE WIPAC GROUP — BUCKINGHAM — BUCKS — ENGLAND

REF. BA3/6

SPECIFICATIONS

MAIN COMPONENTS

Ignition Generator Specification Number	Series	Rotation	H.T. Lead Length	Stator Plate Unit	Flywheel Unit	Cam and Distributor Rotor Unit	Stator Cover Unit	H.T. Lead Wire Group	L.T. Leads Set	H.T. Lead Sleeve	Flywheel Extractor
IG.1100	USE SPECIFICATION No. IG.1358										
IG.1118	S.55	CW	12"	S0377	S0378	S1244	S0381	S1167	S0370	S1220	S1256
IG.1130 A.C.	USE SPECIFICATION No. IG.1452										
IG.1130 D.C.	USE SPECIFICATION No. IG.1450										
IG.1133	OBSOLETE										
IG.1156	OBSOLETE										
IG.1179	OBSOLETE										
I.1204	OBSOLETE										
IG.1217	S.73Mk.2	CW	17½"	S1260	S1265	S1242	S0381	S1167	S0361		S1256
IG.1252	OBSOLETE										
IG.1358	S.73Mk.1	CW	22"	S0363	S1265	S1266	S0381	*S1271	S0361	*S1220	S1256
IG.1450	S.55	CCW	31¼"	S1225	S1239	S1243	S1251	S1255	S0372		S1256
IG.1452	S.55	CCW	22¼"	S1226	S1239	S1243	S1251	S1253	S0370		S1256
IG.1454	USE SPECIFICATION No. IG.1450										
IG.1462	USE SPECIFICATION No. IG.1358										
IG.1552	S.55	CCW	32"	S0824	S1239	S1243	S1251	S1255	S0828	S1220	S1256
IG.1704	S.55	CCW	18"	S3540	S1239	S3794	S1251		S3539		S1256

Each component on this list is made up of several parts and these are shown, on separate lists, headed SUB-COMPONENTS.
* Two required.
For Prices refer to Master Price List.

APPLICATION LIST

IGNITION GENERATOR	LIGHTING OUTPUT	MANUFACTURER	MODEL DETAILS
IG.1358	D.C. 6 Volt	BRITISH ANZANI	Anzani Twin Engine (Special)
IG.1450	D.C. 6 Volt	B.S.A.	All Model Bantams with Full D.C. Lighting to May 66
IG.1452	A.C. 6 Volt 30 Watt	B.S.A.	All Model Bantams with A.C. Lighting (No Battery or Rectifier fitted)
IG.1552	A.C. 6 Volt 30 Watt Trickle Charge	B.S.A.	Model D7 Super to Sept. 63 (One Switch in Headlamp)
IG.1704	A.C. Lights Trickle Charge and Coil Ignition	B.S.A.	Model D7 Super from Oct. 63 to May 66 (Two Switches in Headlamp)
IG.1358	D.C. 6 Volt	COTTON	Cotanza 197 c.c. (Twin)
IG.1217	D.C. 6 Volt	EXCELSIOR	Courier 150 c.c.
IG.1217	A.C. 6 Volt	EXCELSIOR	Monarch 147 c.c.
IG.1358	D.C. 6 Volt	EXCELSIOR	Talisman 250 c.c. (Twin)
IG.1358	D.C. 6 Volt	GREEVES	Fleetwing (Twin) and Fleetmaster (Twin)
IG.1358	D.C. 6 Volt	NORMAN	T.S. 250 c.c. (Twin)
IG.1118	D.C. 6 Volt	ROYAL ENFIELD	R.E. 125 c.c.
IG.1358	D.C. 6 Volt	TANDON	Supreme (Twin) and Viscount (Twin)

RE:- OBSOLETE SPECIFICATIONS. SEE NOTE ON PAGE BA5/6

THE WIPAC GROUP — BUCKINGHAM — BUCKS — ENGLAND

SERVICE INSTRUCTIONS

The ignition generator requires very little maintenance and if the following notes are observed the life of the machine should prove trouble-free.

Check and if necessary re-adjust the contacts once every 5,000 miles.

Occasionally clean the contacts by inserting a dry smooth piece of paper between them and withdrawing while the contacts are in the closed position. Do not allow the engine to run with oil or petrol on the contacts or they will start to burn and blacken, and if they do, lightly polish with a piece of smooth emery cloth.

After every 5,000 miles it is necessary to re-lubricate the cam grease pad. This is done by removing the pad and squeezing and working into it a Summer grade of motor transmission grease which will very closely resemble that used at the factory. **Do not use ordinary grease.**

Obsolete Ignition Generators

It has been found necessary to obsolete certain ignition generator unit specifications. It is therefore recommended, when attention is required, that the user returns the ignition generator unit to our Service Department at Buckingham where every endeavour will be made to carry out a complete repair.

Checking Ignition for Spark

If the engine fails to start and there is indication that the ignition is at fault:—

(a) Disconnect H.T. leads from the spark plugs and hold them about $\frac{3}{16}$" away from some unpainted portion of the frame or engine. Kick-start the engine in the usual way and a spark should jump this gap.

(b) If no spark is visible:—
1. Check H.T. leads for continuity.
2. Check contact breaker points for correct gap setting and see that they are clean.
   Check breaker point adjustment screws for tightness.
3. By removing the cover examine the internal leads for breaks and see they are all properly secured. Make sure covered leads are not chafed and earthing.
4. Make sure there are no metallic particles inside the unit.
5. If the insulation of the H.T. coil has broken down it will show signs of charring on the outside but it is unlikely that this will happen in normal use.

Condenser

A weak or faulty condenser can be detected by badly burnt and pitted contacts or a continuous **intense blue** spark across the contacts when running. A very small white spark across the points when running is normal.

The condenser can be removed by undoing the screw securing it and releasing the lead from the terminal post.

Contact Breaker Points

Adjustment. Turn engine over until points are fully open. See sketch.

Test with feeler gauge between "points". If the "points" require adjustment slacken the fixing screw and carefully move the fixed contact plate by means of a screwdriver until the correct gap is obtained. Tighten screw.

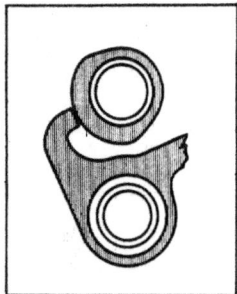

SERIES 55 & 73MK2

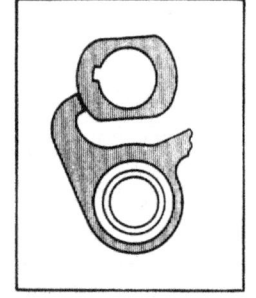

SERIES 73MK1

The breaker point setting should only be adjusted in the manner described and **at no time should the breaker arm be bent to provide adjustment.**

If the contact points need replacing both the fixed and movable points must be replaced at the same time.

DISTRIBUTOR BOARD AND ROTOR

Series 73 Mk. 1 (Twin)

Occasional checks should be made on the tightness of the terminal screws of the "distributor board", and also the insulated surfaces should be wiped clean and dry. Dust-laden moisture will act as a conductor and electrical flash-over may then occur. The metal contact faces of the Spark-jump projections of the distributor board and the distributor Rotor contact should be gently cleaned with fine emery paper. Care should be taken not to remove much metal which will increase the Jump-gap distance, and to finally clean off any metallic dust produced during the cleaning process. The gap distance between the "Distributor Rotor Contact" and the three fixed contacts on the Distributor Board should be .003"—.005". The distance of the gap may be adjusted by gentle tapping on the contact projections in the required direction.

LOW TENSION CURRENT

The low tension windings produce A.C. current.

For D.C. current the A.C. current is rectified by a full-wave rectifier. This provides D.C. for battery charging.

An arrangement is made whereby a day charge of approximately 2 amps. at maximum engine revs, 6,000—7,000 r.p.m. is allowed to pass into the battery.

During night use, with the battery supplying a 30-watt lamp load, a generated balance against this battery drain is accomplished at approximately 2,500 r.p.m. of the engine, and allowing a charge of 1.5 amperes at maximum engine speed.

REPLACEMENT OF IGNITION AND LIGHTING COILS

Series 55 A.C. (Single)

Disconnect H.T. lead from ignition coil and red low tension lead from terminal marked 1, also disconnect primary lead from the movable contact spring terminal. Unscrew the two core clamp nuts, the coil core assembly can then be gently eased off the two stator plate studs. Any of the coils can now be removed. Considerable force may be necessary to remove coil from core as a fibre wedge is used to ensure a tight fit and a varnish adherent is also used to secure the lighting coils.

Series 55 and 73 Mk. 2 (Single) D.C.

Disconnect H.T. lead from ignition coil and white, red and green low tension leads from terminals marked 3, 1 and 4, also disconnect H.T. primary lead from the movable contact spring terminal. Unscrew the two core clamp nuts, the coil core assembly can then be gently eased off the two stator plate stubs. Any of the coils can now be removed. Considerable force may be necessary to remove coil from core as a fibre wedge is used to ensure a tight fit and a varnish adherent is also used to secure the lighting coils.

Series 73 Mk. 1 D.C. (Twin)

Disconnect H.T. lead from ignition coil and white, red and green low tension leads from terminals marked 2, 3 and 4, also disconnect H.T. primary lead from the movable contact spring terminal. Unscrew the two core clamp nuts, the coil core assembly can then be gently eased off the two stator plate studs. Any of the coils can now be removed. Considerable force may be necessary to remove coil from core as a fibre wedge is used to ensure a tight fit and a varnish adherent is also used to secure the lighting coils.

FLYWHEEL

This unit is robustly constructed and it is unlikely to develop any faults in normal use. A KEEPER RING IS NOT NECESSARY WHEN WITHDRAWN FROM THE STATOR PLATE.

REMOVAL

Remove the nut securing the flywheel to the shaft. If a Wipac flywheel extractor, Part No. S.1256 is not available and the flywheel cannot be easily withdrawn, grasp the flywheel firmly and while attempting to pull it off tap the end of the crankshaft with a mallet or lead hammer, being careful during this operation not to damage the crankshaft. When replacing the flywheel make sure metalized dust or small steel items have not been attracted onto the magnet core faces.

THE WIPAC GROUP — BUCKINGHAM — BUCKS — ENGLAND

REF. BA5/6

SPARE PARTS LIST — SUB-COMPONENTS

STATOR PLATE UNITS

DESCRIPTION OF PARTS	These Columns are headed by the Part Numbers of complete units, which include all the Parts shown beneath them.						
Stator Plate Unit	**S0363**	**S0377**	**S0824**	**S1225**	**S1226**	**S1260**	**S3540**
Stator Plate Set	S1262	S1227	S1227	S1227	S1227	S1261	S1227
Coils and Core Set	S0366	S1213	S0825	S1211	S1212	S1211	S3541
L.T. Coils Set	S0367	S0376	S0826	S1234	S1235	S1234	S1235
H.T. Coil Set	S0365	S0206	S0206	S0206	S0206	S0206	
Breaker Point Set	S1233	S1233	S1233	S1233	S1233	S1233	S1233
Breaker Point Fixing Set	S1232	S1232	S1232	S1232	S1232	S1232	S1232
Grease Pad	S1229	S1229	S1229	S1229	S1229	S1229	S1229
Condenser Set	S0364	S1231	S1231	S1231	S1231	S1231	S1231
Condenser Fixing Set	S1230	S1230	S1230	S1230	S1230	S1230	S1230
Lead Outlet Block	S1264	S1238	S1238	S1238	S1238	S1264	S1238
Contact Terminal Block Set	S1228	S1228	S1228	S1228	S1228	S1228	S1228
Distributor Board Set	S0391						
Feed Coil Set							S3542

FLYWHEEL UNITS

DESCRIPTION OF PARTS	These Columns are headed by the Part Numbers of complete units, which include all the Parts shown beneath them.						
Flywheel Unit	**S0378**	**S1239**	**S1265**				
Fixing Set	S1241	S1241	S1241				

BREAKER CAM UNITS

DESCRIPTION OF PARTS	These Columns are headed by the Part Numbers of complete units, which include all the Parts shown beneath them.						
Breaker Cam Unit	**S1242**	**S1243**	**S1244**		**S3794**		
Breaker Cam and Distributor Rotor Unit				**S1266**			
Fixing Set	S1246	S1246	S0389	S0362	S1246		
Distributor Rotor				S1268			

STATOR COVER UNITS

DESCRIPTION OF PARTS	These Columns are headed by the Part Numbers of complete units, which include all the Parts shown beneath them.						
Stator Cover Unit	**S0381**	**S1251**					
Fixing Set	S1252	S1252					

H.T. LEAD GROUPS

DESCRIPTION OF PARTS	These Columns are headed by the Part Numbers of complete units					
H.T. Lead Group	**S1155**	**S1167**	**S1253**	**S1255**	**S1271**	

L.T. LEADS SETS

DESCRIPTION OF PARTS	These Columns are headed by the Part Numbers of complete units					
L.T. Leads Set	**S0361**	**S0370**	**S0372**	**S0828**	**S3539**	

H.T. LEAD SLEEVES

DESCRIPTION OF PARTS	These Columns are headed by the Part Numbers of complete units
H.T. Lead Sleeve	**S1220**

FLYWHEEL EXTRACTORS

DESCRIPTION OF PARTS	These Columns are headed by the Part Numbers of complete units
Flywheel Extractor	**S1256**

The appropriate equipment to which these parts are fitted can be found by referring the Part No. in heavy type to sheets headed MAIN COMPONENTS.

For Prices refer to Master Price List.

THE WIPAC GROUP — BUCKINGHAM — BUCKS — ENGLAND

REF. BA6/6

SERVICE WIPAC INSTRUCTIONS — IG 1555

RUNNING MAINTENANCE

The ignition generator requires very little maintenance and if the following notes are observed the life of the machine should prove trouble-free.

Check and if necessary re-adjust the contacts once every 5,000 miles.

Occasionally clean the contacts by inserting a dry smooth piece of paper between them and withdrawing while the contacts are in the closed position. Do not allow the engine to run with oil or petrol on the contacts or they will start to burn and blacken, and if they do, lightly polish with a piece of smooth emery cloth.

After every 5,000 miles it is necessary to re-lubricate the cam grease pad. This is done by removing the pad and squeezing and working into it a Summer grade of motor transmission grease which will very closely resemble that used at the factory. **Do not use ordinary grease.**

SERVICING

Checking ignition for spark

If the engine fails to start and there is indication that the ignition is at fault:—

(A) Disconnect H.T. lead from the spark plug and hold it about $\frac{3}{16}$" away from some unpainted portion of the frame or engine. Kick-start the engine in the usual way and a spark should jump this gap.

(B) If no spark is visible:—
1. Make sure H.T. lead is screwed right home into Coil box.
2. Check H.T. lead for continuity.
3. Check contact breaker points for correct gap setting and see that they are clean.
Check breaker point adjustment screws for tightness.
4. By removing the flywheel examine the internal leads for breaks and see they are all properly secured. Make sure covered leads are not chafed and earthing.
5. Make sure there are no metallic particles inside the unit.

Condenser

A weak or faulty condenser can be detected by badly burnt and pitted contacts or a continuous **intense blue** spark across the contacts when running. A very small white spark across the points when running is normal.

The condenser can be removed by undoing the screw securing it and releasing the lead from the terminal post.

Contact breaker points

Adjustment. Turn engine over until points are fully open.

Test with feeler gauge between "points". If the "points" require adjustment slacken the fixing screw and carefully move the fixed contact plate by means of a screwdriver until the correct gap is obtained. Tighten screw.

The breaker point setting should only be adjusted in the manner described and **at no time should the breaker arm be bent to provide adjustment.**

If the contact points need replacing both the fixed and movable points must be replaced at the same time.

Replacement of ignition and lighting coils

Removal. First release ignition coil primary leads, then with a gentle pull the coil can be withdrawn from the core. Considerable force may be necessary to remove L.T. coils from core as a fibre wedge is used to ensure a tight fit and a varnish adherent is also used to secure the lighting coils.

THIS IGNITION GENERATOR IS FITTED AS STANDARD EQUIPMENT TO THE

B.S.A. SUNBEAM B1.
175c.c. SCOOTER

AND

TRIUMPH TS1. TIGRESS
175c.c. SCOOTER

MAIN DETAILS	
Wipac Type	Series 141
Engine cylinder	Single
Rotation	CCW
Flywheel weight	4 lbs. 12 ozs.
Flywheel dia. Body	$5\frac{1}{2}$"
Fan	$6\frac{3}{8}$"
Ignition	Direct from magneto
Lighting	6 volt A.C./D.C. Trickle Charge
H.T. Lead	24" (5 mm.)
Breaker point setting	.018"
Flywheel extractor	S0073
Recommended spark plug	P90 (Wipac)

Flywheel

This flywheel is robustly constructed with the cam integral with the flywheel boss and it is unlikely to develop any faults in normal use. **A KEEPER RING IS NOT NECESSARY WHEN WITHDRAWING IT FROM THE STATOR PLATE.**

Removal. Remove the nut securing the flywheel to the shaft. If an extractor is not available and the flywheel cannot be easily withdrawn, grasp the flywheel firmly and while attempting to pull it off, tap the end of the crankshaft with a mallet or lead hammer, being careful during this operation not to damage the crankshaft. When replacing the flywheel make sure metallized dust or small steel items have not been attracted onto the magnets.

THE WIPAC GROUP — BUCKINGHAM — BUCKS.
TELEPHONE: BUCKINGHAM 3031   TELEGRAMS: WICOMAGSCO BUCKINGHAM

REF. B 1555

IG 1555 SPARE PARTS LIST

PARTS IN EXPLODED VIEW	COMPONENTS	SETS	UNITS
		S1072 Inspection Cover Set	
			S1071 Flywheel and Cam Unit (includes S1072)
	S0052 Condenser Fixing Set	S0051 Condenser Set (includes S0052)	
		S0054 Contact Breaker Fixing Set	
		S1178 Contact Breaker Point Set	
	S1048 L.T. Coils Set		
	S0057 Core and Plate Assembly Set (includes S0055)	S1047 H.T., L.T. Coils and Core Unit	S1045 Stator Unit
	S1046 H.T. Coil Set		
	S0055 Grease Pad Set		
		S1208 H.T. & L.T. Leads Fixing Bracket Set	
		S1049 L.T. Leads Set	
		S0773 H.T. Lead Wire Group (24")	
			S1220 H.T. Lead Sleeve

BRITISH BUILT BY THE WIPAC GROUP

REF. B1555

SERVICE WIPAC INSTRUCTIONS   IG 1586

RUNNING MAINTENANCE

The ignition generator requires very little maintenance and if the following notes are observed the life of the machine should prove trouble-free.

Check and if necessary re-adjust the contacts once every 5,000 miles.

Occasionally clean the contacts by inserting a dry smooth piece of paper between them and withdrawing while the contacts are in the closed position. Do not allow the engine to run with oil or petrol on the contacts or they will start to burn and blacken, and if they do, lightly polish with a piece of smooth emery cloth.

After every 5,000 miles it is necessary to re-lubricate the cam grease pad. This is done by removing the pad and squeezing and working into it a Summer grade of motor transmission grease which will very closely resemble that used at the factory. **Do not use ordinary grease.**

SERVICING

Checking ignition for spark

If the engine fails to start and there is indication that the ignition is at fault:—

(A) Disconnect H.T. lead from the spark plug and hold it about $\frac{3}{16}''$ away from some unpainted portion of the frame or engine. Kick-start the engine in the usual way and a spark should jump this gap.

(B) If no spark is visible:—
 1. Make sure H.T. lead is screwed right home into Coil box.
 2. Check H.T. lead for continuity.
 3. Check contact breaker points for correct gap setting and see that they are clean.
    Check breaker point adjustment screws for tightness.
 4. By removing the flywheel examine the internal leads for breaks and see they are all properly secured. Make sure covered leads are not chafed and earthing.
 5. Make sure there are no metallic particles inside the unit.

Condenser

A weak or faulty condenser can be detected by badly burnt and pitted contacts or a continuous **intense blue** spark across the contacts when running. A very small white spark across the points when running is normal.

The condenser can be removed by undoing the screw securing it and releasing the lead from the terminal post.

Contact breaker points

Adjustment. Turn engine over until points are fully open.

Test with feeler gauge between "points". If the "points" require adjustment slacken the fixing screw and carefully move the fixed contact plate by means of a screwdriver until the correct gap is obtained. Tighten screw.

The breaker point setting should only be adjusted in the manner described and at no time should the breaker arm be bent to provide adjustment.

If the contact points need replacing both the fixed and movable points must be replaced at the same time.

Replacement of ignition and lighting coils

Removal. First release ignition coil primary leads, then with a gentle pull the coil can be withdrawn from the core. Considerable force may be necessary to remove L.T. coils from core as a fibre wedge is used to ensure a tight fit and a varnish adherent is also used to secure the lighting coils.

THIS IGNITION GENERATOR IS FITTED AS STANDARD EQUIPMENT TO THE

JAMES 150c.c. FLYING CADET
AND
FRANCIS-BARNETT 150c.c. PLOVER 86

MAIN DETAILS

Wipac Type	Series 141
Engine cylinder	Single
Rotation	Clockwise
Flywheel weight	3 lbs. 13 ozs.
Flywheel diameter	$5\frac{1}{4}''$
Ingition	Direct from magneto
Lighting	6 volt A.C. 28.8 watts at 2,800 r.p.m.
H.T. lead	21" (5 mm.)
Breaker point setting	.018"

Flywheel

This flywheel is robustly constructed with the cam integral with the flywheel boss and it is unlikely to develop any faults in normal use. **A KEEPER RING IS NOT NECESSARY WHEN WITHDRAWING IT FROM THE STATOR PLATE.**

Removal. Remove the nut securing the flywheel to the shaft. If an extractor is not available and the flywheel cannot be easily withdrawn, grasp the flywheel firmly and while attempting to pull it off, tap the end of the crankshaft with a mallet or lead hammer, being careful during this operation not to damage the crankshaft. When replacing the flywheel make sure metallized dust or small steel items have not been attracted onto the magnets.

THE WIPAC GROUP — BUCKINGHAM — BUCKS — ENGLAND
TELEPHONE: BUCKINGHAM 3031   TELEGRAMS: WICOMAGSCO · BUCKINGHAM

REF. B. 1586/1

IG 1586 SPARE PARTS LIST

PARTS IN EXPLODED VIEW	COMPONENTS	SETS	UNITS
(Flywheel illustration)			S1032 Flywheel and Cam Unit
(Condenser)	S0052 Condenser Fixing Set	S1051 Condenser Set (includes S0052)	S1052 Stator Unit
(Breaker point parts)	S0054 Breaker Point Fixing Set	S0577 Breaker Point Set	
(L.T. Coil)	S1053 L.T. Coil Set		
(Core and plate assembly)	S0057 Core and Plate Assembly (includes S0055)	S1055 H.T., L.T. Coils and Core Unit	
(H.T. Coil)	S1046 H.T. Coil Set		
(Grease pad)	S0055 Grease Pad Set		
(L.T. Lead)	S1054 L.T. Lead Set		
(H.T. Lead Wire)	S0716 H.T. Lead Wire Group (21")		
(Sleeve)	S1220 Sleeve		
(Grommet)	S1168 Grommet		

BRITISH BUILT BY THE WIPAC GROUP

REF. B. 1586/1

SERVICE WIPAC INSTRUCTIONS IG 1649

RUNNING MAINTENANCE

The ignition generator requires very little maintenance and if the following notes are observed the life of the machine should prove trouble-free.

Check and if necessary re-adjust the contacts once every 5,000 miles.

Occasionally clean the contacts by inserting a dry smooth piece of paper between them and withdrawing while the contacts are in the closed position. Do not allow the engine to run with oil or petrol on the contacts or they will start to burn and blacken, and if they do, lightly polish with a piece of smooth emery cloth.

After every 5,000 miles it is necessary to re-lubricate the cam grease pad. This is done by removing the pad and squeezing and working into it a Summer grade of motor transmission grease which will very closely resemble that used at the factory. **Do not use ordinary grease.**

SERVICING

Checking ignition for spark

If the engine fails to start and there is indication that the ignition is at fault:—

(A) Disconnect H.T. lead from the spark plug and hold it about $\tfrac{3}{16}''$ away from some unpainted portion of the frame or engine. Kick-start the engine in the usual way and a spark should jump this gap.

(B) If no spark is visible:—
1. Make sure H.T. lead is screwed right home into Coil box.
2. Check H.T. lead for continuity.
3. Check contact breaker points for correct gap setting and see that they are clean.
   Check breaker point adjustment screw for tightness.
4. By removing the flywheel examine the internal leads for breaks and see they are all properly secured. Make sure covered leads are not chafed and earthing.
5. Make sure there are no metallic particles inside the unit.

Condenser

A weak or faulty condenser can be detected by badly burnt and pitted contacts or a continuous **intense blue** spark across the contacts when running. A very small white spark across the points when running is normal.

The condenser can be removed by undoing the screw securing it and releasing the lead by unsoldering from the terminal post.

Contact breaker points

Adjustment. Turn engine over until points are fully open.

Test with feeler gauge between "points". If the "points" require adjustment slacken the fixing screw and carefully move the fixed contact plate by means of a screwdriver until the correct gap is obtained. Tighten screw.

The breaker point setting should only be adjusted in the manner described and **at no time should the breaker arm be bent to provide adjustment.**

If the contact points need replacing both the fixed and movable points must be replaced at the same time.

Ignition Coil

First release the ignition coil primary leads at the earth tag and contact breaker.

Next carefully lift the coil retaining clip clear from the lamination stack centre bore and with a gentle pull the coil can be withdrawn from the core complete with clip.

Lighting Coils

It may be necessary to use rather more force to remove the lighting coil units as a varnish adherent is used to secure these to the coil core limbs. As an additional safeguard, the top lamination is also opened up and it is essential to close this gap before attempting removal.

THIS IGNITION GENERATOR IS FITTED AS STANDARD EQUIPMENT TO THE

TRIUMPH "TINA"
100 c.c. SCOOTER

MAIN DETAILS	
Wipac Type	Series 191
Engine cylinder	Single
Rotation	CCW
Flywheel weight	4 lbs.
Flywheel dia.	
Body	$4\tfrac{1}{2}''$
Fins	$6\tfrac{1}{2}''$
Ignition	Direct from magneto
Lighting	6 volt A.C. 22.8 watts at 3,000 r.p.m.
H.T. Lead	16" (5 mm.)
Breaker point setting	.018"
Flywheel extractor	S0073

See separate leaflets for Standard Models
Wiring Diagram	WD/35/830
Lighting Equipment	LE.2
Data Sheet	T.D.2

See separate leaflets for models fitted with Stop Lamp Set
Wiring Diagram	WD/67/901/1
Lighting Equipment	LE.6
Data Sheet	T.D.2

Flywheel

This flywheel is robustly constructed with the cam integral with the flywheel boss and it is unlikely to develop any faults in normal use. A KEEPER RING IS NOT NECESSARY WHEN WITHDRAWING IT FROM THE STATOR PLATE.

Removal. Remove the nut securing the flywheel to the shaft. If an extractor is not available and the flywheel cannot be easily withdrawn, grasp the flywheel firmly and while attempting to pull it off, tap the end of the crankshaft with a mallet or lead hammer, being careful during this operation not to damage the crankshaft. When replacing the flywheel make sure metallized dust or small steel items have not been attracted onto the magnets.

THE WIPAC GROUP — BUCKINGHAM — BUCKS.
TELEPHONE: BUCKINGHAM 3031   TELEGRAMS: WICOMAGSCO BUCKINGHAM

REF. B. 1649/1

IG 1649 — SPARE PARTS LIST

UNITS	SETS	COMPONENTS AND ASSEMBLIES	PARTS IN EXPLODED VIEW
S2729 Flywheel Unit (includes S2841)		S2841 Inspection Cover Set	
S3663 Stator Unit		S2849 Grease Pad Set	
		S3440 Contact Breaker Point Unit	S2850 Contact Breaker Point Fixing Set
		S2847 Condenser Set (includes S2848)	S2848 Condenser Fixing Set
		S3666 Stator Core and Lighting Coils Set	S3664 Lighting Coils Set (includes Part of S2853) / S2843 Stator Core Set
		S3646 H.T. Coil Set	
		S2853 L.T. Leads Set	
		S3665 H.T Lead Set	
			S1220 Sleeve

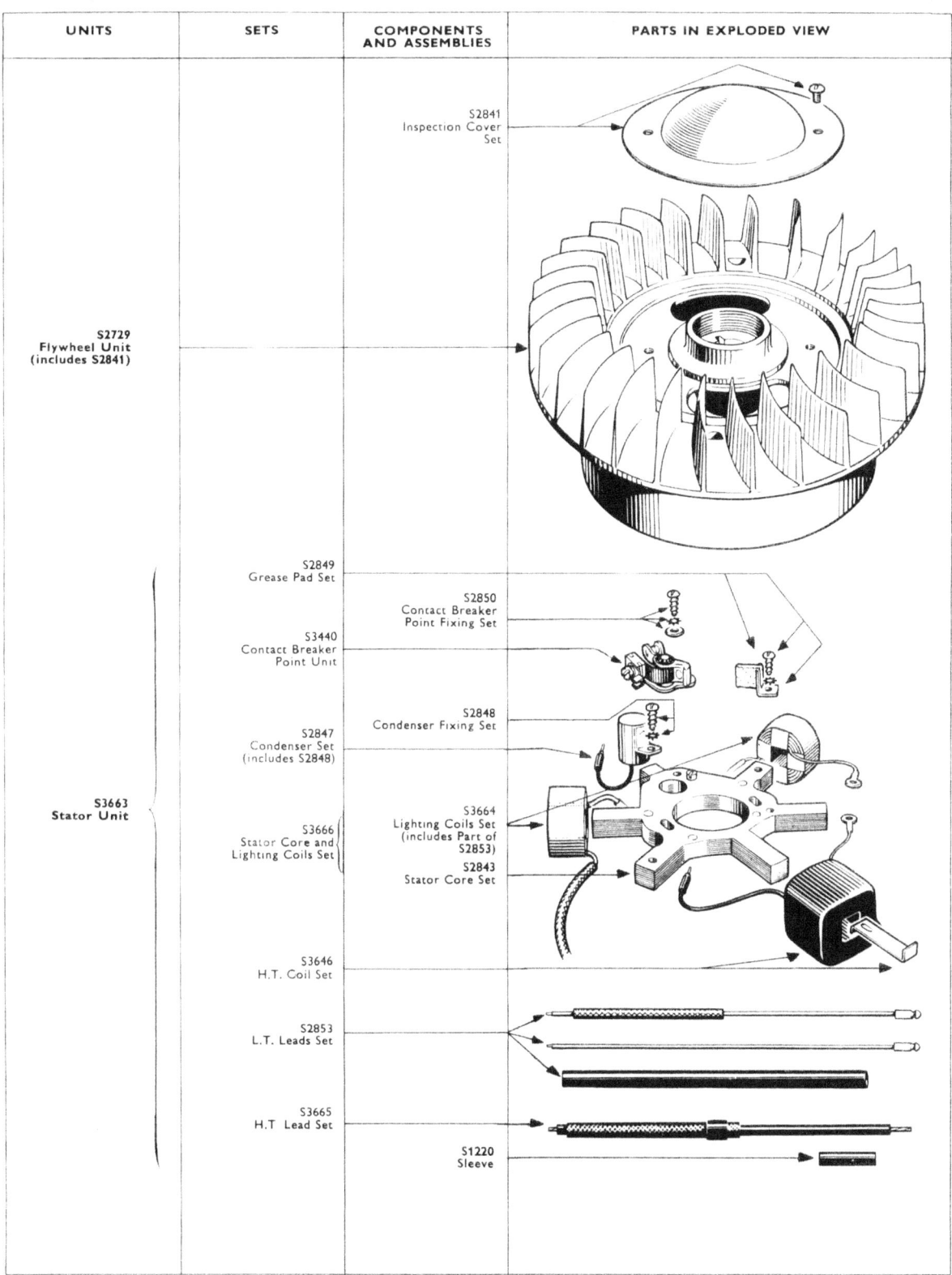

BRITISH BUILT BY THE WIPAC GROUP

REF B.1649/3

SERVICE WIPAC INSTRUCTIONS   IG 1688

RUNNING MAINTENANCE

The ignition generator requires very little maintenance and if the following notes are observed the life of the machine should prove trouble-free.

Check and if necessary re-adjust the contacts once every 5,000 miles.

Occasionally clean the contacts by inserting a dry smooth piece of paper between them and withdrawing while the contacts are in the closed position. Do not allow the engine to run with oil or petrol on the contacts or they will start to burn and blacken, and if they do, lightly polish with a piece of smooth emery cloth.

After every 5,000 miles it is necessary to re-lubricate the cam grease pad. This is done by removing the pad and squeezing and working into it a Summer grade of motor transmission grease which will very closely resemble that used at the factory. **Do not use ordinary grease.**

SERVICING

Checking ignition for spark

If the engine fails to start and there is indication that the ignition is at fault:—

(A) Disconnect H.T. lead from the spark plug and hold it about $\frac{3}{16}''$ away from some unpainted portion of the frame or engine. Kick-start the engine in the usual way and a spark should jump this gap.

(B) If no spark is visible:—
1. Make sure H.T. lead is screwed right home into Coil box.
2. Check H.T. lead for continuity.
3. Check contact breaker points for correct gap setting and see that they are clean.
   Check breaker point adjustment screw for tightness.
4. By removing the flywheel examine the internal leads for breaks and see they are all properly secured. Make sure covered leads are not chafed and earthing.
5. Make sure there are no metallic particles inside the unit.

Condenser

A weak or faulty condenser can be detected by badly burnt and pitted contacts or a continuous **intense blue** spark across the contacts when running. A very small white spark across the points when running is normal.

The condenser can be removed by undoing the screw securing it and releasing the lead by unsoldering from the terminal post.

Contact breaker points

Adjustment. Turn engine over until points are fully open.

Test with feeler gauge between "points". If the "points" require adjustment slacken the fixing screw and carefully move the fixed contact plate by means of a screwdriver until the correct gap is obtained. Tighten screw.

The breaker point setting should only be adjusted in the manner described and **at no time should the breaker arm be bent to provide adjustment.**

If the contact points need replacing both the fixed and movable points must be replaced at the same time.

Ignition Coil

First release the ignition coil primary leads at the earth tag and contact breaker.

Next carefully lift the coil retaining clip clear from the lamination stack centre bore and with a gentle pull the coil can be withdrawn from the core complete with clip.

Lighting Coils

It may be necessary to use rather more force to remove the lighting coil units as a varnish adherent is used to secure these to the coil core limbs. As an additional safeguard, the top lamination is also opened up and it is essential to close this gap before attemping removal.

THIS IGNITION GENERATOR IS FITTED AS STANDARD EQUIPMENT TO THE

ARIEL "PIXIE" 50 c.c.
LIGHTWEIGHT MOTORCYCLE

AND

B.S.A. "BEAGLE" 75 c.c.
LIGHTWEIGHT MOTORCYCLE

MAIN DETAILS	
Wipac Type	Series 191
Engine cylinder	Single
Rotation	CW
Flywheel type	Plain
" bore	Taper
" weight	2 lbs. 5 ozs.
" dia.	4 $\frac{11}{16}$"
Ignition	Direct from magneto
Lighting	6 volt A.C. 22.8 watts at 4,000 r.p.m.
H.T. Lead	14" (5 mm.)
Breaker point setting	.018"
Flywheel extractor	S0282

See separate leaflets for "Pixie"
Wiring Diagram	WD/63/904/1
Lighting Equipment	L.E.9
Data Sheet	TD.2

See separate leaflets for "Beagle"
Wiring Diagram	WD/64/903
Lighting Equipment	L.E.7
Data Sheet	TD.2

Flywheel

This flywheel is robustly constructed with the cam integral with the flywheel boss and it is unlikely to develop any faults in normal use. **A KEEPER RING IS NOT NECESSARY WHEN WITHDRAWING IT FROM THE STATOR PLATE.**

Removal. Remove the nut securing the flywheel to the shaft. If an extractor is not available and the flywheel cannot be easily withdrawn, grasp the flywheel firmly and while attempting to pull it off, tap the end of the crankshaft with a mallet or lead hammer, being careful during this operation not to damage the crankshaft. When replacing the flywheel make sure metallized dust or small steel items have not been attracted onto the magnets.

THE WIPAC GROUP — BUCKINGHAM — BUCKS.
TELEPHONE: BUCKINGHAM 3031   TELEGRAMS: WICOMAGSCO BUCKINGHAM

REF. B. 1688

IG 1688   SPARE PARTS LIST

UNITS	SETS	COMPONENTS AND ASSEMBLIES	PARTS IN EXPLODED VIEW
	S3382 Flywheel Unit		
S3404 Stator Unit	S2849 Grease Pad Set		
	S3440 Contact Breaker Point Unit	S2850 Contact Breaker Point Fixing Set	
	S2847 Condenser Set (includes S2848)	S2848 Condenser Fixing Set	
	S3550 Stator Core and Lighting Coils Set	S3557 Lighting Coils Set (includes Part of S3559)	
		S2843 Stator Core Set	
	S2846 H.T. Coil Set		
	S3559 L.T. Leads Set		
	S3405 H.T. Lead Set	S1220 Sleeve	

BRITISH BUILT BY THE WIPAC GROUP

REF. B.1688.

SERVICE WIPAC INSTRUCTIONS — IG 1741

RUNNING MAINTENANCE

The ignition generator on the T.10 Automatic operates on the Energy Transfer principle, requiring very little maintenance and if the following notes are observed the life of the machine should prove trouble free.

Check and if necessary re-adjust the contacts once every 5,000 miles.

Occasionally clean the contacts by inserting a dry smooth piece of paper between them and withdrawing whilst the contacts are in the closed position. Do not allow the engine to run with oil or petrol on the contacts, or they will burn and blacken, and if they do, lightly polish with a piece of smooth emery cloth.

After every 5,000 miles it is necessary to re-lubricate the cam grease pad. This can be done by removing the pad and squeezing and working into it, a little high melting point grease (H.M.P.). Alternatively, the cam can be very lightly smeared with H.M.P. Grease through the Inspection apertures in the face of the flywheel.

Do not use ordinary grease as this tends to become fluid under heat, and the contacts may become contaminated.

SERVICING

Checking engine for spark

If the engine fails to start and there is indication that the ignition is at fault:—
(A) Disconnect the H.T. lead from the spark plug and hold it about $\tfrac{3}{16}''$ away from some unpainted portion of the frame or engine. Kick-start the engine in the usual way and a spark should jump this gap.
(B) If no spark is visible:—
1. Unplug the violet lead from the engine governor centrifugal switch from the machine harness and re-check as described at (A). This check will give an indication that the fault does not lie in the governor switch.
2. Disconnect the violet lead from the seat switch to the main harness and again re-check as at (A). This will give an indication as to whether the fault lies in the seat switch.
3. Make sure that the H.T. lead is correctly fitted into the coil box, and check H.T. lead for continuity.
4. Check contact breaker point for correct gap setting, and see that they are clean. Check breaker point adjustment screw for tightness.
5. By removing the flywheel, examine the internal leads for breaks, and see that they are all properly secured. Make sure that covered leads are not chafed or earthing.

Condenser

A weak or faulty condenser or condenser connections can be detected by badly burned and pitted contacts, or a continuous intense blue spark across the contacts when running. A very small white spark across the points when running is normal.

The condenser can be removed by undoing the screw securing it, and releasing the lead by unsoldering from the contact breaker terminal.

Contact Breaker points.

Adjustment. Turn the engine over until the contact breaker heel is on the highest portion of the cam.

Test with a feeler gauge between the "points". If the "points" require adjustment, slacken the fixing screw and carefully move the fixed contact plate by means of a screwdriver until the correct gap is obtained. Tighten Screw.

The breaker points should only be adjusted in the manner described, and at no time should the breaker arm be bent to provide adjustment.

If the contact points need replacing, both the fixed and movable points must be replaced at the same time.

Ignition Coil

This is mounted externally from the ignition generator and requires only periodic checking as to security and cleanliness, particularly at lead connections.

Low Tension Coils

Four low tension coils are to be found mounted on the various core limbs of the stator plate. When viewing the stator plate with the contact breaker group in the downwards position, the uppermost coil and the coil to the right of the contact breaker group (i.e. situated between the contact breaker and the condenser) are the lighting feed coils. These coils are connected in series with one end earthed to provide A/C lights for the machine.

The remaining two coils, i.e. those on the left of the stator plate, are the ignition feed coils.

A varnish adherent is used to secure these coils to the coil core limbs. As an additional safeguard, the top lamination of the stator core is formed into a retaining tab and it is essential to close down this tab before an attempt is made to remove the coils.

THIS IGNITION GENERATOR IS FITTED AS STANDARD EQUIPMENT TO THE

TRIUMPH T.10 AUTOMATIC
100 c.c. SCOOTER

MAIN DETAILS

Wipac Type	Series 191
Engine cylinder	Single
Rotation	CCW
Flywheel weight	4 lbs.
Flywheel dia.	
Body	$4\tfrac{1}{2}''$
Fins	$6\tfrac{1}{2}''$
Ignition	Energy Transfer
Lighting	6 volt A.C. 22.8 watts at 3,000 r.p.m.
H.T. Lead	16" (5 mm.)
Breaker point setting	.018"

See separate leaflets for

Wiring Diagram	WD/85/1013
Lighting Equipment	L.E.20
Data Sheet	T.D.7.

Replacing Feed Coils

As it is essential that the link wires between the coils be sufficiently short as to prevent their fouling the flywheel during service, replacement coils are not supplied pre-connected. After fitting replacement coils to the stator plate, it will be necessary to connect these together in series, and in the case of both the lighting and feed coils, one end earthed. An earth tag is provided, on the appropriate coils, and these should be secured under the cam grease felt support. The coils bearing the earth connection terminals are positioned on the core limbs closest to the cam grease felt.

Connecting Low Tension Coils

Refer to T.10 Technical Data sheet.

Flywheel

The flywheel is constructed with the cam integral with the flywheel boss, and is unlikely to develop faults in normal use. A KEEPER RING IS NOT NECESSARY WHEN WITHDRAWING IT FROM THE STATOR PLATE.

Removal. Remove the nut securing the flywheel to the crankshaft. The wheel can then be removed with the appropriate flywheel extractor. When replacing the flywheel ensure that no metallized dust or small steel items have been attracted onto the magnets.

THE WIPAC GROUP — BUCKINGHAM — BUCKS.
TELEPHONE: BUCKINGHAM 3031   TELEGRAMS: WICOMAGSCO BUCKINGHAM

REF. B. 1741

IG 1741   SPARE PARTS LIST

UNITS	SETS	COMPONENTS AND ASSEMBLIES	PARTS IN EXPLODED VIEW
S2729 Flywheel Unit (includes S2841)		S2841 Inspection Cover Set	
S3851 Stator Unit	S2849 Grease Pad Set		
	S3853 Contact Breaker Point Unit	S2850 Contact Breaker Point Fixing Set	
	S2847 Condenser Set (includes S2848)	S2848 Condenser Fixing Set	
	S3852 Stator Core and Lighting Coils Set	S4006 Feed Coils Set	
		S2843 Stator Core Set	
		S4007 Lighting Coils Set	
	S3854 L.T. Leads Set		

BRITISH BUILT BY THE WIPAC GROUP

REF. B. 1741

THE FOLLOWING PAGES 45-79 CONTAIN ILLUSTRATED PARTS LISTS FOR LIGHTING EQUIPMENT FITTED TO WIPAC EQUIPED MOTORCYCLES, SCOOTERS AND MOPEDS.

THIS LISTING IS IN ALPHABETICAL ORDER BY MANUFACTURER/MODEL. HOWEVER, PLEASE NOTE THAT THE MODEL LISTING MAY NOT BE SEQUENTIAL.
(FOR A.J.S. SEE MATCHLESS)

NOTES

ARIEL "PIXIE" 50 c.c.
LIGHTWEIGHT MOTORCYCLE
MODELS PRODUCED FROM OCTOBER 1963 TO AUG. 1965

- S3492 REFLECTOR AND GLASS SET 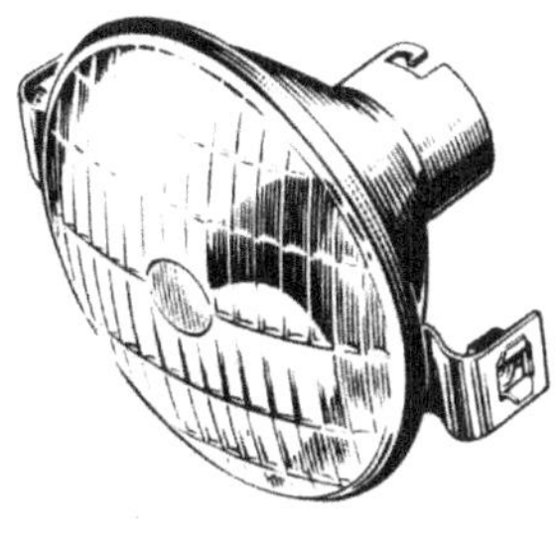
- S0215 FIXING SET (2 OFF)
- S0213 REAR/PARK LAMP
- S0214 COVER SET
- S0837 SWITCH UNIT
- S0939 SWITCH KNOB SET 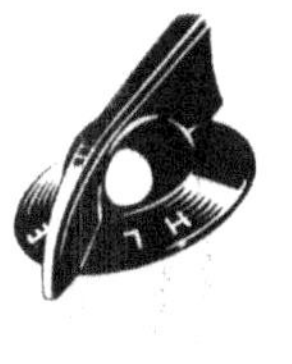
- S0768 BULB HOLDER (MAIN) 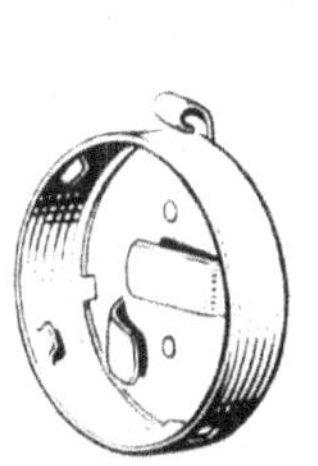 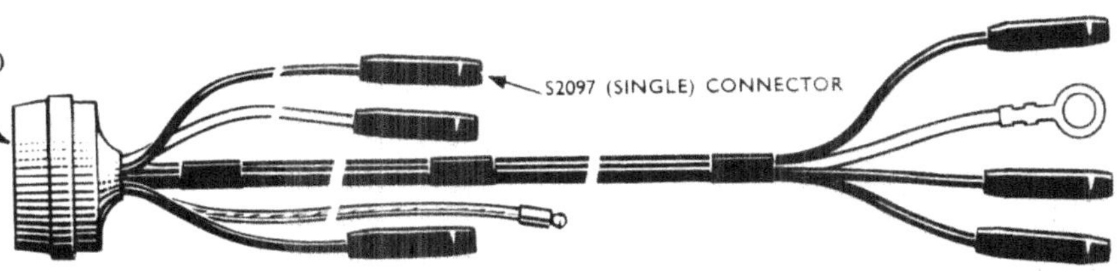
- S3491 HEADLAMP UNIT
- S0526 (BLUE) PLUG UNIT
- S2097 (SINGLE) CONNECTOR
- S3494 HARNESS (MAIN)

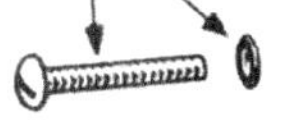

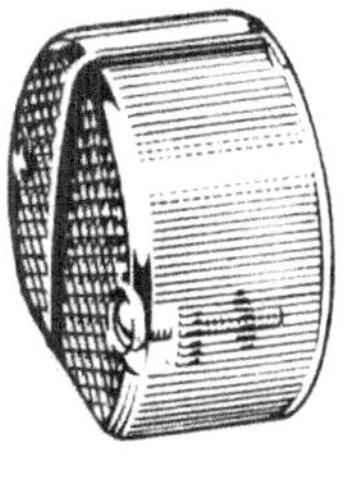

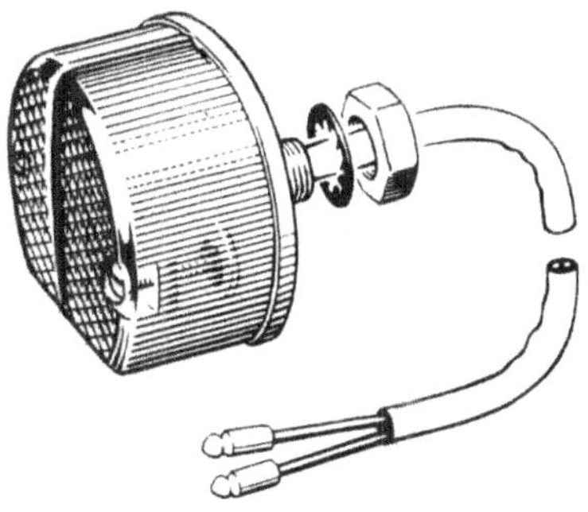

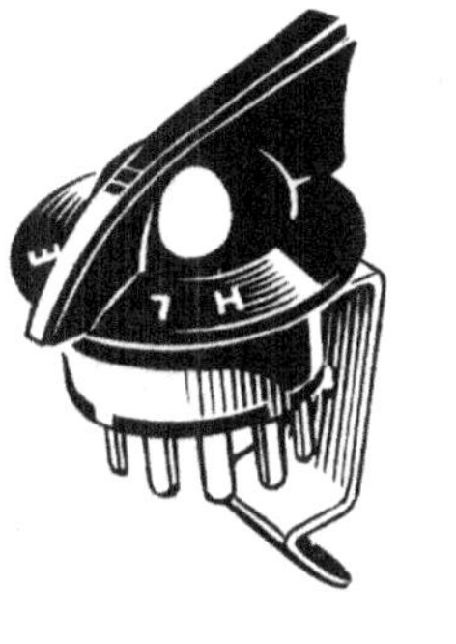

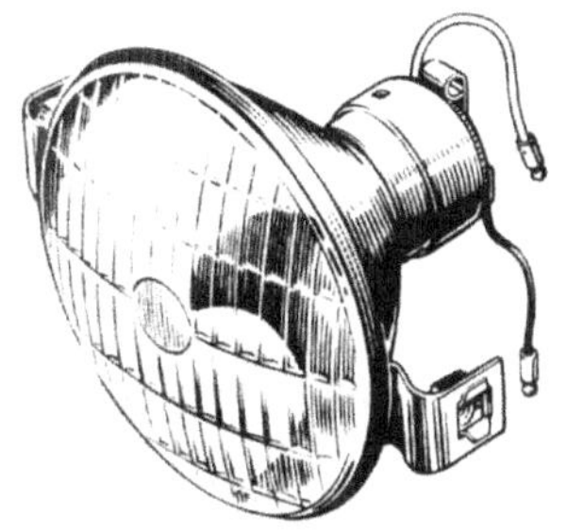

THE WIPAC GROUP — BUCKINGHAM — BUCKS.
TELEPHONE: BUCKINGHAM 3031   TELEGRAMS: WICOMAGSCO BUCKINGHAM

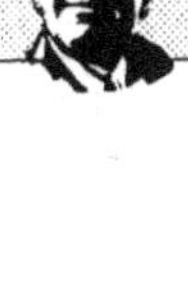

REF. L.E. 8/1/1/4

B.S.A. BANTAM SUPER D7
AC LIGHTING
FROM OCTOBER 1958

S0873 RIM	S2669 LAMP FRONT UNIT	S0507 REFLECTOR AND GLASS SET
S0768 BULB HOLDER UNIT (MAIN)	S0856 HEADLAMP UNIT	S0781 SWITCH (LIGHTS)
S0877 BULB HOLDER (PILOT)		S0783 SWITCH COVER UNIT (LIGHTS)
S0909 RIM LOCKING SET	S0874 LAMP ADJUSTER SET	S2796 PLUG UNIT RETAINER CLIP
S0887 REFLECTOR CLIP SET (SET OF 4)		

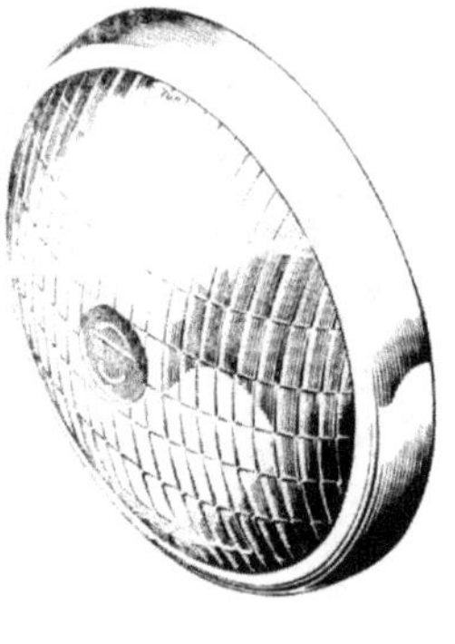

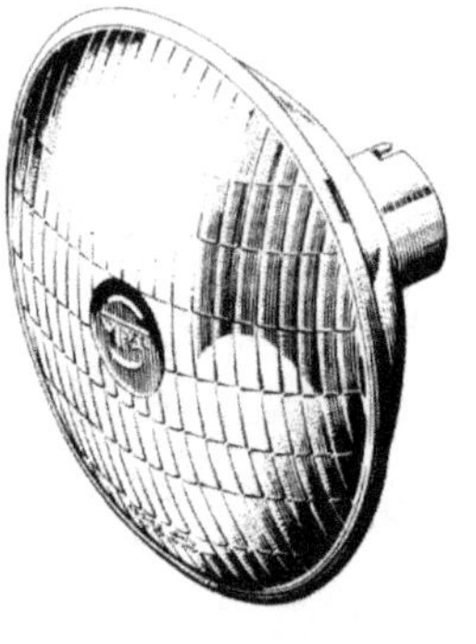

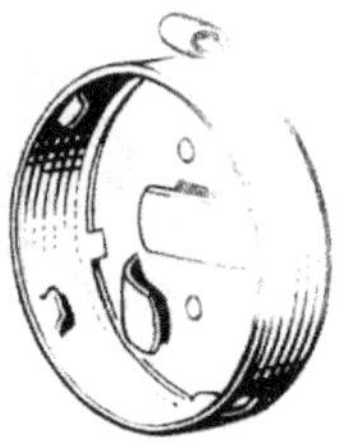

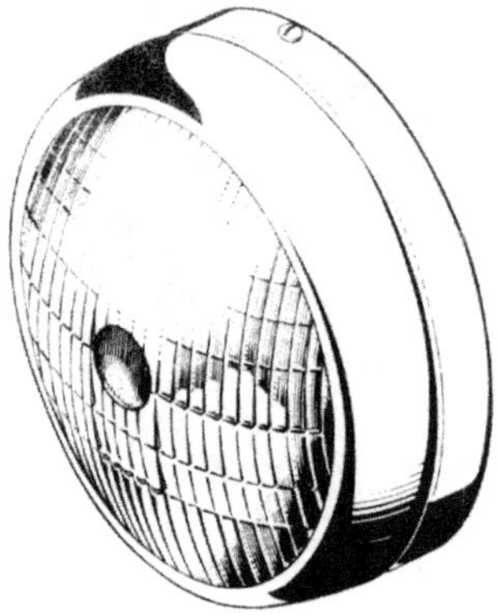

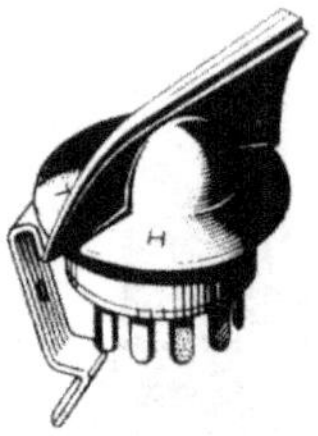

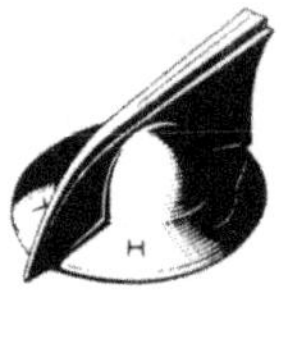

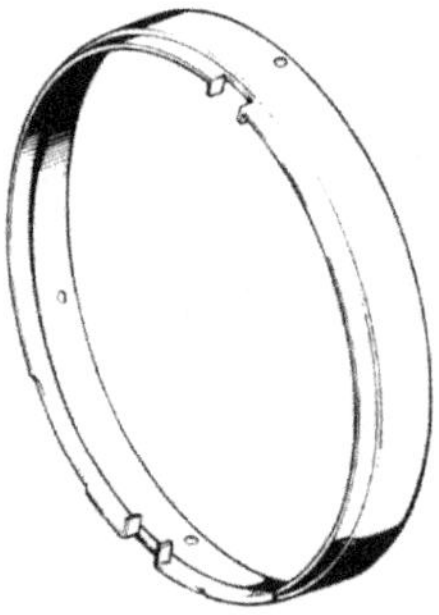

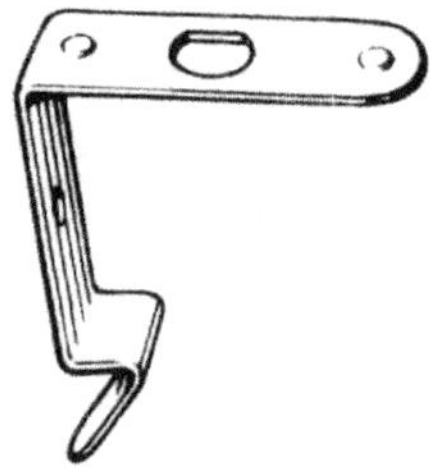

THE WIPAC GROUP — BUCKINGHAM — BUCKS.
TELEPHONE: BUCKINGHAM 3031   TELEGRAMS: WICOMAGSCO BUCKINGHAM

REF. LE.13/1/2

LIGHTING EQUIPMENT (Continued)

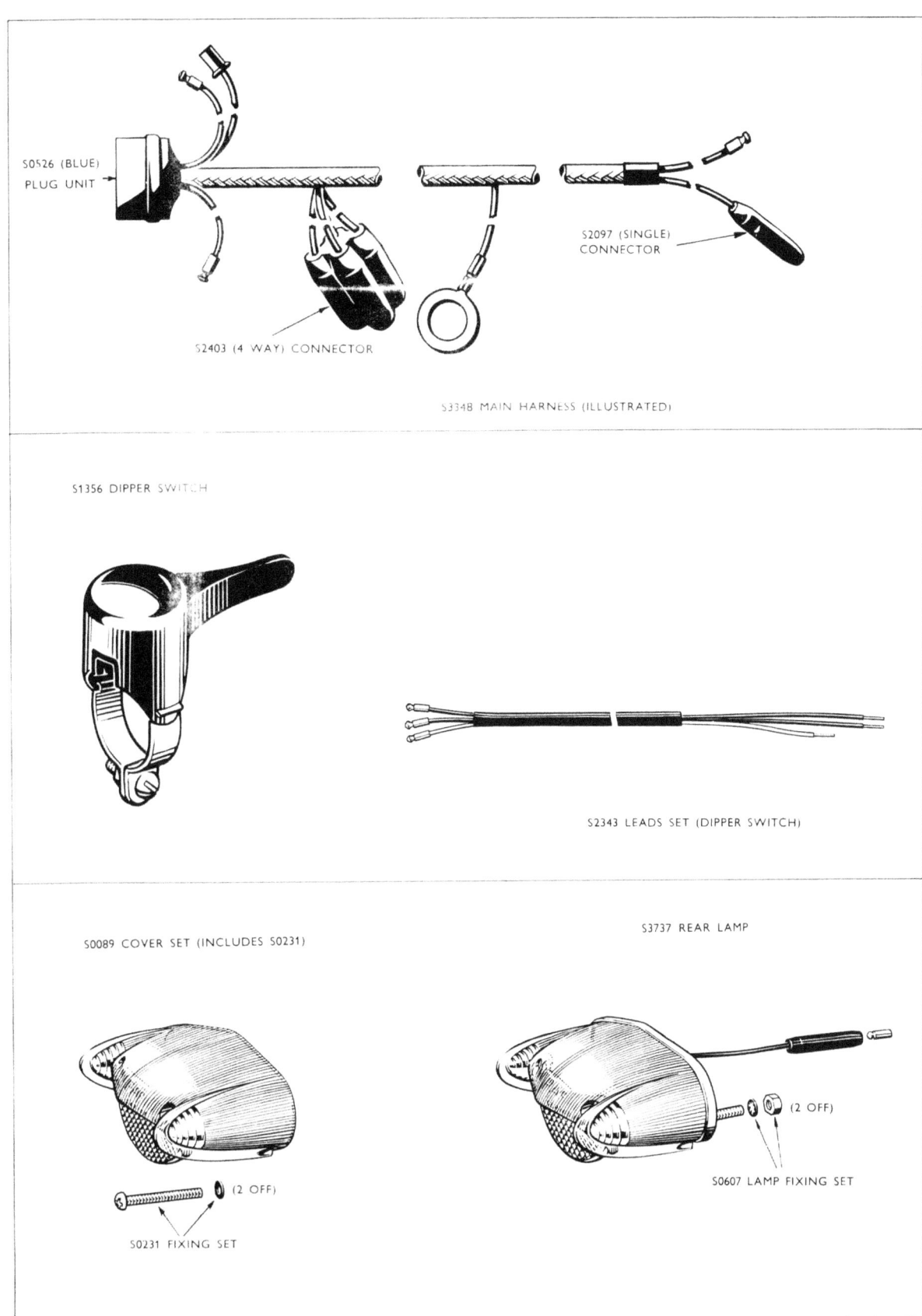

B.S.A. BANTAM SUPER D7
AC/DC TRICKLE CHARGE
FROM JULY 1959

S0873 RIM	S2669 LAMP FRONT UNIT	S0507 REFLECTOR AND GLASS SET
S0768 BULB HOLDER UNIT (MAIN)	S0891 HEADLAMP UNIT	S0781 SWITCH (LIGHTS)
S0877 BULB HOLDER (PILOT)	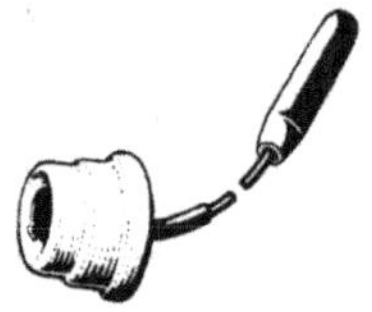	S0783 SWITCH COVER UNIT (LIGHTS)
S0909 RIM LOCKING SET	S0874 LAMP ADJUSTER SET	
S0887 REFLECTOR CLIP SET (SET OF 4)		S2796 PLUG UNIT RETAINER CLIP

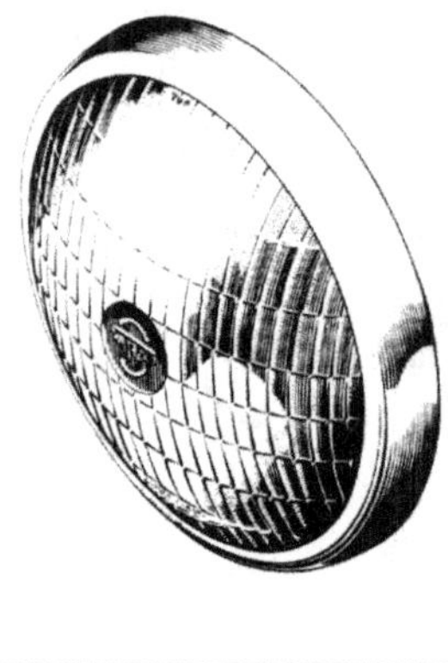

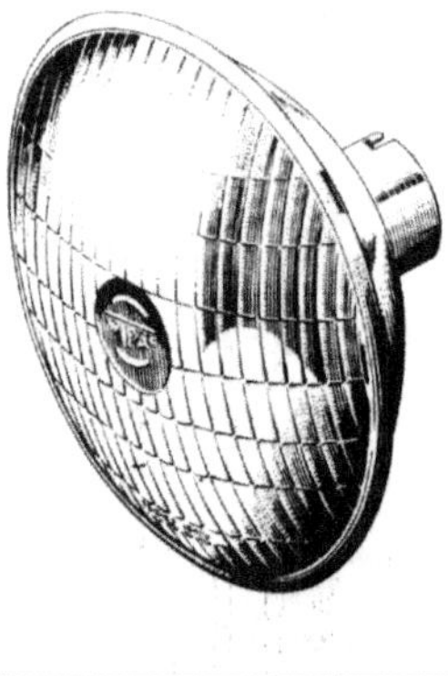

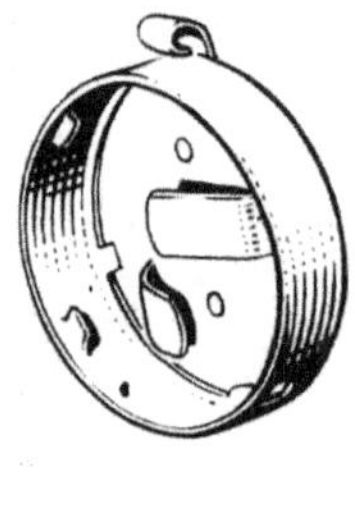

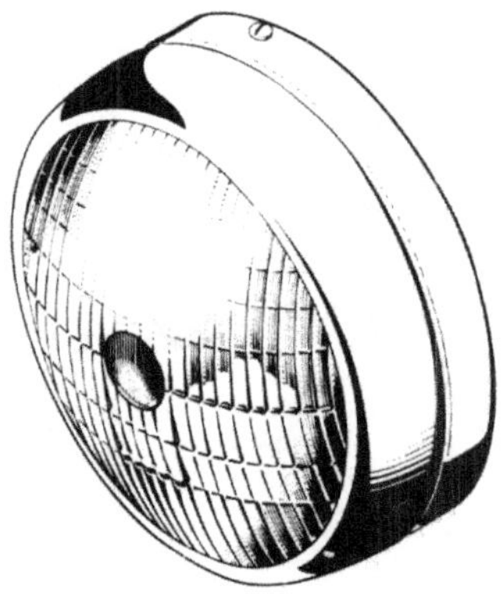

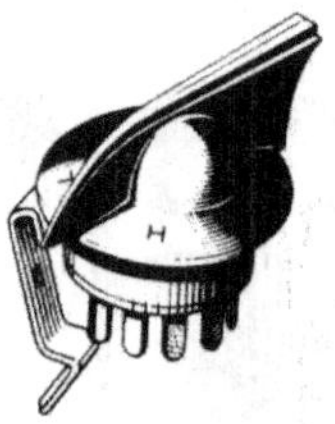

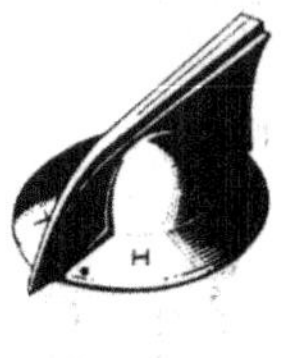

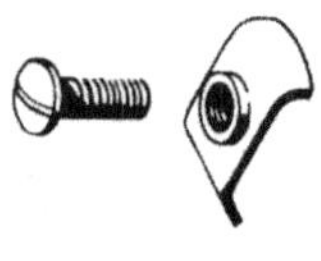

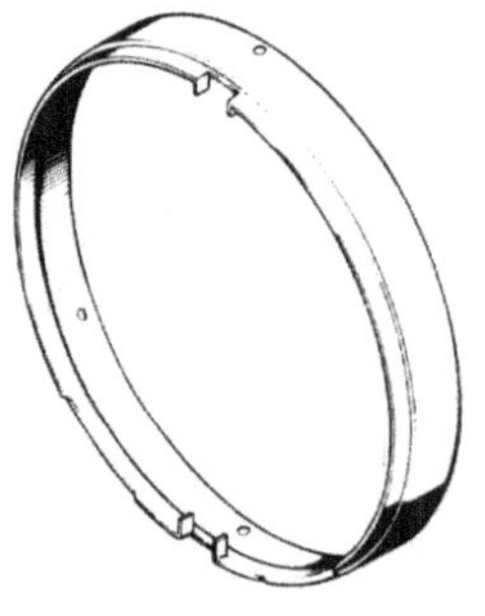

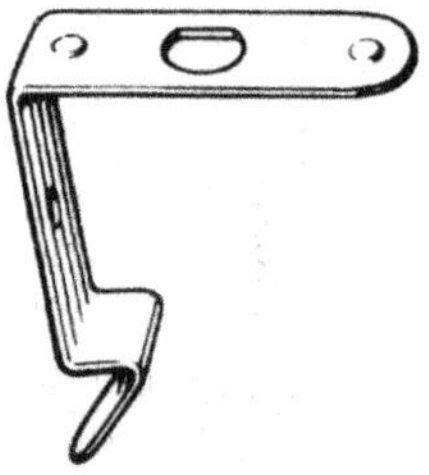

THE WIPAC GROUP — BUCKINGHAM — BUCKS.
TELEPHONE: BUCKINGHAM 3031   TELEGRAMS: WICOMAGSCO BUCKINGHAM

REF. LE.14/1/2

LIGHTING EQUIPMENT (Continued)

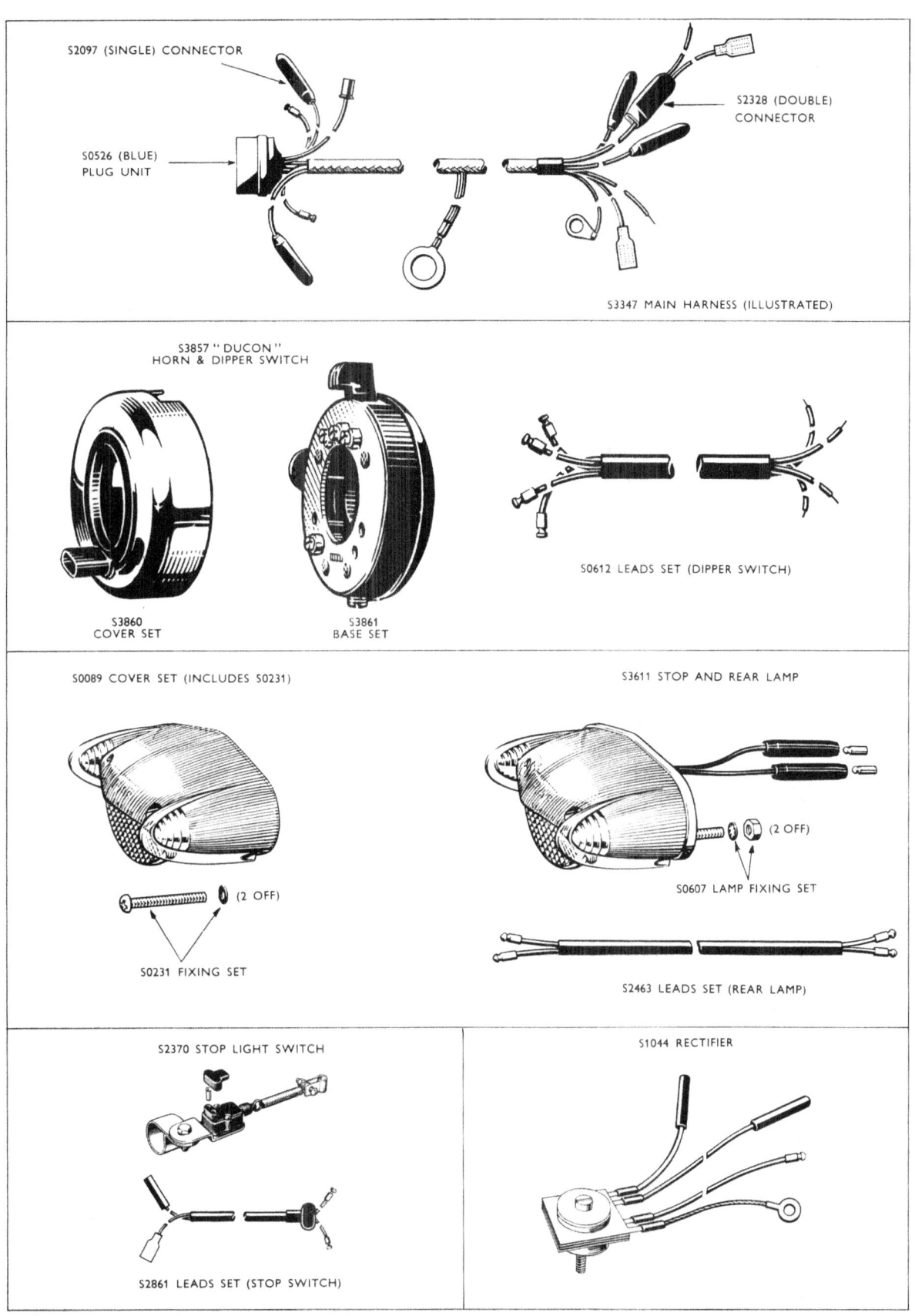

B.S.A. BANTAM SUPER D7
AC/DC TRICKLE CHARGE WITH COIL IGNITION
FROM OCTOBER 1963

S0873	RIM
S2669	LAMP FRONT UNIT
S0507	REFLECTOR AND GLASS SET
S0768	BULB HOLDER UNIT (MAIN)
S0891	HEADLAMP UNIT
S0781	SWITCH (LIGHTS)
S0782	SWITCH (IGNITION)
S0877	BULB HOLDER (PILOT)
S0783	SWITCH COVER UNIT (LIGHTS)
S0784	SWITCH COVER UNIT (IGNITION)
S0909	RIM LOCKING SET
S0874	LAMP ADJUSTER SET
S2796	PLUG UNIT RETAINER CLIP
S0887	REFLECTOR CLIP SET (SET OF 4)

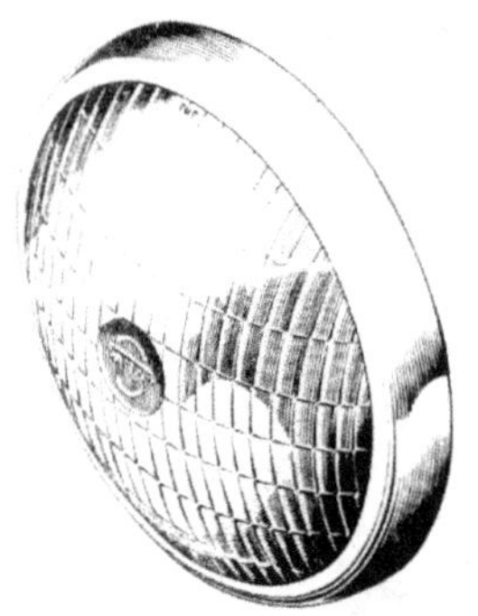

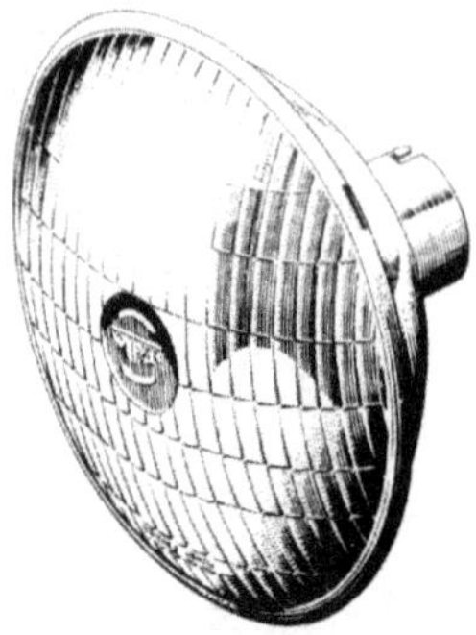

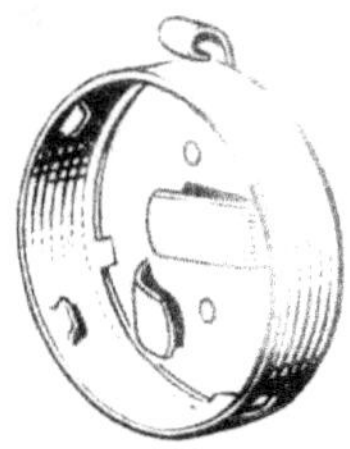

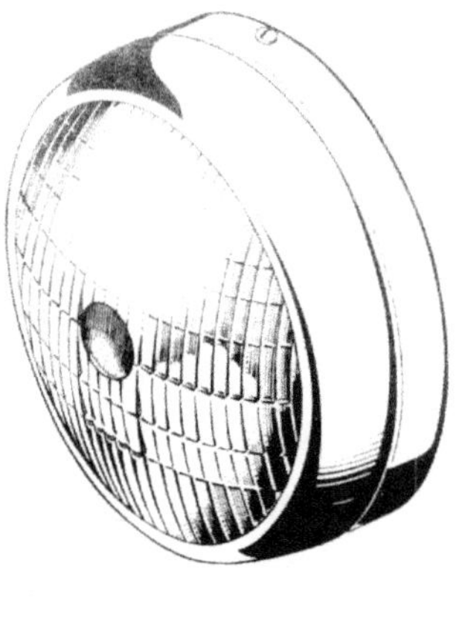

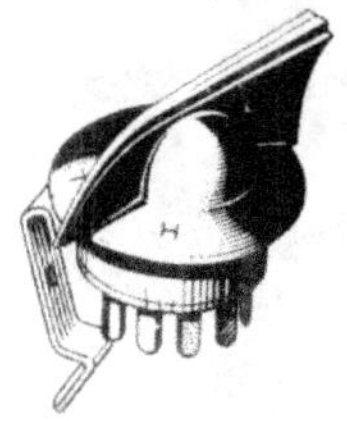

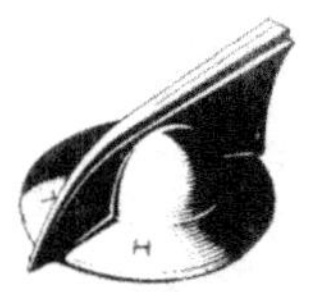

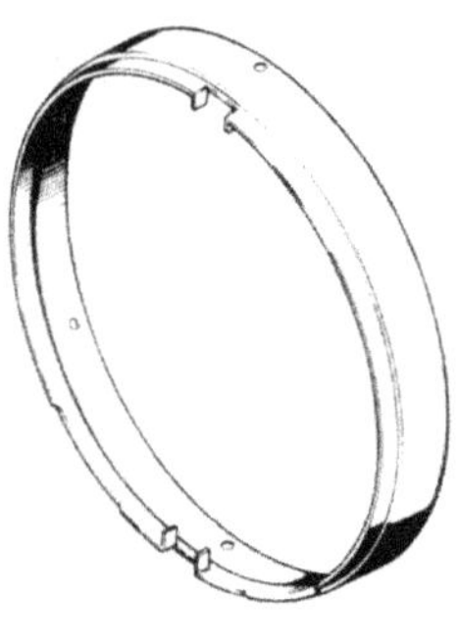

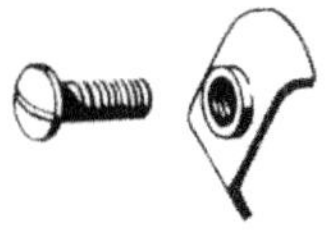

THE WIPAC GROUP — BUCKINGHAM — BUCKS.
TELEPHONE: BUCKINGHAM 3031   TELEGRAMS: WICOMAGSCO BUCKINGHAM

REF. LE.16/1/2

LIGHTING EQUIPMENT (Continued)

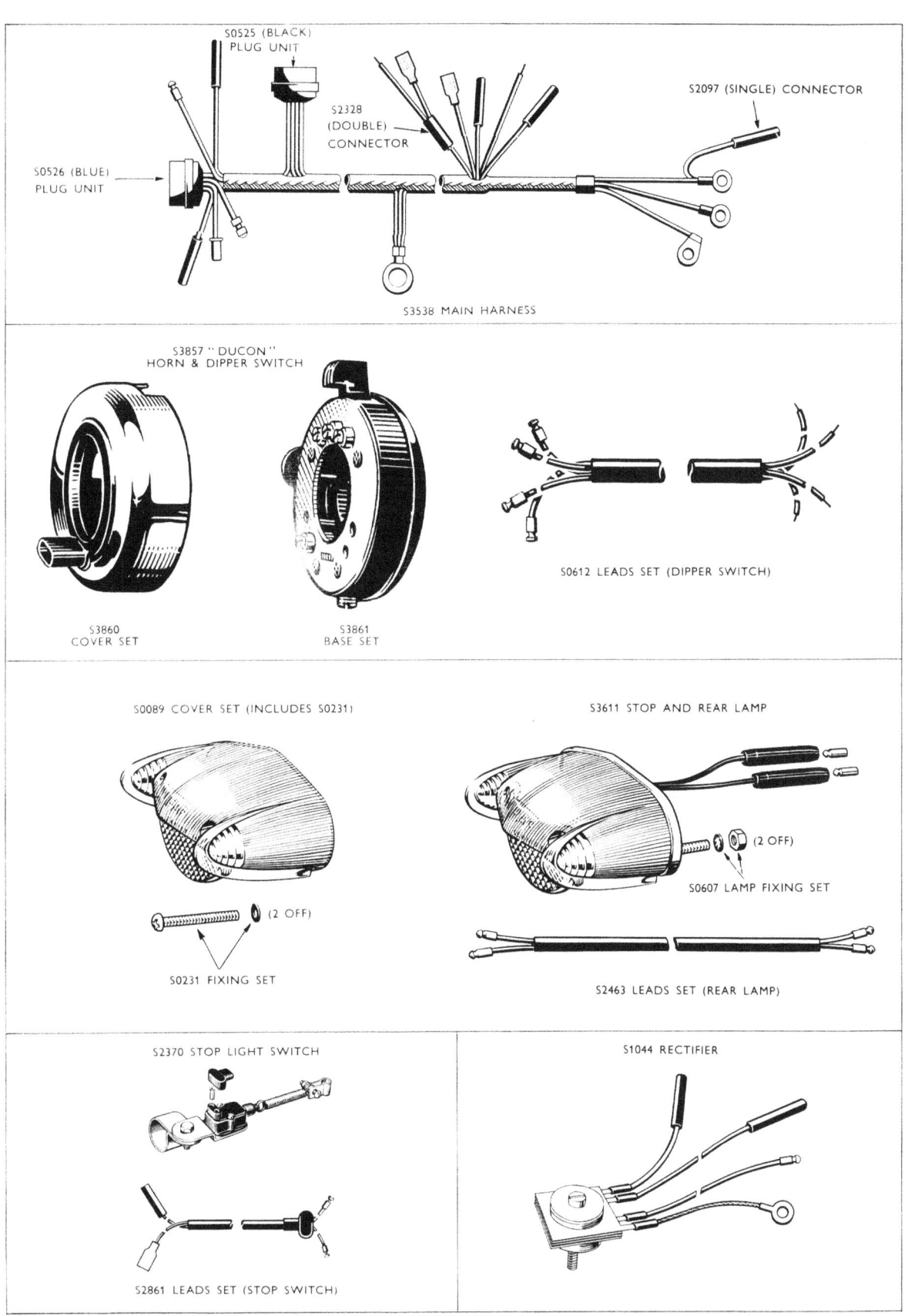

B.S.A. Bantam D10 and D14
FULL D.C. LIGHTING WITH COIL IGNITION
FROM JUNE 1966

S0873 RIM	S2669 LAMP FRONT UNIT	S0507 REFLECTOR AND GLASS SET
S0768 BULB HOLDER UNIT (MAIN)	S4067 HEADLAMP UNIT	S0781 SWITCH (LIGHTS) / S0782 SWITCH (IGNITION)
S0877 BULB HOLDER (PILOT)		S0783 SWITCH COVER UNIT (LIGHTS)
S0909 RIM LOCKING SET	S0874 LAMP ADJUSTER SET	S0784 SWITCH COVER UNIT (IGNITION)
S0887 REFLECTOR CLIP SET (SET OF 4)		S2796 PLUG UNIT RETAINER CLIP

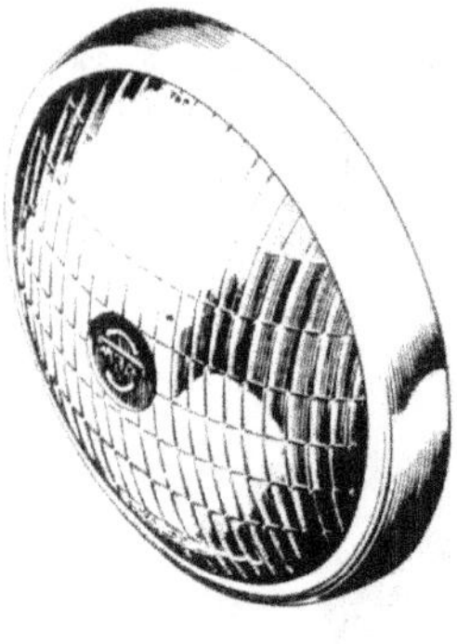

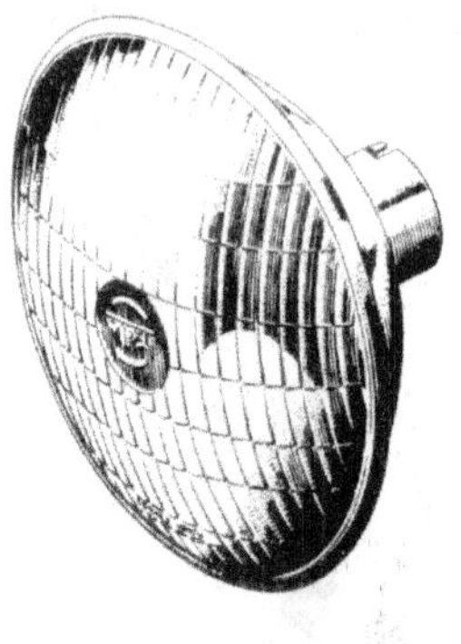

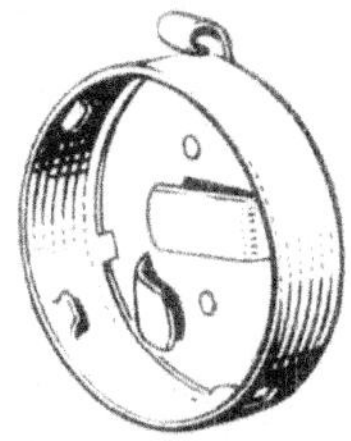

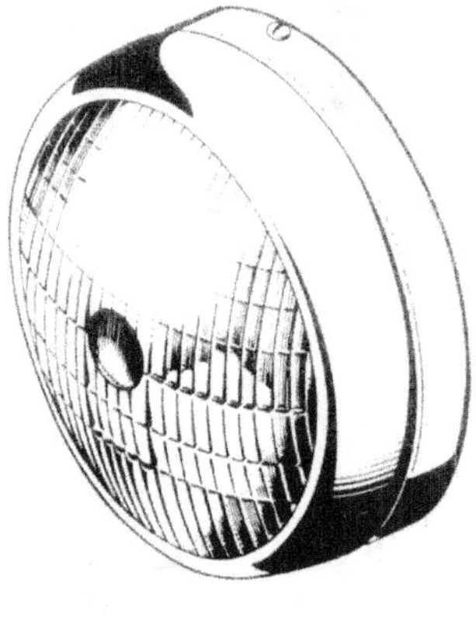

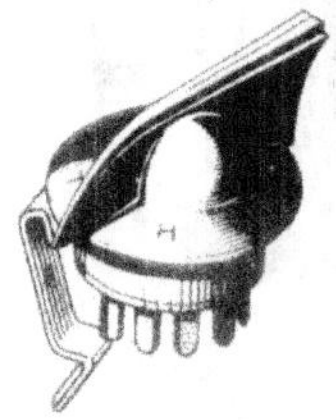

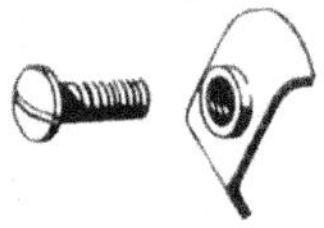

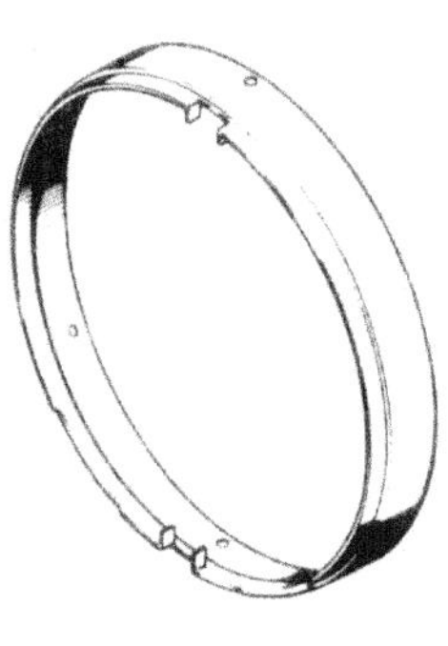

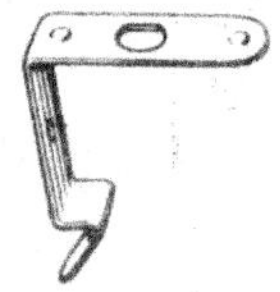

THE WIPAC GROUP — BUCKINGHAM — BUCKS.
TELEPHONE: BUCKINGHAM 3031   TELEGRAMS: WICOMAGSCO BUCKINGHAM

REF. LE. 24/1/2/A

LIGHTING EQUIPMENT (Continued)

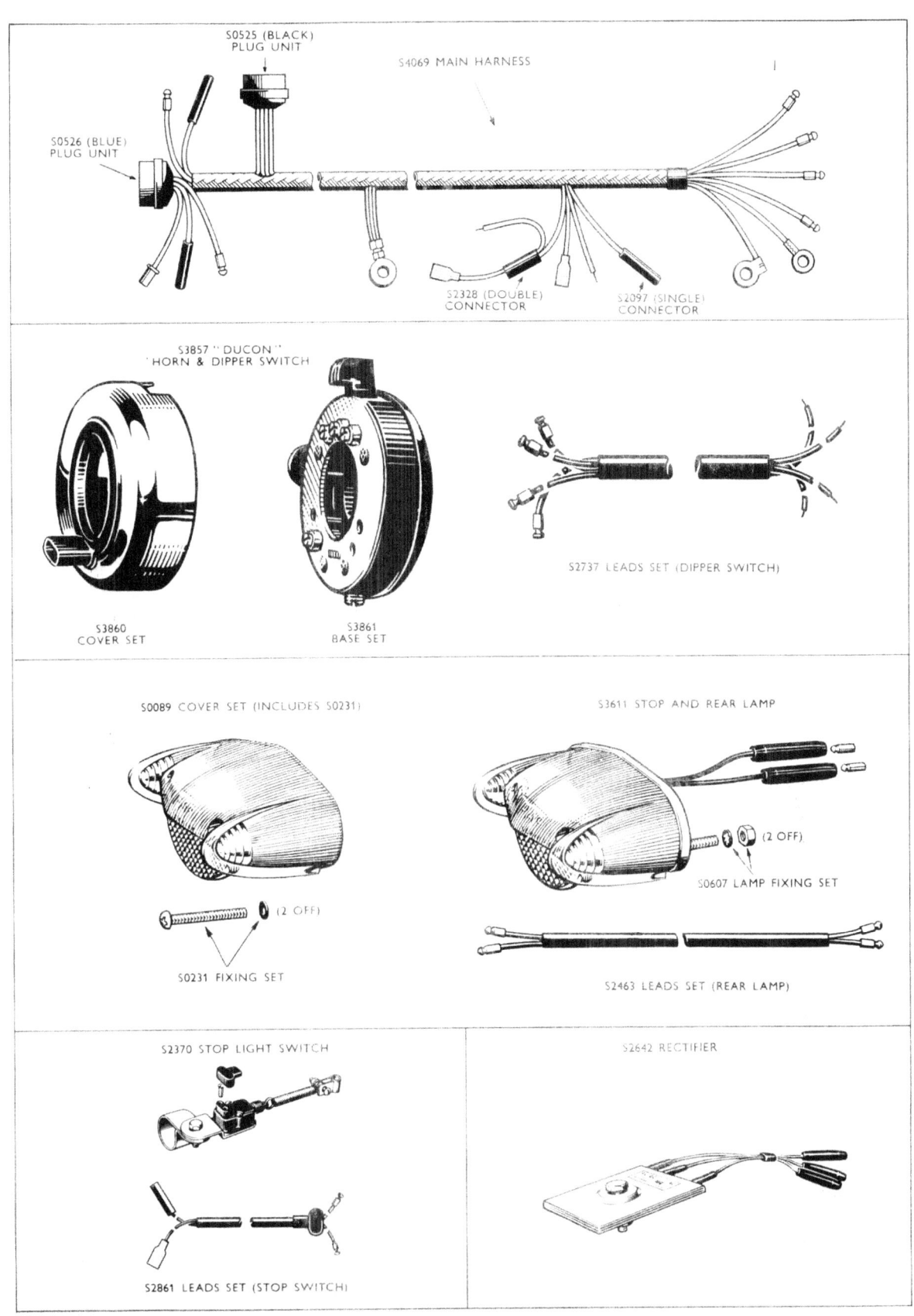

B.S.A. "BEAGLE" 75 c.c.
LIGHTWEIGHT MOTORCYCLE
MODELS PRODUCED FROM OCTOBER 1963 TO AUG. 1965

S3487 FRONT UNIT	S0348 GLASS SET	S3489 REFLECTOR AND GLASS SET
S0349 RIM	S3484 HEADLAMP UNIT	S0907 SWITCH UNIT
S0877 BULB HOLDER (PILOT)	S3486 LAMP BODY UNIT	S0908 SWITCH KNOB SET
S3488 MAIN BULB CONTACT SET		S0887 REFLECTOR CLIP SET (SET OF 4)
S0064 RIM LOCKING SET	S0238 HEADLAMP FIXING SET	S2796 PLUG UNIT RETAINER CLIP

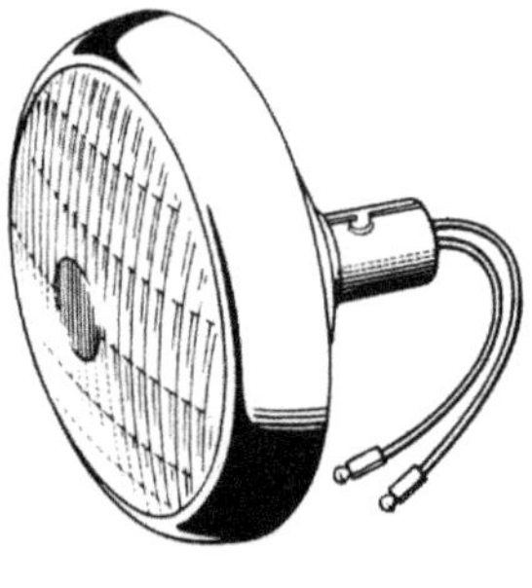

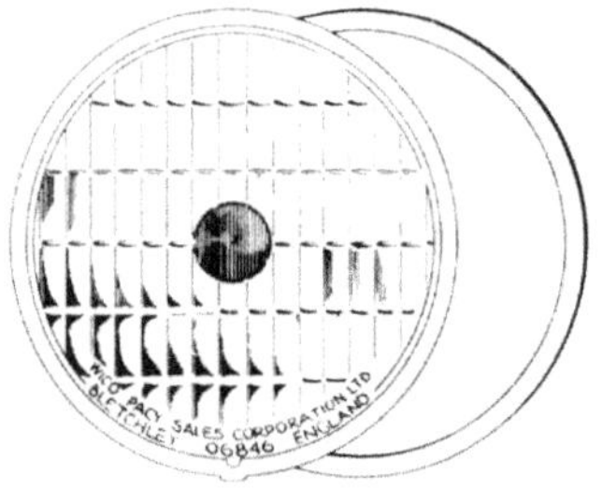

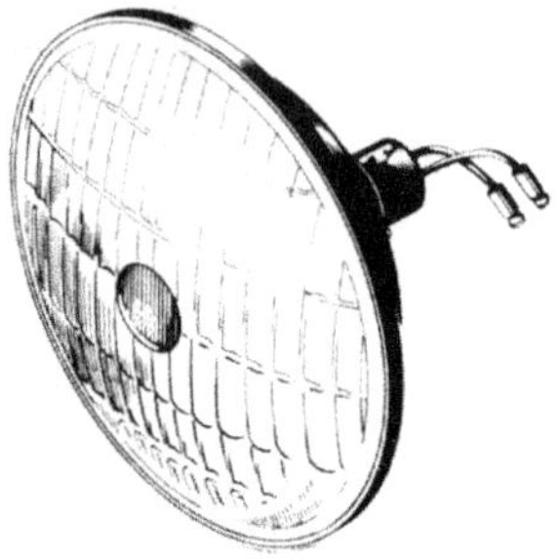

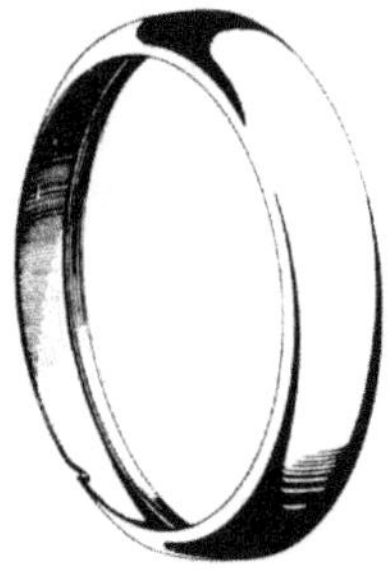

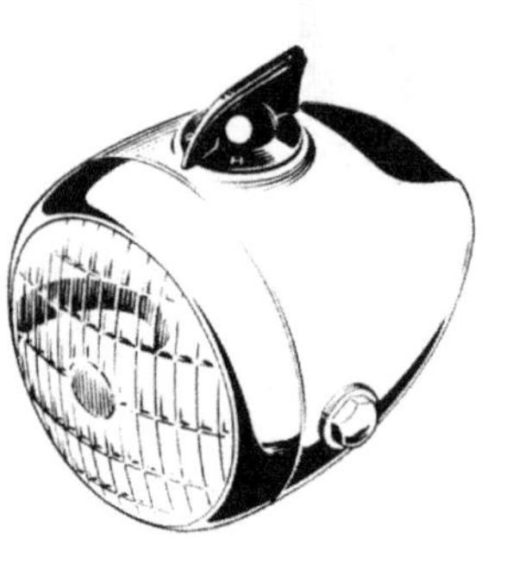

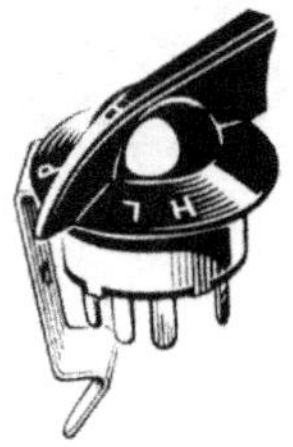

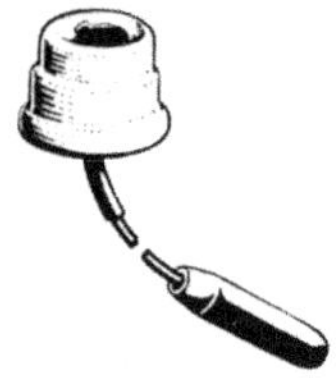

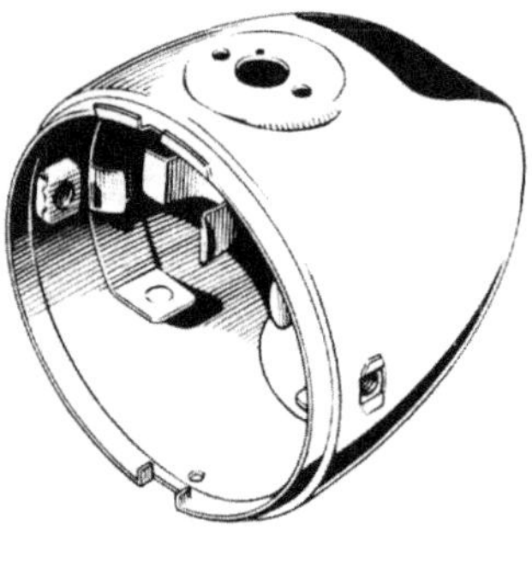

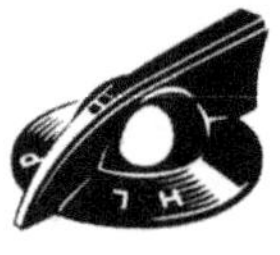

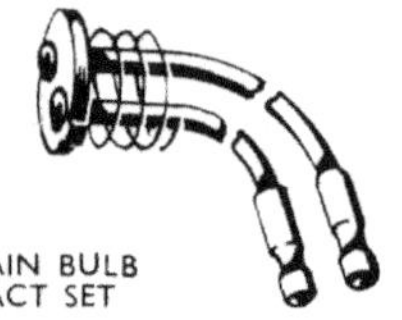

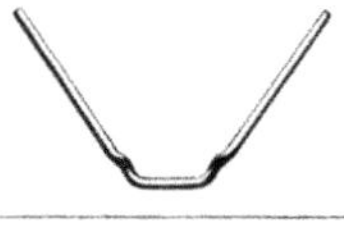

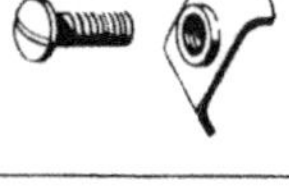

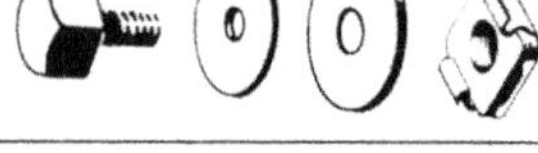

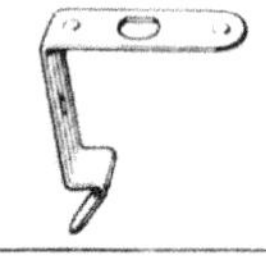

THE WIPAC GROUP — BUCKINGHAM — BUCKS.
TELEPHONE: BUCKINGHAM 3031   TELEGRAMS: WICOMAGSCO BUCKINGHAM

REF. L.E. 7/1/2/4

LIGHTING EQUIPMENT (CONTINUED)

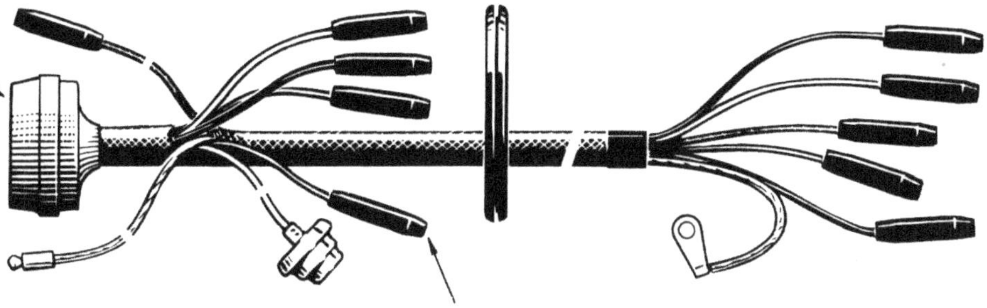

S0526 (BLUE) PLUG UNIT

S2097 (SINGLE) CONNECTOR

S3485 HARNESS (MAIN)

S0214 COVER SET

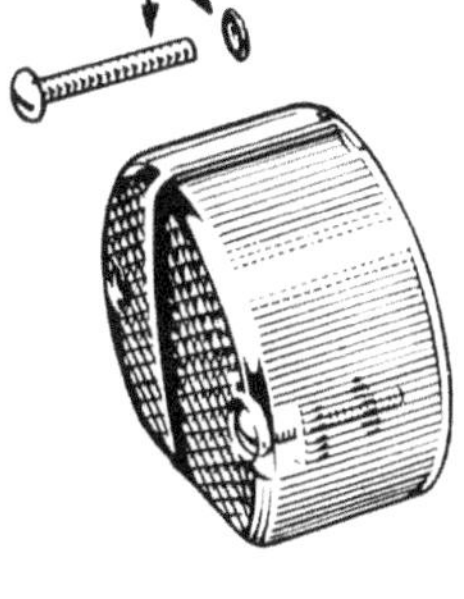

S0215 FIXING SET (2 OFF)

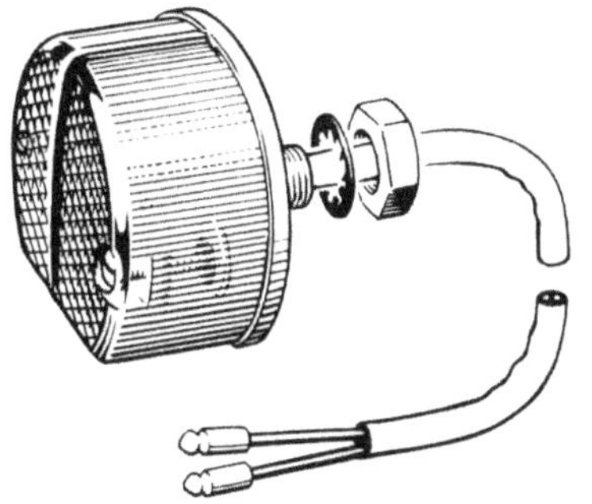

S0213 REAR/PARK LAMP

S3490 IGNITION SWITCH UNIT

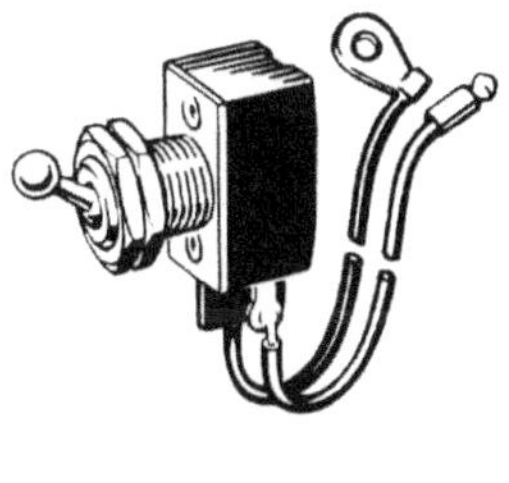

REF. L.E. 7/2/2/A

B.S.A. "BEAGLE" 75 C.C.
LIGHTWEIGHT MOTORCYCLE (FITTED WITH STOP LAMP)
MODELS PRODUCED FROM MARCH 1964 TO AUG. 1965

S3639 FRONT UNIT	S0348 GLASS SET	S3640 REFLECTOR AND GLASS SET
S0349 RIM	S3636 HEADLAMP UNIT	S0907 SWITCH UNIT
S0887 REFLECTOR CLIP SET (SET OF 4)	S3637 LAMP BODY UNIT	S0908 SWITCH KNOB SET
S3488 MAIN BULB CONTACT SET		S2796 PLUG UNIT RETAINER CLIP
S0064 RIM LOCKING SET	S0238 HEADLAMP FIXING SET	

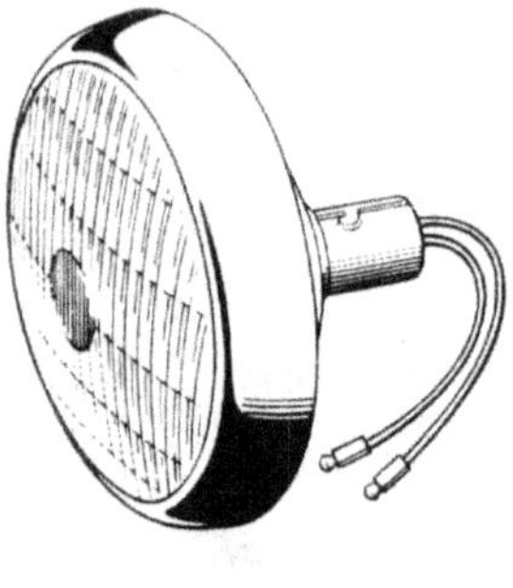

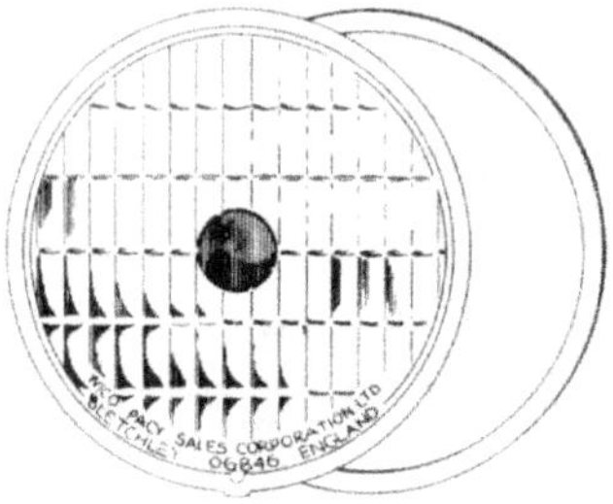

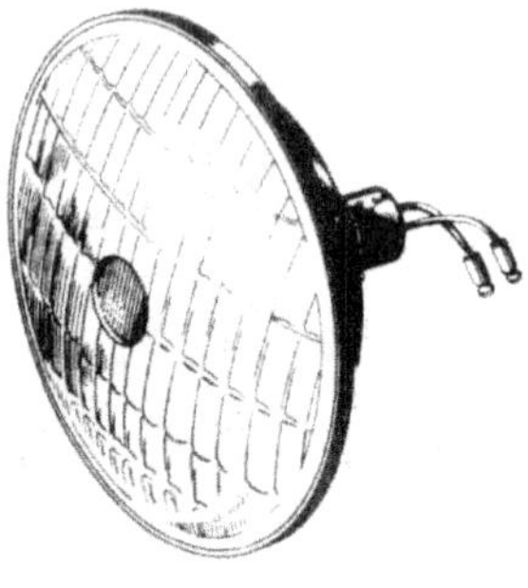

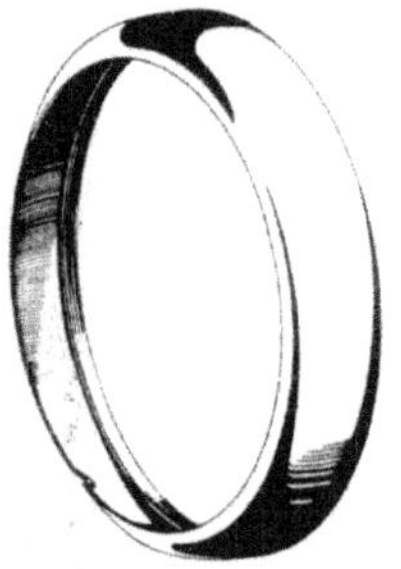

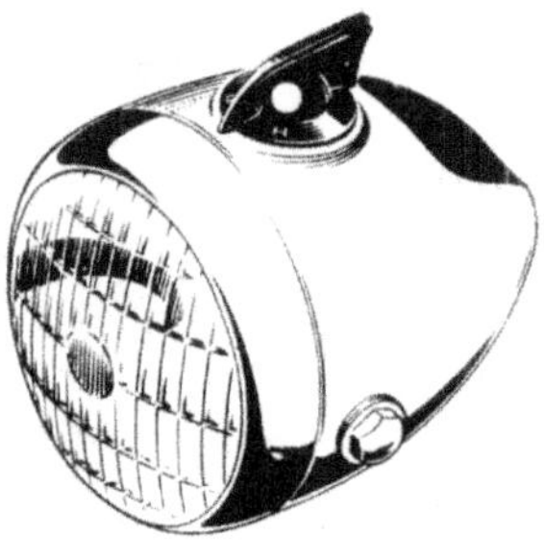

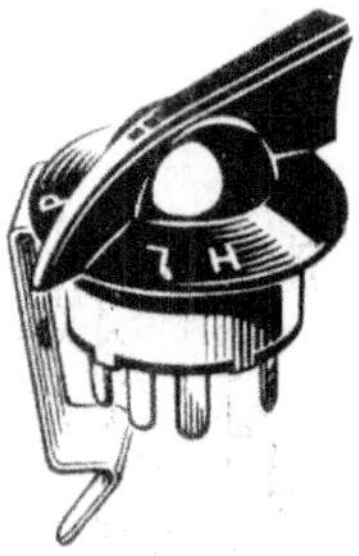

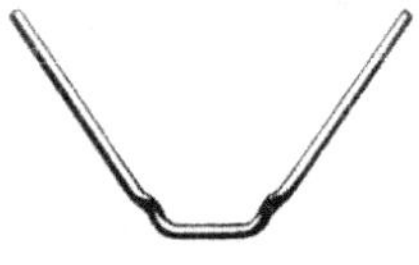

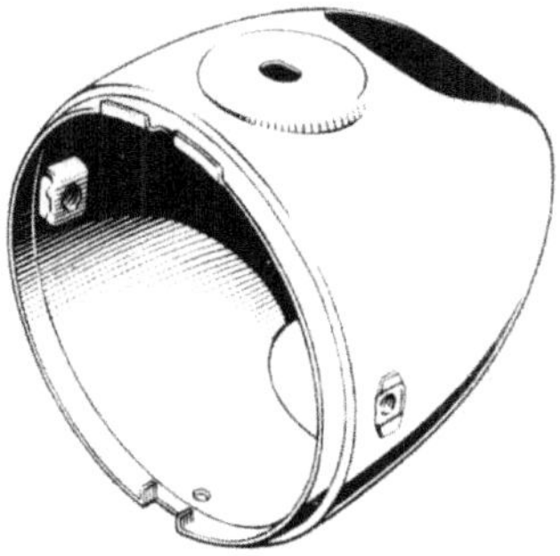

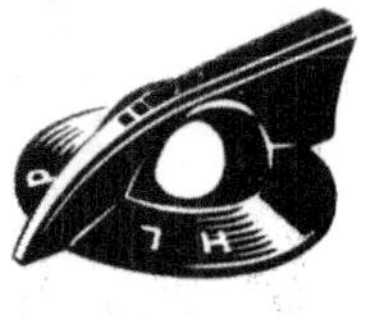

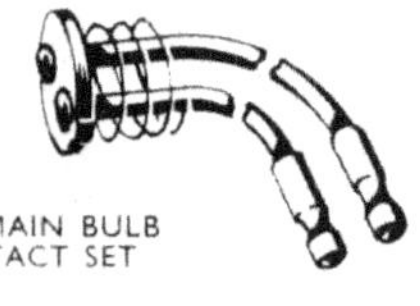

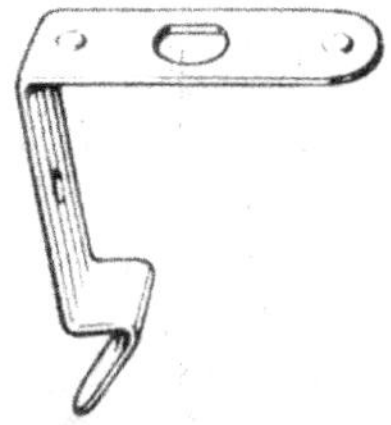

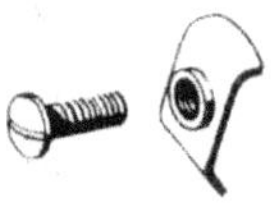

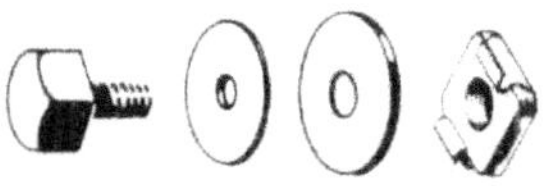

THE WIPAC GROUP — BUCKINGHAM — BUCKS.
TELEPHONE: BUCKINGHAM 3031   TELEGRAMS: WICOMAGSCO BUCKINGHAM

REF. L.E.10.1.2.A

LIGHTING EQUIPMENT (CONTINUED)

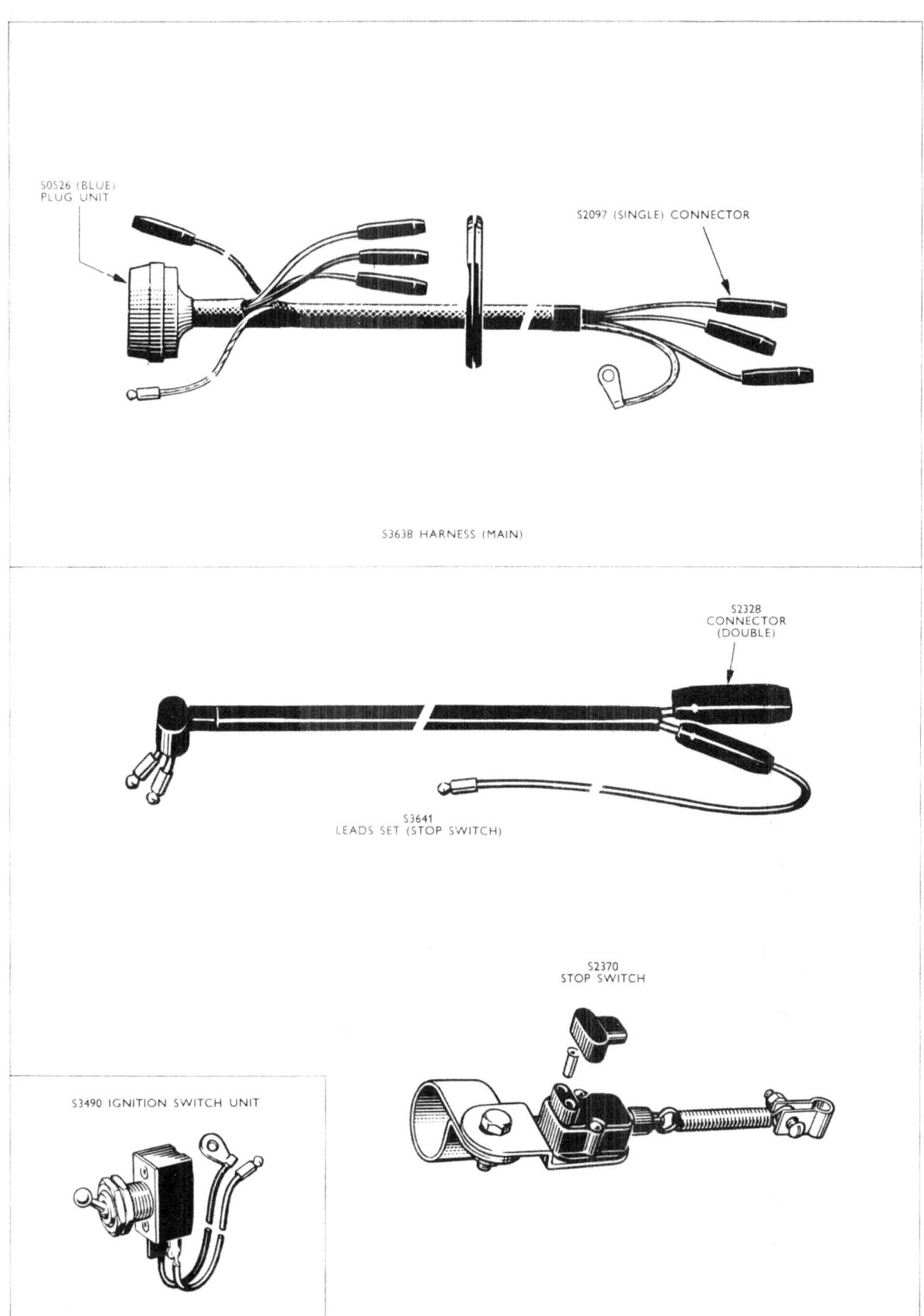

WIPAC LIGHTING EQUIPMENT

FRANCIS-BARNETT 250 c.c. CRUISER 80
MODELS PRODUCED FROM AUGUST 1956 TO DECEMBER 1964

- S0066 RIM 
- S0237 FRONT UNIT 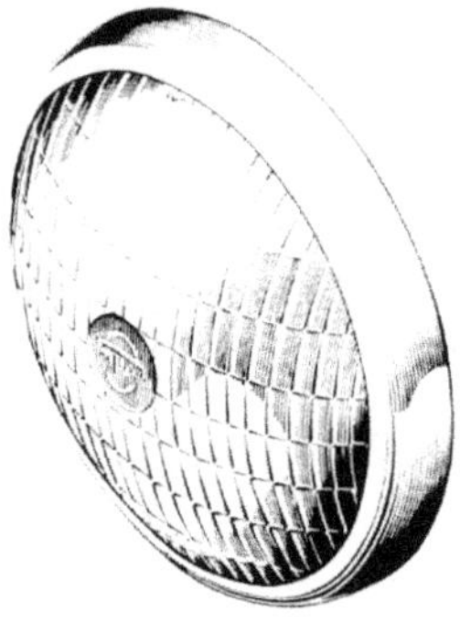
- S0507 REFLECTOR AND GLASS SET 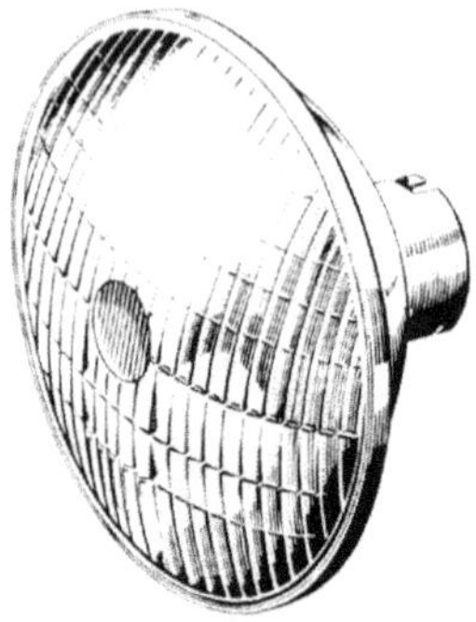
- S0768 BULB HOLDER UNIT (MAIN) 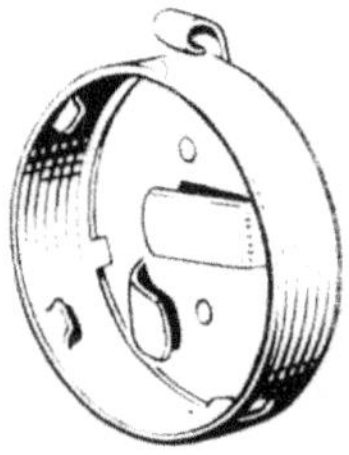
- S0902 HEADLAMP UNIT 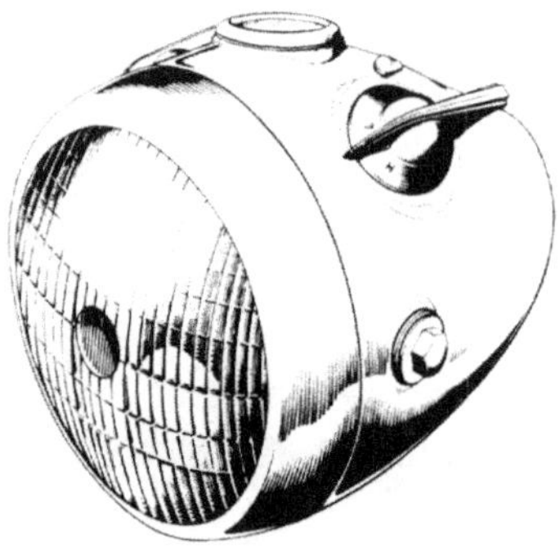
- S0781 SWITCH (LIGHTS)
- S0782 SWITCH (IGNITION) 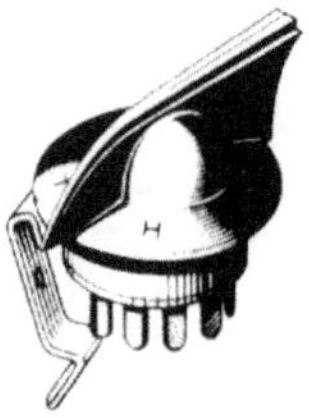
- S0877 BULB HOLDER (PILOT) 
- S0783 SWITCH COVER UNIT (LIGHTS)
- S0062 AMMETER UNIT
- S1101 SEALING RING 
- S0904 BODY UNIT
- S0784 SWITCH COVER UNIT (IGNITION) 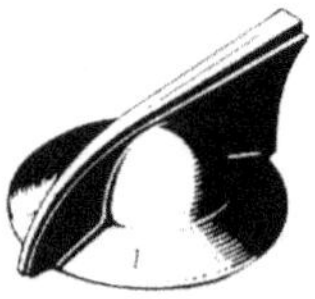
- S0070 REFLECTOR CLIP SET (SET OF 4) 
- S2796 PLUG UNIT RETAINER CLIP 
- S0064 RIM LOCKING SET 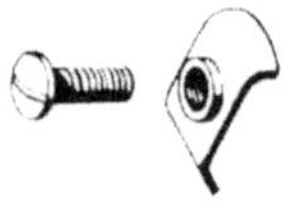
- S0238 HEADLAMP FIXING SET

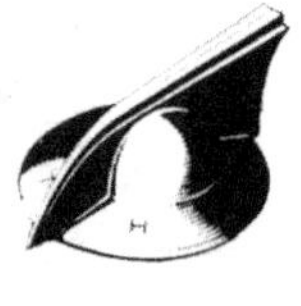

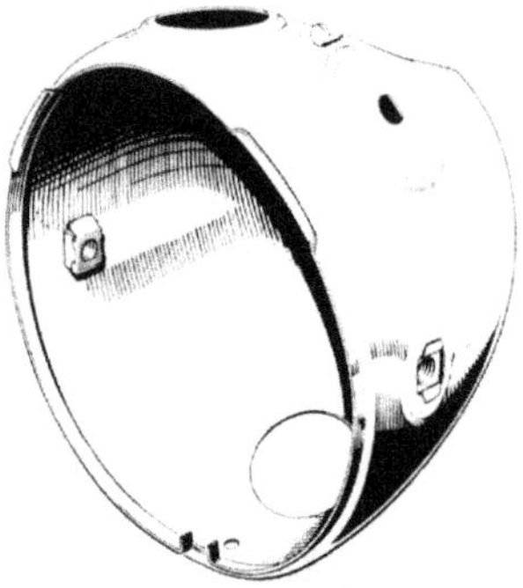

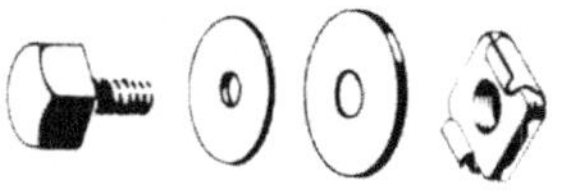

THE WIPAC GROUP — BUCKINGHAM — BUCKS.
TELEPHONE: BUCKINGHAM 3031   TELEGRAMS: WICOMAGSCO BUCKINGHAM

REF. L.E. 19/1/2

LIGHTING EQUIPMENT (CONTINUED)

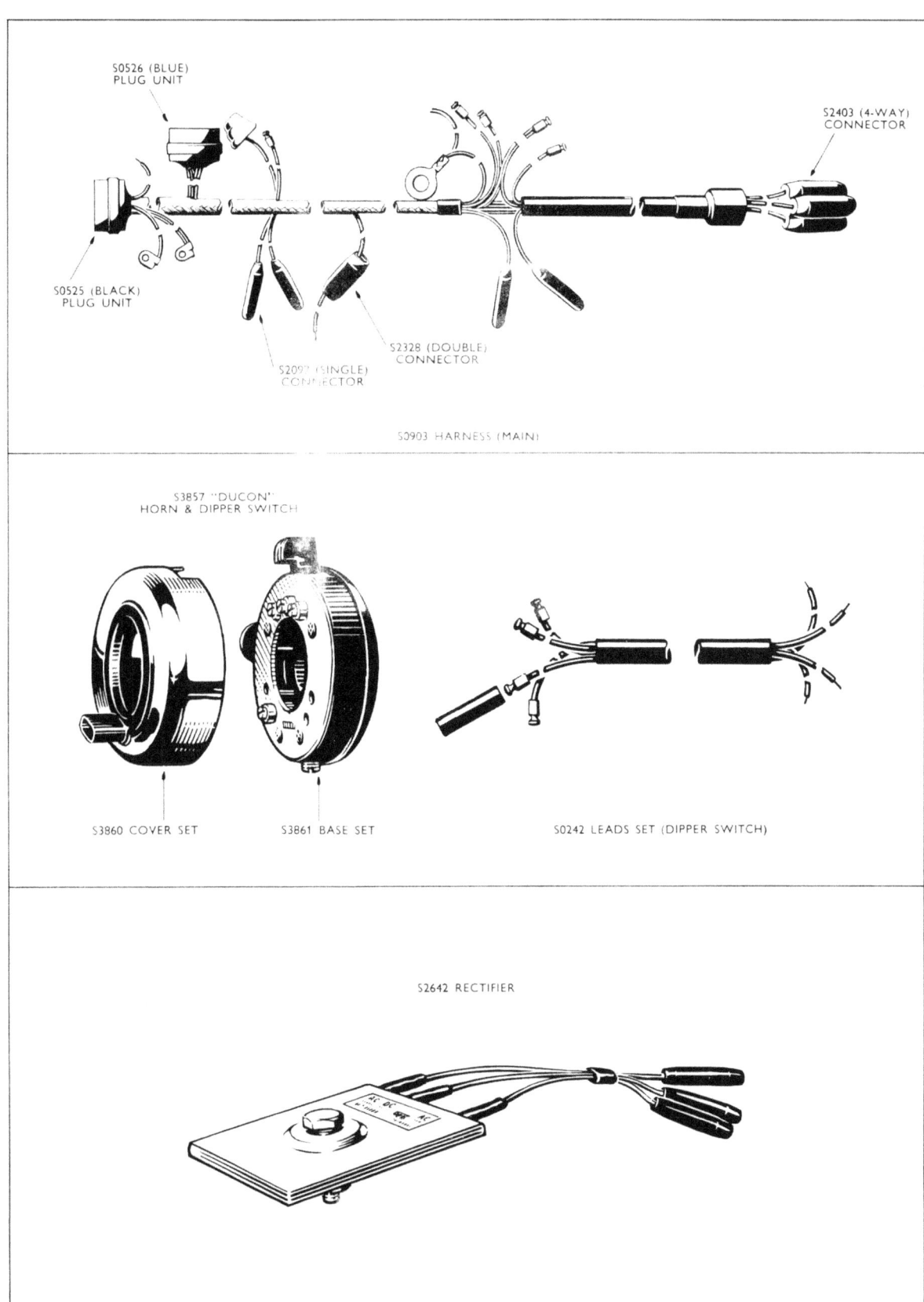

JAMES 250 c.c. COMMODORE
(D.C. CIRCUIT)
MODELS PRODUCED FROM AUGUST 1956 TO JULY 1963

S0066 RIM	S0237 FRONT UNIT	S0507 REFLECTOR AND GLASS SET
S0768 BULB HOLDER UNIT (MAIN)	S0777 HEADLAMP UNIT	S0781 SWITCH (LIGHTS) / S0782 SWITCH (IGNITION)
S0877 BULB HOLDER (PILOT)		S0783 SWITCH COVER UNIT (LIGHTS)
S0062 AMMETER UNIT / S1101 SEALING RING	S0752 BODY UNIT	S0784 SWITCH COVER UNIT (IGNITION)
S0070 REFLECTOR CLIP SET (SET OF 4)		S2796 PLUG UNIT RETAINER CLIP
S0064 RIM LOCKING SET	S0238 HEADLAMP FIXING SET	

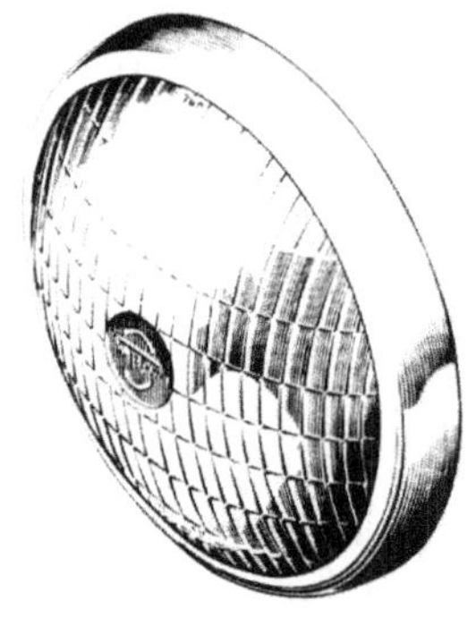

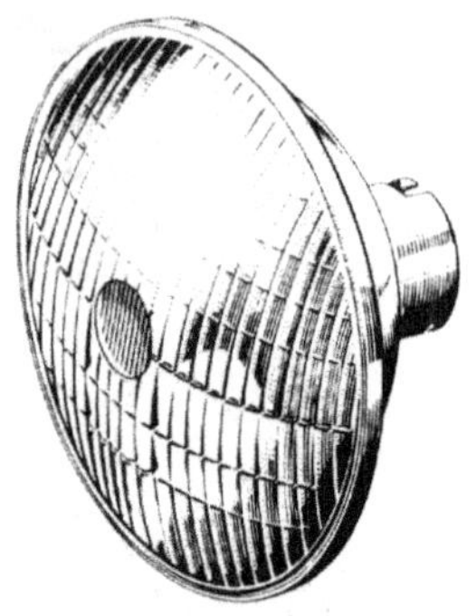

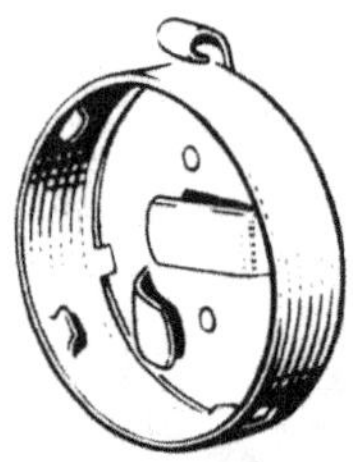

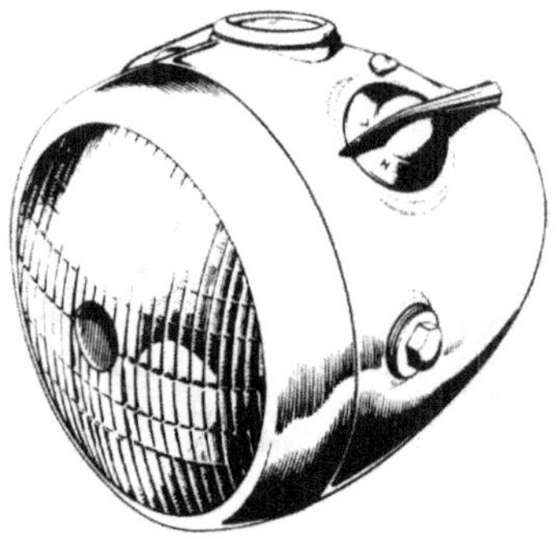

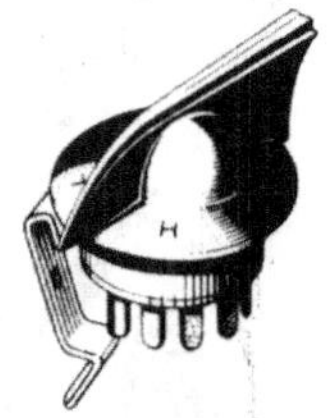

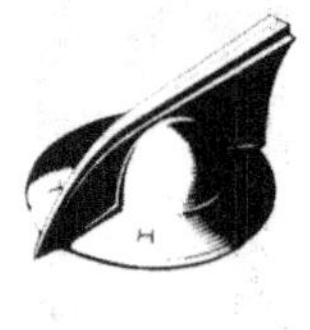

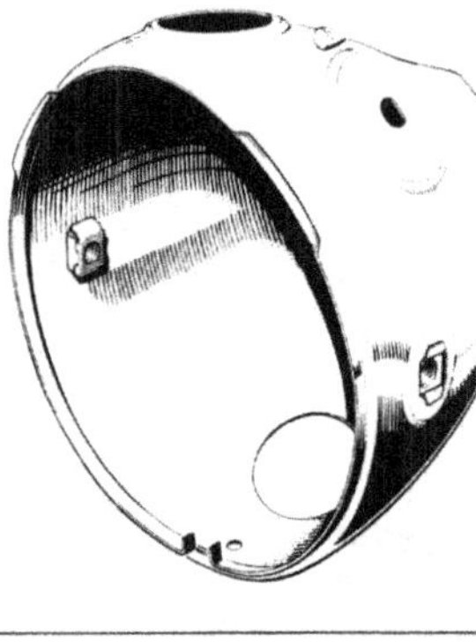

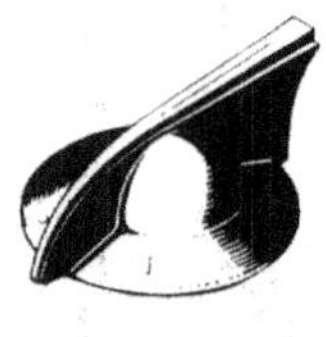

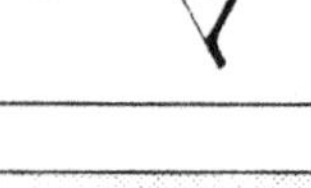

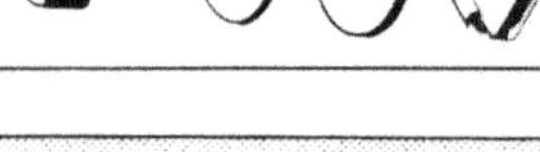

THE WIPAC GROUP — BUCKINGHAM — BUCKS.
TELEPHONE: BUCKINGHAM 3031   TELEGRAMS: WICOMAGSCO BUCKINGHAM

REF. L.E. 18/1/2

LIGHTING EQUIPMENT (CONTINUED)

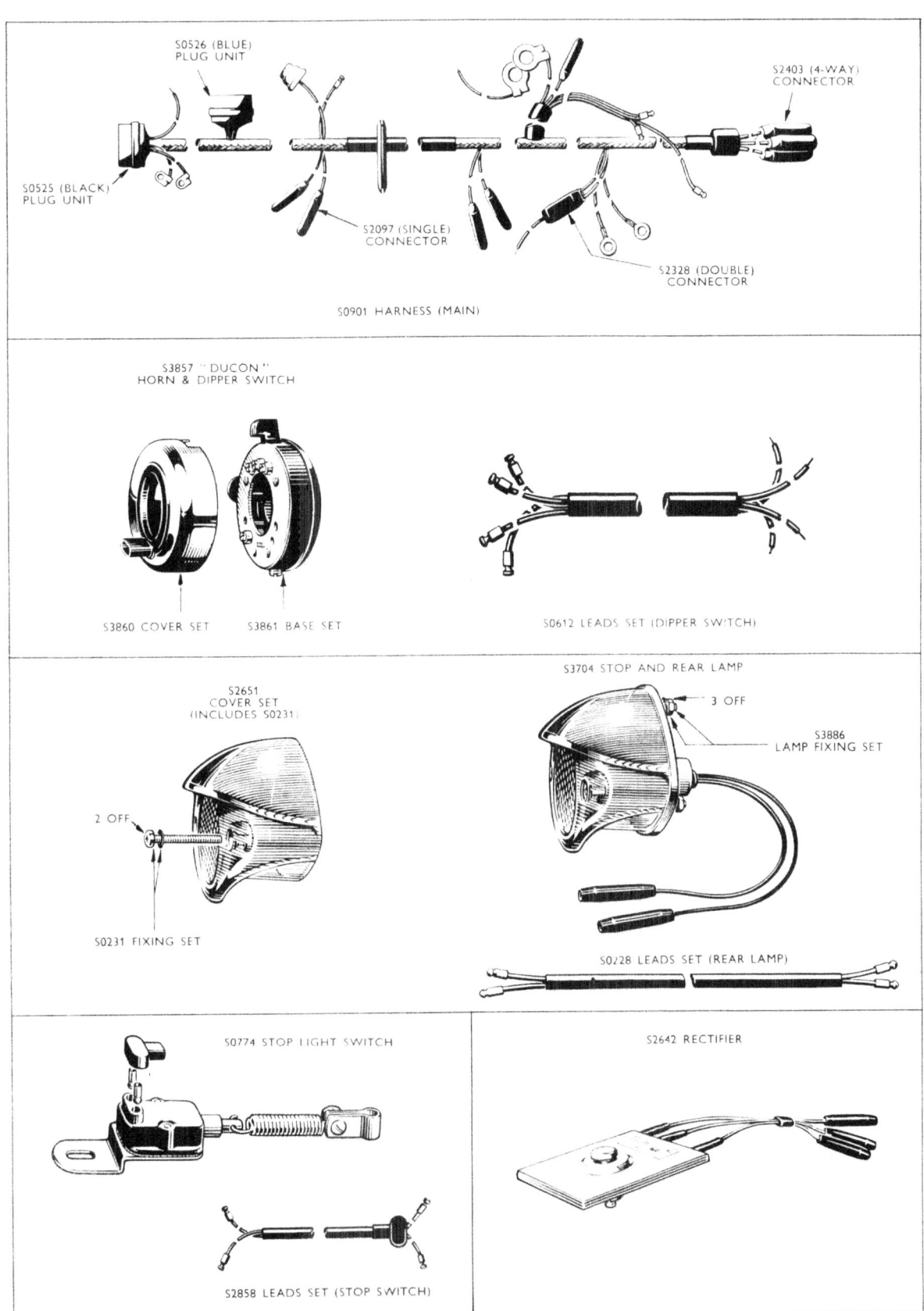

MATCHLESS G2 AND A.J.S. MODEL 14
250 c.c. O.H.V.
MODELS PRODUCED FROM MAY 1958 TO SEPTEMBER 1959

S0066 RIM	S0237 FRONT UNIT	S0507 REFLECTOR AND GLASS SET
S0768 BULB HOLDER UNIT (MAIN)	S0777 HEADLAMP UNIT	S0781 SWITCH (LIGHTS) / S0782 SWITCH (IGNITION)
S0877 BULB HOLDER (PILOT)		S0783 SWITCH COVER UNIT (LIGHTS)
S0062 AMMETER UNIT / S1101 SEALING RING	S0752 BODY UNIT	S0784 SWITCH COVER UNIT (IGNITION)
S0070 REFLECTOR CLIP SET (SET OF 4)		S2796 PLUG UNIT RETAINER CLIP
S0064 RIM LOCKING SET	S0238 HEADLAMP FIXING SET	

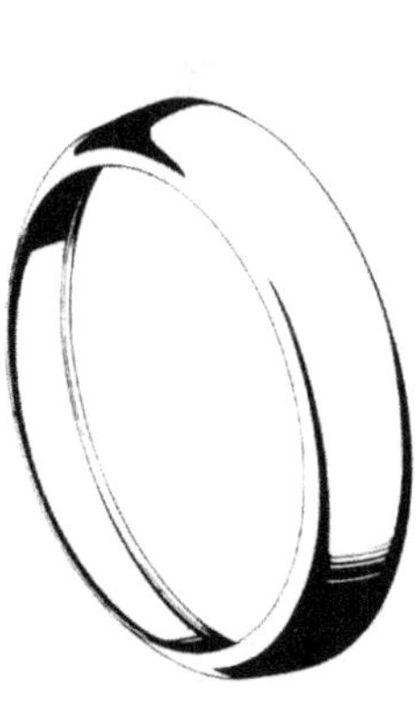

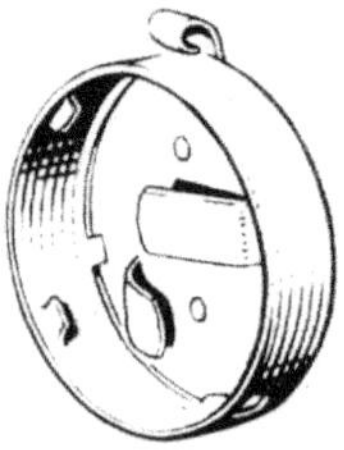

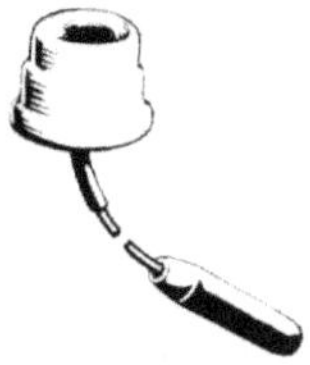

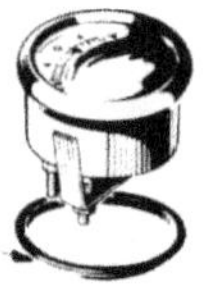

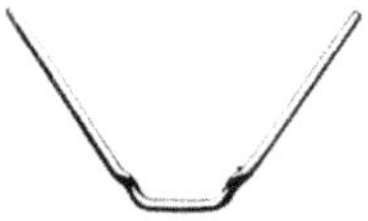

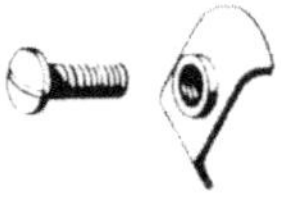

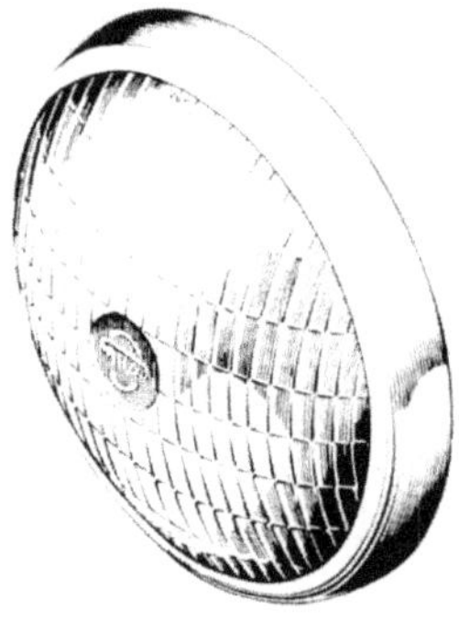

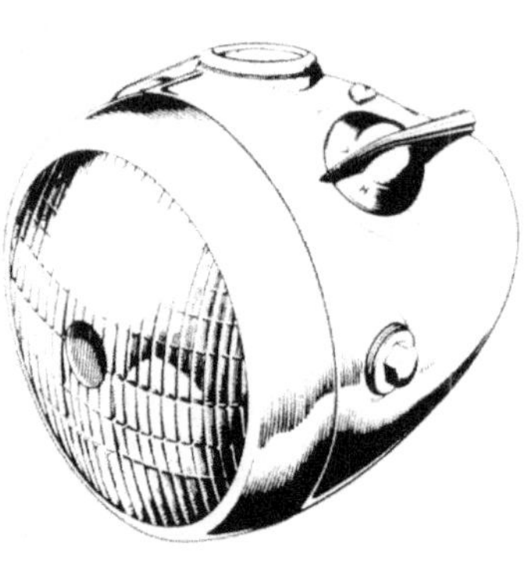

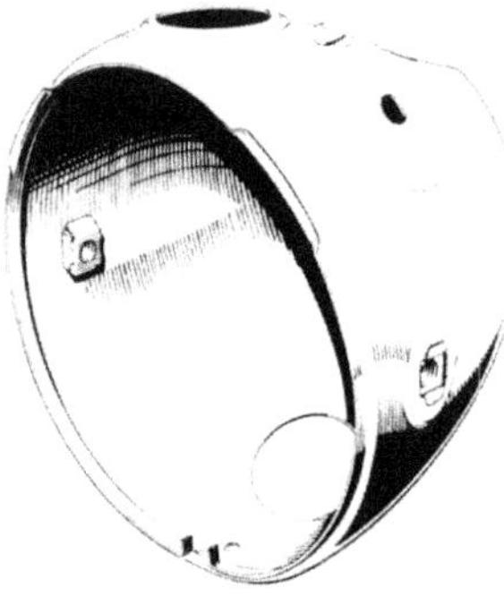

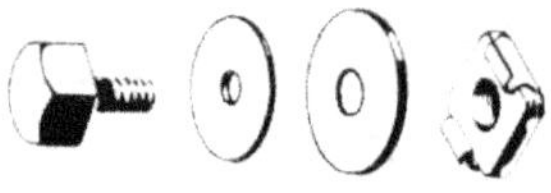

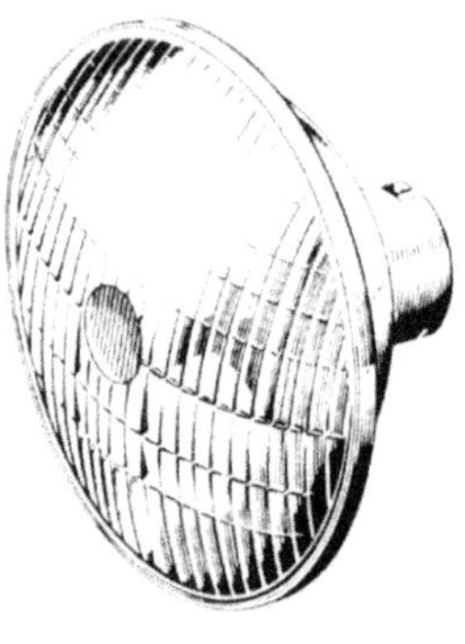

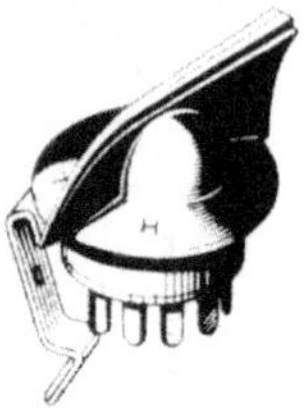

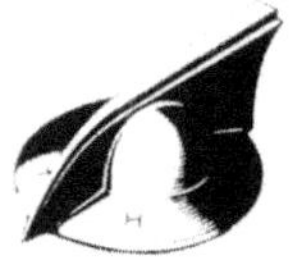

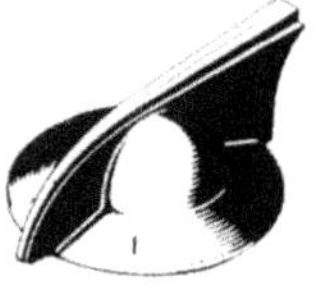

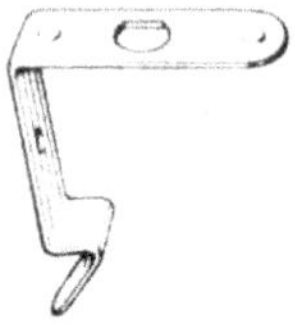

THE WIPAC GROUP — BUCKINGHAM — BUCKS.
TELEPHONE: BUCKINGHAM 3031   TELEGRAMS: WICOMAGSCO BUCKINGHAM

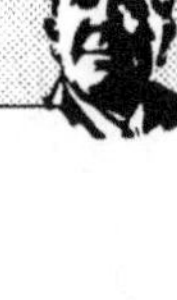

REF. L.E. 21/1/2

LIGHTING EQUIPMENT (CONTINUED)

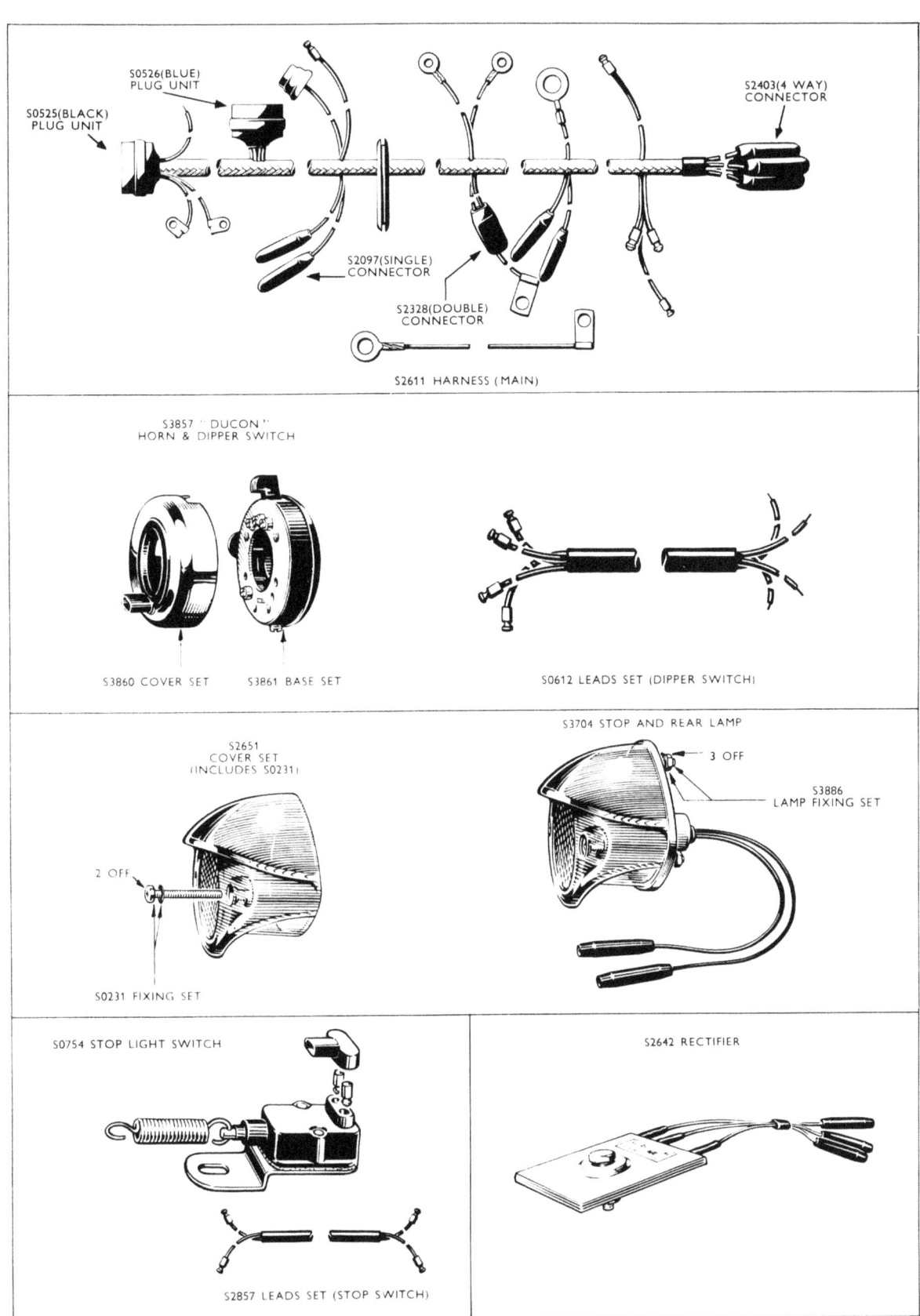

MATCHLESS G2 250 c.c., G5 350 c.c. AND A.J.S. MODELS 14 250 c.c., 8 350 c.c.
MODELS PRODUCED FROM AUGUST 1959 TO DECEMBER 1964

- S2617 RIM 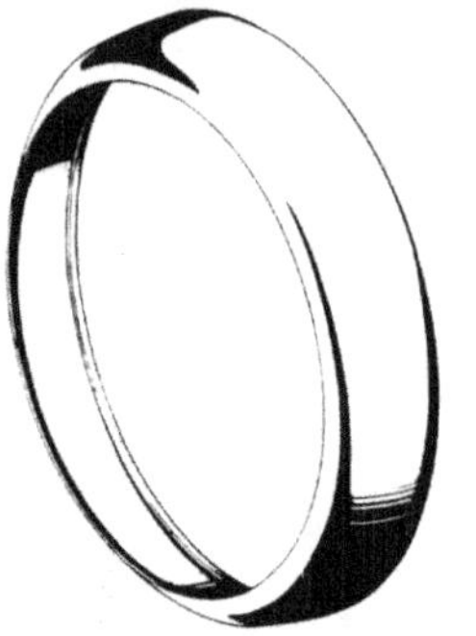
- S2618 FRONT UNIT
- S2612 REFLECTOR AND GLASS SET
- S0768 BULB HOLDER UNIT (MAIN) 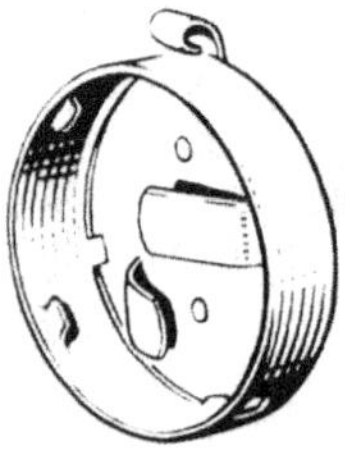
- S2615 HEADLAMP UNIT
- S0781 SWITCH (LIGHTS)
- S0782 SWITCH (IGNITION)
- S0877 BULB HOLDER (PILOT) 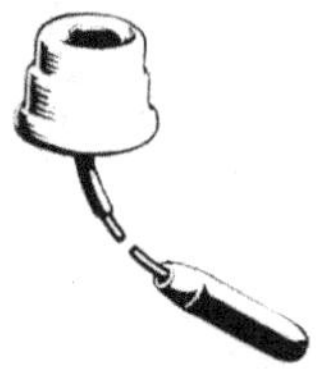
- S0783 SWITCH COVER UNIT (LIGHTS)
- S2611 BODY UNIT
- S0062 AMMETER UNIT
- S1101 SEALING RING 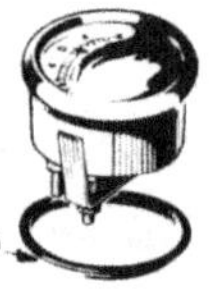
- S0784 SWITCH COVER UNIT (IGNITION)
- S0070 REFLECTOR CLIP SET (SET OF 4)
- S2796 PLUG UNIT RETAINER CLIP
- S0064 RIM LOCKING SET
- S2688 HEADLAMP FIXING SET

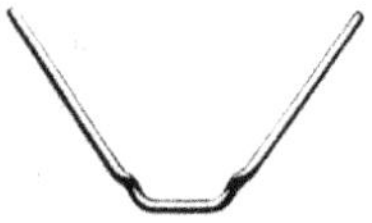

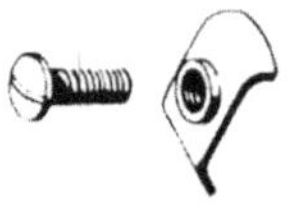

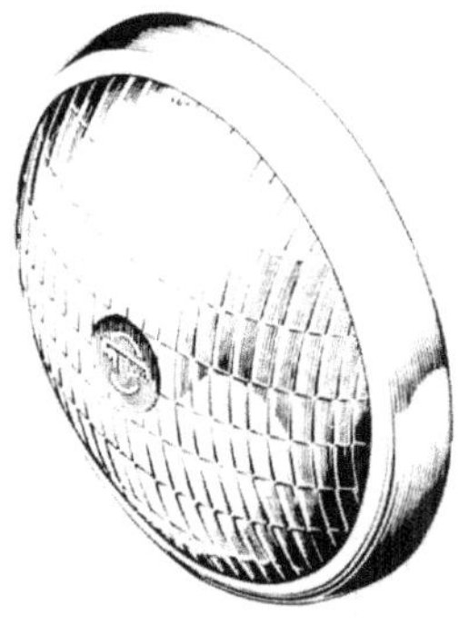

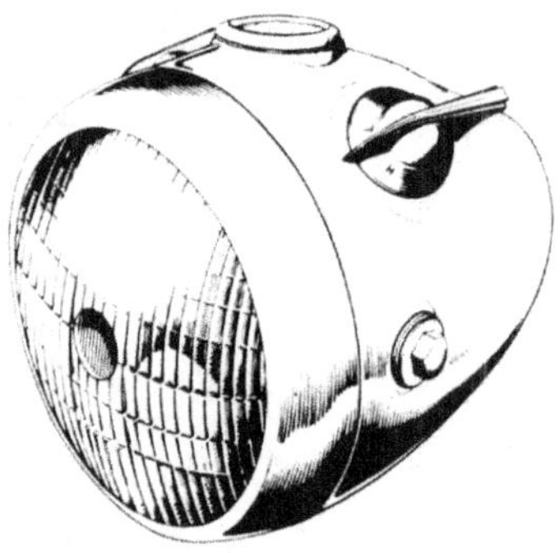

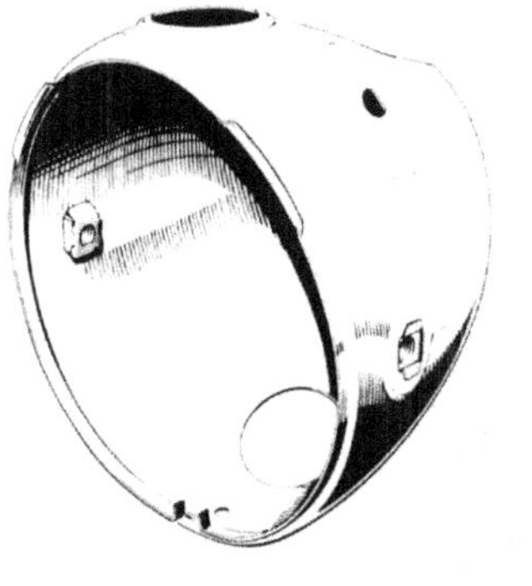

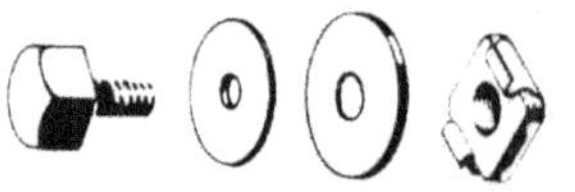

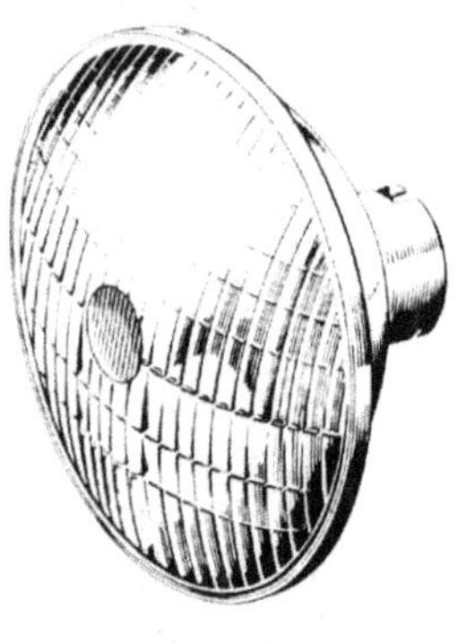

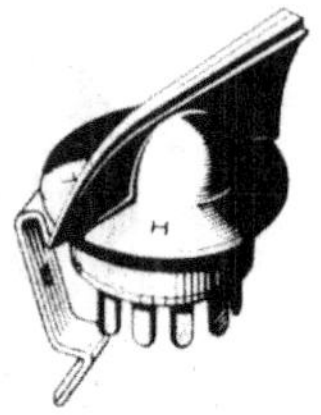

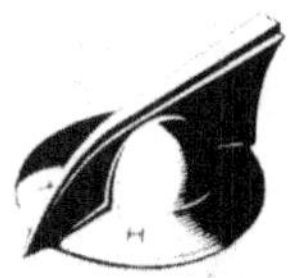

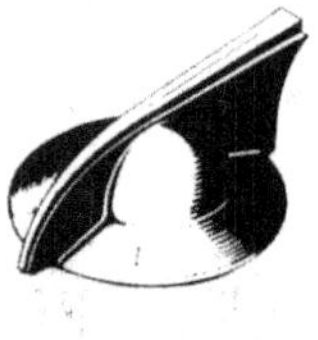

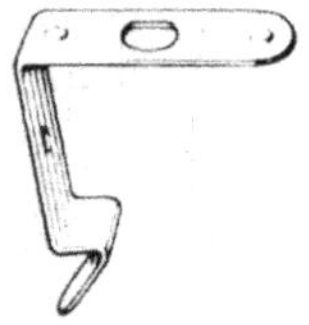

THE WIPAC GROUP — BUCKINGHAM — BUCKS.
TELEPHONE: BUCKINGHAM 3031   TELEGRAMS: WICOMAGSCO BUCKINGHAM

REF. L.E. 22/1/2/A

LIGHTING EQUIPMENT (CONTINUED)

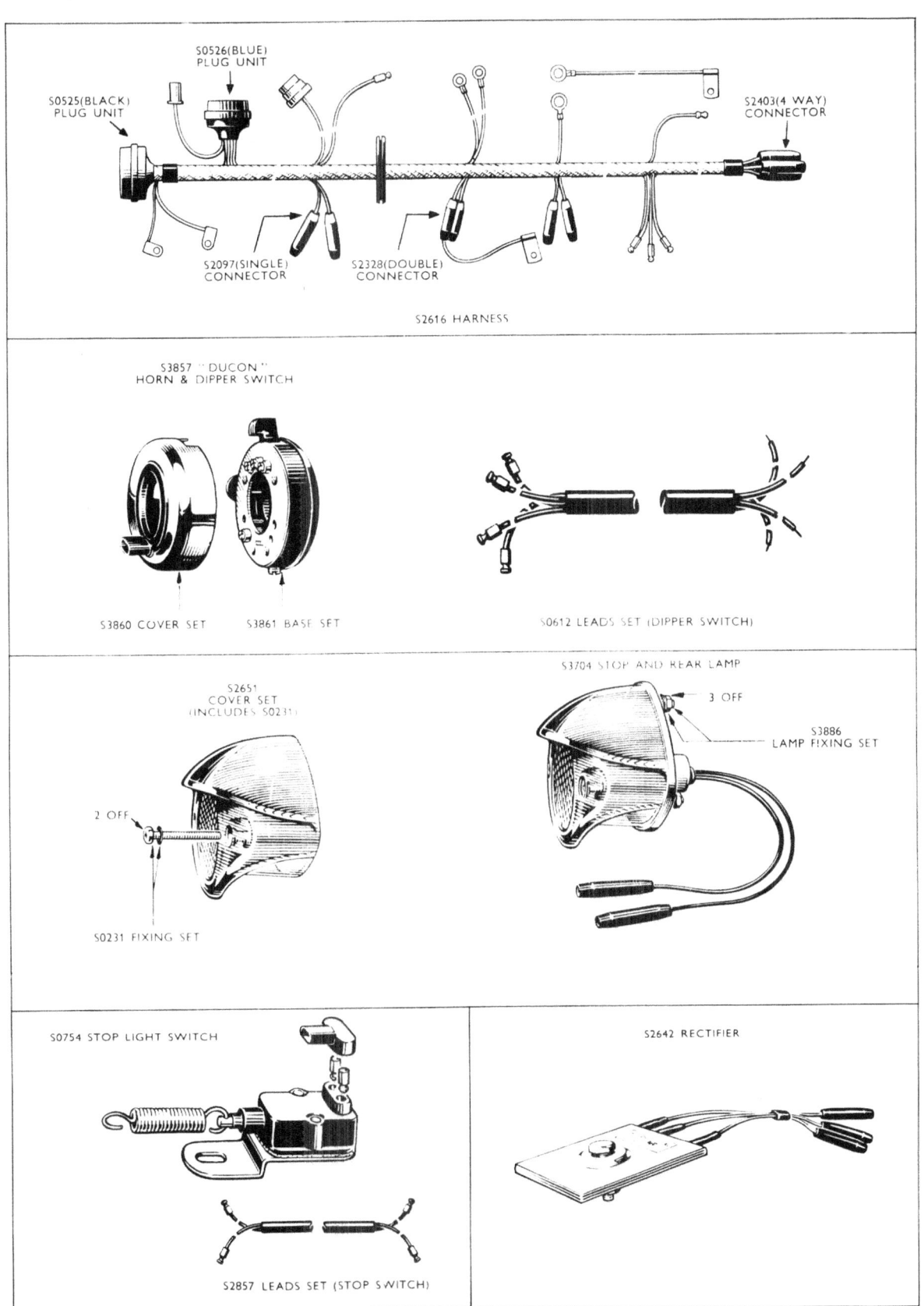

WIPAC LIGHTING EQUIPMENT

MATCHLESS G2 C.S.R. 250 c.c. AND A.J.S. MODEL 14 C.S.R. 250 c.c. SAPPHIRE NINETY
MODELS PRODUCED FROM MARCH 1965

- S2617 RIM 
- S2618 FRONT UNIT 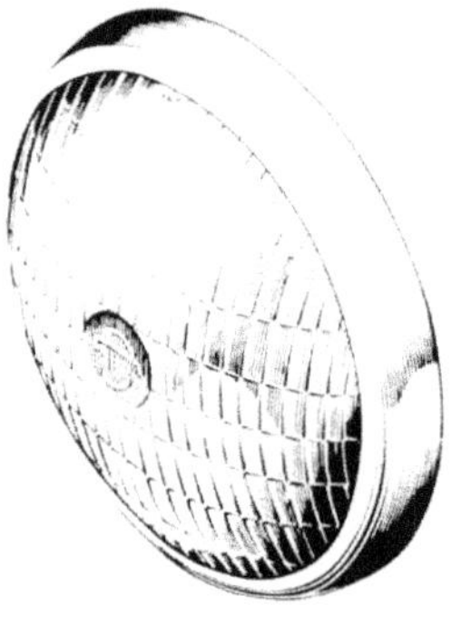
- S2612 REFLECTOR AND GLASS SET 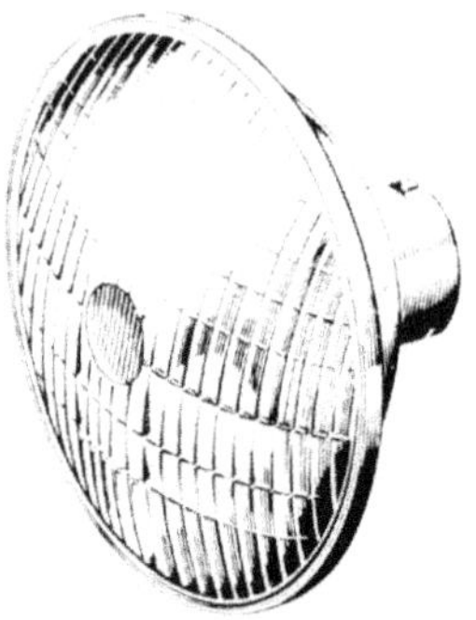
- S0768 BULB HOLDER UNIT (MAIN) 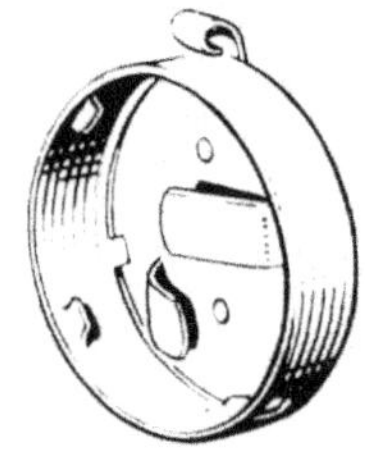
- S2615 HEADLAMP UNIT 
- S0781 SWITCH (LIGHTS)
- S0782 SWITCH (IGNITION) 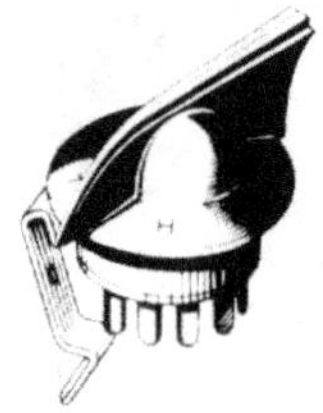
- S0877 BULB HOLDER (PILOT) 
- S0783 SWITCH COVER UNIT (LIGHTS)
- S0062 AMMETER UNIT
- S1101 SEALING RING 
- S2611 BODY UNIT
- S0784 SWITCH COVER UNIT (IGNITION) 
- S0070 REFLECTOR CLIP SET (SET OF 4) 
- S2796 PLUG UNIT RETAINER CLIP 
- S0064 RIM LOCKING SET 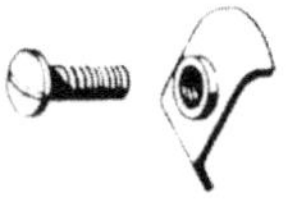
- S2688 HEADLAMP FIXING SET

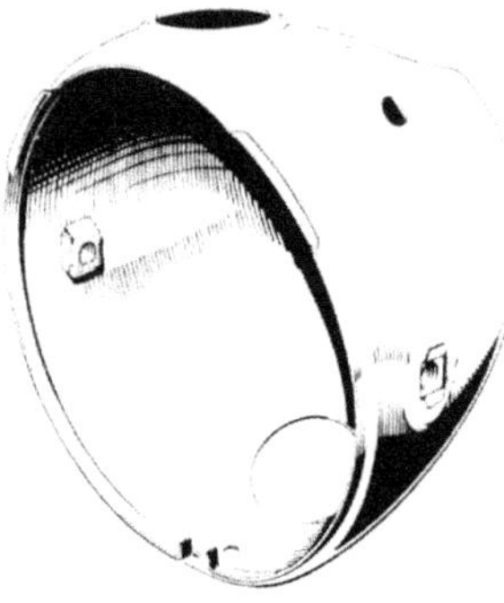

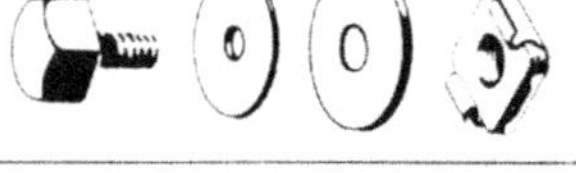

THE WIPAC GROUP — BUCKINGHAM — BUCKS.
TELEPHONE: BUCKINGHAM 3031   TELEGRAMS: WICOMAGSCO BUCKINGHAM

REF. L.E. 23/1/2 A

LIGHTING EQUIPMENT (CONTINUED)

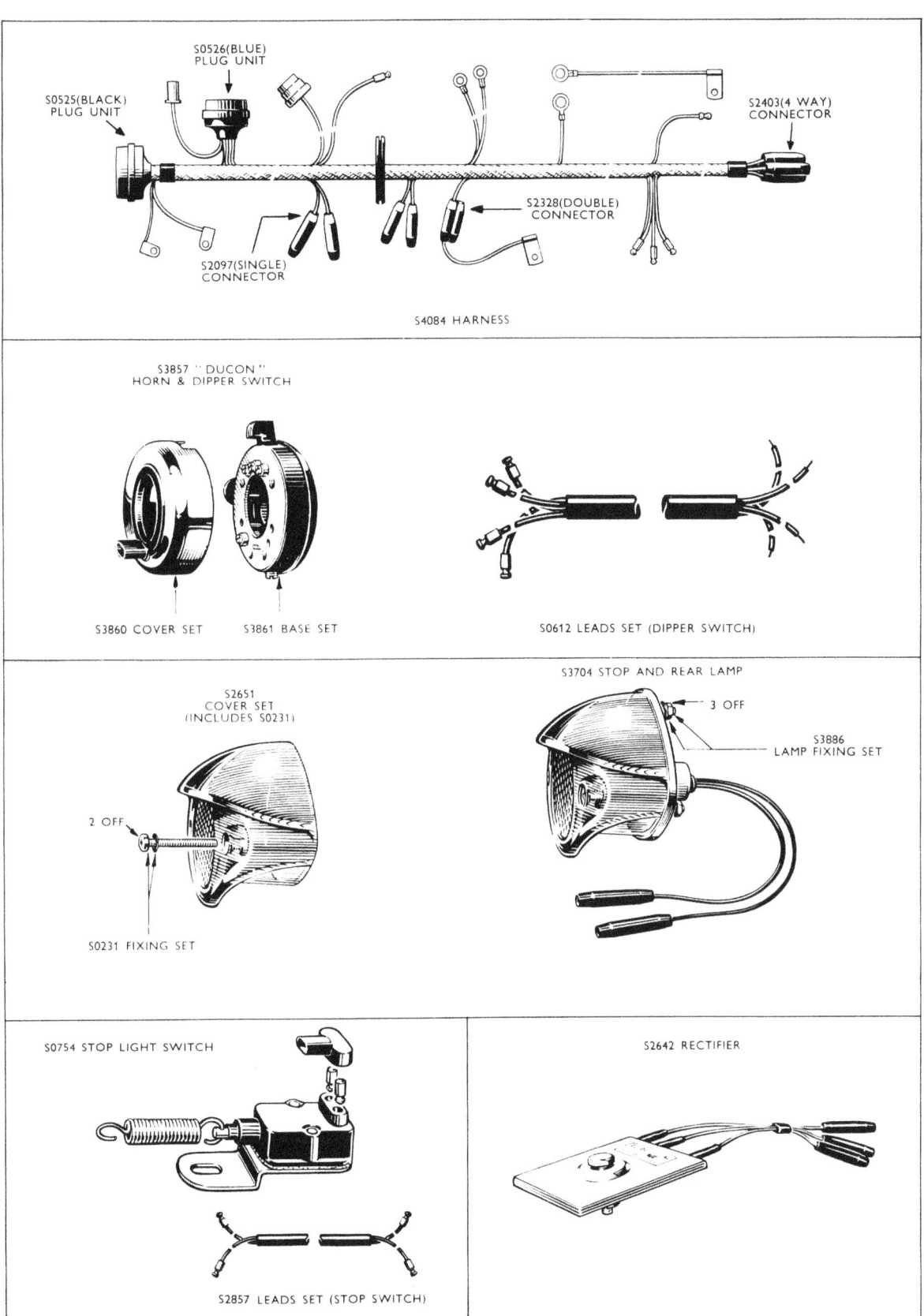

 **NORTON JUBILEE 250 c.c. TWIN**
MODELS PRODUCED FROM NOVEMBER 1958 TO AUGUST 1960

S0529 RIM SET	S3231 FRONT UNIT (COMPLETE)	S0507 REFLECTOR AND GLASS SET
S0768 BULB HOLDER UNIT (MAIN)	S1084 HEADLAMP UNIT	S0062 AMMETER SET
S0895 BULB HOLDER (PILOT)		S0783 SWITCH KNOB SET (LIGHTS)
S0064 RIM LOCKING SET	S0752 LAMP BODY UNIT	SWITCH S0781 (LIGHTS) S0782 (IGNITION)
S0070 REFLECTOR CLIP SET (SET OF 4)		
S2796 PLUG UNIT RETAINER CLIP	S0238 HEADLAMP FIXING SET	S0784 SWITCH KNOB SET (IGNITION)

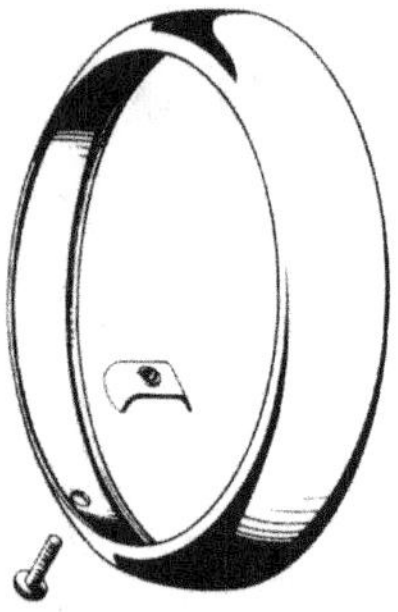

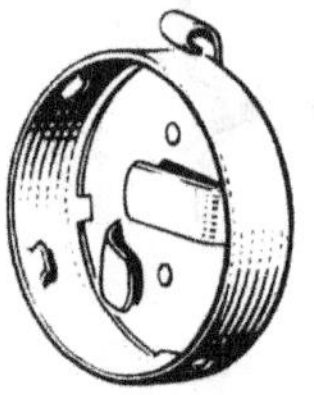

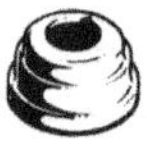

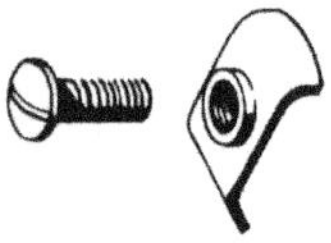

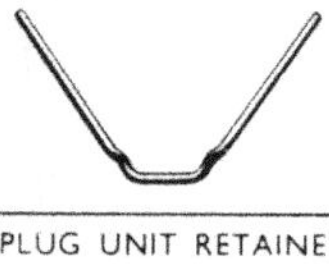

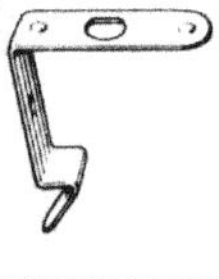

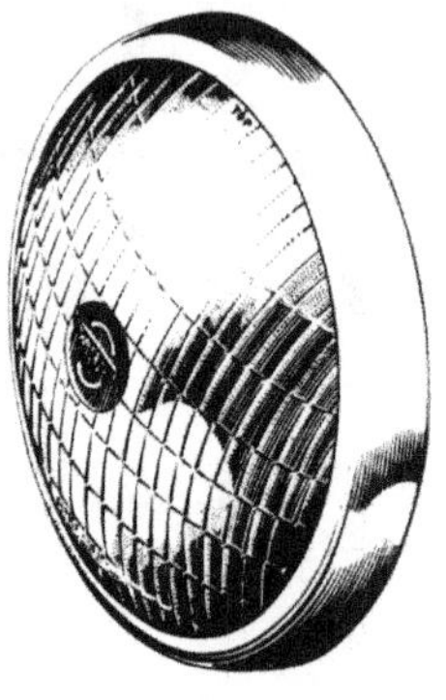

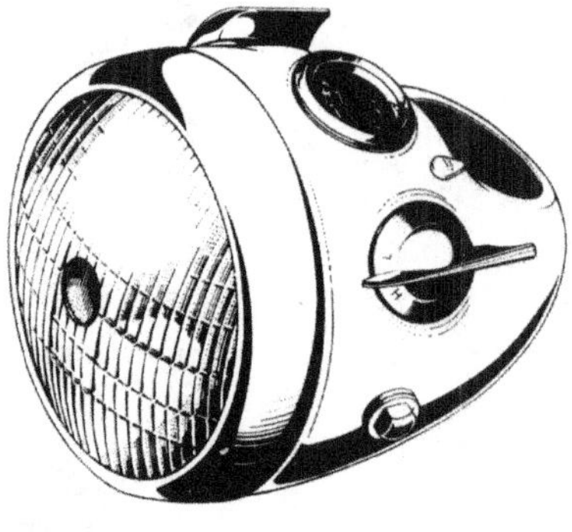

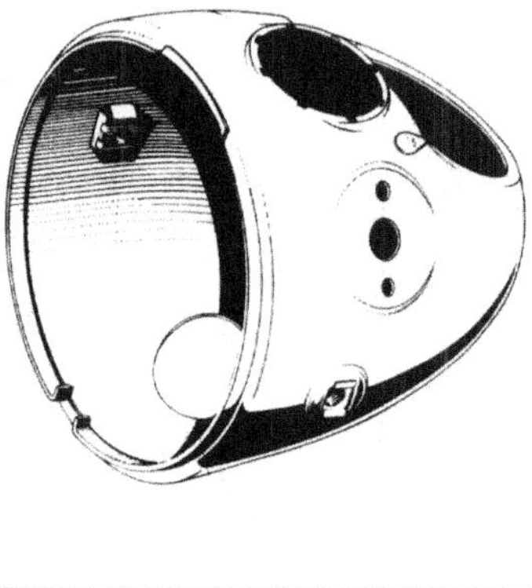

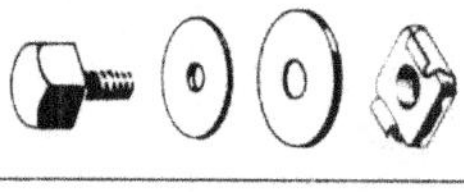

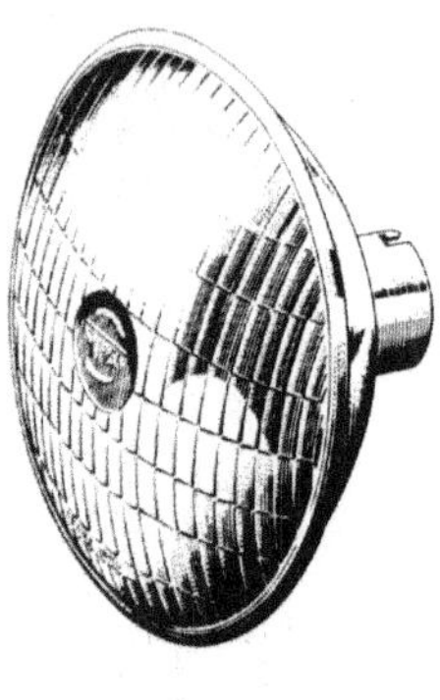

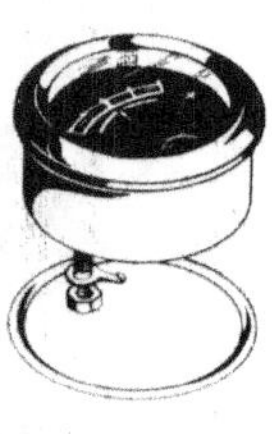

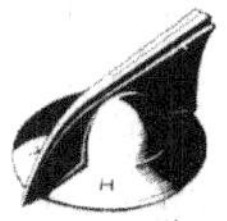

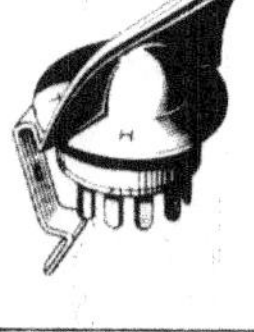

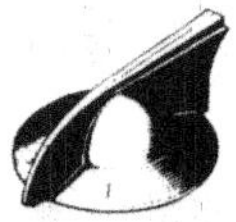

THE WIPAC GROUP — BUCKINGHAM — BUCKS.
TELEPHONE: BUCKINGHAM 3031   TELEGRAMS: WICOMAGSCO BUCKINGHAM

REF. LE.12/1/2

LIGHTING EQUIPMENT (Continued)

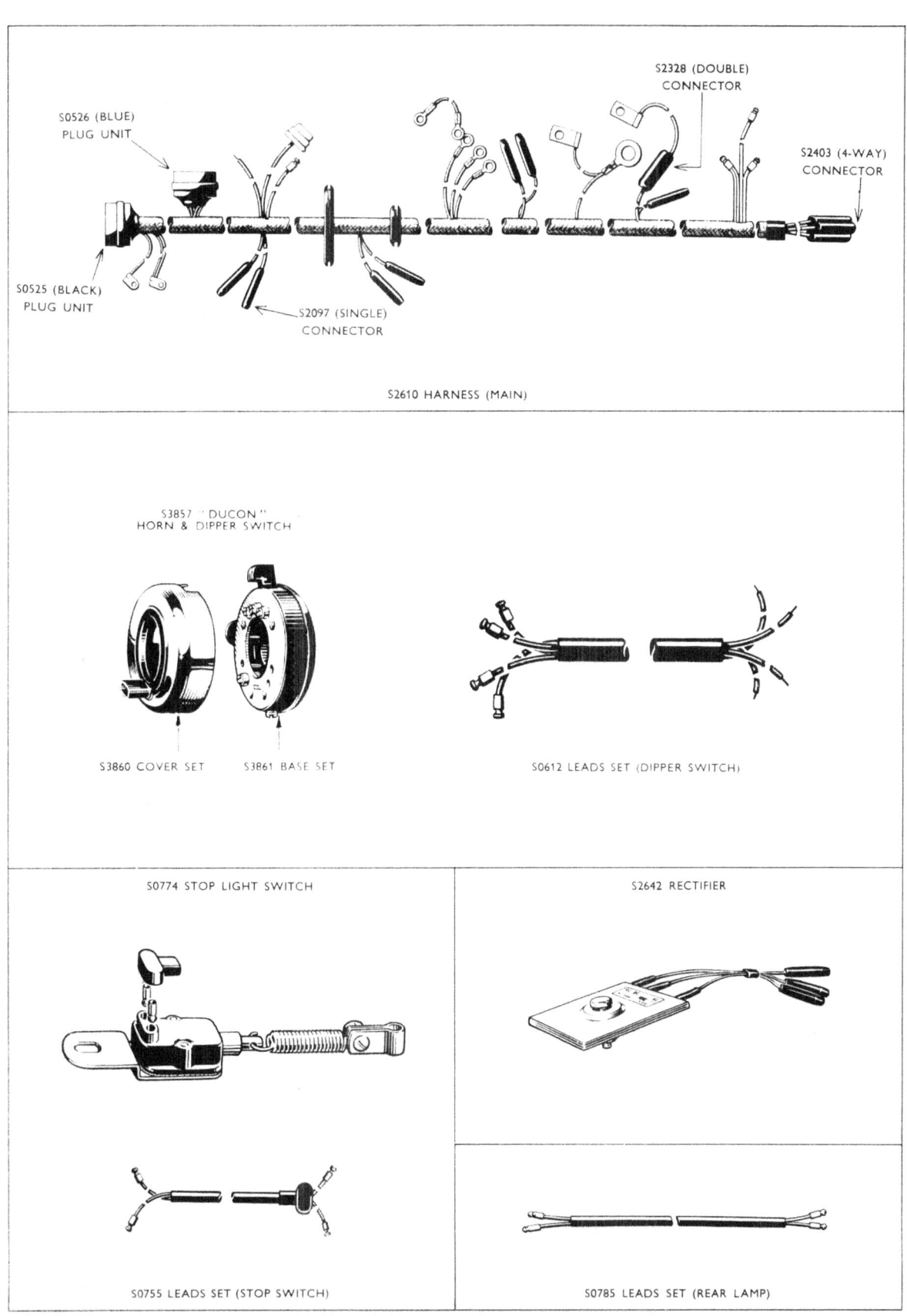

WIPAC LIGHTING EQUIPMENT

Norton Jubilee 250 c.c. & Navigator 350 c.c.
MODELS PRODUCED FROM SEPT. 1960 TO SEPT. 1962

S2617	RIM
S2618	FRONT UNIT (COMPLETE)
S2612	REFLECTOR AND GLASS SET
S0768	BULB HOLDER UNIT (MAIN)
S2615	HEADLAMP UNIT
S0062	AMMETER SET
S0877	BULB HOLDER (PILOT)
S0783	SWITCH KNOB SET (LIGHTS)
S2664	REFLECTOR CLIP SET (SET OF 5)
S2611	LAMP BODY UNIT
S0781	SWITCH UNIT (LIGHTS)
S0782	SWITCH UNIT (IGNITION)
S0064	RIM LOCKING SET
S0784	SWITCH KNOB SET (IGNITION)
S2796	PLUG UNIT RETAINER CLIP
S2688	HEADLAMP FIXING SET

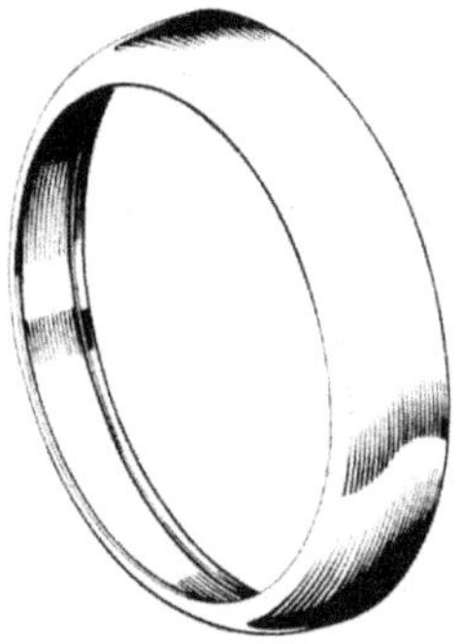

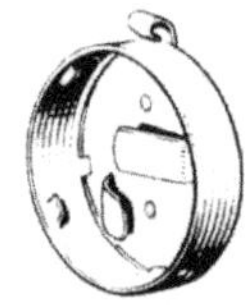

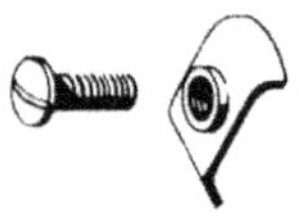

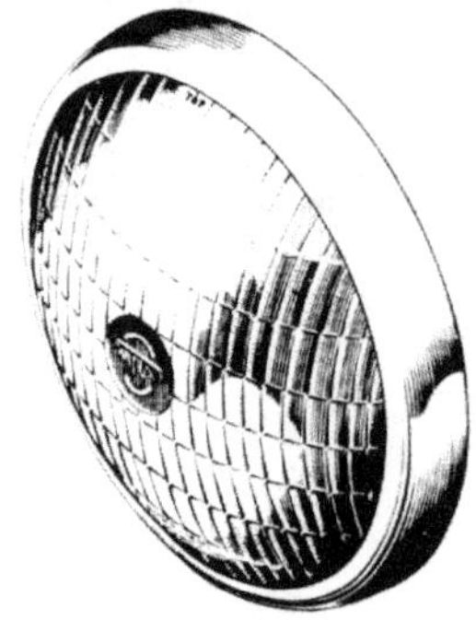

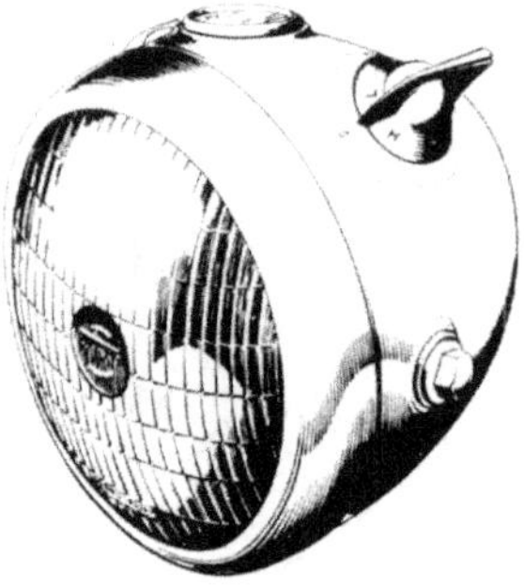

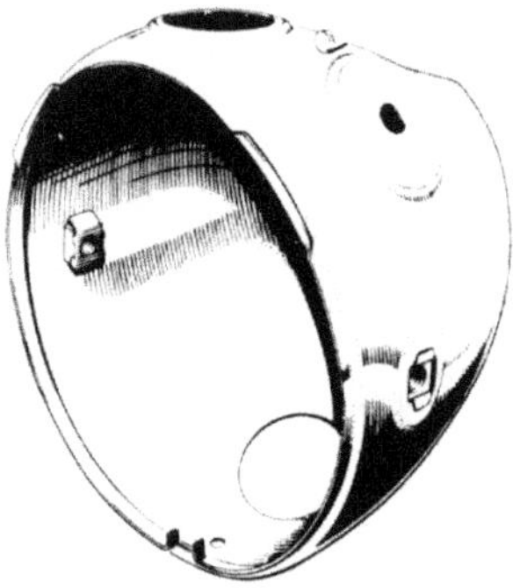

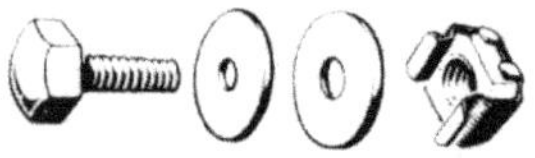

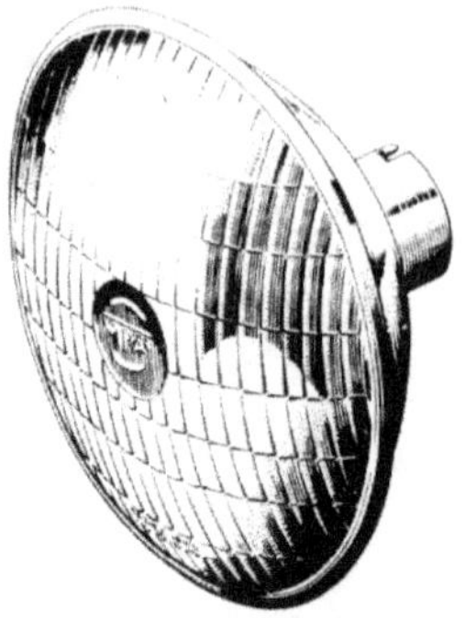

THE WIPAC GROUP — BUCKINGHAM — BUCKS.
TELEPHONE: BUCKINGHAM 3031   TELEGRAMS: WICOMAGSCO BUCKINGHAM

REF. L.E.1/1/2

LIGHTING EQUIPMENT (Continued)

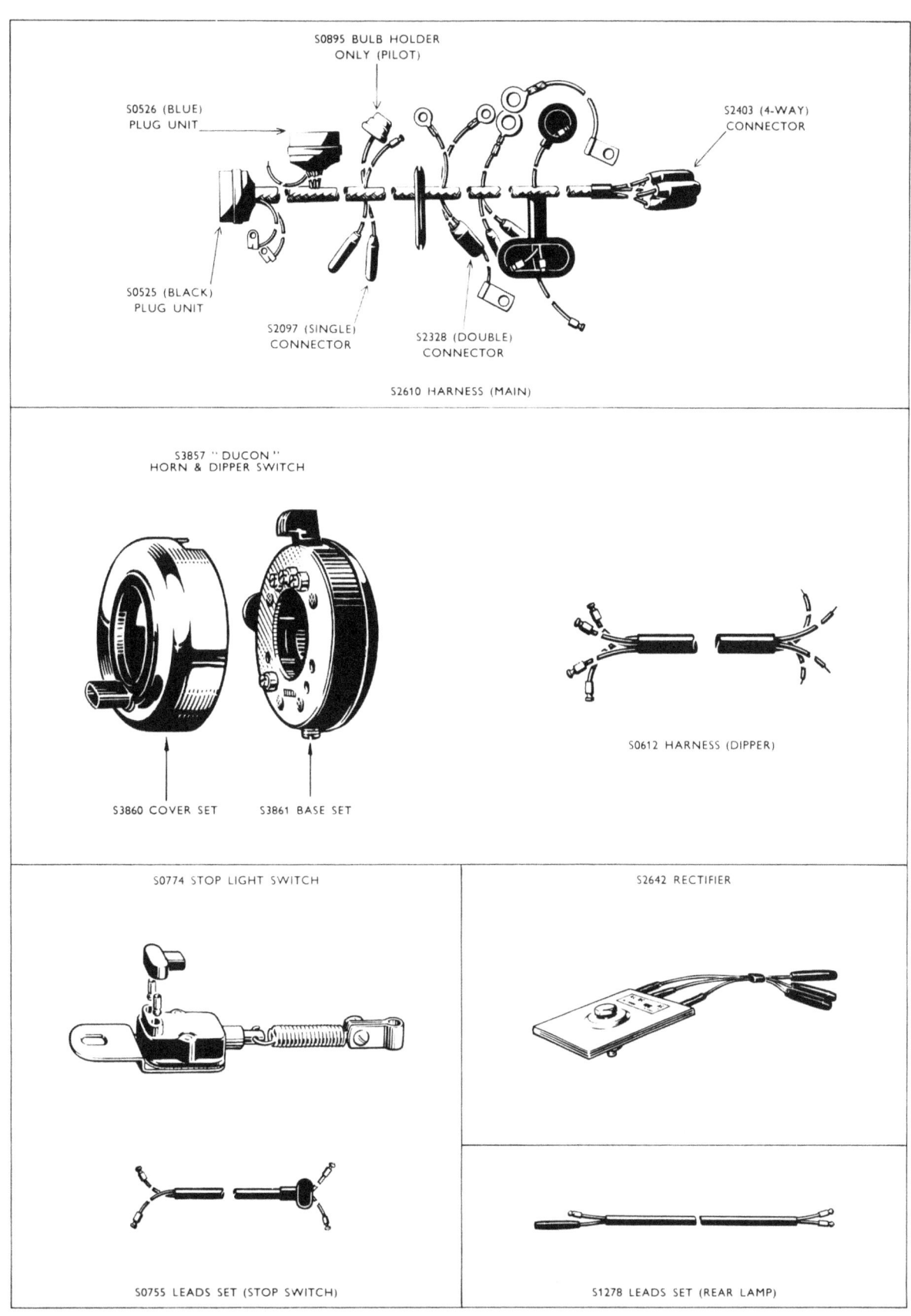

RALEIGH MOPED
MODELS RM8 AND RM9.
MODELS PRODUCED FROM MAY 1964.

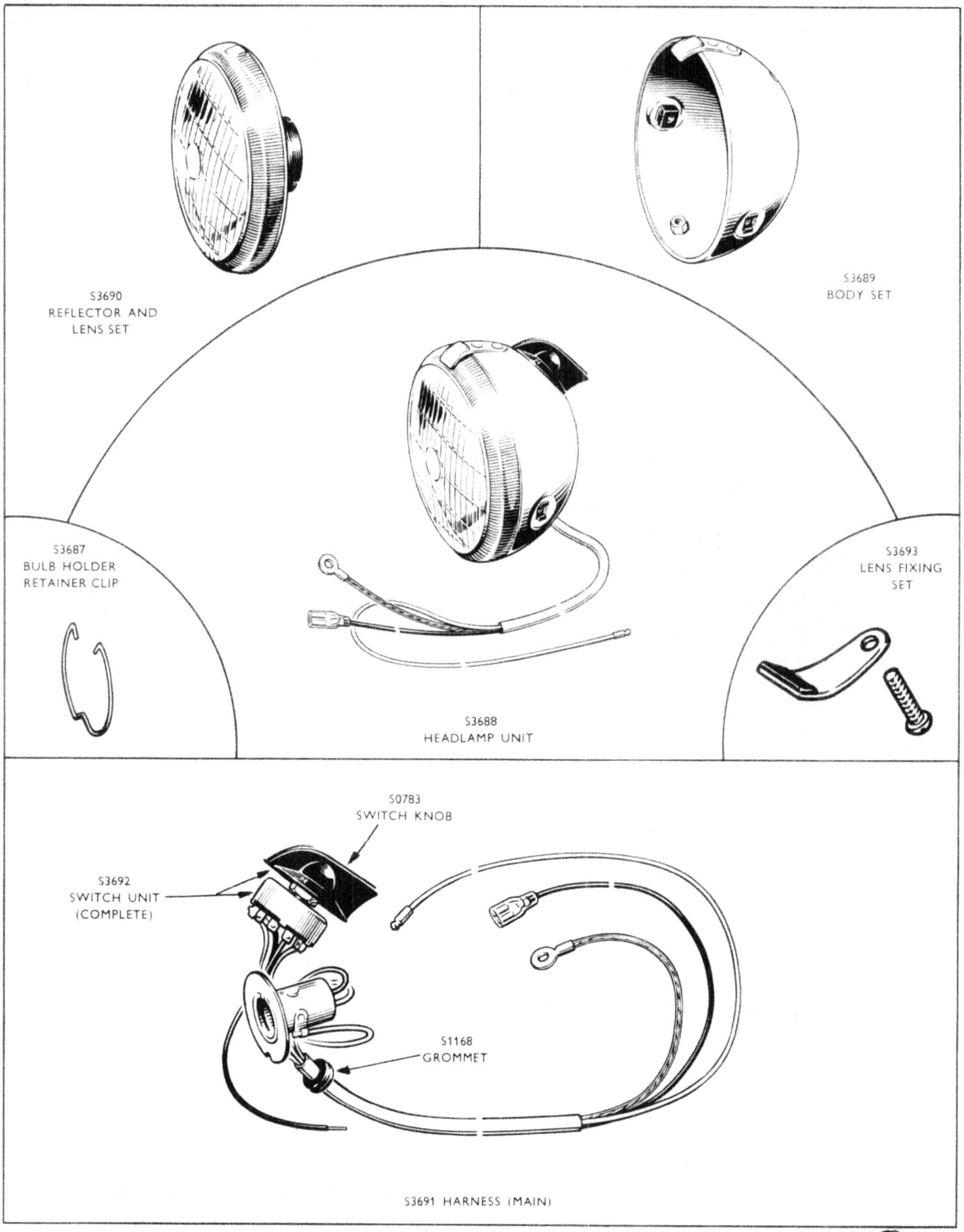

S3690 REFLECTOR AND LENS SET

S3689 BODY SET

S3687 BULB HOLDER RETAINER CLIP

S3693 LENS FIXING SET

S3688 HEADLAMP UNIT

S0783 SWITCH KNOB

S3692 SWITCH UNIT (COMPLETE)

S1168 GROMMET

S3691 HARNESS (MAIN)

THE WIPAC GROUP — BUCKINGHAM — BUCKS.
TELEPHONE: BUCKINGHAM 3031   TELEGRAMS: WICOMAGSCO BUCKINGHAM

LE 11/1/2

LIGHTING EQUIPMENT (Continued)

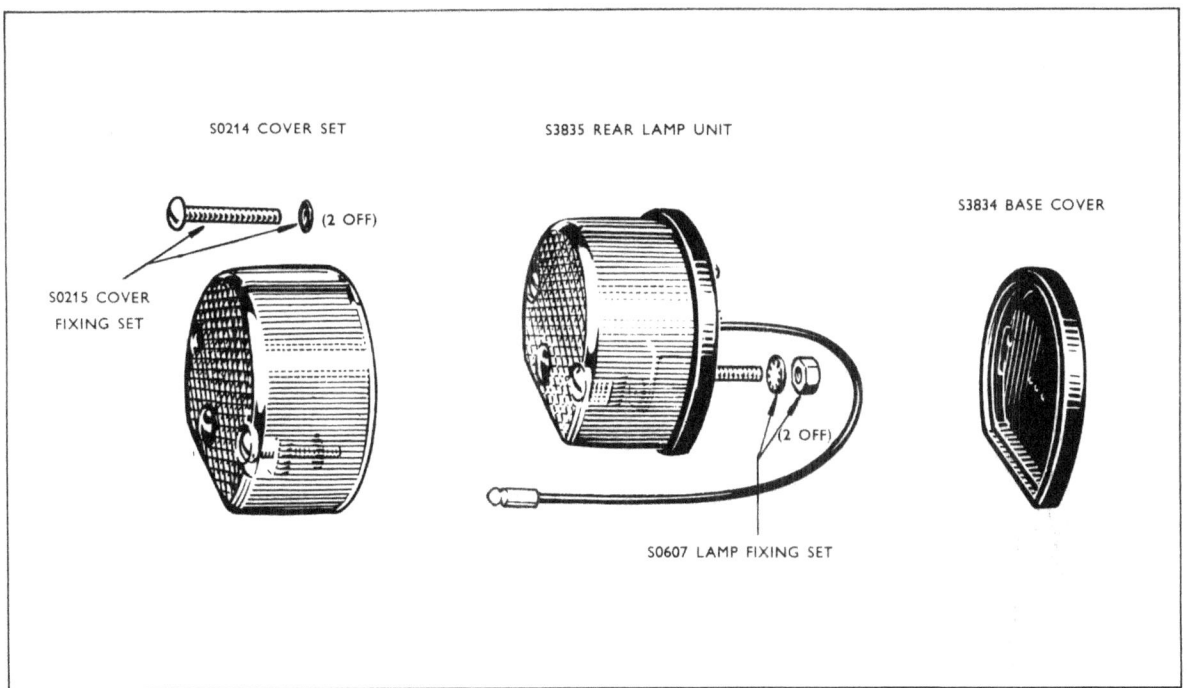

WIPAC LIGHTING EQUIPMENT

TRIUMPH "TINA" 100 c.c. SCOOTER
MODELS PRODUCED FROM OCTOBER 61

S0348 GLASS SET	S2910 FRONT UNIT	S2909 REFLECTOR AND GLASS SET
S0349 RIM	S2906 HEADLAMP UNIT	S2907 LAMP BODY UNIT
S0347 MAIN BULB CONTACT SET	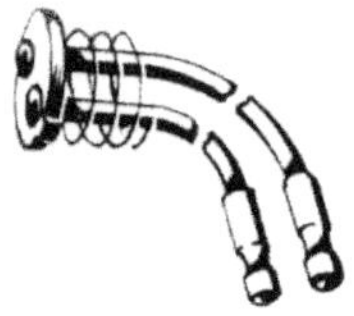	S0351 BULB HOLDER (PILOT)
S2796 PLUG UNIT RETAINER CLIP	S0783 SWITCH KNOB SET	S0781 SWITCH UNIT	S0064 RIM LOCKING SET
S0887 REFLECTOR CLIP SET (SET OF 4)	S2908 HEADLAMP FIXING SET		S2340 CONNECTOR (3-WAY)
			S1975 GROMMET

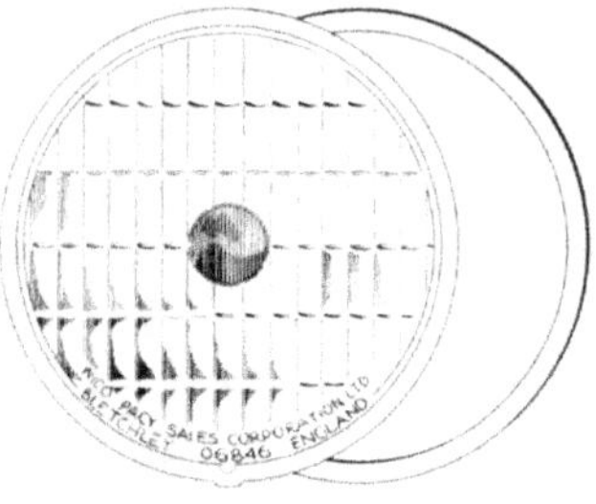

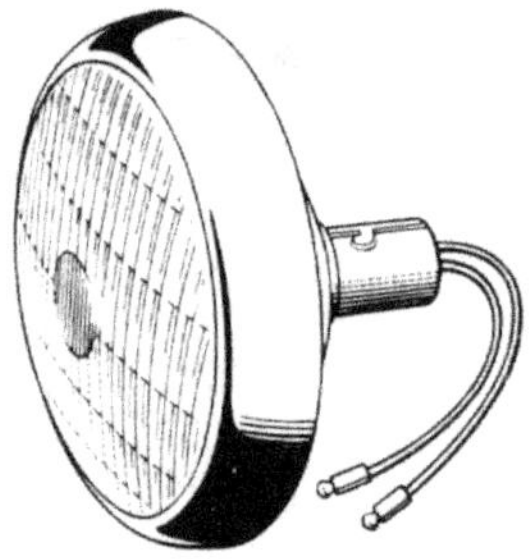

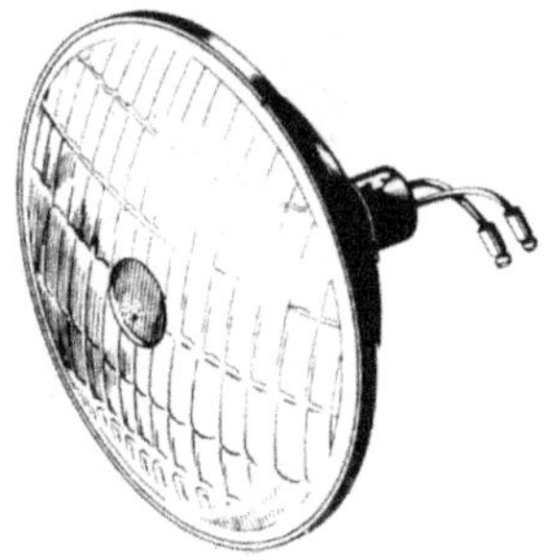

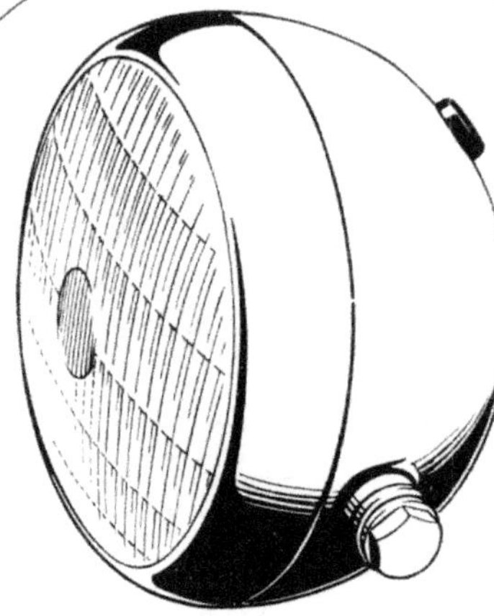

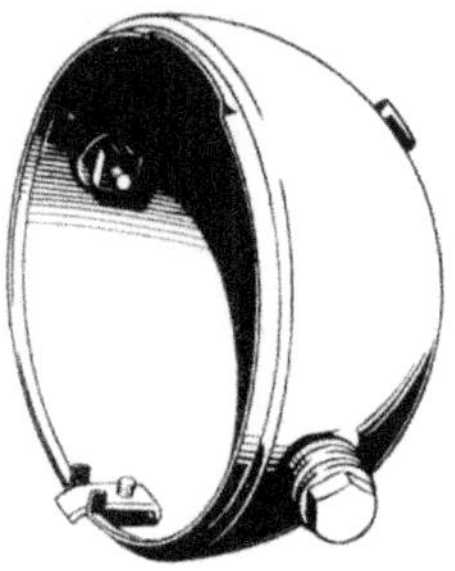

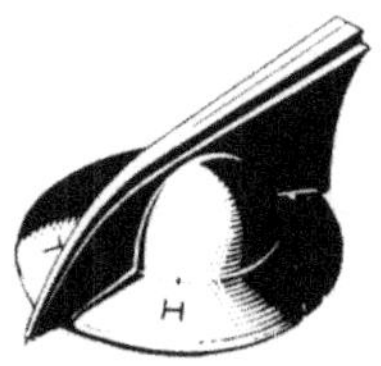

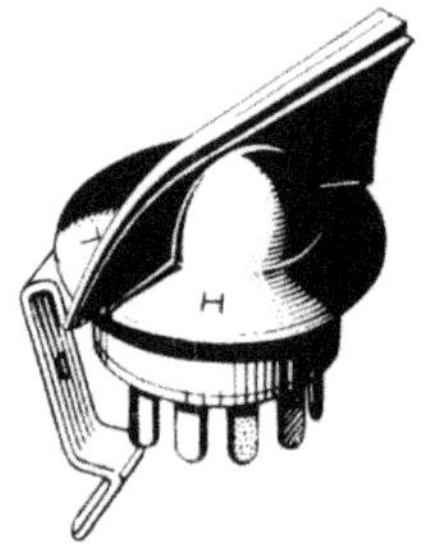

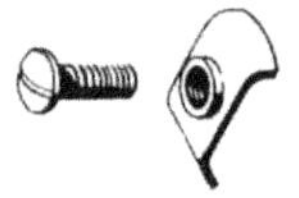

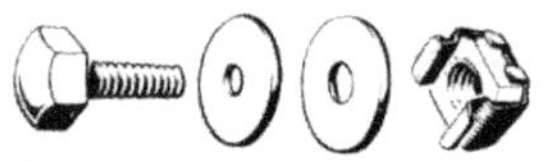

THE WIPAC GROUP — BUCKINGHAM — BUCKS.
TELEPHONE: BUCKINGHAM 3031   TELEGRAMS: WICOMAGSCO BUCKINGHAM

REF. L.E. 2/1/3

LIGHTING EQUIPMENT (Continued)

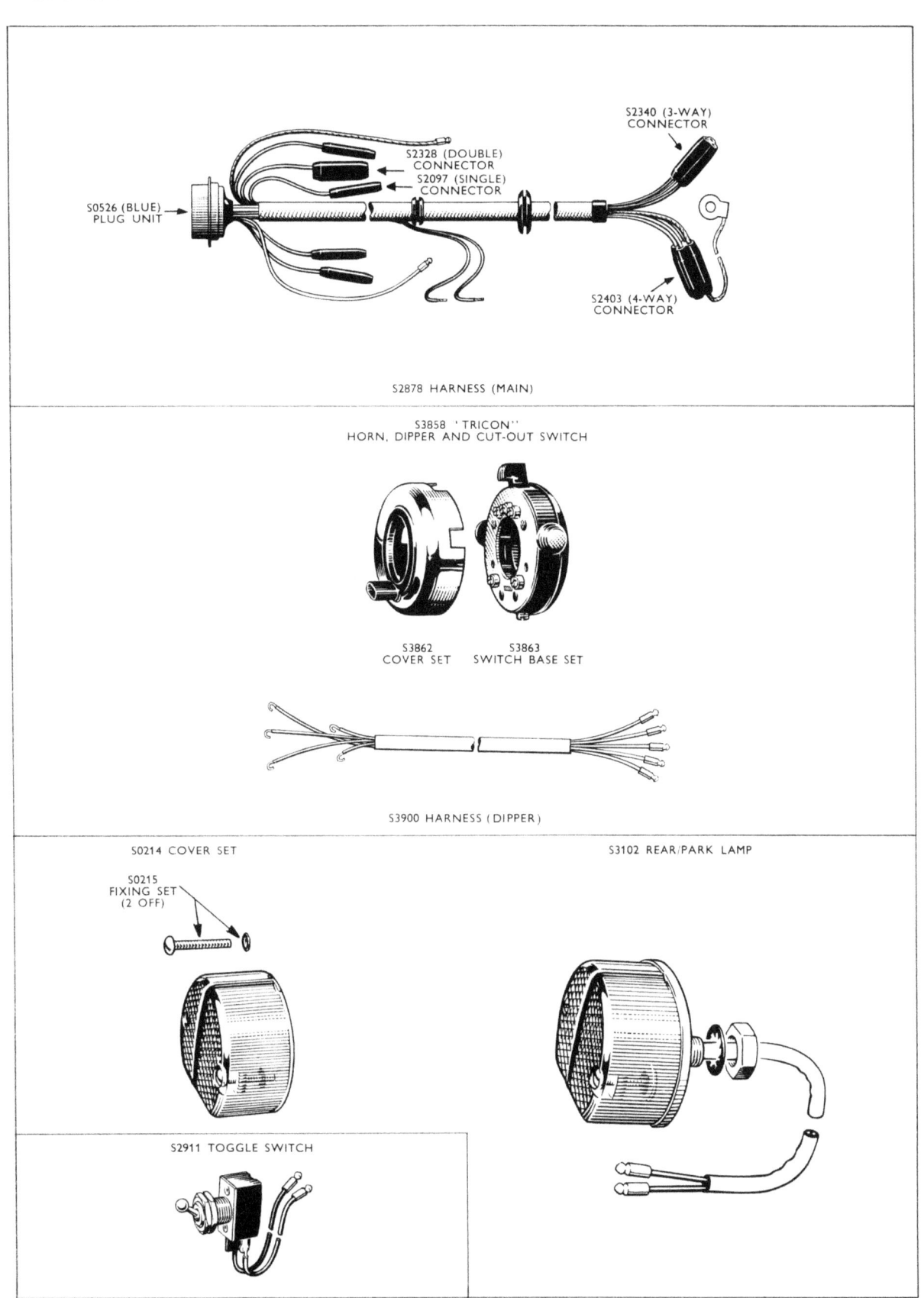

WIPAC LIGHTING EQUIPMENT

TRIUMPH T10 AUTOMATIC 100 c.c. SCOOTER
MODELS PRODUCED FROM APRIL 1965

- S0348 GLASS SET 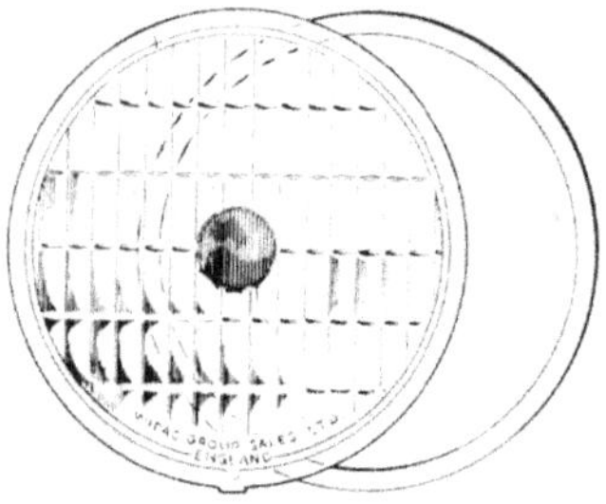
- S2910 FRONT UNIT 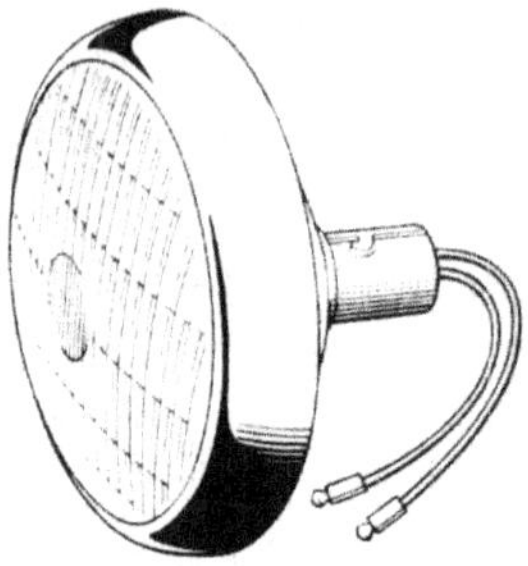
- S2909 REFLECTOR AND GLASS SET 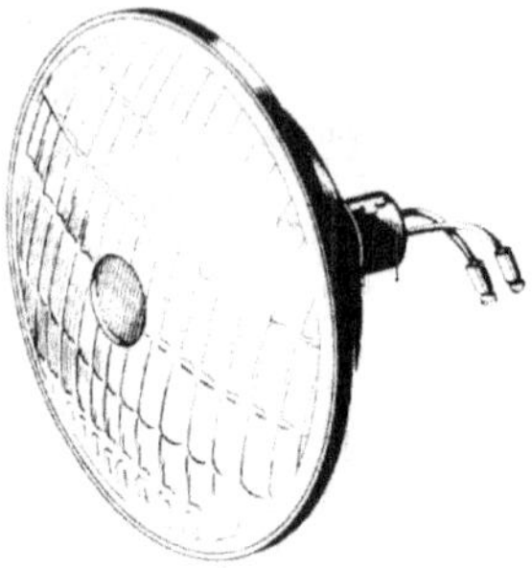
- S0349 RIM
- S2907 LAMP BODY UNIT 
- S0347 MAIN BULB CONTACT SET 
- S2906 HEADLAMP UNIT
- S0351 BULB HOLDER (PILOT) 
- S2796 PLUG UNIT RETAINER CLIP 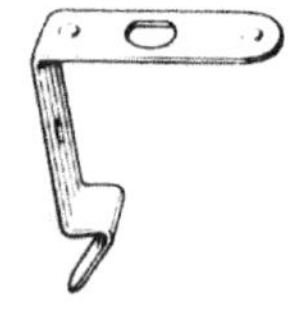
- S0783 SWITCH KNOB SET 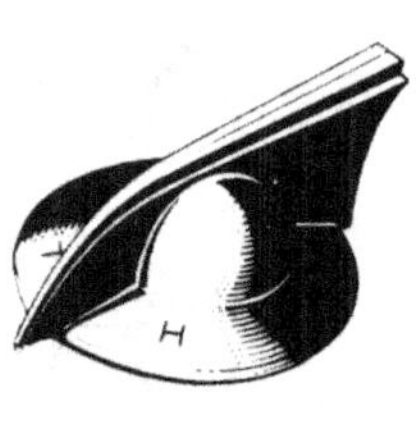
- S0781 SWITCH UNIT 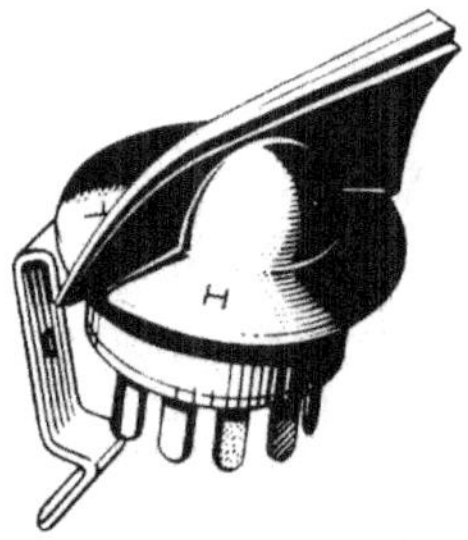
- S0064 RIM LOCKING SET 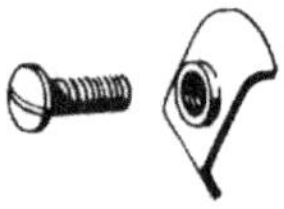
- S2340 CONNECTOR (3-WAY) 
- S0887 REFLECTOR CLIP SET (SET OF 4) 
- S2908 HEADLAMP FIXING SET 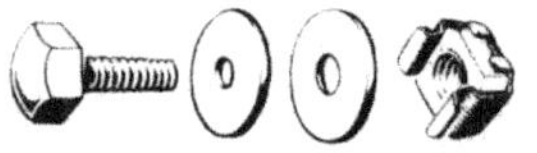
- S1975 GROMMET

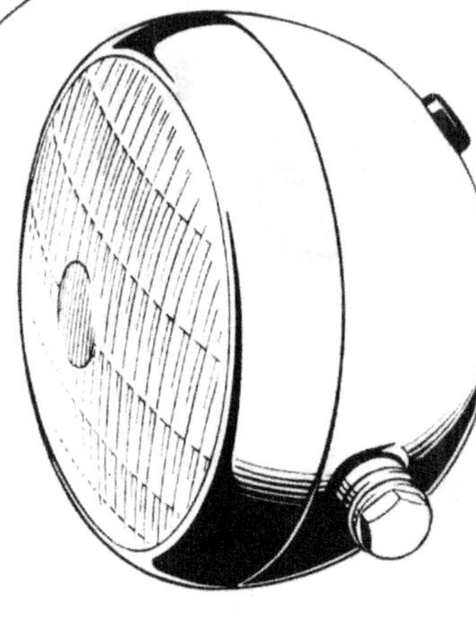

THE WIPAC GROUP — BUCKINGHAM — BUCKS.
TELEPHONE: BUCKINGHAM 3031   TELEGRAMS: WICOMAGSCO BUCKINGHAM

REF. L.E.20/1/2

LIGHTING EQUIPMENT (Continued)

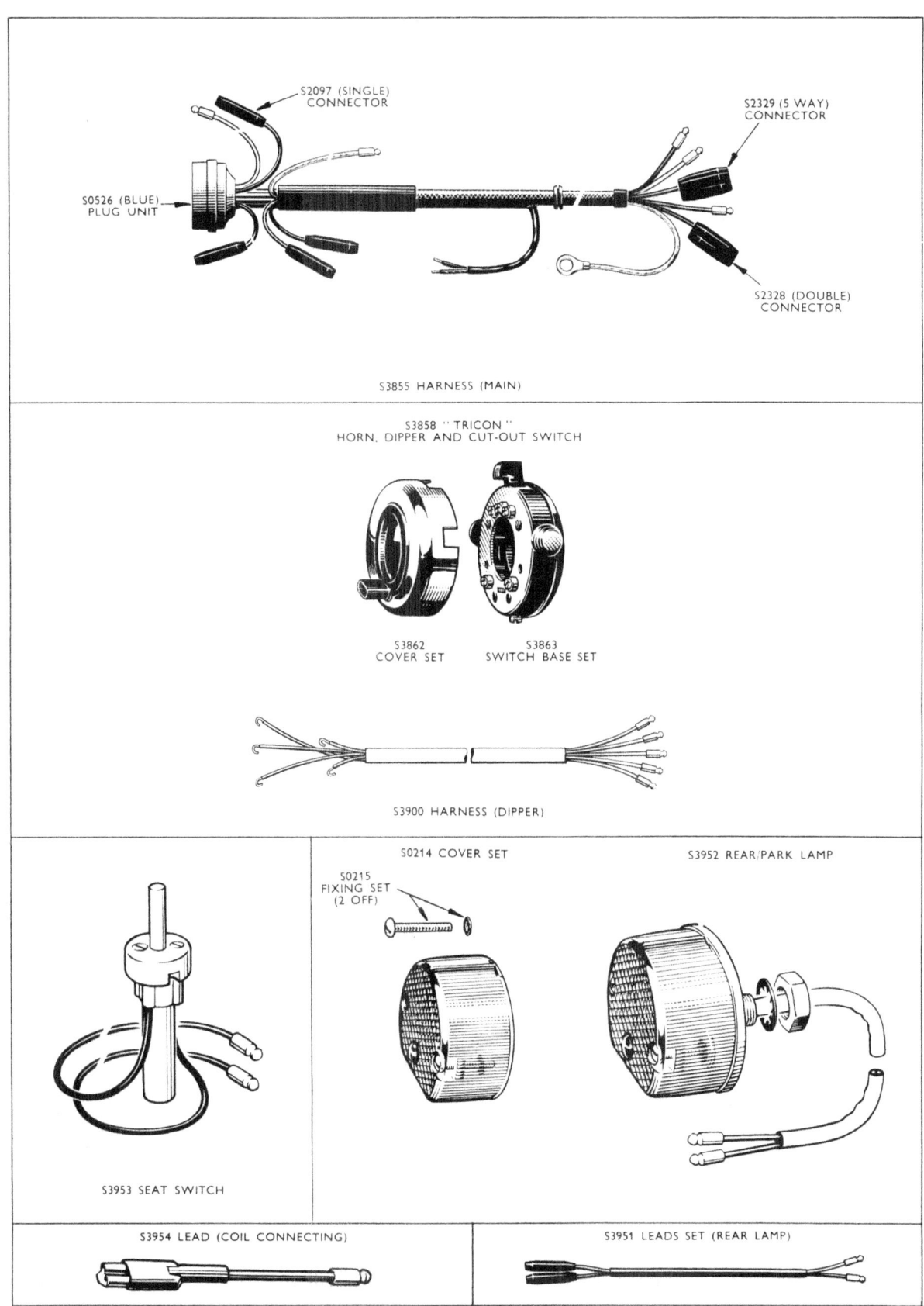

REF. L.E.20/2/2

TRIUMPH 199 c.c. SUPER CUB T20
Full D.C. Lighting with Coil Ignition
FROM JANUARY 1967

S0066 RIM	S4086 FRONT UNIT	S4087 REFLECTOR AND GLASS SET
S0768 BULB HOLDER UNIT (MAIN)	S4187 HEADLAMP UNIT	S0781 SWITCH (LIGHTS) / S0782 SWITCH (IGNITION)
S4089 BULB HOLDER UNIT (PILOT)	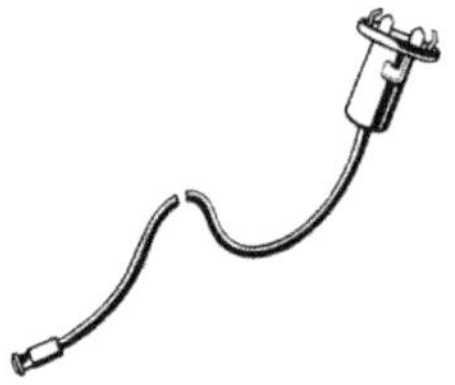	S0783 SWITCH COVER UNIT (LIGHTS)
S0070 REFLECTOR CLIP SET (SET OF 4)	S4088 BODY UNIT	S0784 SWITCH COVER UNIT (IGNITION)
S0064 RIM LOCKING SET	S0238 HEADLAMP FIXING SET	S2796 PLUG UNIT RETAINER CLIP

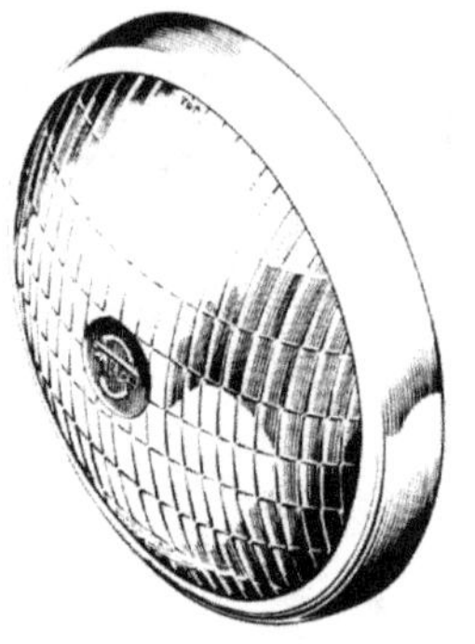

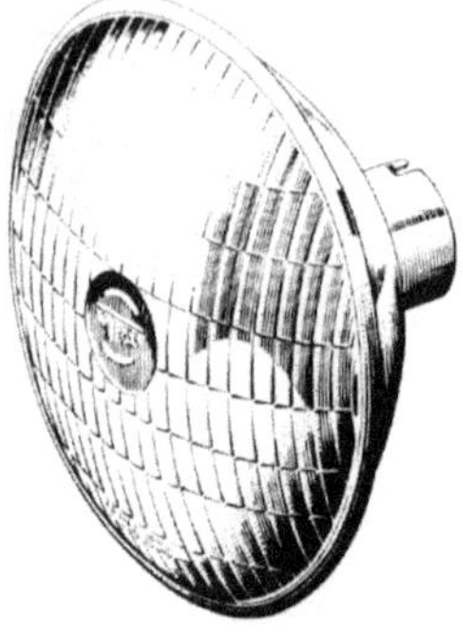

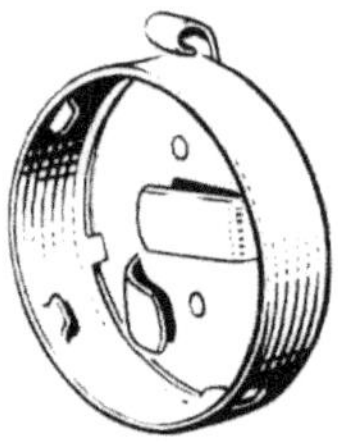

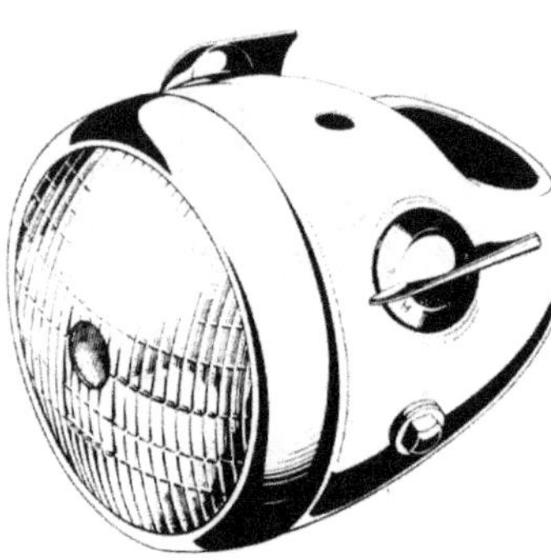

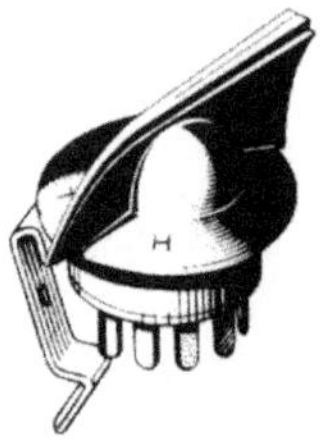

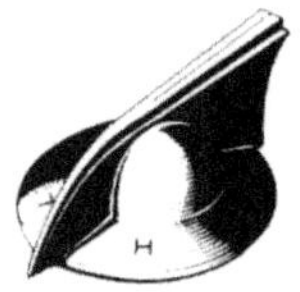

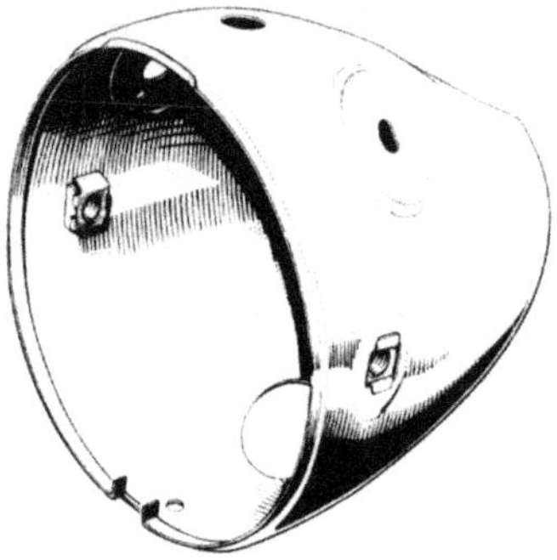

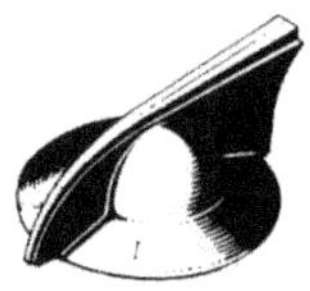

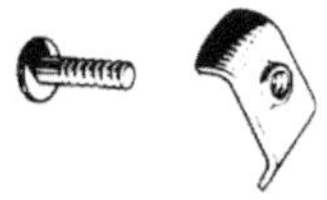

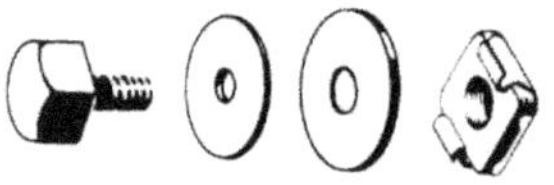

THE WIPAC GROUP — BUCKINGHAM — BUCKS.
TELEPHONE: BUCKINGHAM 3031   TELEGRAMS: WICOMAGSCO BUCKINGHAM

REF.L.E. 25/1/2

LIGHTING EQUIPMENT (CONTINUED)

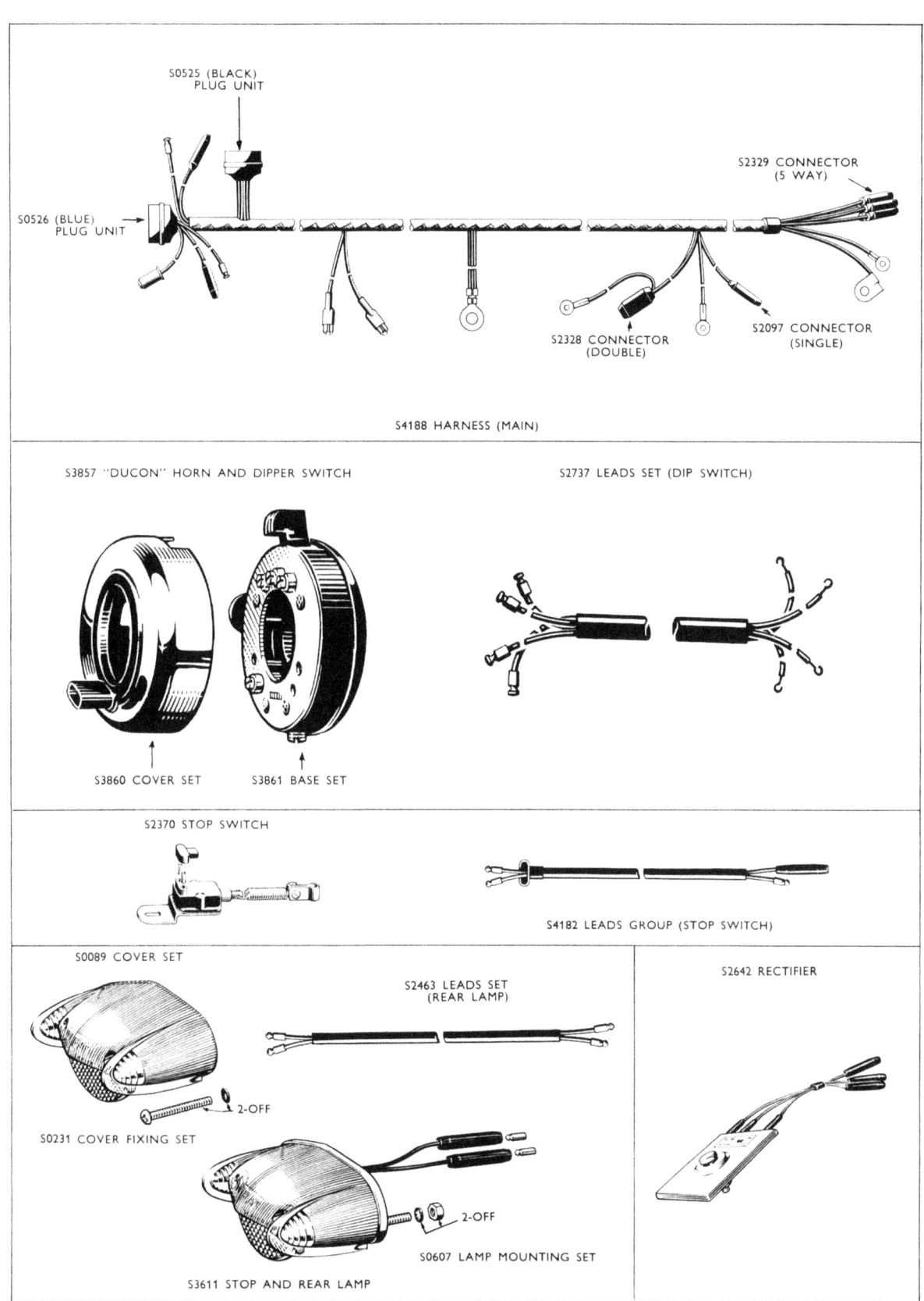

INDEX TO WIRING DIAGRAMS — PAGES

A.J.S.
Model 14, 14S, 14CSR & 8	143
Model 14CSR	144
Model 14CS	145 - 146

ARIEL
Colt	81 - 86
Pixie	87

B.S.A.
C10L (see also page 84)	88 - 91
Bantam (D1 through D14)	92 - 106
Dandy	107 - 109
Sunbeam (Scooter)	110 - 111
Beagle	112 - 113

DAYTON
Flamenco (Scooter)	114
Albatross (Scooter)	115

DUNKLEY Whippet (Scooterette)   116 - 117

EXCELSIOR Talisman   118 - 119

FRANCIS-BARNETT
Cruiser 80	120
Trials 83	121
Cruiser 84	122
Trials 85	123 - 124
Plover 86	125 - 126
Falcon 87	127
Model 88	128 - 129
Cruiser 89	130
Cruiser 91	131

JAMES
Commodore	132
Super Swift	133
Comet	134 - 135
Scooter	136
Flying Cadet	137 - 138
Captain	139
Model M.15	140 - 141
Model M. 16	142

MATCHLESS
Model G2, G5, G2S & G2CSR	143
Model G2CSR	144
Model G2CS	145 - 146

NORTON
Jubilee	147
Jubilee & Navigator	148 - 150
Navigator	151
Electra	152

PIATTI Scooter   153

RALEIGH MOPED RM8 & RM9   154

TRIUMPH
T10 Scooter	155
T20 Super Cub	156
Tina Scooter	157
Tigress Scooter	110 - 111

WIRING WIPAC DIAGRAM

ARIEL model "Colt" L.H.
FROM AUGUST 1953 TO MAY 1954

THE WIPAC GROUP · BUCKINGHAM · ENGLAND

NOTE

Prior to ordering spare parts refer to Wipac Service Bulletin Ref. R 3/63/A.B.

NOTE :— Switches supplied Approx. 1st Oct. 1954 to 1st Jan. 1955 *with* a link between No. 12 top and No. 5 bottom should have this connection removed. (Shown dotted).

REF. WD8P/1

WIRING WIPAC DIAGRAM

ARIEL model "Colt" L.H.
FROM MAY 1954 TO SEPTEMBER 1954

THE WIPAC GROUP · BUCKINGHAM · ENGLAND

NOTE

Prior to ordering spare parts refer to Wipac Service Bulletin Ref. R 3/63/A.B.

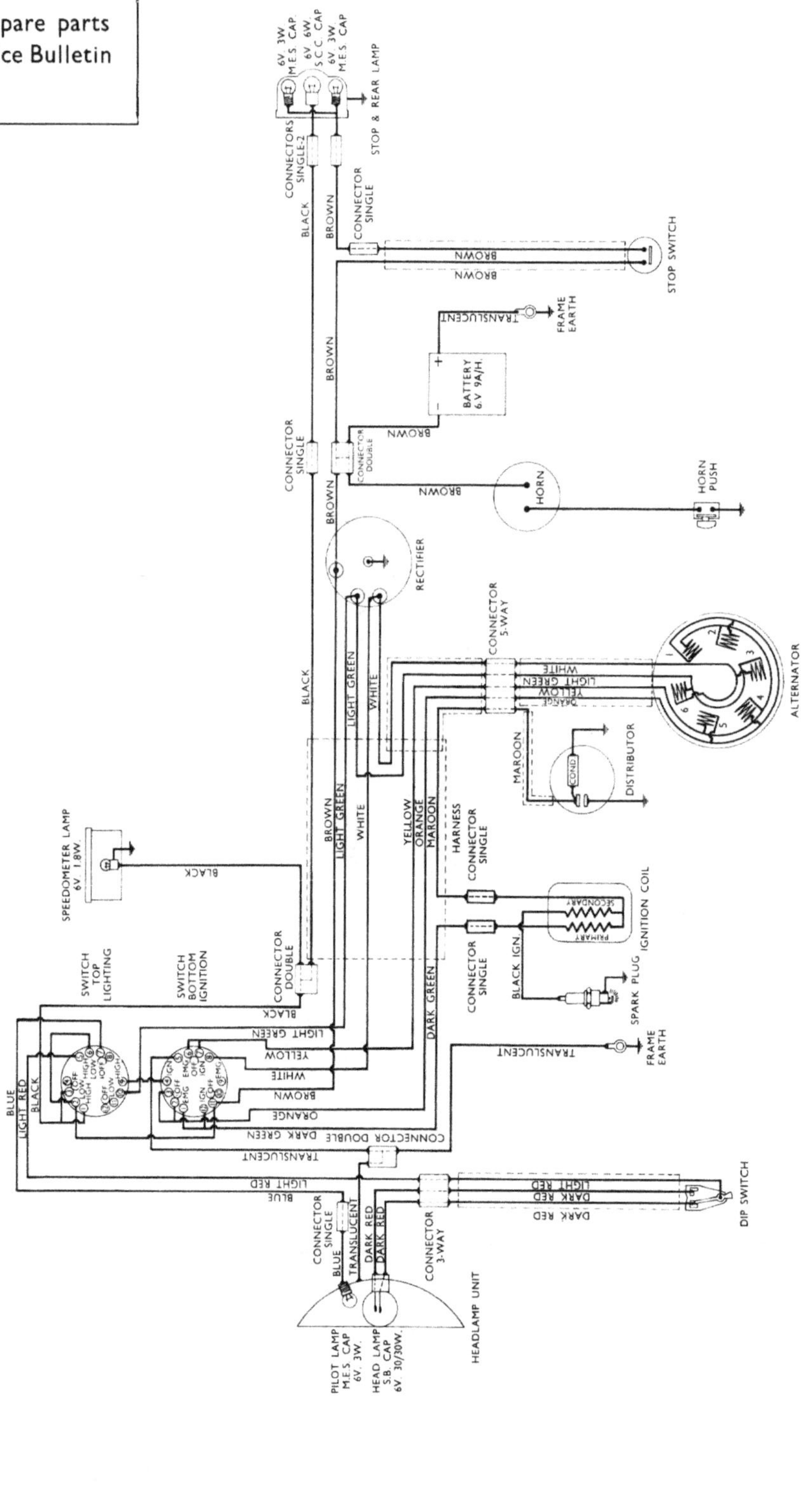

REF. WD8P/2

WIRING WIPAC DIAGRAM

ARIEL "Colt" Model L.H.
FROM OCTOBER 1954 TO JULY 1955

THE WIPAC GROUP · BUCKINGHAM · ENGLAND

NOTE

Prior to ordering spare parts refer to Wipac Service Bulletin Ref. R 3/63/A.B.

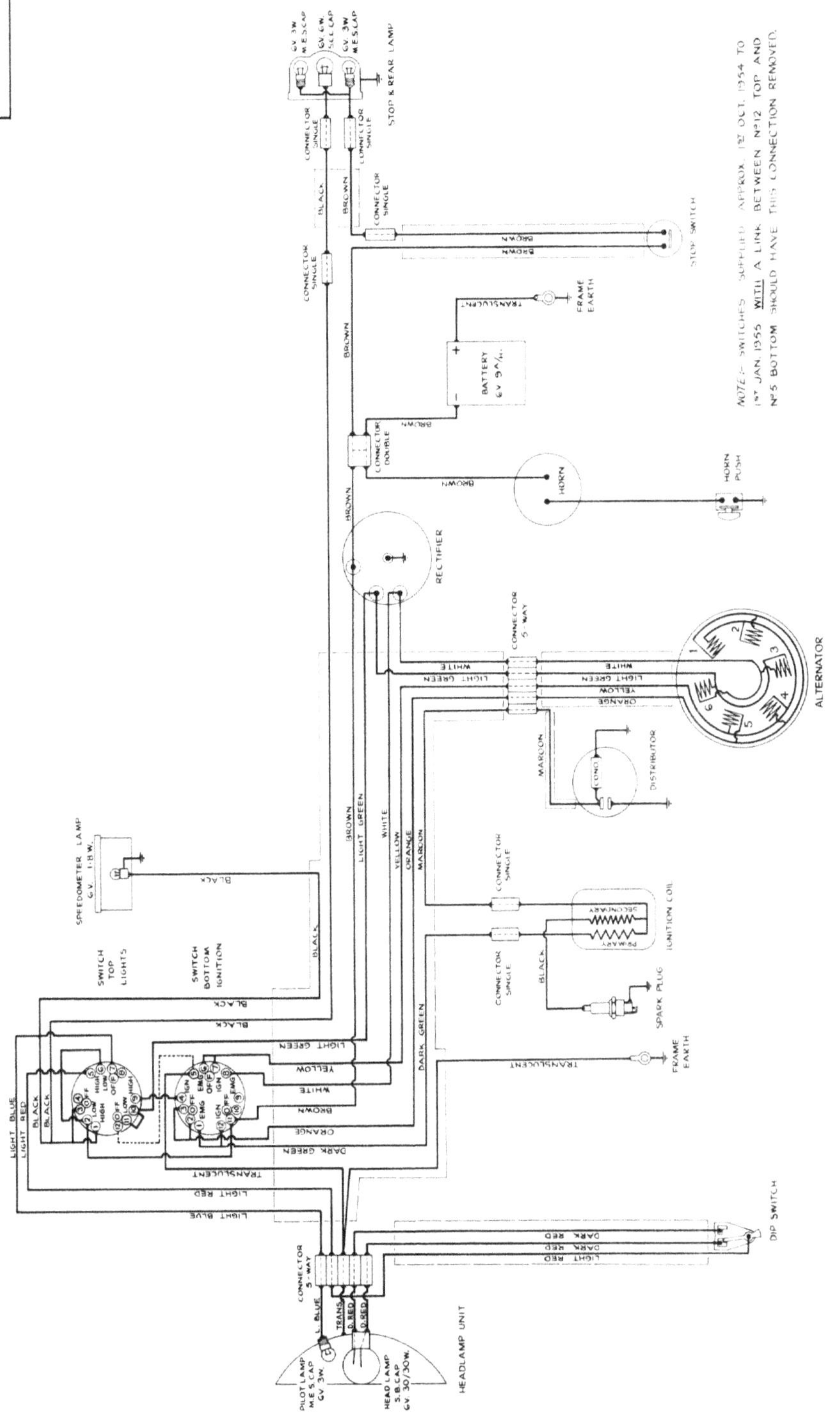

NOTE :- Switches supplied Approx. 1st Oct. 1954 to 1st Jan. 1955 *with* a link between No. 12 top and No. 5 bottom should have this connection removed. (Shown dotted).

REF. WD85/1

WIRING WIPAC DIAGRAM

ARIEL COLT L.H. & B.S.A. C.10.L. PRIOR TO SEPT. 1955
FITTED WITH CURRENT REPLACEMENT PARTS

REPLACEMENTS	PART No.
Headlamp (less harness)	S0720
Harness (Main)	S0719
Dip Switch	S1356
Dip Switch Harness	S2343
Alternator	G1583
Distributor	S2469
Rectifier	SEE NOTE
Coil—6v. Ignition	S0973
Stop & Tail Lamp	S0088
Stop Switch	S2370
Stop Switch Leads	S2337

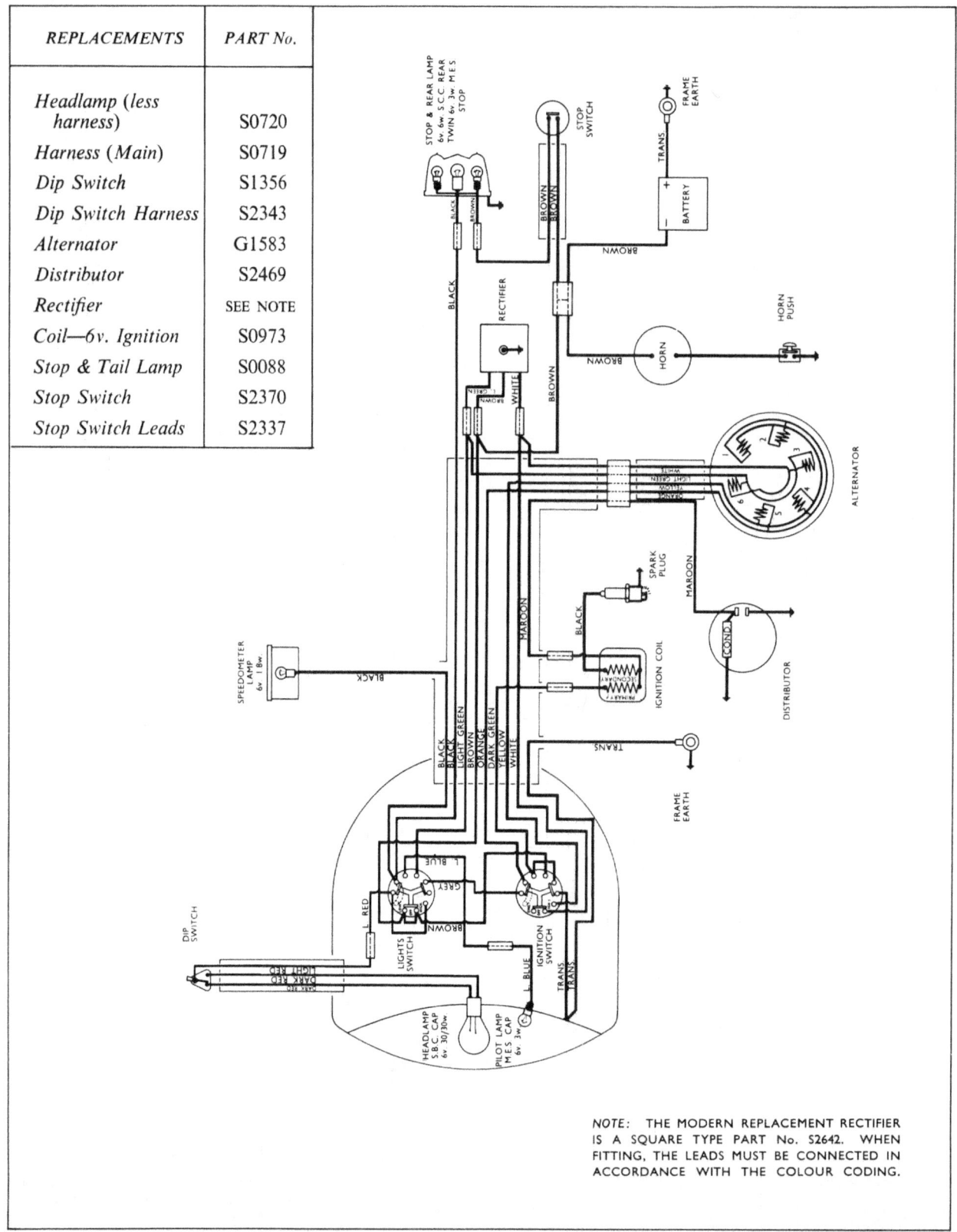

NOTE: THE MODERN REPLACEMENT RECTIFIER IS A SQUARE TYPE PART No. S2642. WHEN FITTING, THE LEADS MUST BE CONNECTED IN ACCORDANCE WITH THE COLOUR CODING.

REF. WD/49/916

WIRING DIAGRAM — WIPAC

ARIEL model "Colt" L.H.
MODELS PRODUCED FROM AUGUST 1955 TO JULY 1956

THE WIPAC GROUP · BUCKINGHAM · ENGLAND

SPARES UNITS	PART No.
Headlamp (less harness)	S0720
Harness (Main)	S2389
Dip Switch	S1356
Dip Switch Harness	S2343
Alternator	G1584
Distributor	S2469
Rectifier	S2642
Coil—6v. Ignition	S0793
Stop & Tail Lamp	S0088
Stop Switch	S2370
Stop Switch Leads	S2337

REF. WD8T/2

WIRING WIPAC DIAGRAM

ARIEL model "Colt" L.H.

MODELS PRODUCED FROM AUGUST 1956 TO SEPT. 1959

THE WIPAC GROUP · BUCKINGHAM · ENGLAND

SPARES UNITS	PART No.
Headlamp (less harness and Ammeter)	S0917
Harness (Main)	S0087
Dip Switch	S1356
Dip Switch Harness	S2343
Alternator	G1584
Distributor	S2469
Rectifier	S2642
Coil—6v. Ignition	S0793
Stop & Rear Lamp	S0088
Stop Switch	S2370
Stop Switch Leads	S2337
Ammeter Unit	S0062

REF. WD/8/669/1

WIRING WIPAC DIAGRAM

ARIEL PIXIE 50 c.c.
A.C. LIGHTING
MODELS PRODUCED FROM OCTOBER 1963 TO AUG. 1965

THE WIPAC GROUP · BUCKINGHAM · BUCKS

SPARES UNITS	PART No.
Headlamp (less harness)	S3491
Harness (Main)	S3494
Switch Unit (Lights)	S0837
Rear and Park Lamp	S0213
Ignition Generator	I.G.1688

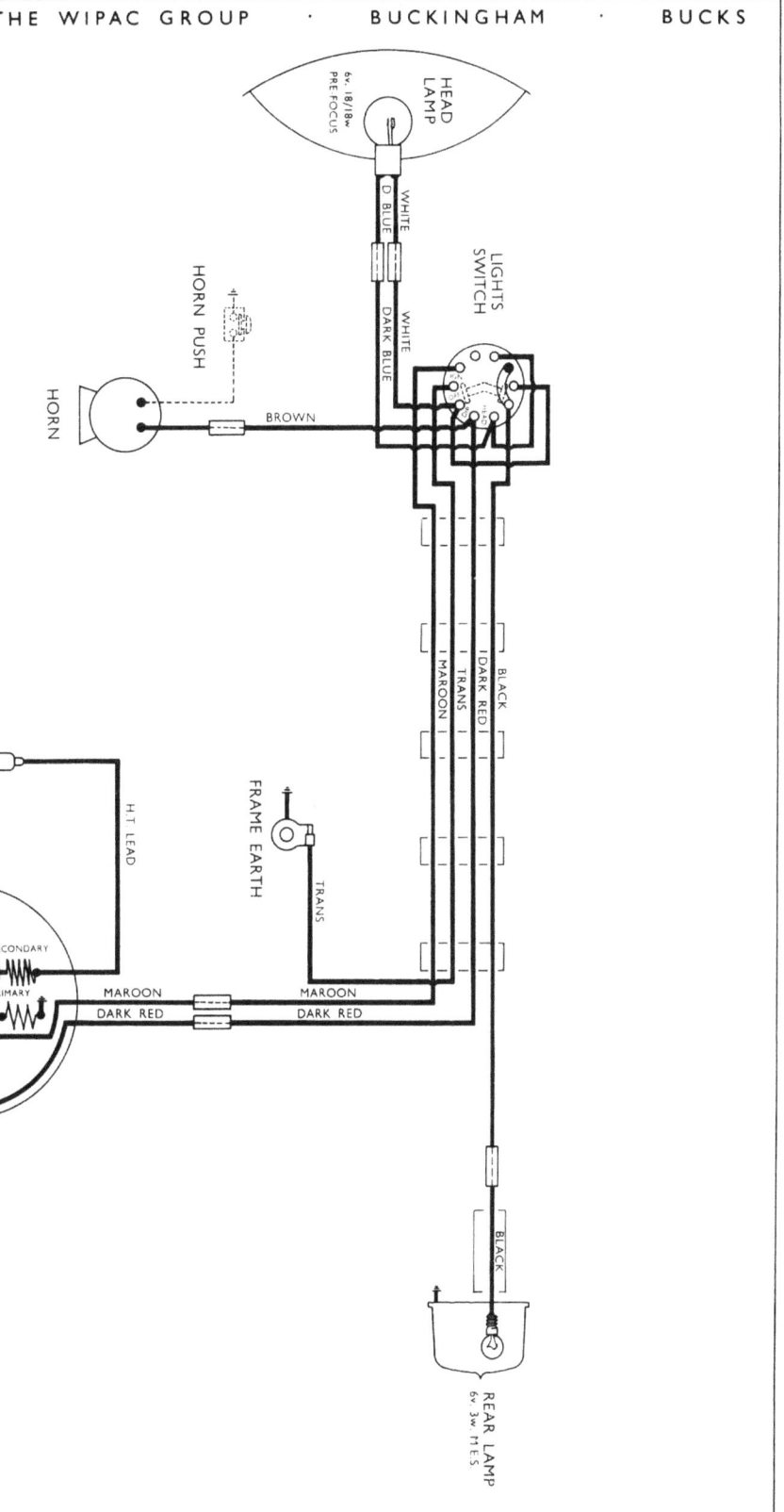

REF. WD/63/904/2

B.S.A. model C.10.L.
FROM AUGUST 1953 TO AUGUST 1954

THE WIPAC GROUP · BUCKINGHAM · ENGLAND

NOTE

Prior to ordering spare parts refer to Wipac Service Bulletin Ref. R 3/63/A.B.

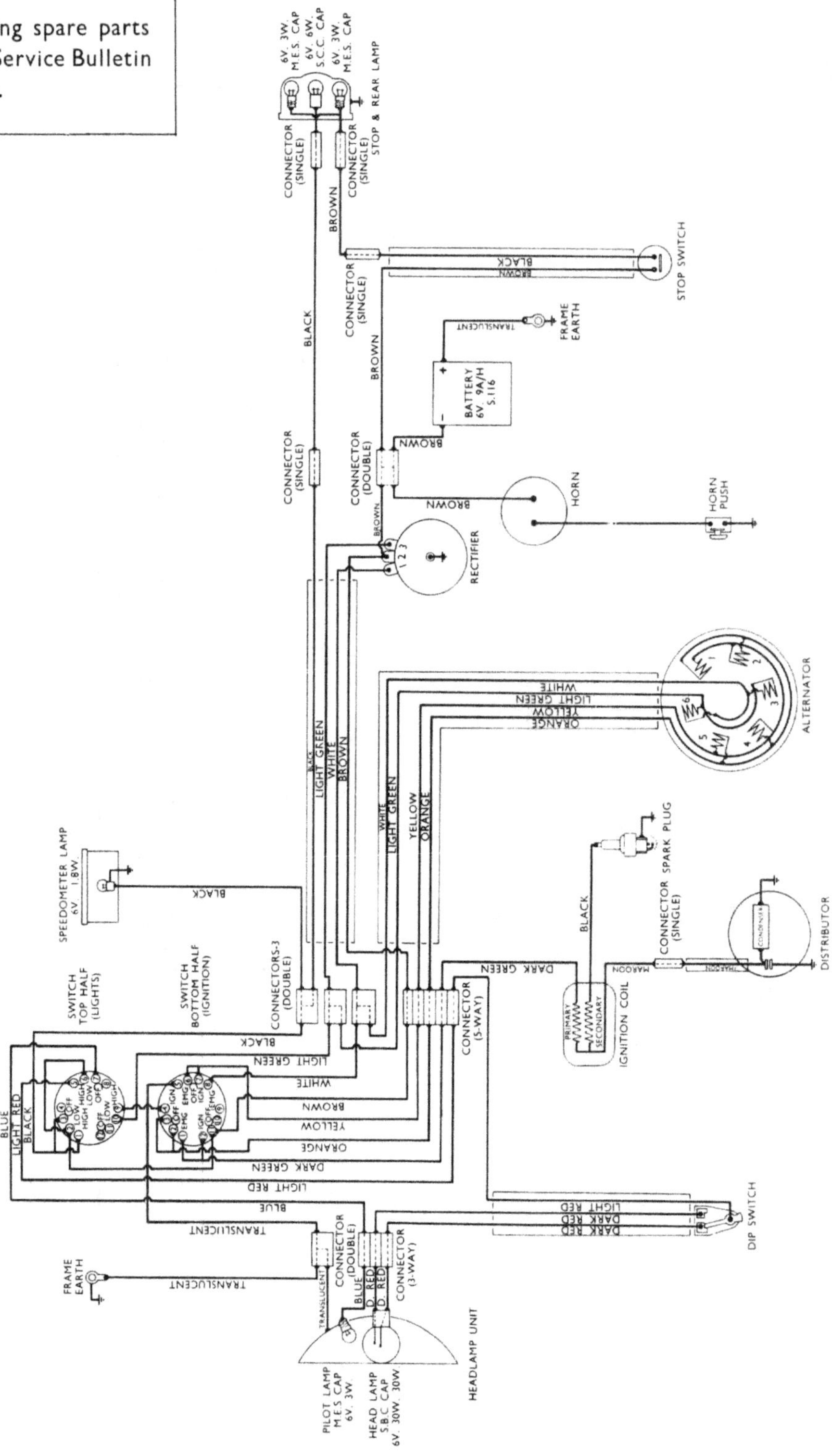

REF. WD3P/2

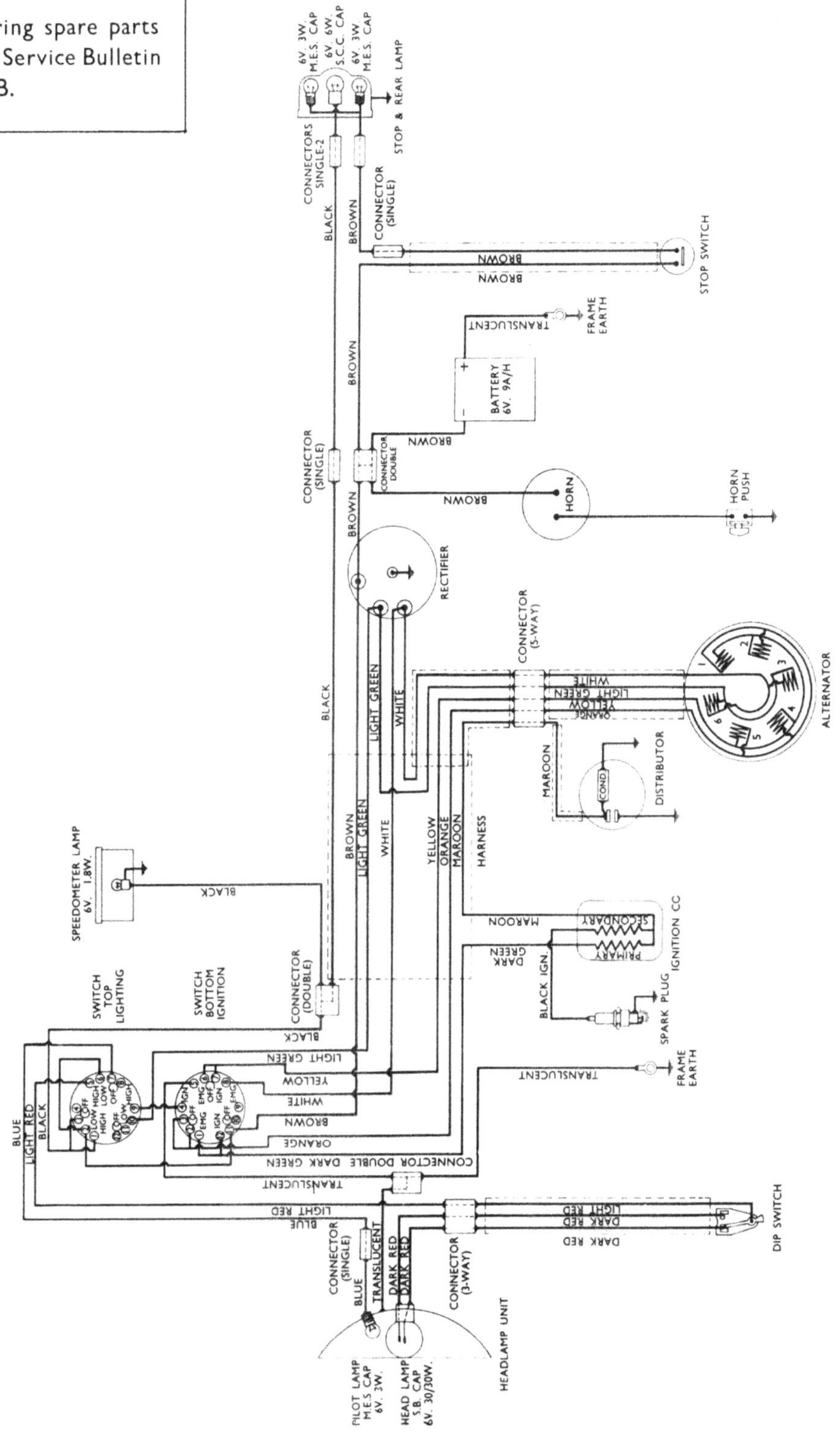

WIRING DIAGRAM WIPAC

B.S.A. Model C.10.L.
FROM OCTOBER 1954 TO JULY 1955

THE WIPAC GROUP · BUCKINGHAM · ENGLAND

NOTE

Prior to ordering spare parts refer to Wipac Service Bulletin Ref. R 3/63/A.B.

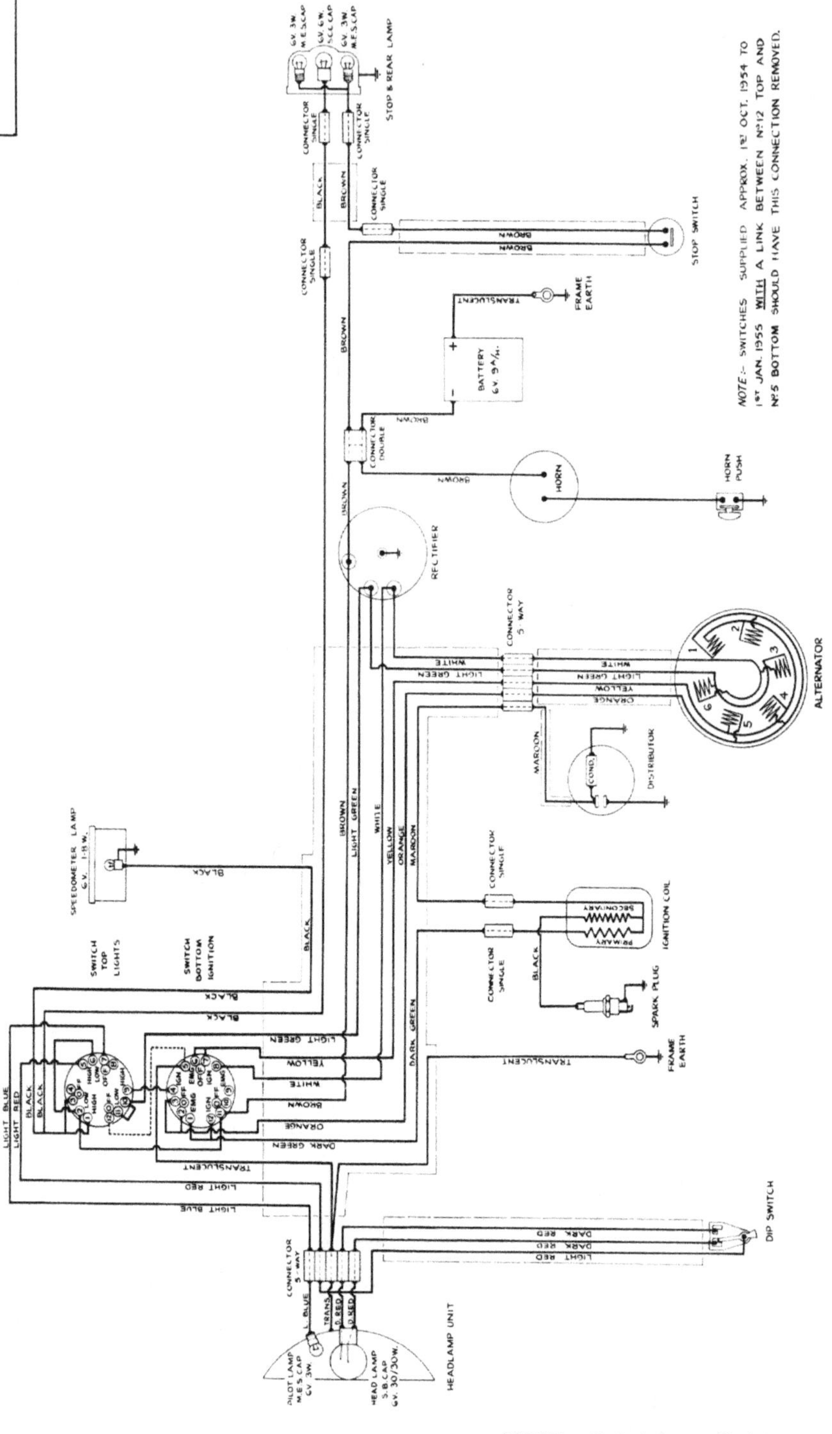

NOTE :- Switches supplied Approx. 1st Oct. 1954 to 1st Jan. 1955 *with* a link between No. 12 top and No. 5 bottom should have this connection removed. (Shown dotted).

REF. WD3S/1

WIRING WIPAC DIAGRAM

B.S.A. model C.10.L.

MODELS PRODUCED FROM AUGUST 1955 TO SEPT. 1958

THE WIPAC GROUP · BUCKINGHAM · ENGLAND

EQUIPMENT	PART No.
Headlamp	S0720
Harness (Main)	S2389
Alternator	G1584
Coil—6V. Ignition	S0793
Distributor	S2469
Dip Switch	S1356
Dip Switch Leads	S2343
Stop & Rear Lamp	S0088
Stop & Rear Lamp Leads	S2463
Stop Switch	S2370
Rectifier	S2642

REF. WD3T/1

WIRING WIPAC DIAGRAM

B.S.A. Bantam Models
A.C. Circuit
FROM JUNE 1950 TO OCTOBER 1953

THE WIPAC GROUP · BUCKINGHAM · BUCKS

EQUIPMENT	Original Part No.	Replacement No.
Ignition Generator	I.G.1130 AC	I.G.1452 AC
Headlamp	03520	*S0890
Dip Switch	06196	S1356
Headlamp Switch	03625	S2453
Harness	03649	S2455
Rear Lamp	05160	S0210

* When S0890 Headlamp is fitted as a replacement, harness S2388 must be included at the same time.

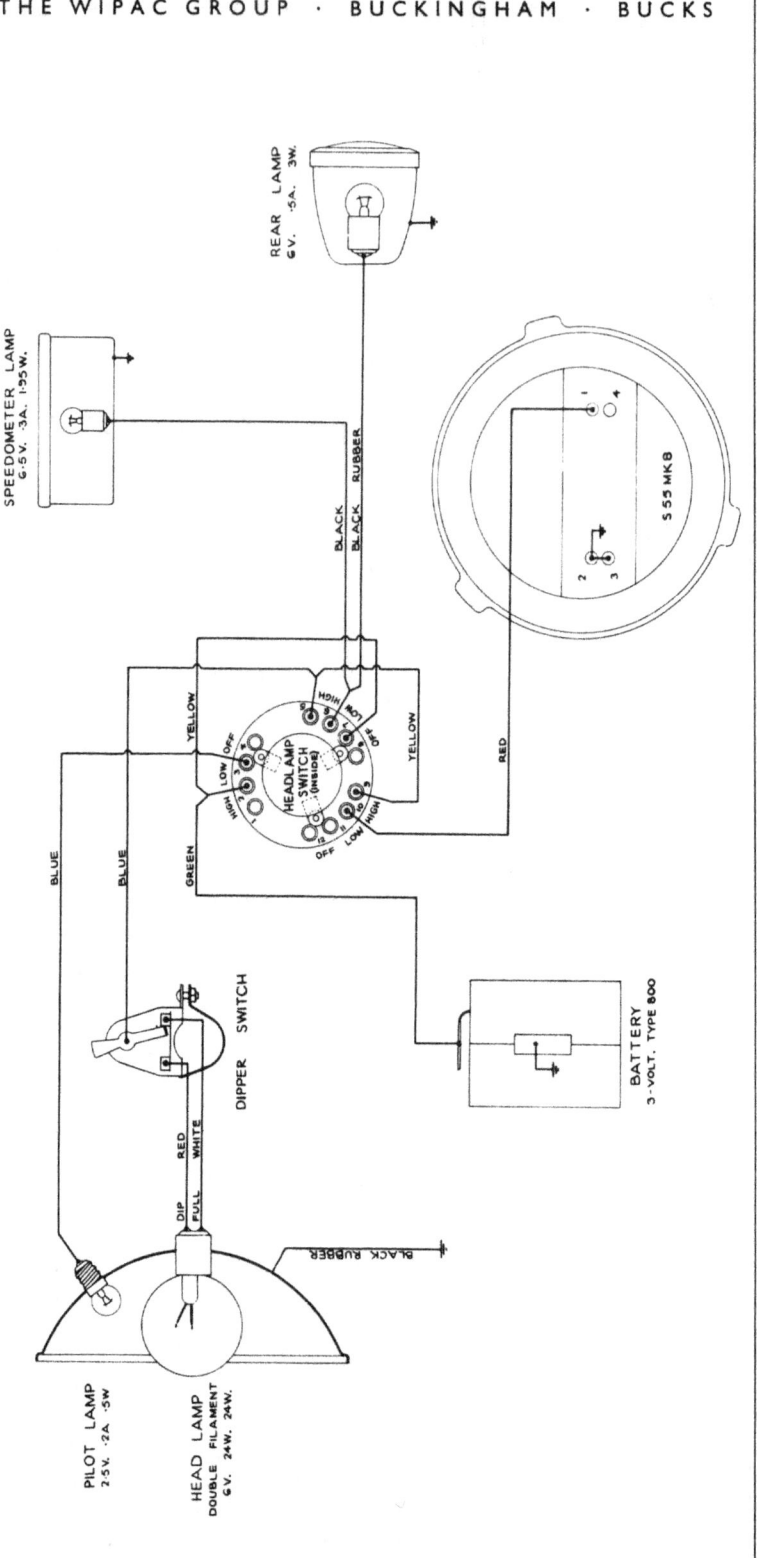

REF. WD/58/597

WIRING DIAGRAM — WIPAC

B.S.A. Bantam
D.C. Circuit
FROM JUNE 1950 TO OCTOBER 1953

THE WIPAC GROUP · BUCKINGHAM · BUCKS

EQUIPMENT	Original Part No.	Replacement Part No.
Ignition Generator	I.G.1130 DC	I.G.1454 DC
Headlamp	03648	*S0900
Harness (Main)	03751	S2457
Dip Switch	06196	S1356
Rear Lamp	05160	S0213
Rectifier	03658	†S2642

* When S0900 Headlamp is fitted as a replacement, harness S0573 must be included at the same time.

† See Service Bulletin S5255/2 before fitting.

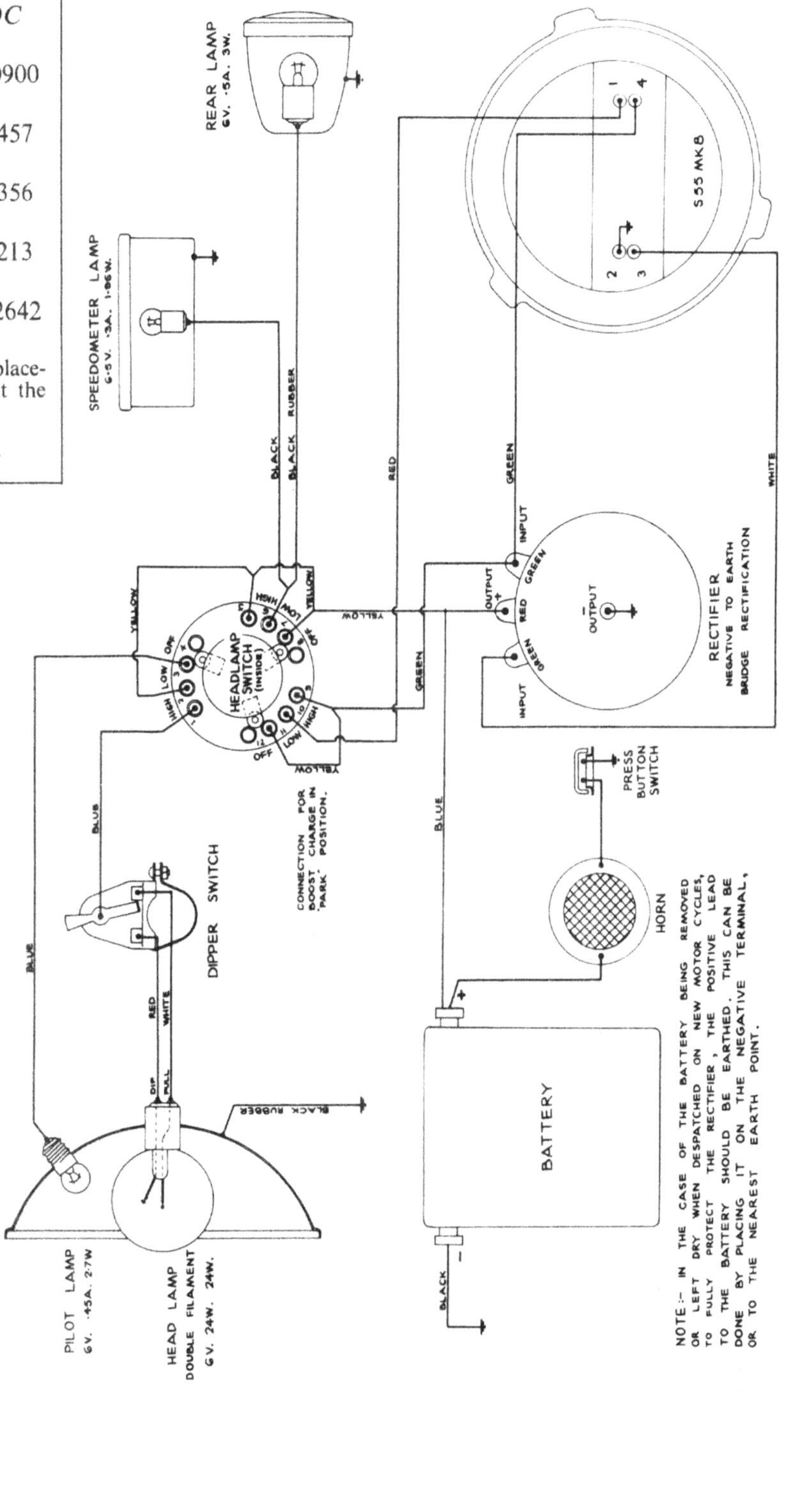

REF. WD/54/598

WIRING WIPAC DIAGRAM

B.S.A. Bantam and Bantam Major
A.C. Circuit
FROM OCTOBER 1953 TO JULY 1955

THE WIPAC GROUP · BUCKINGHAM · BUCKS

EQUIPMENT	Original Part No.	Replacement Part No.
Headlamp	02163	*S0890
Rear Lamp	02306	S0814
Dip Switch	06196	S1356
Ignition Generator	I.G.1130 AC	I.G.1452 AC
Headlamp Switch	03625	S2453

* When S0890 Headlamp is fitted as a replacement, harness S2388 must be included at the same time.

REF. WD/60/538

WIRING WIPAC DIAGRAM

B.S.A. Bantam and Bantam Major
D.C. Circuit
FROM OCTOBER 1953 TO AUGUST 1954

THE WIPAC GROUP · BUCKINGHAM · BUCKS

EQUIPMENT	Original Part No.	Replacement Part No.
Harness (Main)	03751	S2457
Headlamp	02143	*S0900
Dip Switch	06196	S1356
Rectifier	02145	†S2642
Ignition Generator	I.G.1130 DC	I.G.1454 DC
Stop & Rear Lamp	02300	S0088
Stop Switch	03402	S2370

* When S0900 Headlamp is fitted as a replacement, harness S0573 must be included at the same time.

† See Service Bulletin 5255/2 before fitting.

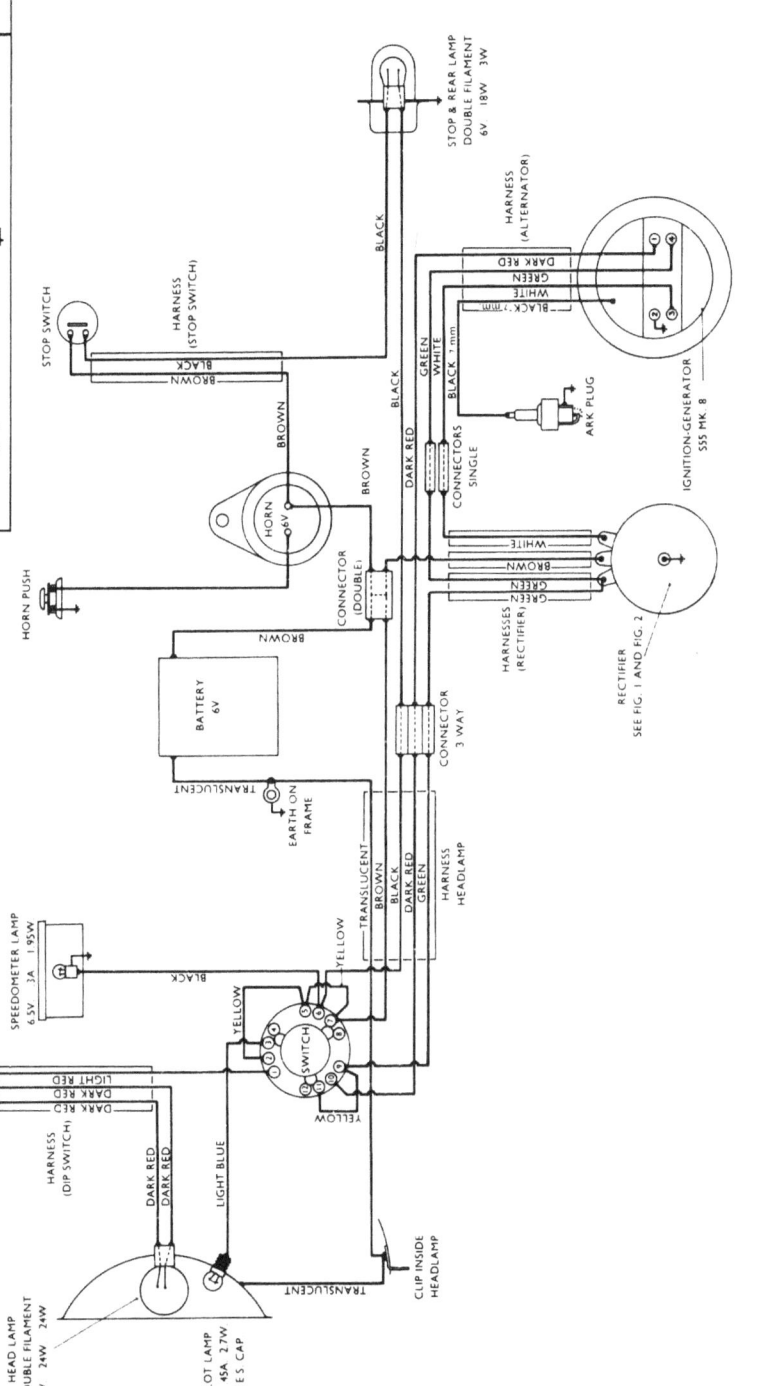

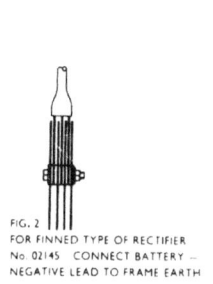

FIG. 1
FOR FLAT TYPE OF RECTIFIER
No. 02196 CONNECT BATTERY
POSITIVE LEAD TO FRAME EARTH

FIG. 2
FOR FINNED TYPE OF RECTIFIER
No. 02145 CONNECT BATTERY
NEGATIVE LEAD TO FRAME EARTH

REF. WD/53/539

B.S.A. Bantam and Bantam Major
D.C. Circuit
FROM AUGUST 1954 TO JULY 1955

THE WIPAC GROUP   BUCKINGHAM   BUCKS

EQUIPMENT	Original Part No.	Replacement Part No.
Headlamp	02143	*S0900
Harness (Main)	03751	S2457
Dip Switch	06196	S1356
Ignition Generator	I.G.1130 DC	I.G.1454 DC
Rectifier	04400	†S2642
Rear Lamp	02300	S0088
Stop Switch	03402	S2370

* When S0900 Headlamp is fitted as a replacement, harness S0573 must be included at the same time.

† See Service Bulletin 5255/2 before fitting.

REF. WD/55/569

B.S.A. Bantam and Bantam Major
A.C. Circuit
MODELS PRODUCED FROM AUGUST 1955

THE WIPAC GROUP · BUCKINGHAM · BUCKS

EQUIPMENT	PART No.
Harness (Main)	S2388
Dip Switch	S1356
Ignition—Generator	I.G.1452
Rear Lamp	S3611

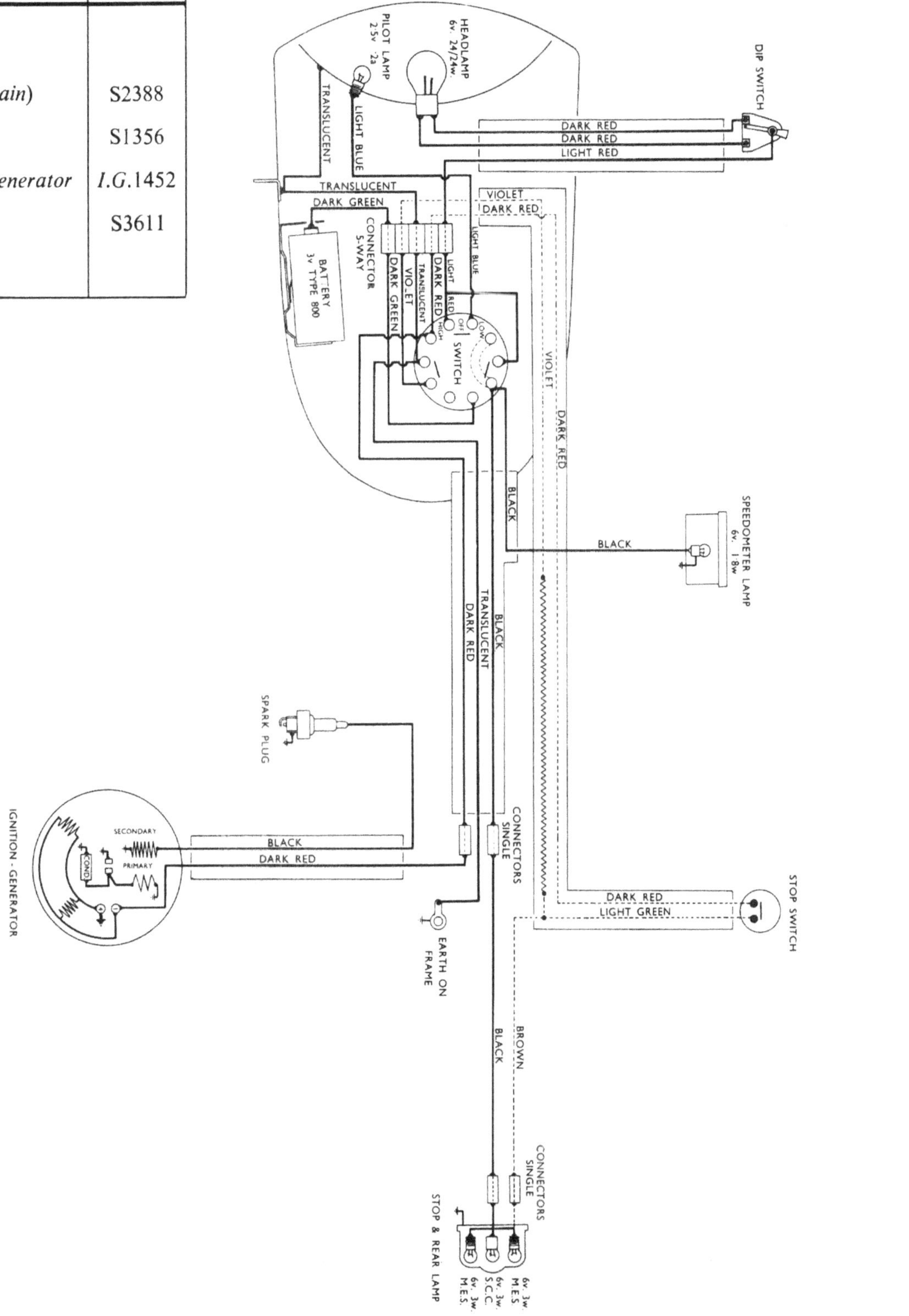

Ref. WD/59/621/1

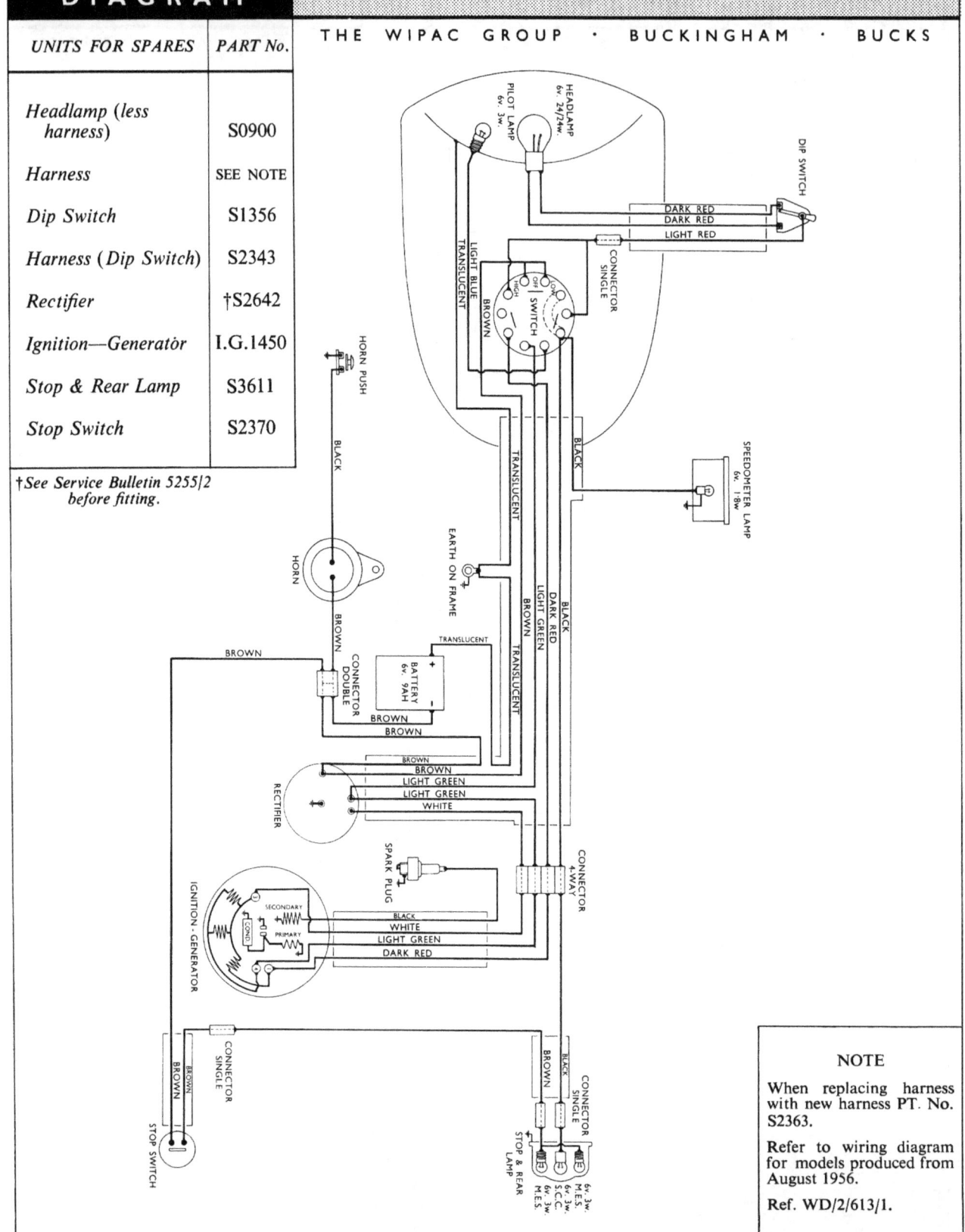

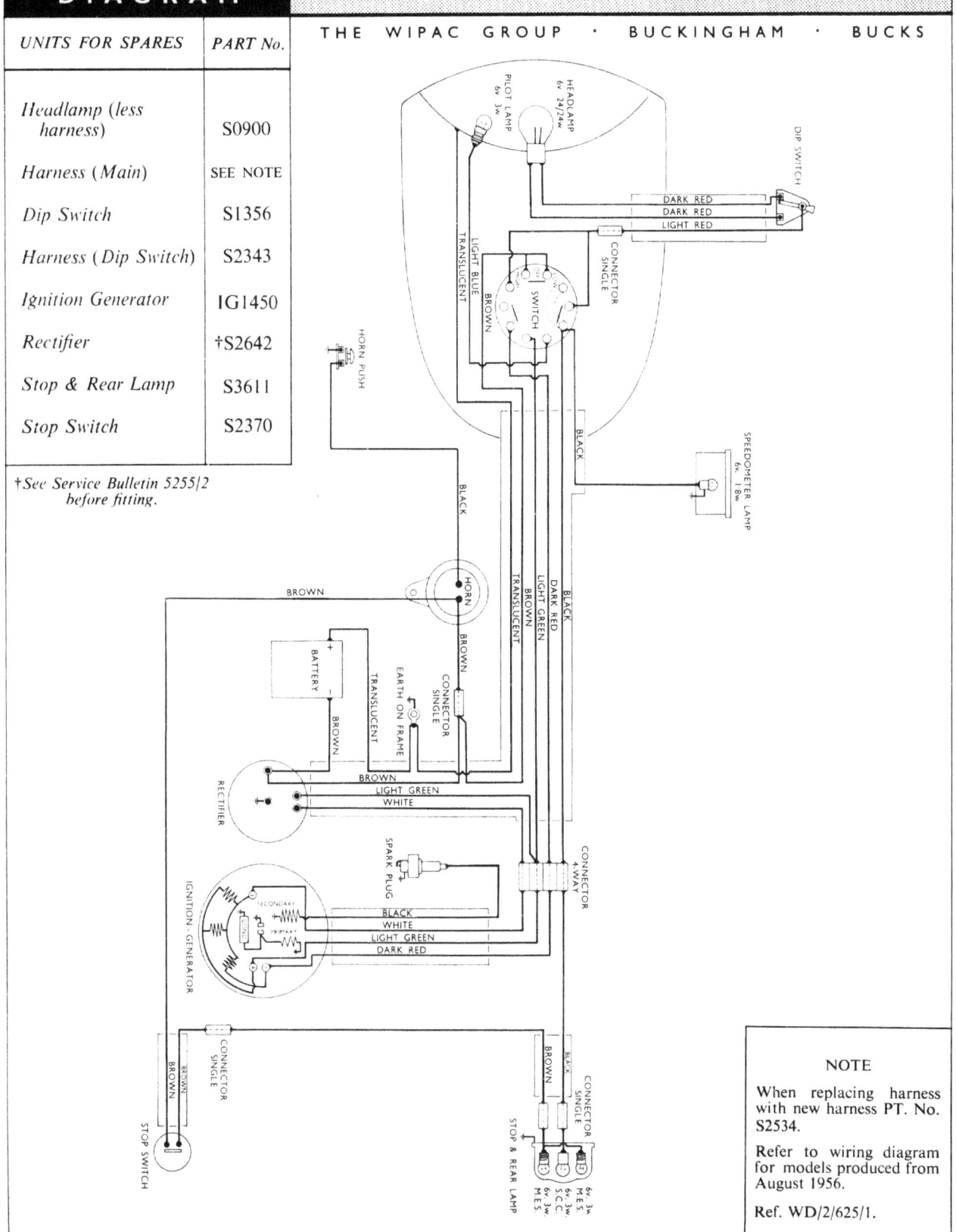

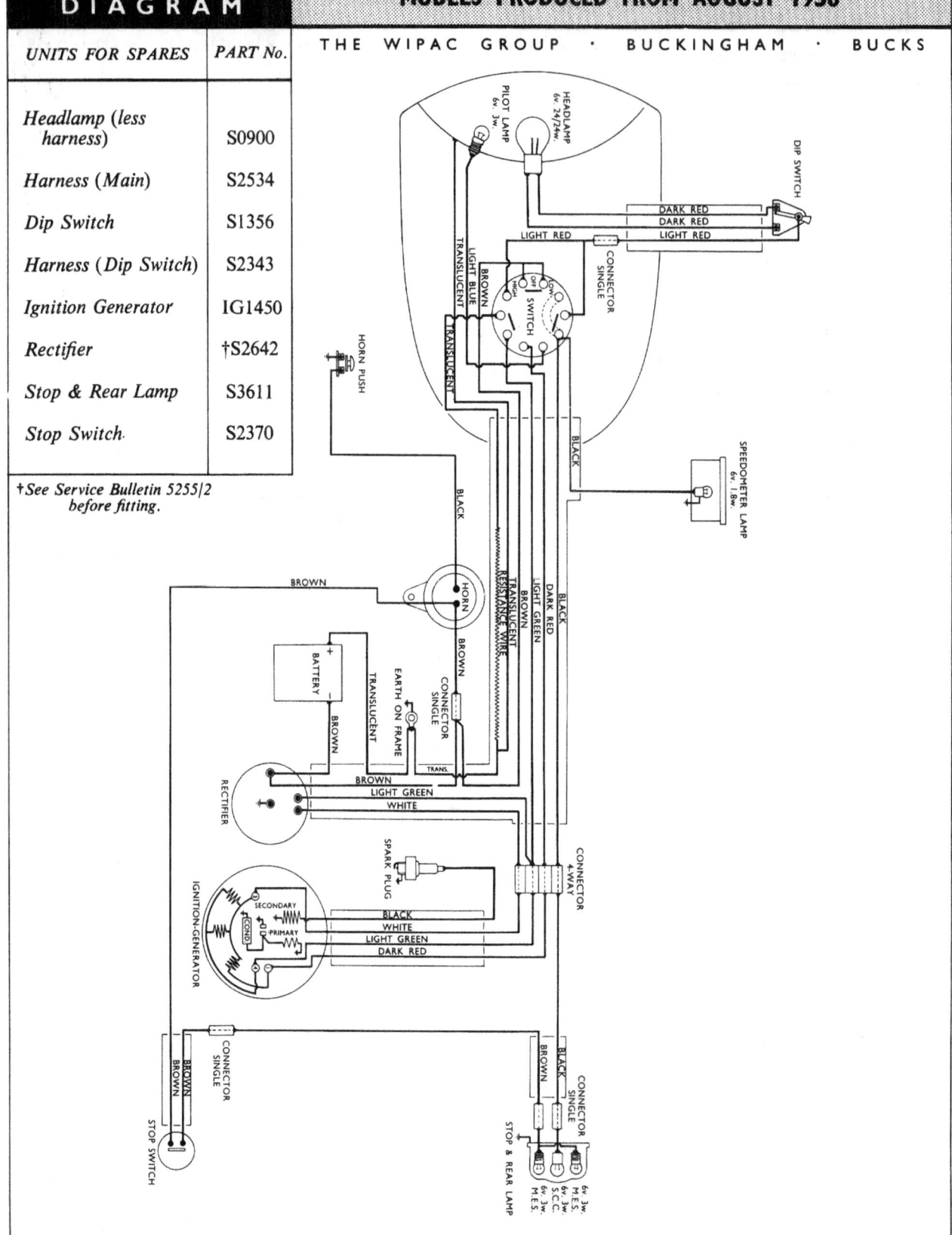

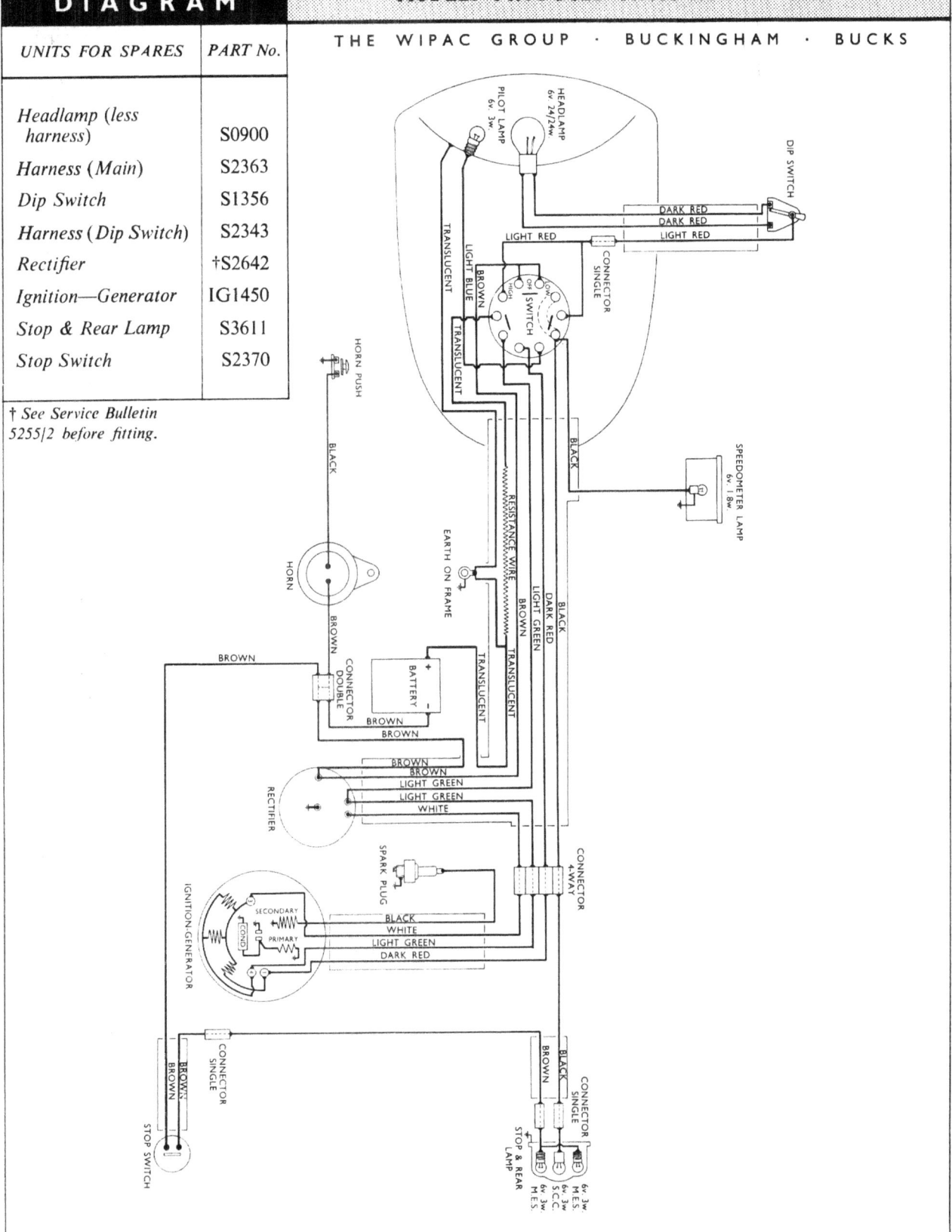

WIRING WIPAC DIAGRAM

B.S.A. Bantam Super D7
A.C. Circuit
FROM OCTOBER 1958 to MAY 1966

THE WIPAC GROUP · BUCKINGHAM · BUCKS

UNITS FOR SPARES	PART No.
Ignition Generator	IG1452
Headlamp Unit	S0856
Dip Switch	S1356
Harness (Dip Switch)	S2343
Harness (Main)	S3348
Rear Lamp	S3737
Switch Unit (Lights)	S0781

REF. WD./50/621/1

WIRING WIPAC DIAGRAM

B.S.A. Bantam Super D7
AC/DC Trickle Charge
FROM OCTOBER 1958 to MAY 1966

THE WIPAC GROUP · BUCKINGHAM · BUCKS.

UNIT FOR SPARES	PART No.
Ignition Generator	IG1552
Headlamp Unit	S0891
Dip Switch	S3857
Harness (Dip Switch)	S0612
Harness (Main)	S3347
Stop & Rear Lamp (state bulbs required)	S3611
Rectifier Unit	S1044
Stop Switch Unit	S2370
Leads (Stop Switch)	S2861
Switch Unit (Lights)	S0781

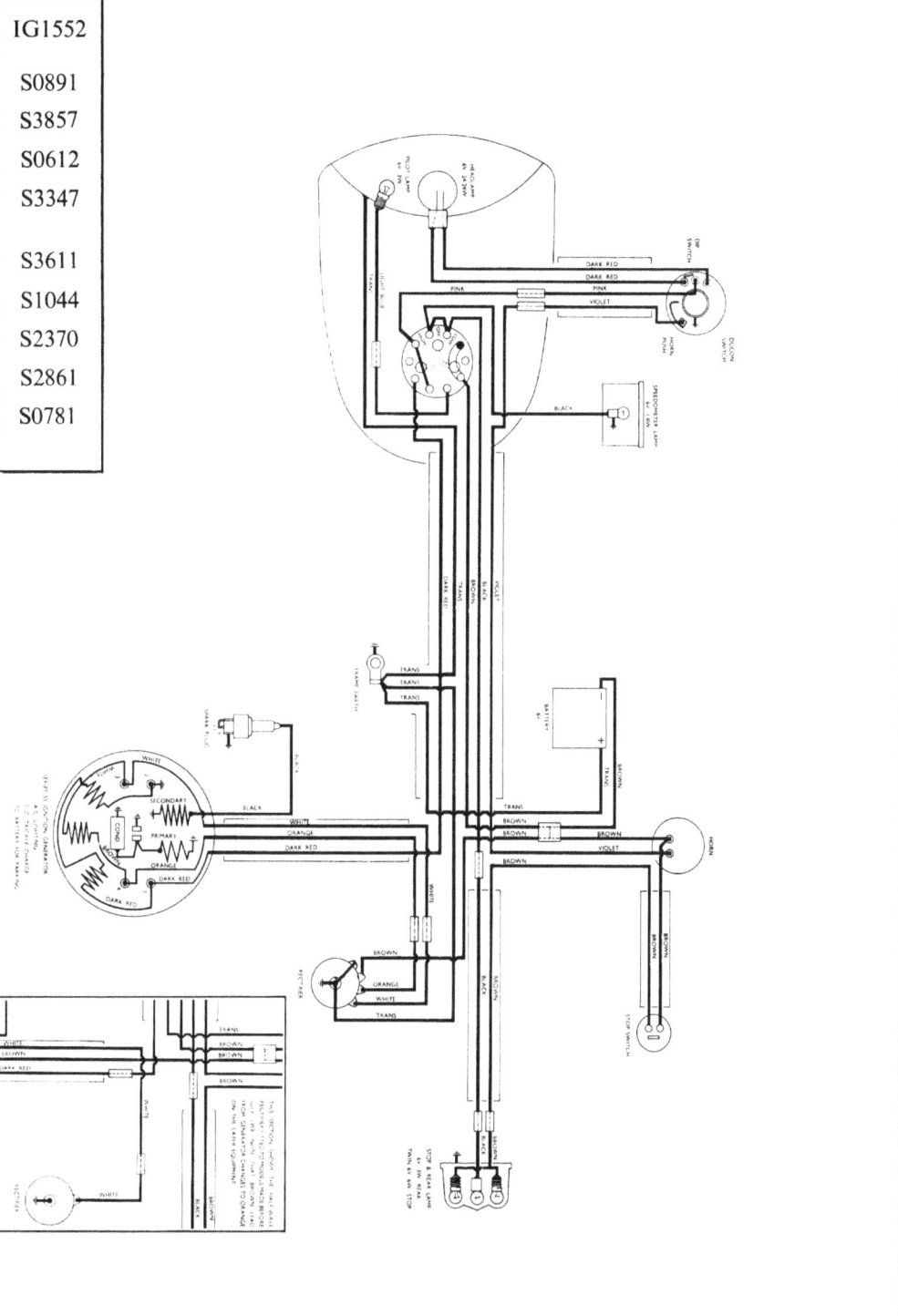

REF. WD./51/767/1

WIRING WIPAC DIAGRAM

B.S.A. Bantam Super D7
D.C. Circuit
FROM JUNE 1959

THE WIPAC GROUP · BUCKINGHAM · BUCKS

EQUIPMENT	PART No.
Ignition Generator	IG1450
Headlamp Unit	S0891
Dip Switch	S0613
Leads (Dip Switch)	S0612
Harness (Main)	S1077
Rectifier	S2642
Rear Lamp	S0088
Leads (Rear Lamp)	S2463
Switch Unit (Lights)	S0781
Stop Switch	S2370
Leads (Stop Switch)	S2861

REF. WD/52/778

WIRING WIPAC DIAGRAM

B.S.A. Bantam Super D7
AC/DC Trickle Charge With Coil Ignition
FROM OCTOBER 1963 TO JUNE 1966

THE WIPAC GROUP · BUCKINGHAM · BUCKS

UNIT FOR SPARES	PART No.
Ignition Generator	IG1704
Headlamp Unit	S0891
Horn & Dip Switch	S3857
Harness (Dip Switch)	S0612
Harness (Main)	S3538
Stop & Rear Lamp (state bulbs required)	S3611
Leads Set (Rear Lamp)	S2463
Rectifier Unit	S1044
Stop Switch Unit	S2370
Leads Set (Stop Switch)	S2861
Switch Unit (Lights)	S0781
Switch Unit (Ignition)	S0782
Ignition Coil	S0769

Ref. WD/62/923/2

WIRING DIAGRAM — WIPAC

B.S.A. Bantam D10 and D14
Full D.C. Lighting with Coil Ignition
FROM JUNE 1966

THE WIPAC GROUP · BUCKINGHAM · BUCKS

UNIT FOR SPARES	PART No.
Alternator Unit	G1767
Distributor Unit	S4060
Headlamp Unit	S4067
Horn & Dip Switch	S3857
Harness (Dip Switch)	S2737
Harness (Main)	S4069
Stop & Rear Lamp (state bulb required)	S3611
Leads Set (Rear Lamp)	S2463
Rectifier Unit	S2642
Stop Switch Unit	S2370
Leads Set (Stop Switch)	S2861
Switch Unit (Lights)	S0781
Switch Unit (Ignition)	S0782
Ignition Coil	S0769

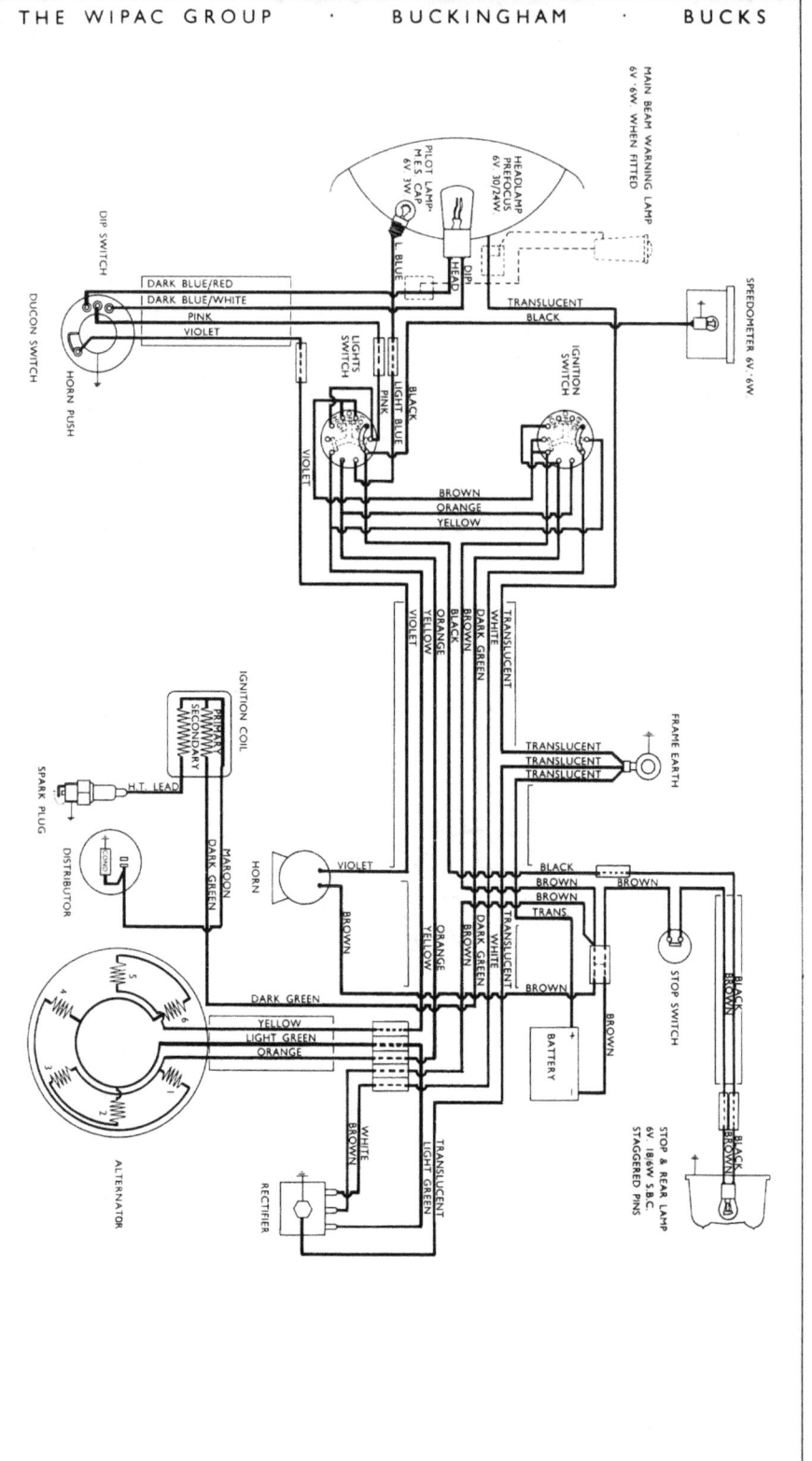

Ref. WD/88/1051/2

WIRING WIPAC DIAGRAM

B.S.A. DANDY SEVENTY LIGHT SCOOTER
MODELS PRODUCED FROM OCTOBER 1956 TO APRIL 1957

WIPAC GROUP · BUCKINGHAM · BUCKS

EQUIPMENT	Original Equipment	Replacement Spares
Ignition Generator	I.G.1493	I.G.1596
*Headlamp (less harness)	S0342	S0938
Harness (Main)	S0344	S0344
Horn and Dip Switch Harness	S0345	SEE NOTE
Horn and Dip Switch	06205	S1356
Stop and Rear Lamp (quote Bulbs required)	S0213	S0213
Leads Set (Stop and Rear Lamp)		S0822

*Speedometer not supplied by Wipac
NOTE: Now part of Main Harness S0344

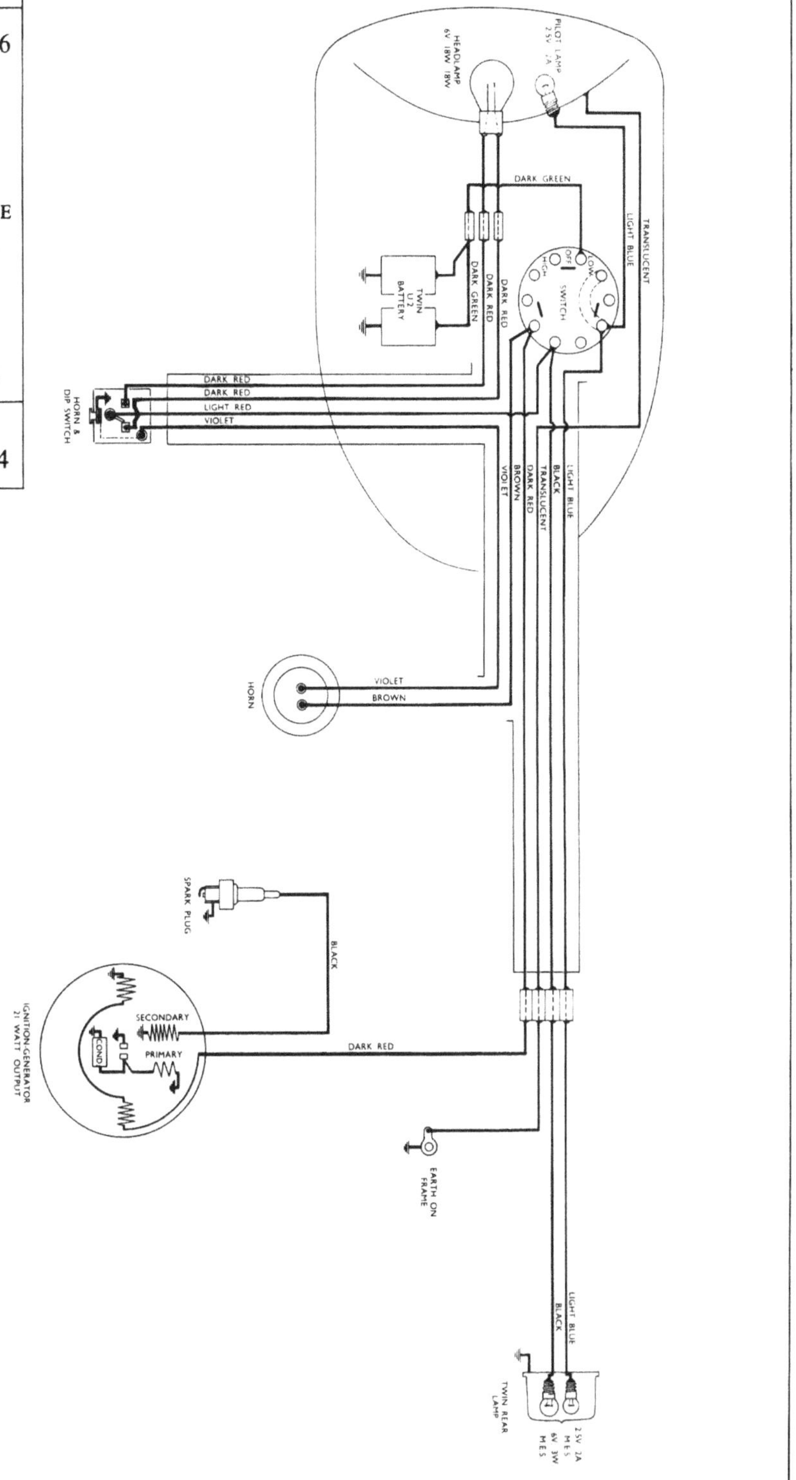

REF. WD/13/673/2

WIRING WIPAC DIAGRAM

B.S.A. DANDY SEVENTY LIGHT SCOOTER
MODELS PRODUCED FROM MAY 1957 TO JANUARY 1960

WIPAC GROUP · BUCKINGHAM · BUCKS

EQUIPMENT	Original Equipment	Replacement Spares
Ignition Generator	I.G.1501	I.G.1596
*Headlamp (less harness)	S0342	S0938
Harness (Main)	S0344	S0344
Horn and Dip Switch	06205	S1356
Stop and Rear Lamp (quote Bulbs required)	S0213	S0213
Leads Set (Stop and Rear Lamp)		S0822

*Speedometer not supplied by Wipac

REF. WD/15/708/1

WIRING WIPAC DIAGRAM

B.S.A. DANDY SEVENTY LIGHT SCOOTER
MODELS PRODUCED FROM FEB. 1960

THE WIPAC GROUP · BUCKINGHAM · BUCKS

EQUIPMENT	PART No.
Ignition Generator	I.G.1596
*Headlamp (less harness)	S0938
Harness (Main)	S0344
Horn and Dip Switch	S0613
Stop and Rear Lamp (quote Bulbs required)	S0213
Leads Set (Stop and Rear Lamp)	S0822

*Speedometer not supplied by Wipac

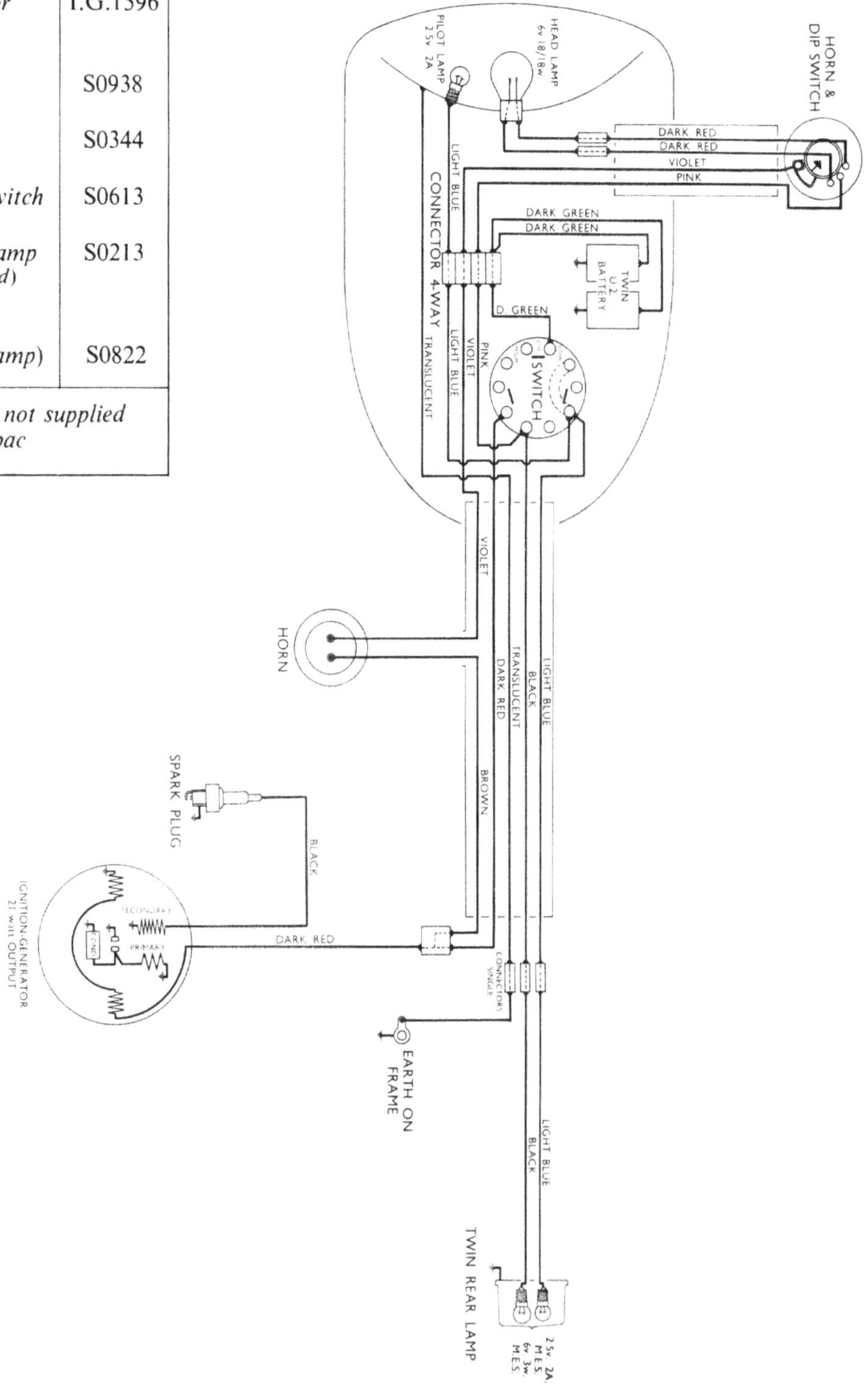

Ref. WD/65/673

WIRING DIAGRAM — WIPAC

B.S.A. SUNBEAM AND TRIUMPH TIGRESS
175 c.c. SCOOTER, (A.C. LIGHTS, D.C. TRICKLE CHARGE)
MODELS PRODUCED FROM OCT. 1958 TO SEPT. 1963

THE WIPAC GROUP · BUCKINGHAM · BUCKS

UNIT FOR SPARES	PART No.
Headlamp Unit	S0867
Harness (Main)	S0869
Switch Unit (Lights)	S0781
Dipper Switch	S3858
Rectifier	S1044
Stop Switch	S2370
Leads Set (Stop Switch)	S0870
Stop and Rear Lamp	S3611
Ignition Generator	IG1555

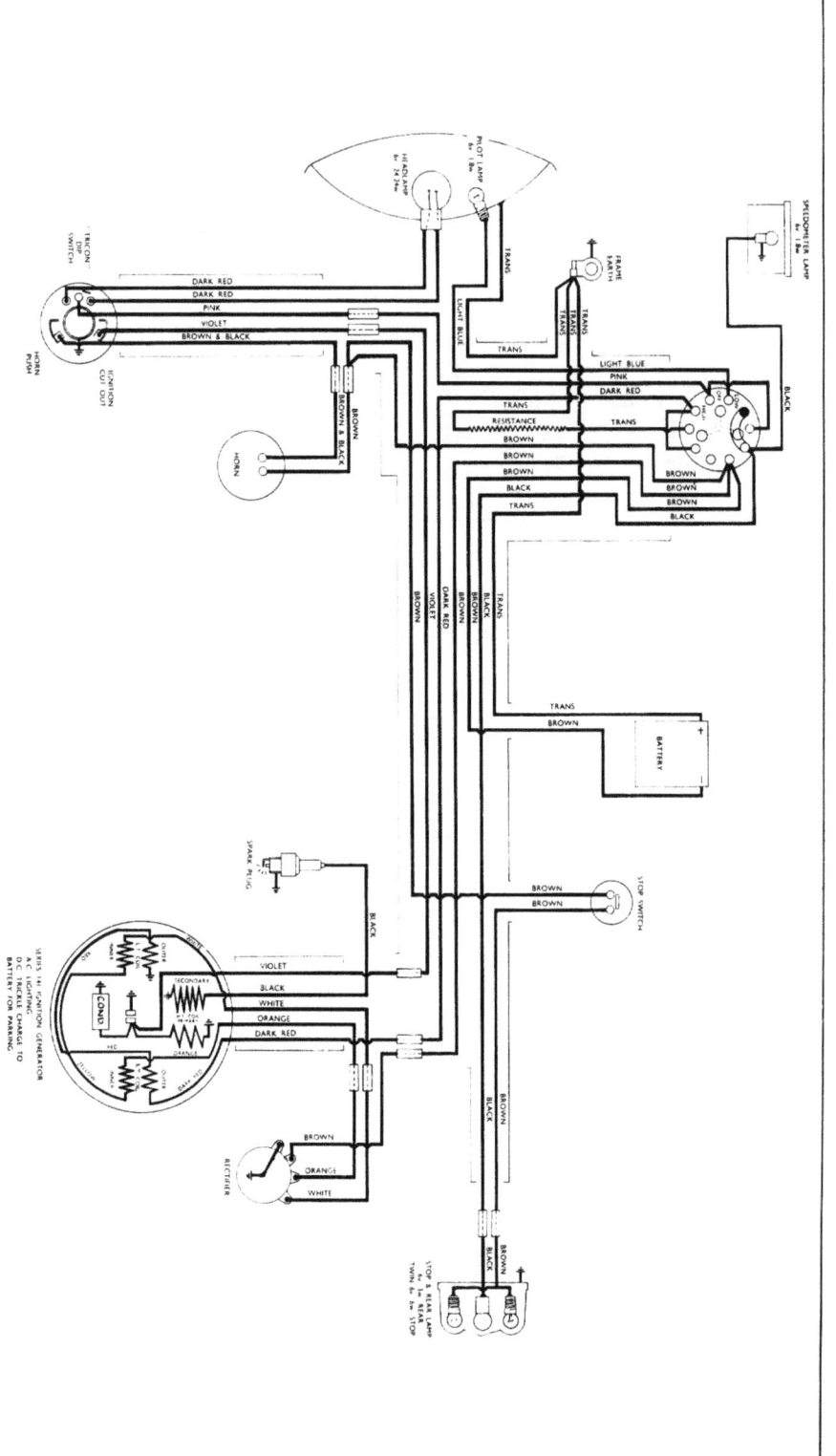

Ref. WD/27/742/3

WIRING WIPAC DIAGRAM

B.S.A. SUNBEAM AND TRIUMPH TIGRESS
175 c.c. SCOOTER, (D.C. COIL IGNITION)
MODELS PRODUCED FROM OCTOBER 1963 TO AUG. 1965

THE WIPAC GROUP · BUCKINGHAM · BUCKS

UNIT FOR SPARES	PART No.
Headlamp Unit	S0867
Harness (Main)	S3544
Switch Unit (Lights)	S0781
Switch Unit (Ignition)	S0782
Dipper Switch	S3857
Leads Set (Dip Switch)	S1217
Rectifier	S1044
Stop Switch	S2370
Leads Set (Stop Switch)	S2862
Stop and Rear Lamp	S3611
Ignition Generator	I.G.1676
Ignition Coil	S0769

Ref. WD/66/925/2

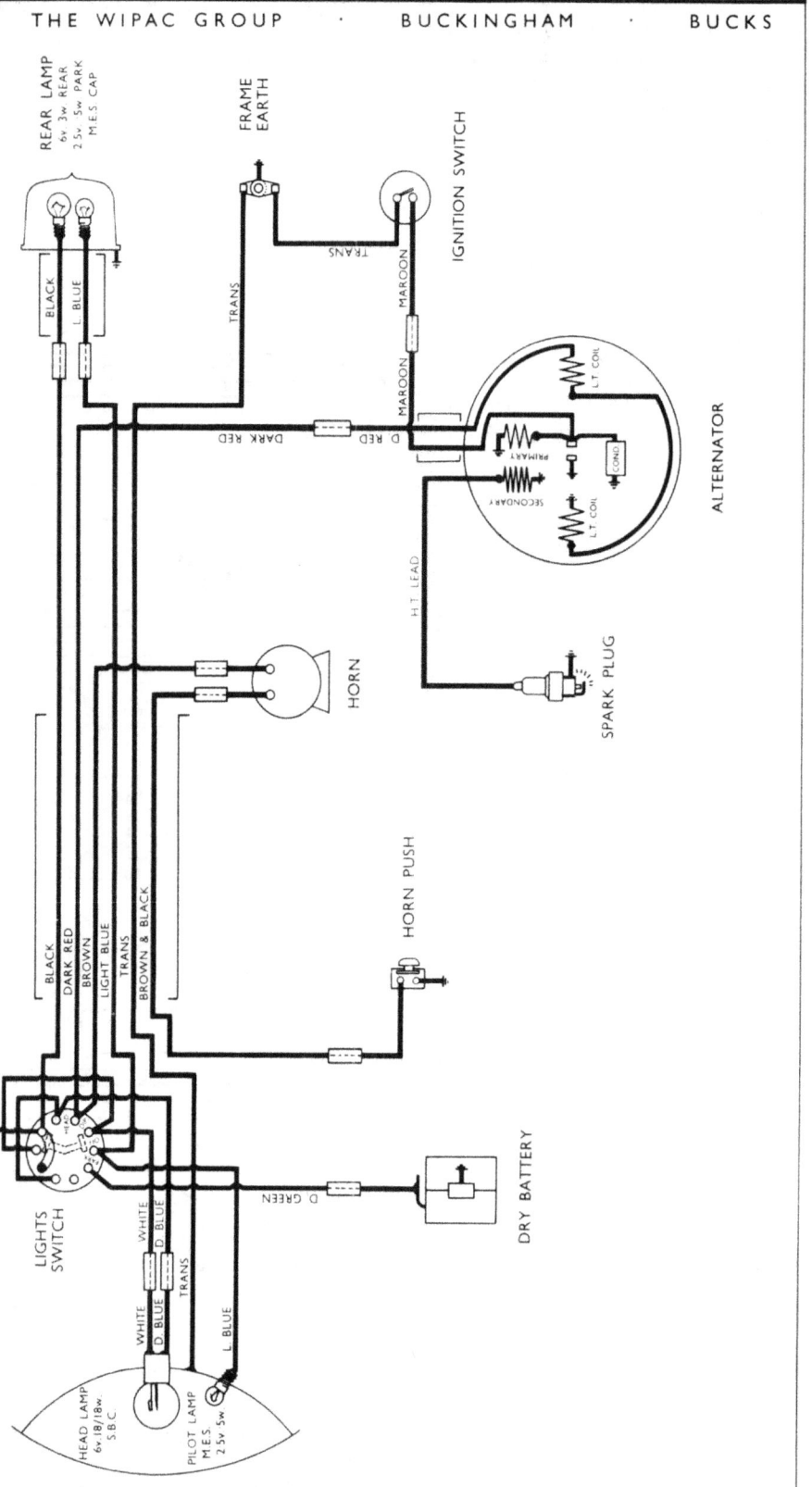

WIRING WIPAC DIAGRAM

B.S.A. BEAGLE 75 c.c.
A.C. LIGHTING
(FITTED WITH STOP LAMP)
MODELS PRODUCED FROM MARCH 1964 TO AUG. 1965

THE WIPAC GROUP · BUCKINGHAM · BUCKS

EQUIPMENT	PART No.
Headlamp Unit	S3636
Harness (Main)	S3638
Switch (Ignition)	S3490
Stop Switch	S2370
Leads Set (Stop Switch)	S3641
Ignition Generator	I.G.1715

Ref. WD/80/973/1

WIRING WIPAC DIAGRAM

DAYTON FLAMENCO 175 c.c. SCOOTER
MODELS PRODUCED FROM NOVEMBER 1958 to AUGUST 1959

THE WIPAC GROUP · BUCKINGHAM · BUCKS

UNIT FOR SPARES	PART No.
Headlamp Unit	S0863
Harness (*Main*)	S0864
Dipper Switch	S0640
Leads Set (*Dip Switch*)	S0865
Switch Unit (*Lights*)	S0781
Stop Switch	S0866
Leads Set (*Stop Switch*)	S2863

REF. WD/28/747/1

WIRING WIPAC DIAGRAM

DAYTON ALBATROSS 250 c.c. TWIN SCOOTER
MODELS PRODUCED FROM SEPTEMBER 1959 to AUGUST 1960

THE WIPAC GROUP · BUCKINGHAM · BUCKS

UNIT FOR SPARES	PART No.
Headlamp Unit	S0863
Harness (Main)	S1124
Switch Unit (Lights)	S0781
Dipper Switch	S0613
Leads Set (Dip Switch)	S1131
Stop Switch	S0866
Leads Set (Stop Switch)	S2863
Rear Lamp	S0213
Ammeter	S0062

REF. WD/29/781/1

WIRING WIPAC DIAGRAM

DUNKLEY WHIPPET 60 SCOOTERETTE
MODELS PRODUCED FROM MARCH 1957 to DECEMBER 1959

THE WIPAC GROUP · BUCKINGHAM · BUCKS

UNITS FOR SPARES	PART No.
Headlamp (less harness)	S0943
Harness	S0504
Horn Push	Clear Hooter No. 10
Ignition—Generator	IG1480
Parking & Rear Lamp	S0213

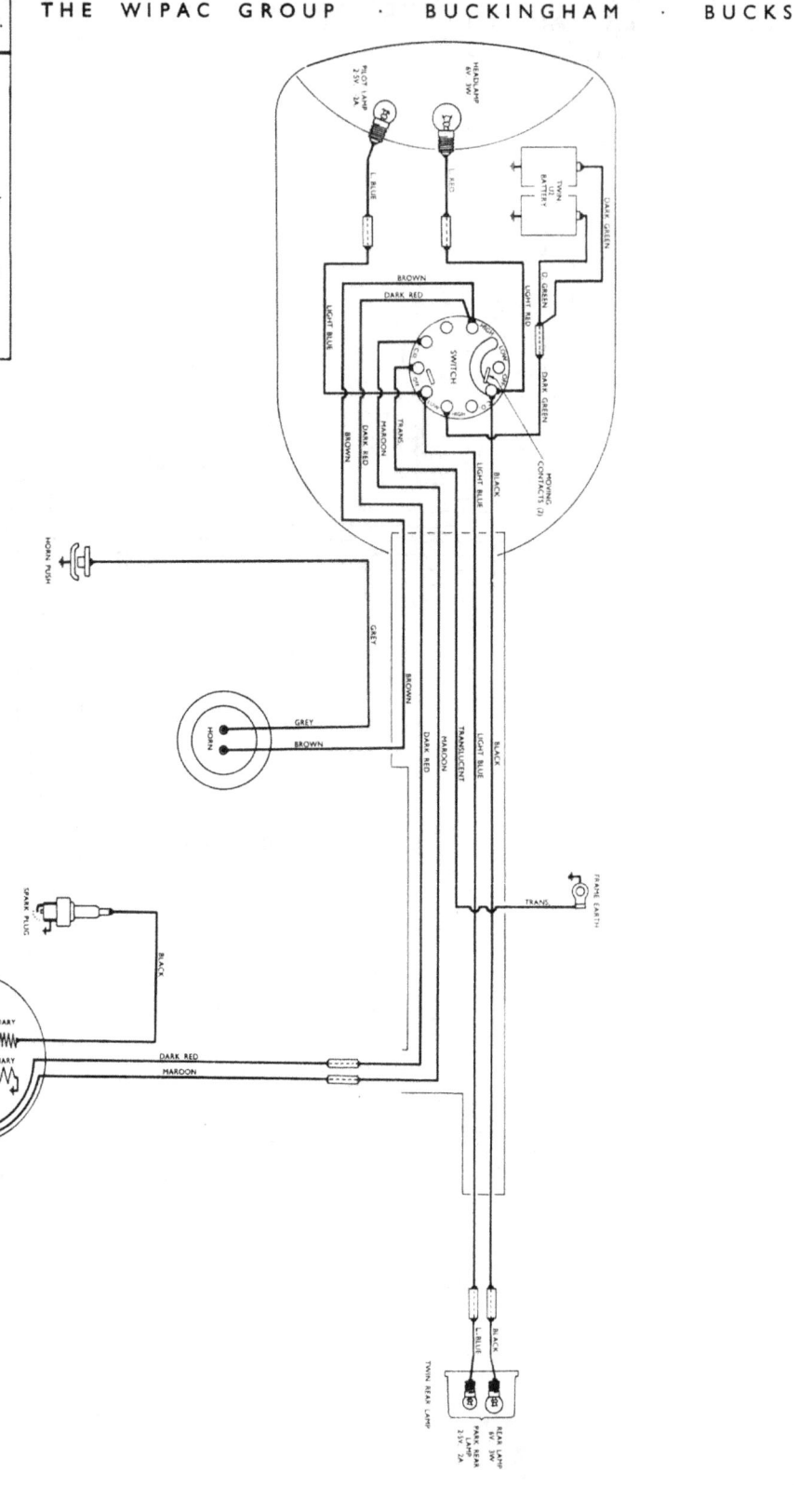

REF. WD/14/688/1

WIRING WIPAC DIAGRAM

DUNKLEY WHIPPET 60 SCOOTERETTE
MODELS PRODUCED FROM JANUARY 1960

THE WIPAC GROUP · BUCKINGHAM · BUCKS

UNITS FOR SPARES	PART No.
Headlamp (less harness)	S0943
Harness	S0942
Horn Push	Clear Hooter No. 10
Ignition—Generator	IG1480
Parking & Rear Lamp	S0213

REF. WD/70/688

EXCELSIOR TALISMAN (TWIN)
D.C. Circuit
FROM AUGUST 1953

THE WIPAC GROUP · BUCKINGHAM · BUCKS

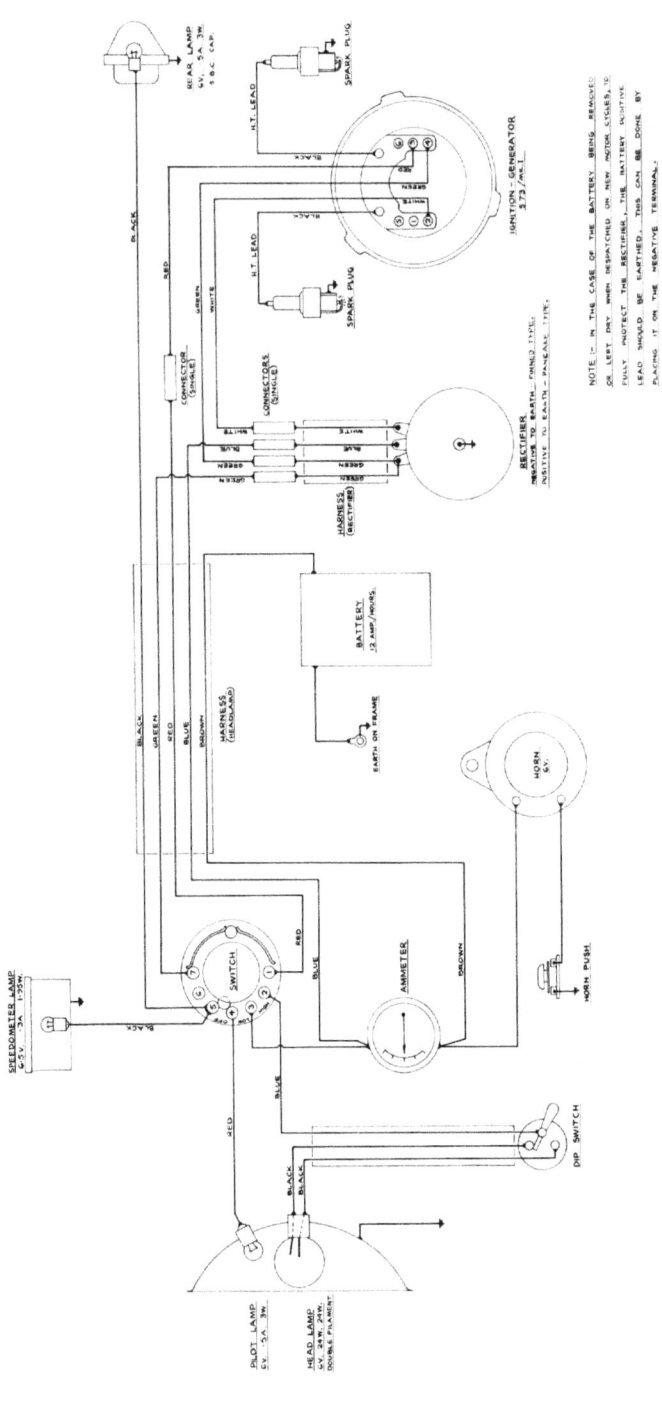

EXCELSIOR TALISMAN (TWIN)
Converted to A.C. Lighting
FROM AUGUST 1953

THE WIPAC GROUP · BUCKINGHAM · BUCKS

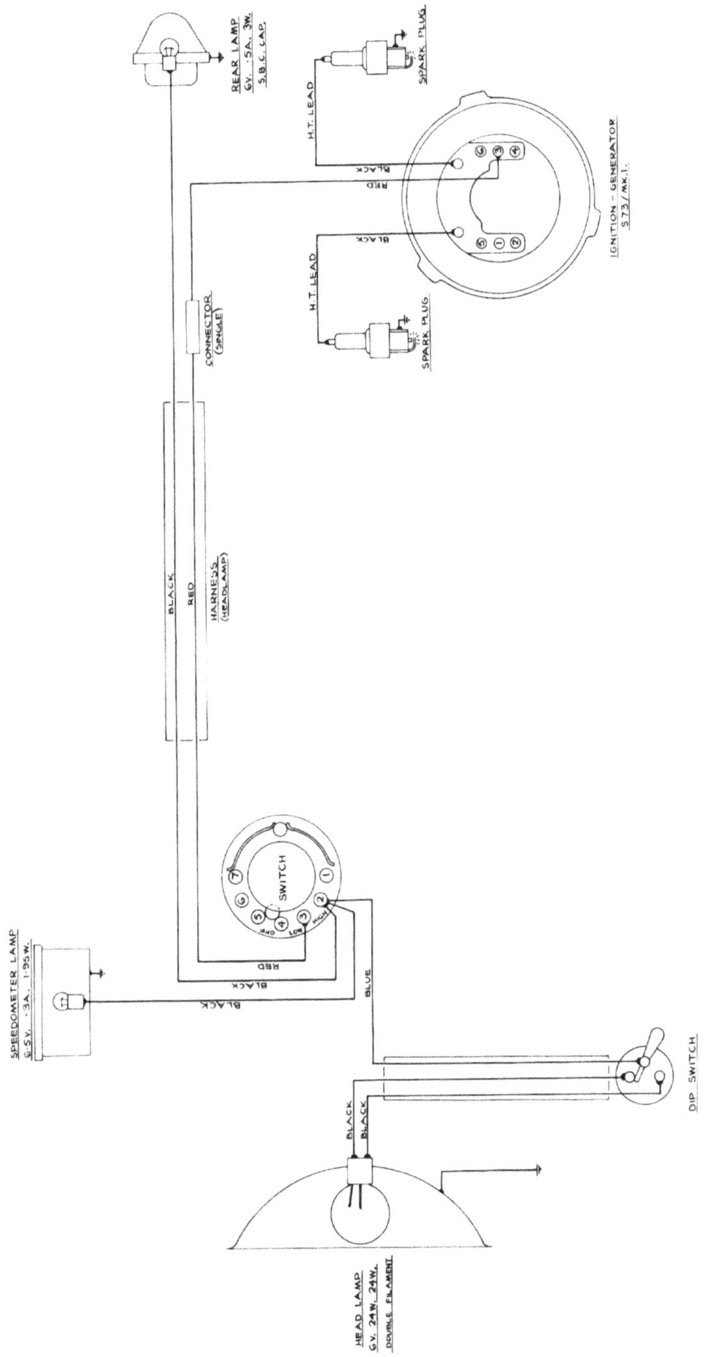

REF. WD/69/550

WIRING WIPAC DIAGRAM

FRANCIS-BARNETT 250 c.c. CRUISER 80
MODELS PRODUCED FROM AUGUST 1956

THE WIPAC GROUP · BUCKINGHAM · ENGLAND

SPARES UNITS	PART No.
*Headlamp (less harness and speedometer)	S0902
Harness (Main)	S0903
Horn and Dip Switch	S3857
Dip Switch Harness	S0242
Alternator	G1585
Distributor Unit	S1024
Rectifier	S2642
Coil—6v. Ignition	S0793
Ammeter Unit	S0062

*Speedometer not supplied by Wipac

NOTE: ON CRUISER 80 MACHINES PRIOR TO 1959, SPEEDO LEAD WAS BLACK AND CONNECTED TO SAME TERMINAL AS REAR LAMP LEAD (BLACK).

REF. WD/11/657/3

WIRING WIPAC DIAGRAM

FRANCIS-BARNETT 250 c.c. TRIALS 83
A.C. LIGHTING

MODELS PRODUCED FROM OCT. 1958 to SEPT. 1959

THE WIPAC GROUP   BUCKINGHAM   BUCKS

SPARES UNITS	PART No.
*Headlamp (less harness)	S0890
Harness (Main)	S0876
Alternator Unit	G1544
Distributor Unit	S1024
Coil-12v. Ignition	S0810
Dipper Switch	S1356
Leads Set (Dipper Switch)	S0885

*Speedometer not supplied by Wipac.

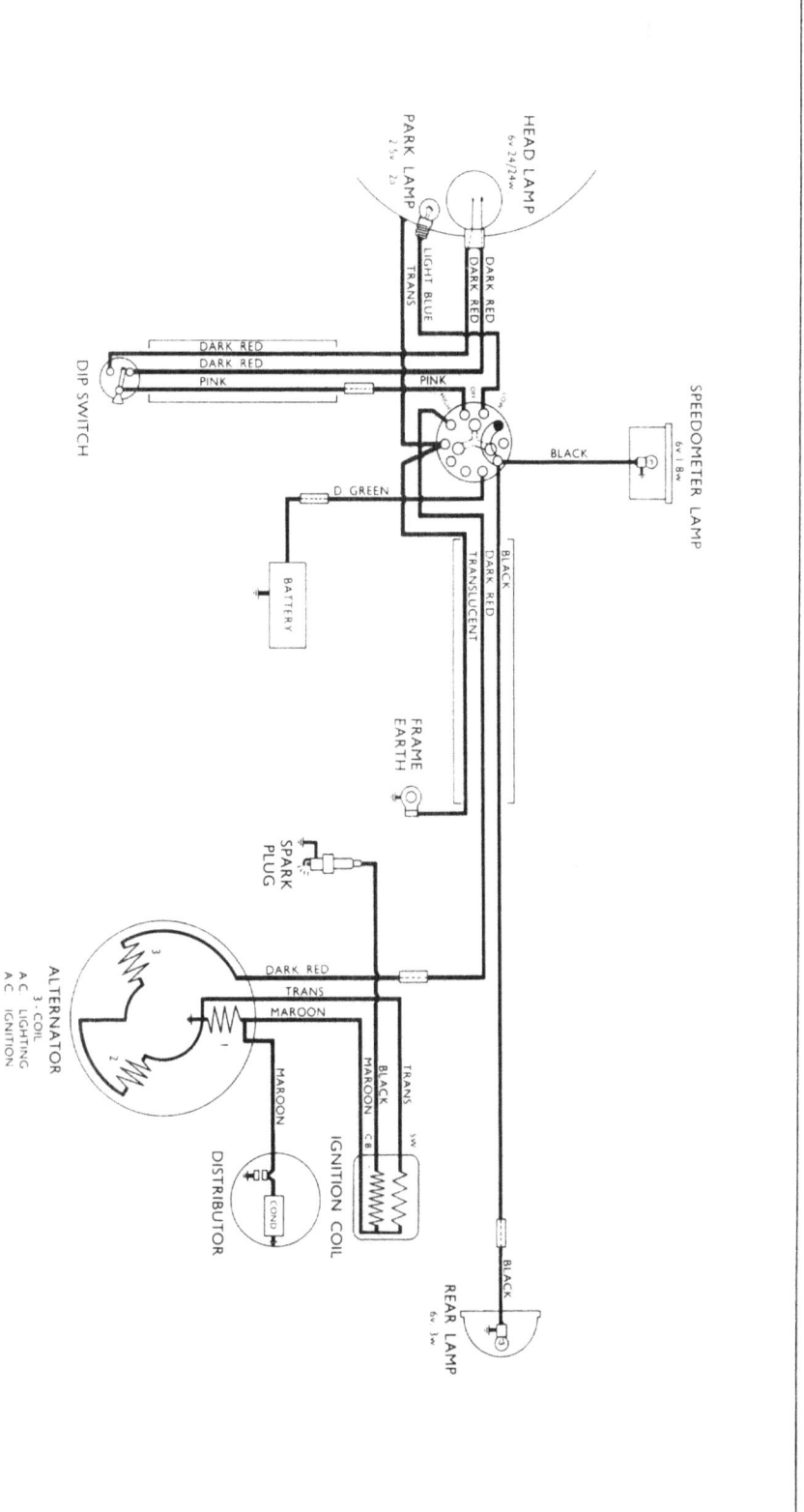

Ref. WD/72/754

WIRING WIPAC DIAGRAM

FRANCIS-BARNETT 250 c.c. CRUISER 84
MODELS PRODUCED FROM MAY 1959 to SEPT. 1963

THE WIPAC GROUP · BUCKINGHAM · ENGLAND

SPARES UNITS	PART No.
*Headlamp (less harness and speedometer)	S0902
Harness (Main)	S0903
Horn and Dip Switch	S3857
Dip Switch Harness	S0242
Alternator	G1585
Distributor Unit	S1024
Rectifier	S2642
Coil—6v. Ignition	S0793
Ammeter Unit	S0062

*Speedometer not supplied by Wipac

NOTE: ON CRUISER 80 MACHINES PRIOR TO 1959, SPEEDO LEAD WAS BLACK AND CONNECTED TO SAME TERMINAL AS REAR LAMP LEAD (BLACK).

Ref. WD/73/657/1

WIRING WIPAC DIAGRAM

FRANCIS-BARNETT 250 c.c. TRIALS 85
A.C. LIGHTING
MODELS PRODUCED OCTOBER 1959 to JANUARY 1960

THE WIPAC GROUP · BUCKINGHAM · BUCKS

SPARES UNITS	PART No.
*Headlamp (less harness)	S1067
Harness (Main)	S1068
Alternator Unit	G1544
Distributor Unit	S1022
Coil-12v. Ignition	S0810
Rear-Park Lamp	S0213

* Speedometer not supplied by Wipac

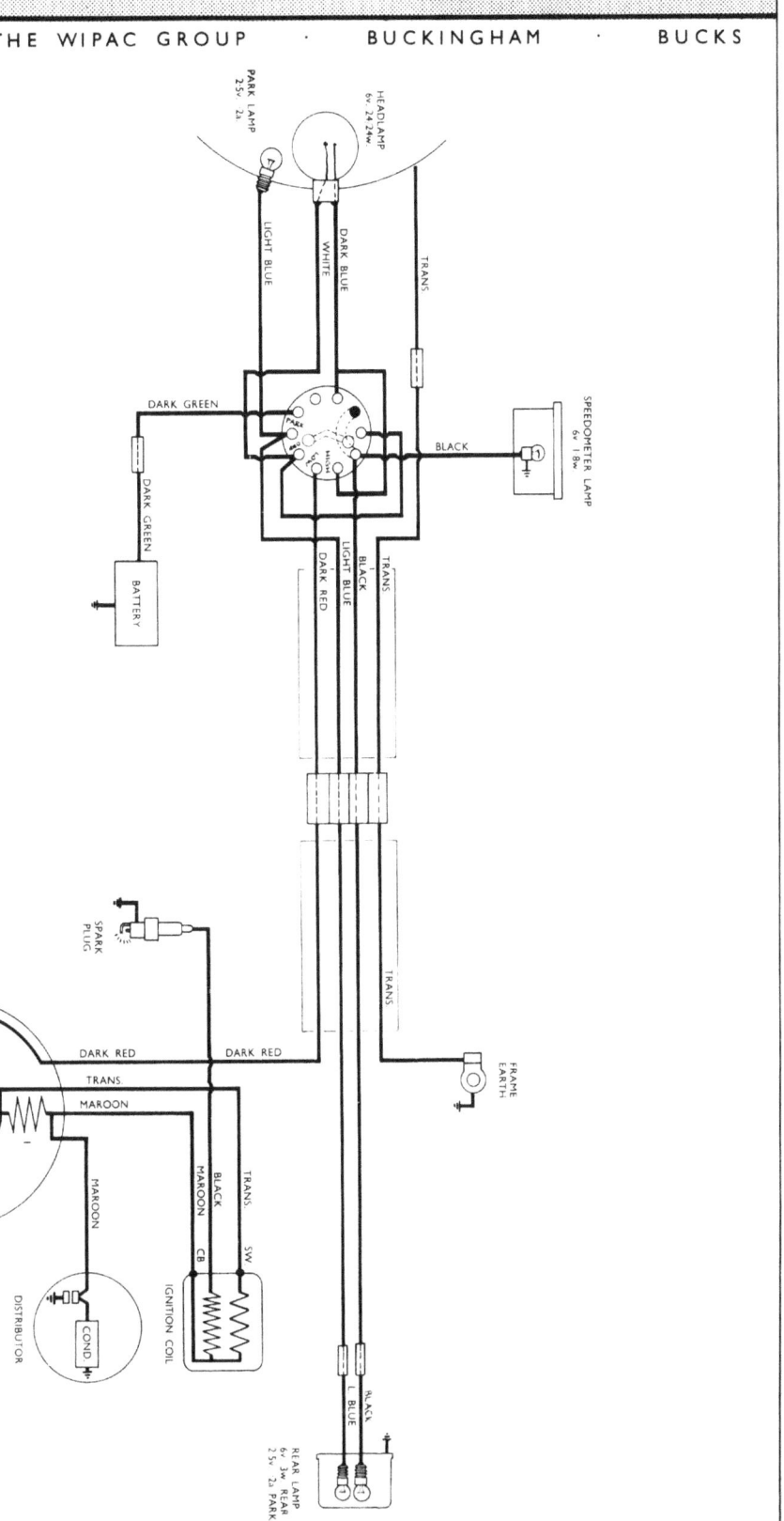

REF. WD/25/772/1

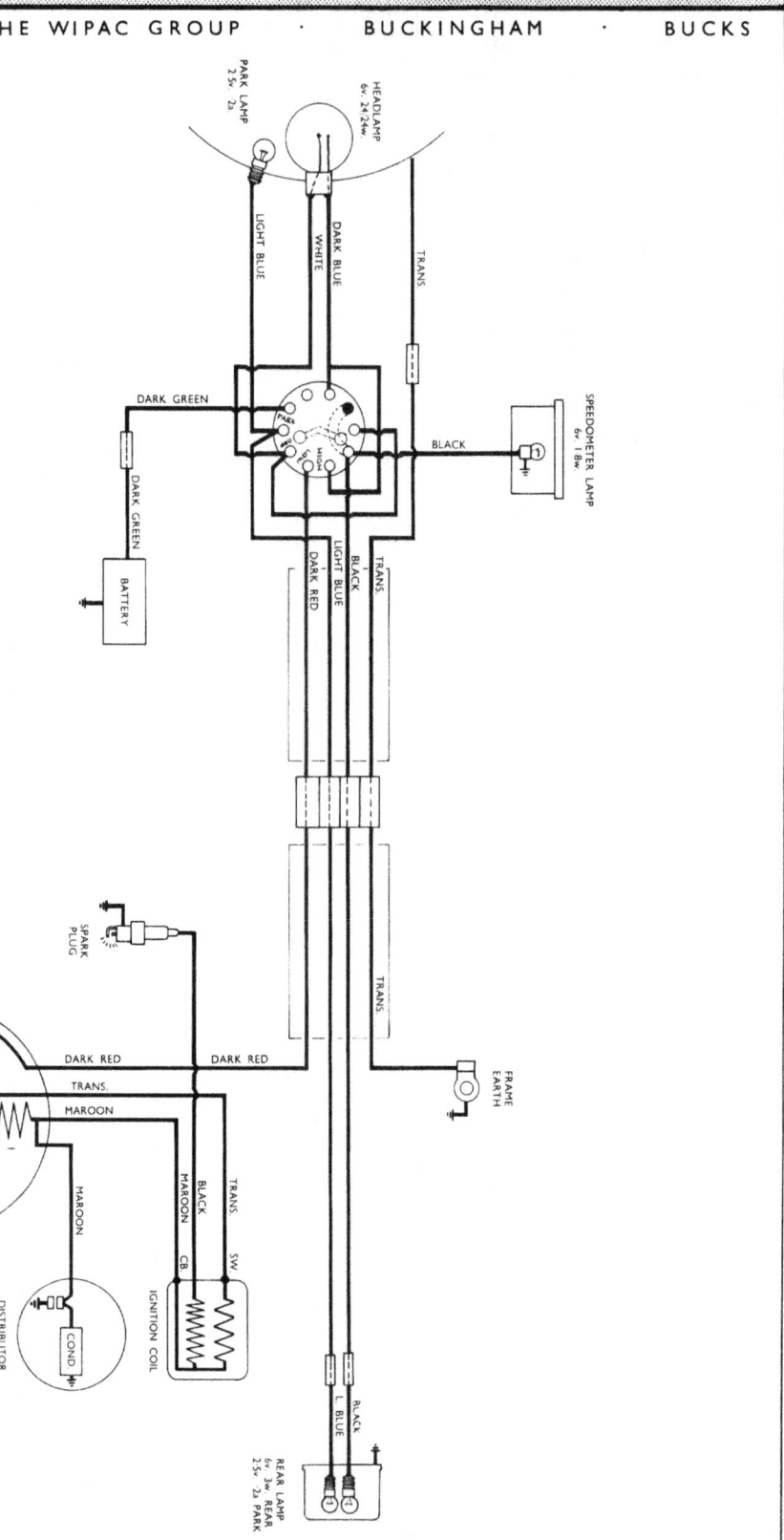

WIRING WIPAC DIAGRAM

FRANCIS-BARNETT "PLOVER 86" 150 CC.
AC LIGHTING
MODELS PRODUCED FROM MAY 1959 TO SEPT. 1960

THE WIPAC GROUP · BUCKINGHAM · BUCKS

UNIT FOR SPARES	PART No.
*Headlamp Unit (less harness)	S1127
Harness (Main)	S0924
Horn and Dipper Switch	S3857
Leads Set (Dipper Switch)	S0612
Stop and Rear Lamp (Quote bulbs required)	S3704
Ignition Generator	IG.1586

*Supplied by Wipac in black only.

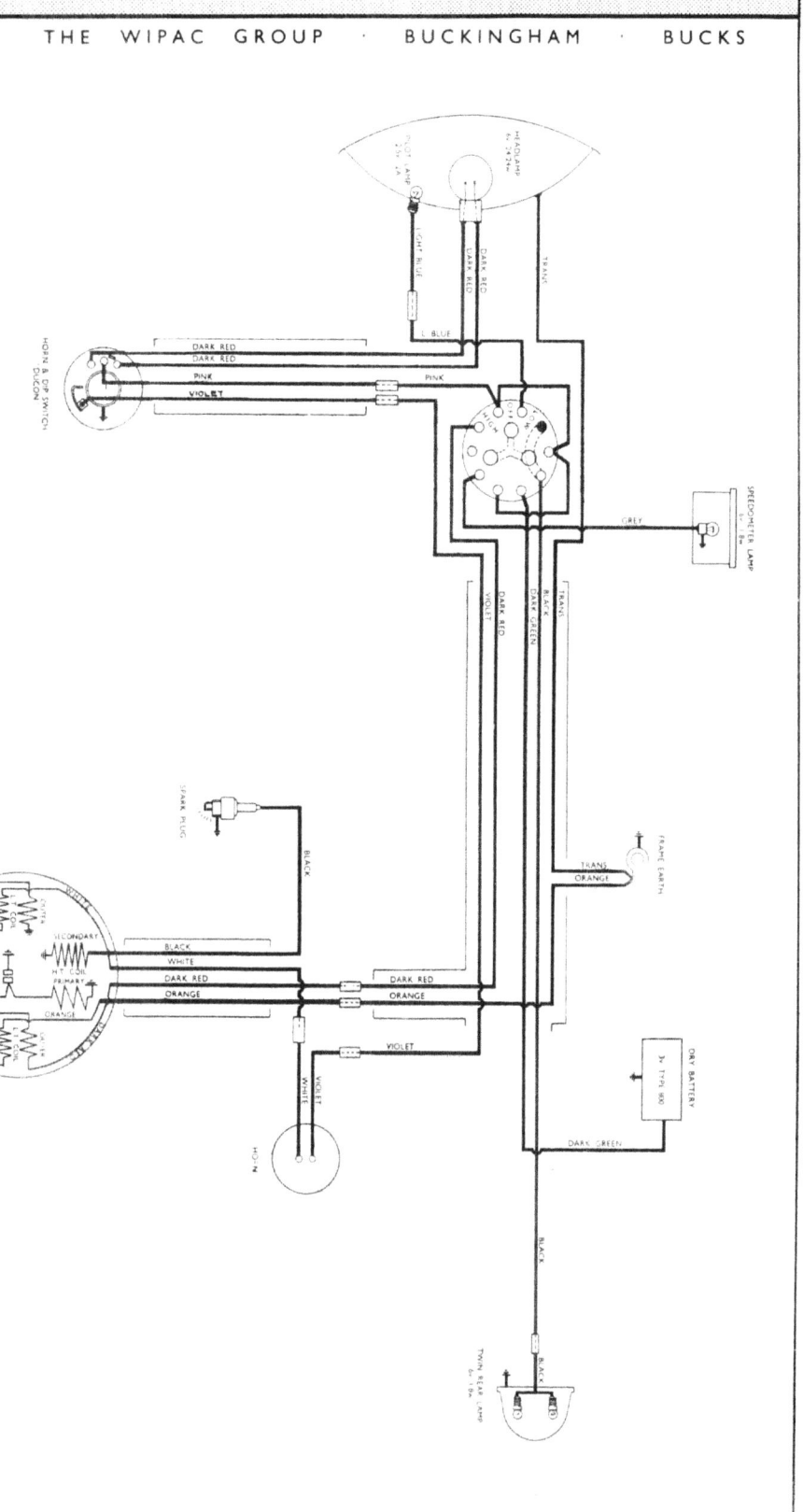

REF. WD/23/755/2

WIRING WIPAC DIAGRAM

FRANCIS-BARNETT "PLOVER 86" 150 CC.
AC/DC TRICKLE CHARGE
MODELS PRODUCED FROM MAY 1959 TO SEPT. 1960

THE WIPAC GROUP · BUCKINGHAM · BUCKS

UNIT FOR SPARES	PART No.
*Headlamp Unit (less harness)	S1057
Harness (Main)	S1058
Horn and Dipper Switch	S3857
Leads Set (Dipper Switch)	S0612
Stop and Rear Lamp (Quote bulbs required)	S3704
Leads Set (Rear Lamp)	S0785
Rectifier	S1044
Stop Switch	S0774
Leads Set (Stop Switch)	S2860
Ignition Generator	IG.1586

*Supplied by Wipac in black only.

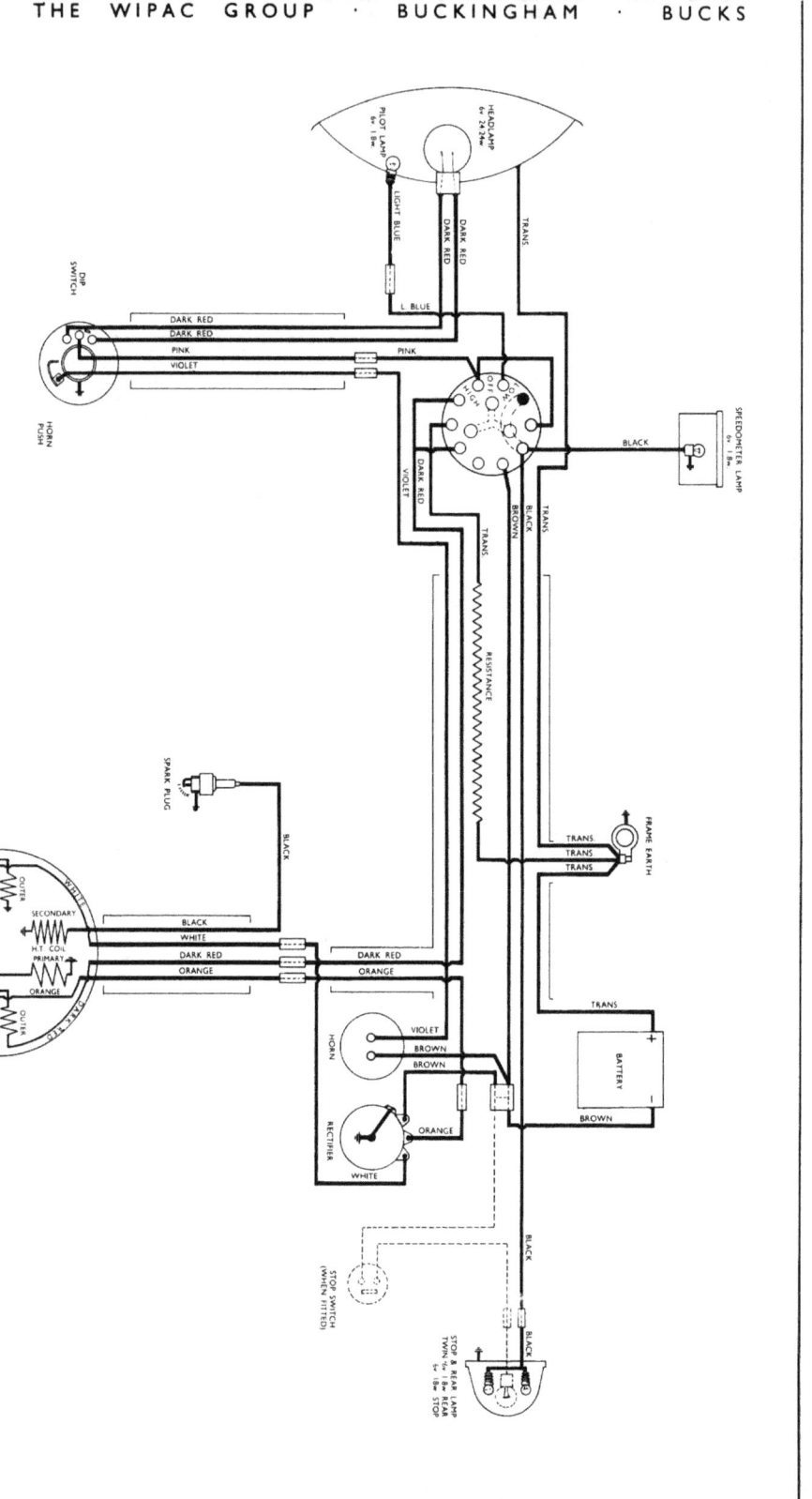

REF. WD/24/765/3

WIRING WIPAC DIAGRAM

FRANCIS-BARNETT 200 c.c. FALCON 87
MODELS PRODUCED FROM AUGUST 1959

THE WIPAC GROUP · BUCKINGHAM · ENGLAND

SPARES UNITS	PART No.
*Headlamp (less harness and speedometer)	S0902
Harness (Main)	S1081
Horn and Dip Switch	S3857
Dip Switch Harness	S0242
Alternator	G1585
Distributor Unit	S1024
Rectifier	S2642
Coil—6v. Ignition	S0793
Ammeter Unit	S0062

*Speedometer not supplied by Wipac

REF. WD/45/657/2

WIRING WIPAC DIAGRAM

FRANCIS-BARNETT MODEL 88. 150 cc.
AC LIGHTING
MODELS PRODUCED FROM OCT. 1961 to AUG. 1965

THE WIPAC GROUP · BUCKINGHAM · BUCKS

UNIT FOR SPARES	PART No.
*Headlamp Unit (less Harness)	S1127
Harness (Main)	S2870
Horn and Dipper Switch)	S3857
Leads Set (Dipper Switch)	S0612
Rear Lamp (Quote bulbs required	S3704
Leads Set	S0785
Ignition Generator	IG.1586
Battery Bracket	S2864

*Supplied by Wipac in black only.

Ref. WD/37/838/1

WIRING WIPAC DIAGRAM

FRANCIS-BARNETT MODEL 88. 150 cc.
AC/DC TRICKLE CHARGE
MODELS PRODUCED FROM OCT. 1961 TO AUG. 1965

THE WIPAC GROUP · BUCKINGHAM · BUCKS

UNIT FOR SPARES	PART No.
*Headlamp Unit (less harness)	S1057
Harness (Main)	S2871
Horn and Dipper Switch	S3857
Leads Set Dipper Switch	S0612
Rear Lamp (Quote bulbs required)	S3704
Leads Set (Rear Lamp)	S0785
Rectifier	S2856
Stop Switch	S3555
Leads Set (Stop Switch)	S3556
Ignition Generator	IG.1586

*Supplied by Wipac in black only.

Ref. WD/38/839/2

WIRING WIPAC DIAGRAM

FRANCIS-BARNETT "CRUISER 89"
250 cc TWIN.
DC LIGHTING
MODELS PRODUCED FROM OCT. 61.

THE WIPAC GROUP · BUCKINGHAM · BUCKS

Ref. WD/43/848/1

WIRING WIPAC DIAGRAM

FRANCIS-BARNETT "CRUISER" 91·SPORTS
250 c.c. TWIN
D.C. LIGHTING

MODELS PRODUCED FROM OCT. 1962 to SEPT. 1963

THE WIPAC GROUP · BUCKINGHAM · BUCKS

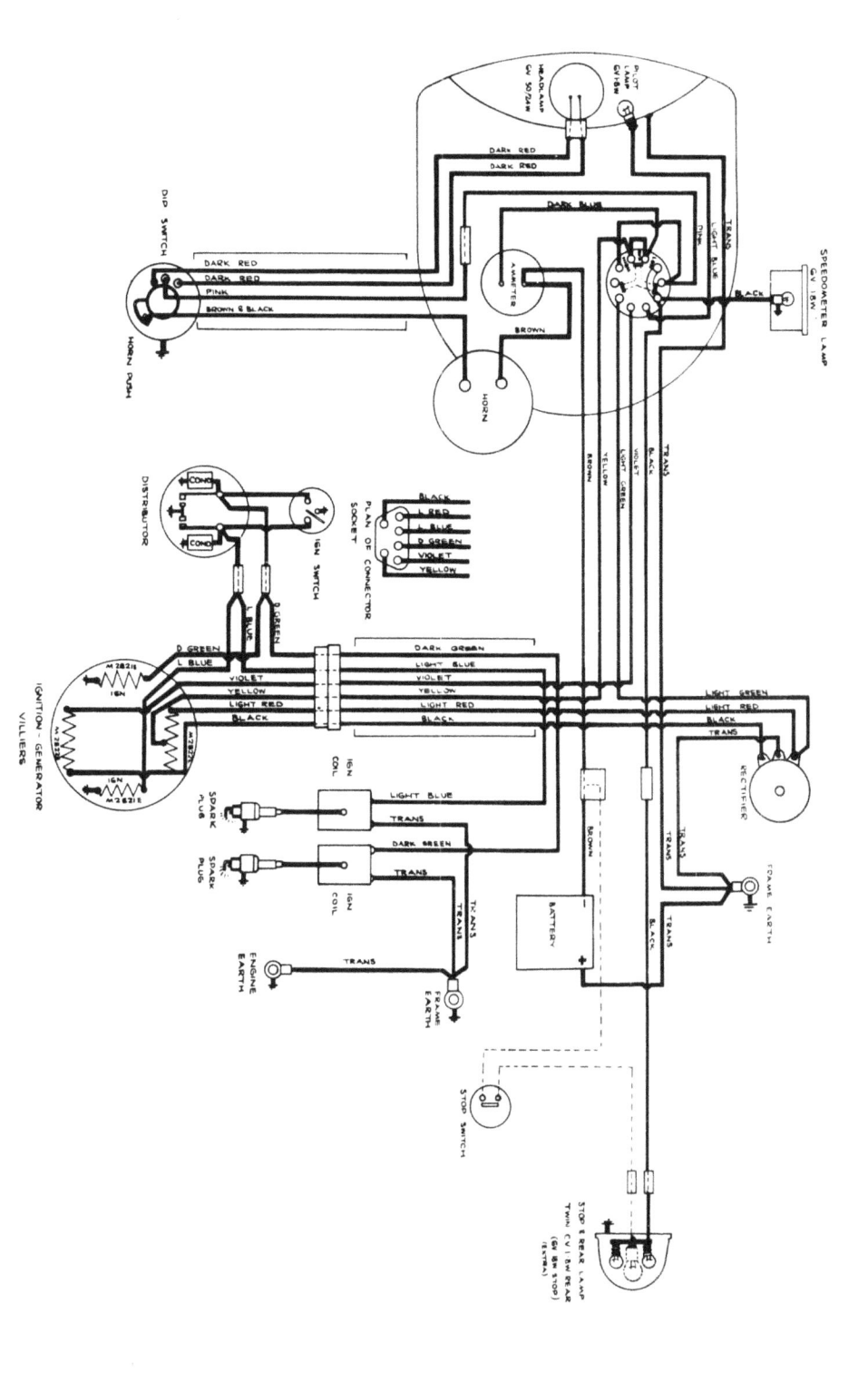

Ref. WD/74/848/1

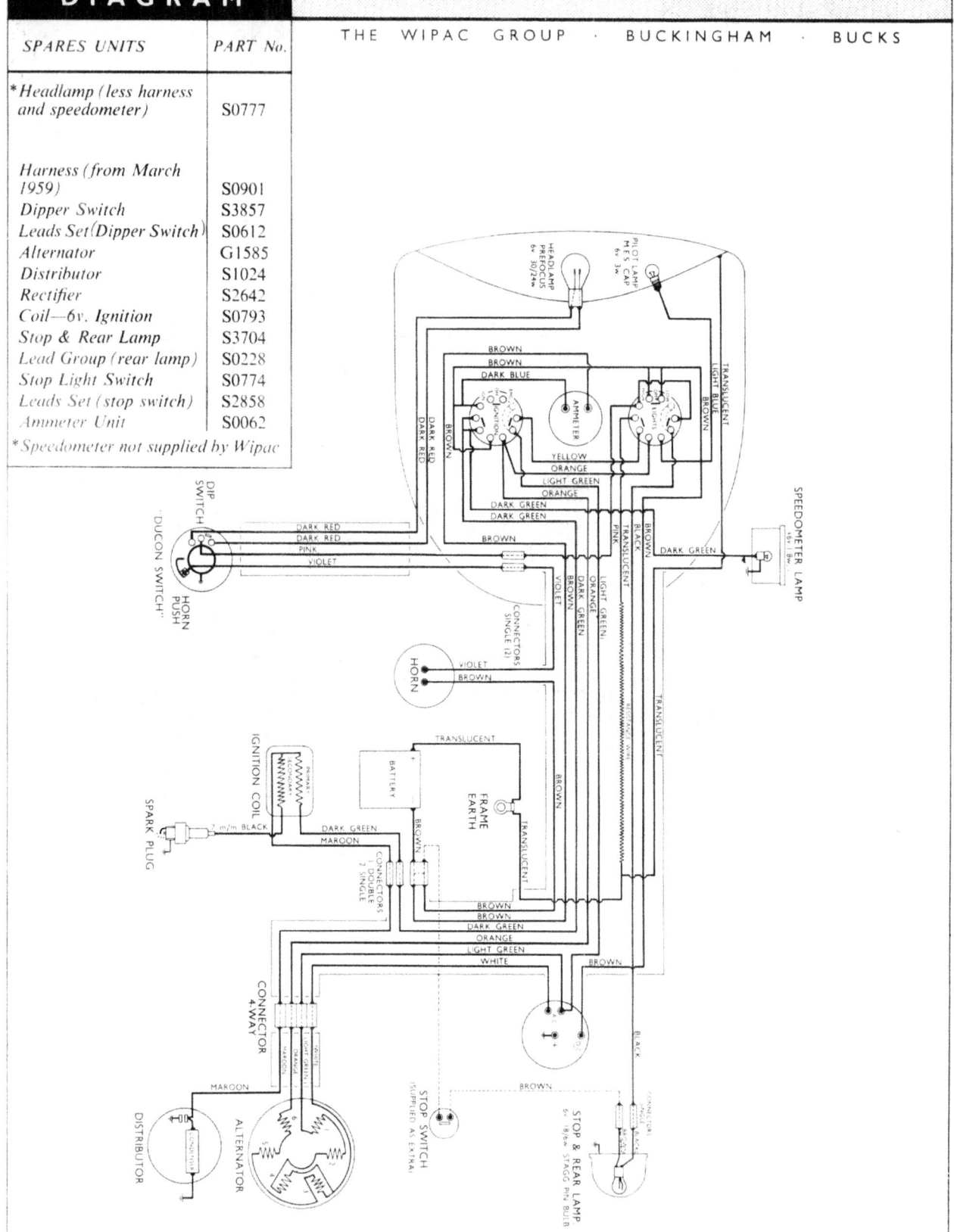

WIRING WIPAC DIAGRAM

JAMES M25 "SUPER SWIFT" 250 c.c. TWIN
DC LIGHTING
MODELS PRODUCED FROM OCT. 1961 TO FEB. 1964

THE WIPAC GROUP · BUCKINGHAM · BUCKS

Ref. WD/42/849/1

WIRING WIPAC DIAGRAM

JAMES "COMET" 98 cc. MODEL 100
AC LIGHTING
MODELS PRODUCED FROM OCTOBER 1959

THE WIPAC GROUP · BUCKINGHAM · BUCKS

UNIT FOR SPARES	PART No.
*Headlamp Unit (less Harness)	S1127
Harness (Main)	S0924
Horn and Dipper Switch	S0613
Leads Set (Dipper Switch)	S0612
Rear Lamp (Quote bulbs required)	S0210

*Supplied by Wipac in black only.

Ref. WD/30/797

WIRING WIPAC DIAGRAM

JAMES "COMET" 98 cc. MODEL 100
AC/DC TRICKLE CHARGE
MODELS PRODUCED FROM JANUARY 1960

THE WIPAC GROUP · BUCKINGHAM · BUCKS

UNIT FOR SPARES	PART No.
*Headlamp Unit (less Harness)	S1302
Harness (Main)	S1301
Horn and Dipper Switch	S0613
Leads Set (Dipper Switch)	S0612
Stop and Rear Lamp (Quote bulbs required)	S0229
Leads Set (Rear Lamp)	S0228
Rectifier	S1066

*Supplied by Wipac in black only.

Ref. WD/31/798

WIRING WIPAC DIAGRAM

JAMES 150cc SCOOTER
A/C D/C LIGHTING (TRICKLE CHARGE)
MODELS PRODUCED FROM JULY 1960

THE WIPAC GROUP · BUCKINGHAM · BUCKS

UNIT FOR SPARES	PART No.
Headlamp Unit (less Harness)	S1425
Harness (Main)	S1286
"Tricon" Dipper Switch	S1424
Leads Set (Dipper Switch)	S1288
Stop and Rear Lamp (Quote bulbs required)	S1287
Leads Set (Rear Lamp)	S1426
Ignition Generator	IG.1630
Rectifier	S1289
Stop Swicth	S1427
Switch Unit	S0781

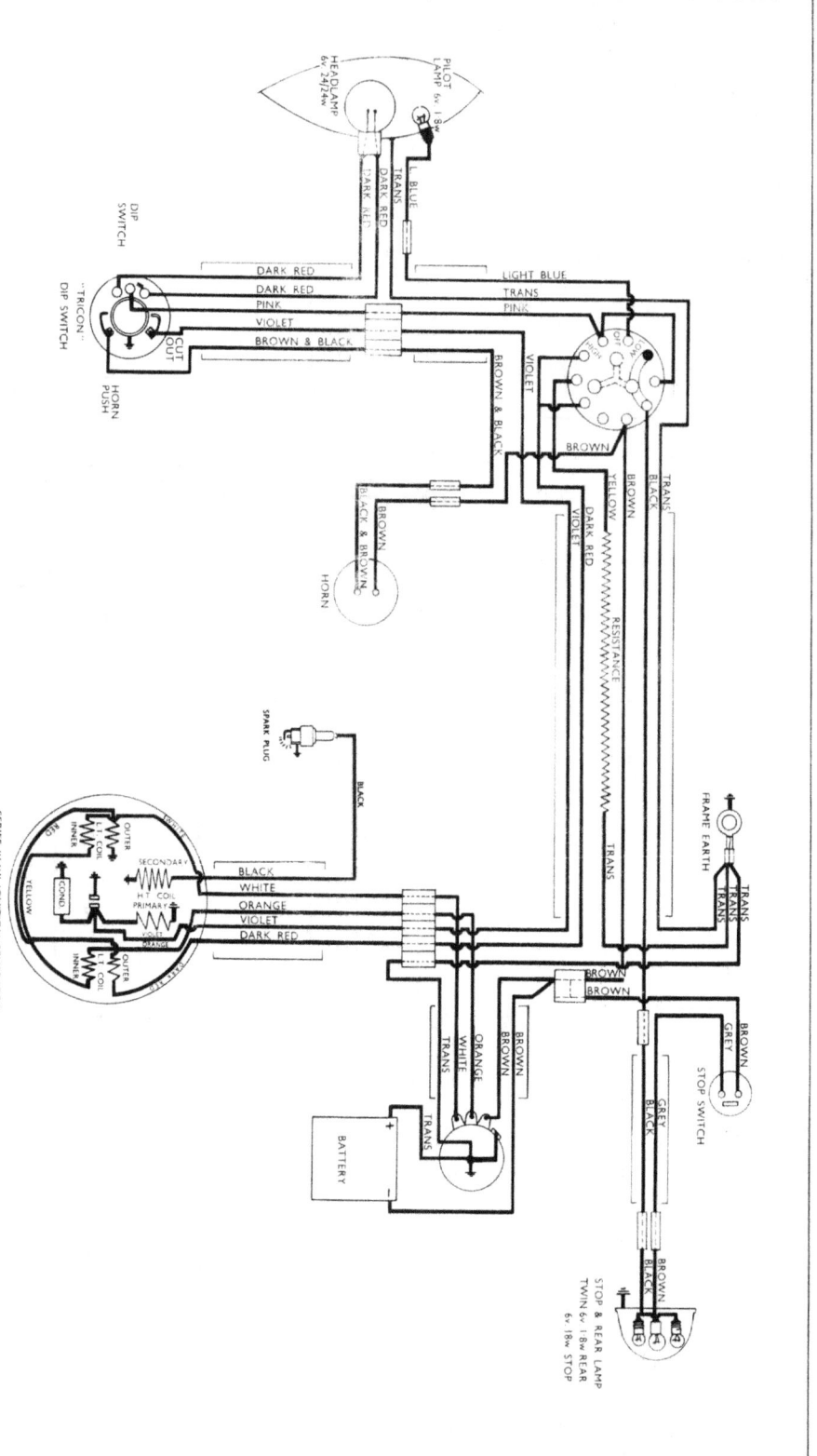

Ref. WD/32/799

WIRING WIPAC DIAGRAM

JAMES "FLYING CADET" MODEL L15 150 cc.
AC LIGHTING
MODELS PRODUCED FROM APRIL 1959 TO SEPT. 1963

THE WIPAC GROUP · BUCKINGHAM · BUCKS

UNIT FOR SPARES	PART No.
*Headlamp Unit (less Harness)	S1127
Harness (Main)	S0924
Horn and Dipper Switch	S3857
Leads Set (Dipper Switch)	S0612
Stop and Rear Lamp (Quote bulb required)	S3704
Ignition Generator	IG.1586

*Supplied by Wipac in black only.

Ref. WD/21/755/1

WIRING WIPAC DIAGRAM

JAMES "FLYING CADET" MODEL L15 150 cc.
AC/DC TRICKLE CHARGE
MODELS PRODUCED FROM APRIL 1959 TO SEPT. 1963

THE WIPAC GROUP · BUCKINGHAM · BUCKS

UNIT FOR SPARES	PART No.
*Headlamp Unit (less harness)	S1057
Harness (Main)	S1058
Horn and Dipper Switch	S3857
Leads Set (Dipper Switch)	S0612
Stop and Rear Lamp (Quote bulb required)	S3704
Leads Set (Rear Lamp)	S0785
Rectifier	S1044
Ignition Generator	IG.1586

*Supplied by Wipac in black only.

Ref. WD/22/765/2

WIRING WIPAC DIAGRAM

JAMES 200 c.c. CAPTAIN
MODELS PRODUCED FROM AUGUST 1959

THE WIPAC GROUP   BUCKINGHAM   BUCKS

SPARES UNITS	PART No.
*Headlamp (less harness and speedometer)	†S0777 ‡S3412
Harness (Main)	S3413
Alternator	G1585
Distributor Unit	S1024
Horn & Dipper Switch	S3857
Leads Set (Dipper Switch)	S0612
Rectifier	S2642
Coil—6v. Ignition	S0793
Stop & Rear Lamp	S3704
Lead Group (rear lamp)	S0785
Stop Switch	S0774
Leads Set (Stop Switch)	S2860
Ammeter Unit	S0062

*Speedometer not supplied by Wipac
†Prior to October 1962
‡From October 1962

REF. WD/33/656/1

WIRING WIPAC DIAGRAM

JAMES MODEL M.15 150 CC.
AC LIGHTING
MODELS PRODUCED FROM OCT. 61.

THE WIPAC GROUP · BUCKINGHAM · BUCKS

UNIT FOR SPARES	PART No.
*Headlamp Unit (less Harness)	†S1057 ‡S1127
Harness (Main)	†S2901 ‡S2870
Horn and Dipper Switch	S3857
Leads Set (Dipper Switch)	S0612
Stop and Rear Lamp (Quote bulb required)	S3704
Ignition Generator	IG1586

*Supplied by Wipac in black only.
†Prior to October 1962
‡From October 1962

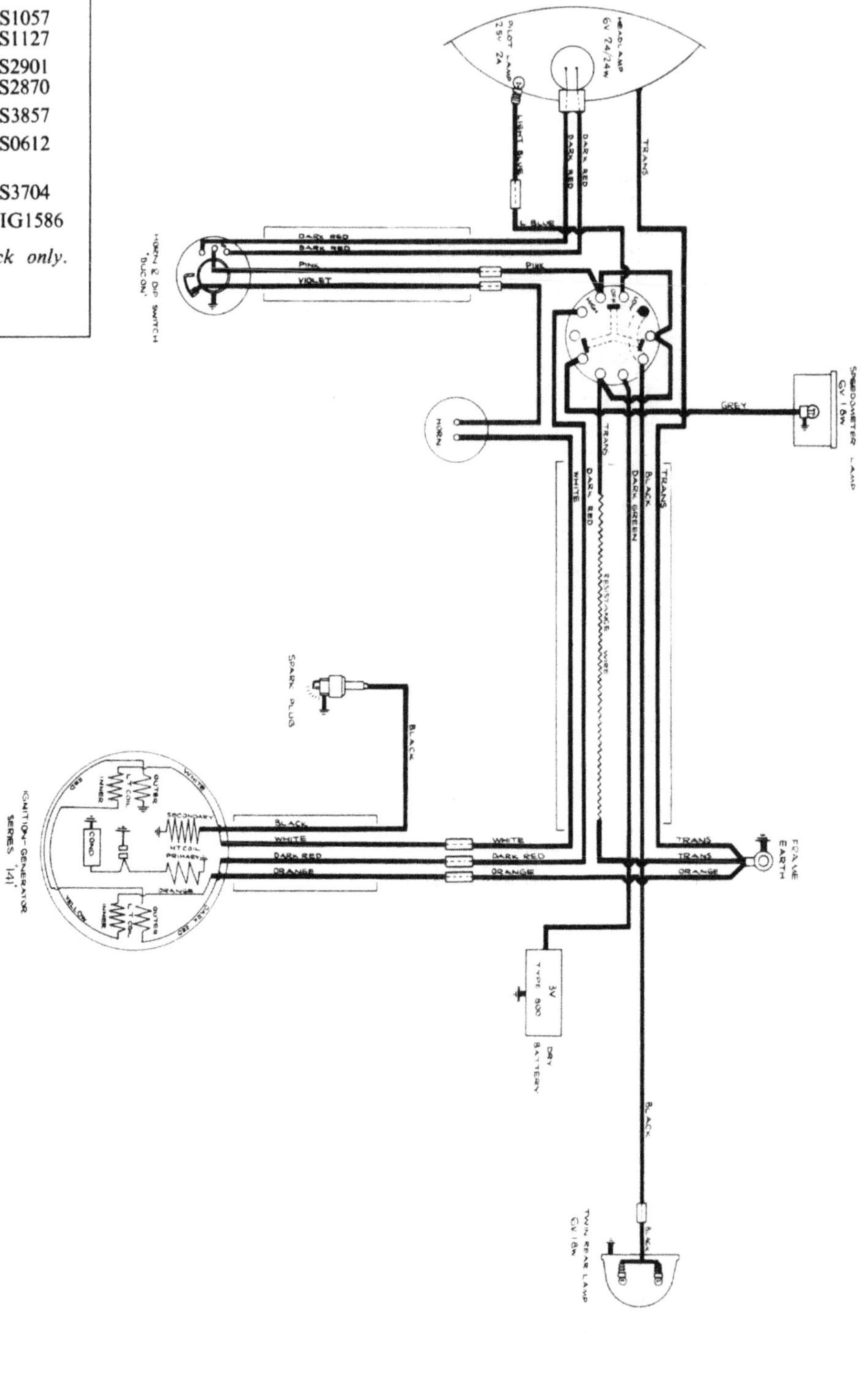

Ref. WD/41/836/1

WIRING WIPAC DIAGRAM

JAMES MODEL M.15 150 cc.
AD/DC (TRICKLE CHARGE)
MODELS PRODUCED FROM OCT. 1961 TO DEC. 1964

THE WIPAC GROUP · BUCKINGHAM · BUCKS

UNIT FOR SPARES	PART No.
*Headlamp Unit (less Harness)	S1057
Harness (Main)	S2871
Rectifier	S1044
Horn and Dipper Switch	S3857
Leads Set (Dipper Switch)	S0612
Stop and Rear Lamp (Quote bulb required)	S3704
Leads Set (Rear Lamp)	S0785
Ignition Generator	IG.1586
Stop Switch	S0774
Leads (Stop Switch)	S2860

*Supplied by Wipac in black only.

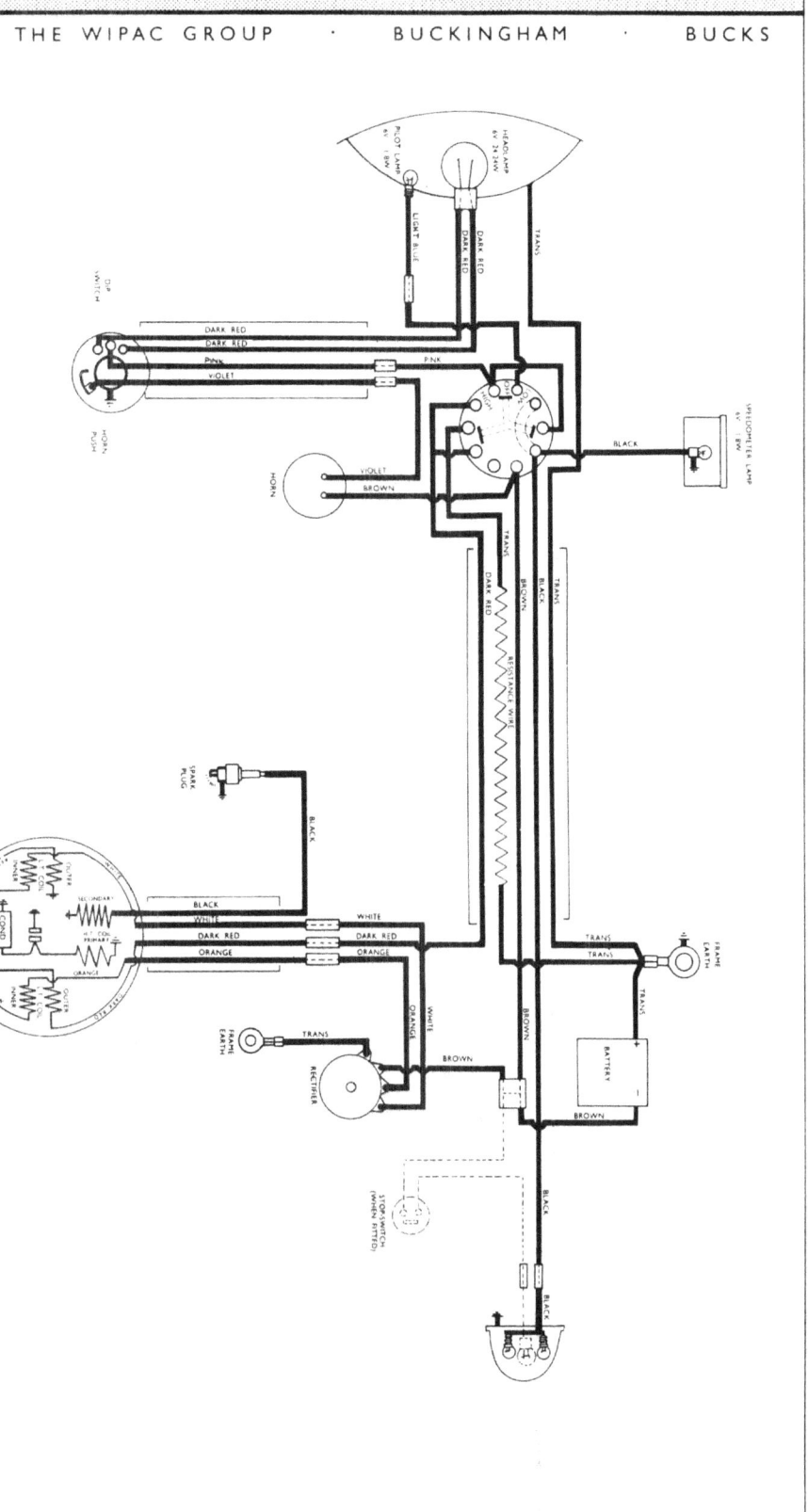

Ref. WD/40/837/1

WIRING WIPAC DIAGRAM

JAMES MODEL M.16 150 cc.
AD/DC (TRICKLE CHARGE)
MODELS PRODUCED FROM JAN. 1965

THE WIPAC GROUP · BUCKINGHAM · BUCKS

UNIT FOR SPARES	PART No.
*Headlamp Unit (less Harness)	S1057
Harness (Main)	S2871
Rectifier	S1044
Horn and Dipper Switch	S3857
Leads Set (Dipper Switch)	S0612
Stop and Rear Lamp (Quote bulb required)	S3704
Leads Set (Rear Lamp)	S0785
Ignition Generator	IG.1586
Stop Switch	S0774
Leads (Stop Switch)	S2860

*Supplied by Wipac in black only.

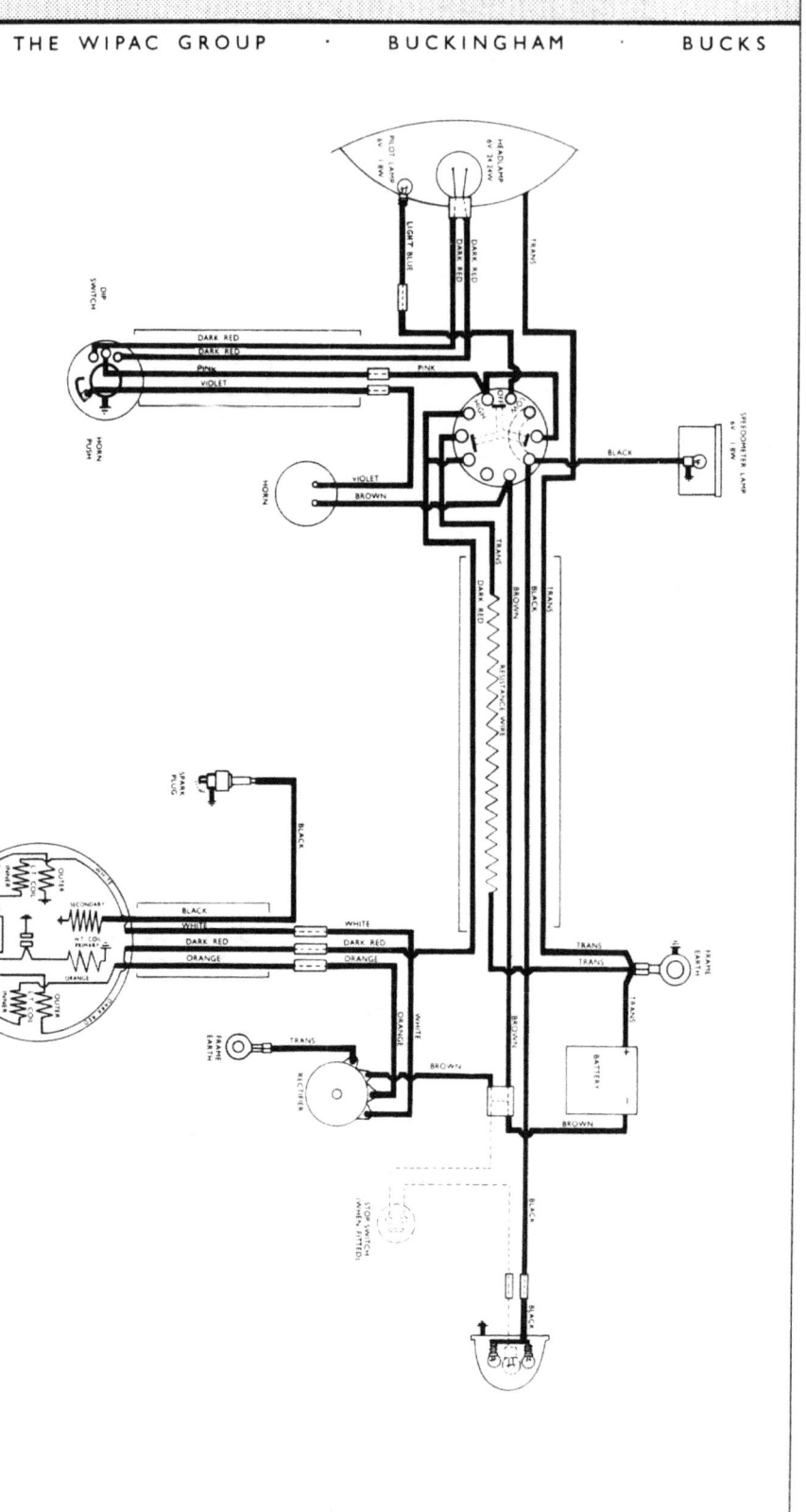

Ref. WD/87/837

WIRING WIPAC DIAGRAM

MATCHLESS G2 250 c.c., G5 350 c.c., G2S, G2CSR
A.J.S. Models 14, 14S, 14CSR 250 c.c., 8 350 c.c.
MODELS PRODUCED FROM MAY 1958 TO DECEMBER 1964

THE WIPAC GROUP · BUCKINGHAM · BUCKS

SPARES UNITS	PART No.
†*Headlamp (less harness and speedometer)	SEE NOTE
Harness (Main)	S2616
Horn and Dipper Switch	S3857
Harness (Dipper Switch)	S0612
Alternator	G1521
Distributor Unit	S1141
Rectifier	S2642
Coil—6v. Ignition	S0793
Stop & Rear Lamp	S3704
Stop Switch	S0754
Leads Set (Stop Switch)	S2857
Ammeter Unit	S0062

*Speedometer not supplied by Wipac

†NOTE. Headlamp Units S0777 fitted from May, 1958 to Sept. 1959 S2615 fitted from Aug. 1959 to Dec. 1964.

REPLACING RECTIFIER

The Square type Rectifier will replace the Round type without any difficulty.

Connections:

White Lead to Terminal A.C.
　　　　　　　　　　　White
Brown Lead to Terminal D.C.
　　　　　　　　　　　Brown
Light Green to Terminal A.C.
　　　　　　　　　　　Green

REAR LAMP REPLACEMENT

From August 1965 the Rear Lamp has been modified to the Ministry of Transport Grade 1 Regulations.

The Three Bulb type is replaced by the Single Bulb (Double Contact) Model.

No rewiring is required.

REF. WD/16/715/1

WIRING WIPAC DIAGRAM

MATCHLESS G2 CSR 250 c.c. and A.J.S. 14 CSR 250 c.c. "SAPPHIRE NINETY"
MODELS PRODUCED FROM MARCH 1965

THE WIPAC GROUP · BUCKINGHAM · BUCKS

SPARES UNITS	PART No.
*Headlamp (less harness and speedometer)	S2615
Harness (Main)	S2611
Horn and Dipper Switch	S3857
Harness (Dipper Switch)	S0612
Alternator	G1521
Distributor Unit	S3881
Rectifier	S2642
Coil—6v. Ignition	S0793
Stop & Rear Lamp	S3704
Stop Switch	S0754
Leads Set (Stop Switch)	S2857
Ammeter Unit	S0062

*Speedometer not supplied by Wipac

REF. WD/86/811/1

WIRING WIPAC DIAGRAM

MATCHLESS G2CS and A.J.S. 14CS
SCRAMBLER MODELS
250 c.c. O.H.V. MOTOR CYCLES
A.C./D.C. TRICKLE CHARGE
MODELS PRODUCED FROM OCTOBER 1958 TO AUGUST 1960

THE WIPAC GROUP · BUCKINGHAM · BUCKS·

SPARES UNITS	PART No.
*Headlamp (less harness and speedometer)	S0910
Harness (Main)	S0911
Dipper Switch Harness	S0860
Alternator Unit	G1569
Distributor Unit	S1122
Rectifier	S0862
Coil-12v. Ignition	S0810
Rear Lamp	S2872
Cut-out, Horn and Dipper Switch	S0497
L.T. Lead Set (Ignition)	S0861

*Speedometer not supplied by Wipac

REF. WD/26/748/1

WIRING WIPAC DIAGRAM

MATCHLESS G2CS and A.J.S. 14CS
SCRAMBLER MODELS
250 c.c. O.H.V. MOTOR CYCLES
A.C./D.C. TRICKLE CHARGE
MODEL PRODUCED FROM SEPTEMBER 1960

THE WIPAC GROUP   BUCKINGHAM   BUCKS

SPARES UNITS	PART No.
*Headlamp (less harness and speedometer)	S0923
Harness (Main)	S2624
Dipper Switch Harness	S2622
Alternator Unit	G1632
Distributor Unit	S1141
Rectifier	S2642
Coil-12v. Ignition	S0792
L.T. Lead Set (Ignition)	S2620
Rear Lamp	S2872
Horn and Dipper Switch	S0613
Harness (Ignition)	S2621

*Speedometer not supplied by Wipac

NOTE:—WHEN THE SET IS SUPPLIED WITHOUT THE LIGHTING EQUIPMENT (i.e. HEADLAMP, REAR LAMP, DIP SWITCH, HORN, LIGHTING SWITCH & HARNESS) THE YELLOW LEAD FROM THE IGNITION SWITCH MUST BE CONNECTED INTO THE DOUBLE CONNECTOR ON THE LIGHT GREEN LEADS.

REF. WD/79/803

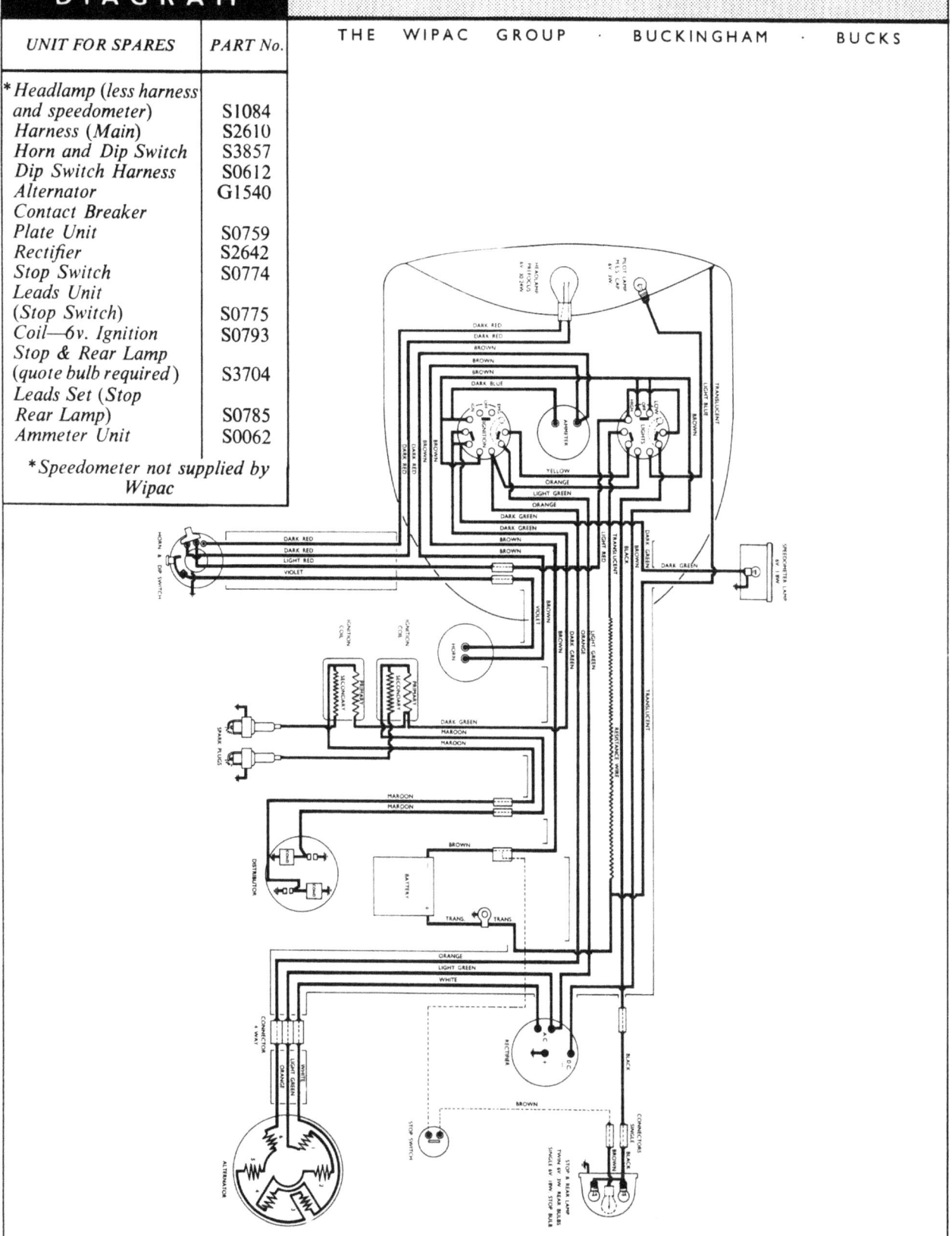

WIRING WIPAC DIAGRAM

NORTON JUBILEE 250 c.c. and NAVIGATOR 350 c.c. TWIN
MODELS PRODUCED FROM SEPT. 1960 to SEPT. 1962

THE WIPAC GROUP · BUCKINGHAM · BUCKS

UNIT FOR SPARES	PART No.
*Headlamp less harness and speedometer	S2615
Harness (Main)	S2610
Horn and Dip Switch	S3857
Dip Switch Harness	S0612
Alternator	G1685
Distributor Unit	S2631
Rectifier	S2642
Stop Switch	S0774
Leads Unit (Stop Switch)	S2840
Coil—6v. Ignition	S0793
Ammeter Unit	S0062

*Speedometer not supplied by Wipac

REF. WD/34/814/3

WIRING WIPAC DIAGRAM

NORTON JUBILEE 250 c.c. and NAVIGATOR 350 c.c. TWIN
MODELS PRODUCED FROM OCT. 1962 to SEPT. 1963

THE WIPAC GROUP · BUCKINGHAM · BUCKS

EQUIPMENT	PART No.
*Headlamp (less harness and speedometer)	S3334
Harness (Main)	S2610
Horn and Dip Switch	S3857
Dip Switch Harness	S0612
Alternator	G1540
Distributor Unit	S2630
Rectifier	S2642
Stop Switch Leads Unit (Stop Switch)	S0774 S2840
Coil—6v. Ignition	S0793
Ammeter Unit	S0062

*Speedometer not supplied by Wipac

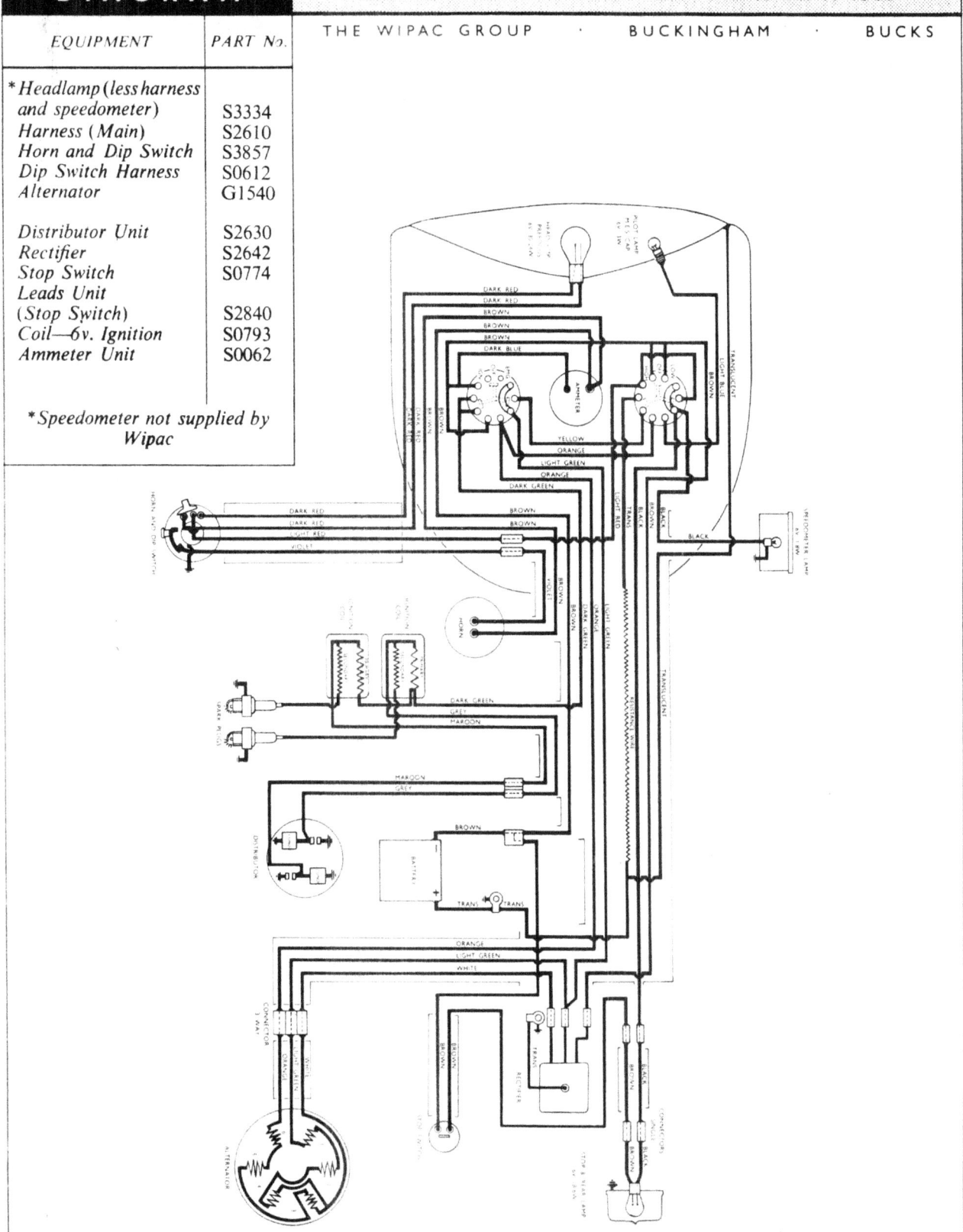

REF. WD/46/814/2

WIRING WIPAC DIAGRAM

NORTON JUBILEE 250 c.c. and NAVIGATOR 350 c.c. TWIN
MODELS PRODUCED FROM OCT. 1963 TO SEPT. 1964

THE WIPAC GROUP · BUCKINGHAM · BUCKS

EQUIPMENT	PART No.
*Headlamp (less harness and speedometer)	S3334
Harness (Main)	S2610
Horn and Dip Switch	S3857
Dip Switch Harness	S0612
Alternator	G1685
Distributor Unit	S2630
Rectifier	S2642
Stop Switch	S0774
Leads Unit (Stop Switch)	S2840
Coil—6v. Ignition	S0793
Ammeter Unit	S0062

*Speedometer not supplied by Wipac

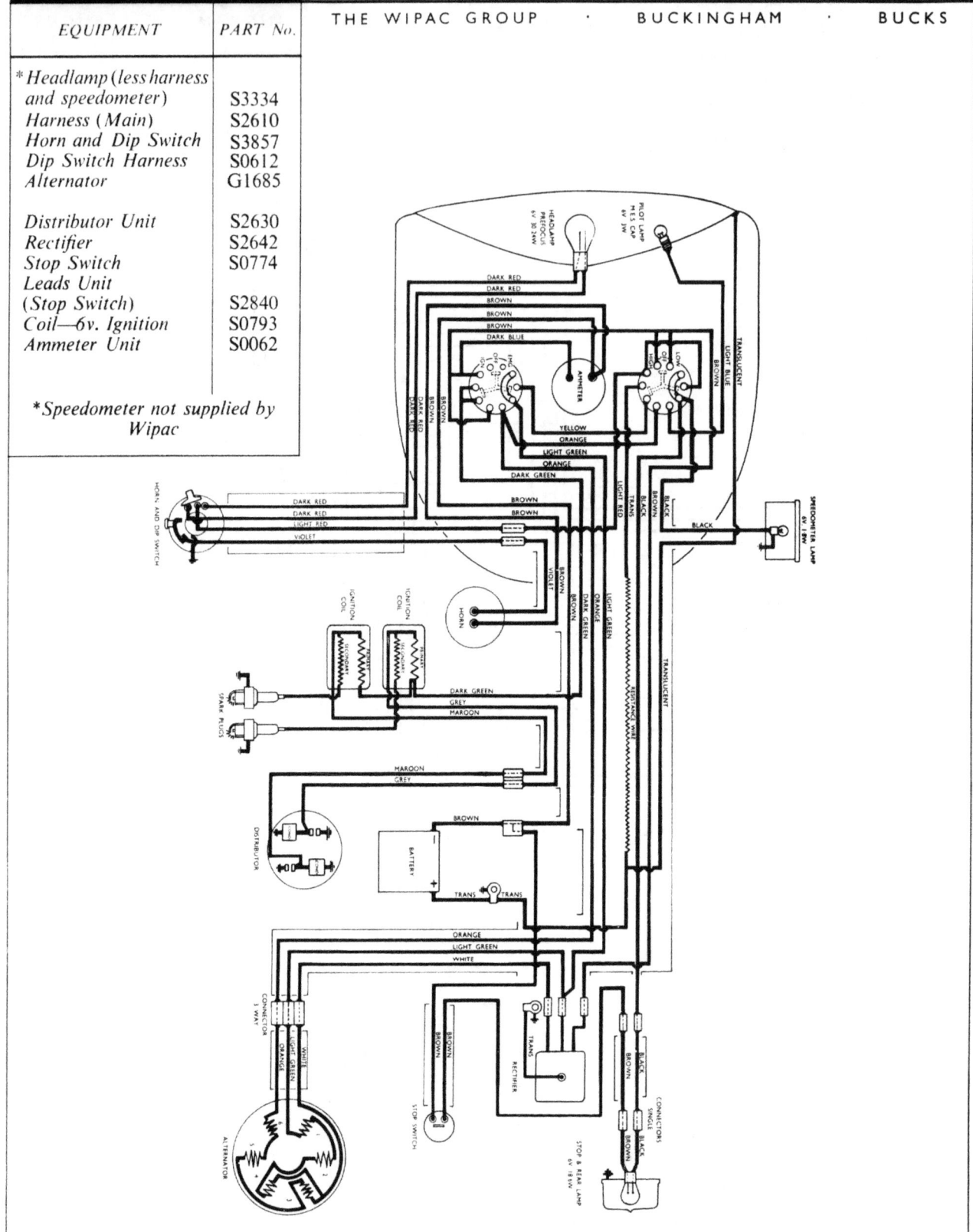

REF. WD/61/814/2

WIRING WIPAC DIAGRAM

NORTON NAVIGATOR 350 c.c. TWIN
MODELS PRODUCED FROM OCT. 1964

THE WIPAC GROUP · BUCKINGHAM · BUCKS

EQUIPMENT	PART No.
*Headlamp (less harness and speedometer)	S3819
Harness (Main)	S2610
Horn and Dip Switch	S3856
Dip Switch Harness	S0612
Alternator	G1685
Distributor Unit	S2630
Rectifier	S2642
Stop Switch	S0774
Leads Unit (Stop Switch)	S2840
Coil—6v. Ignition	S0793
Ammeter Unit	S0062

*Speedometer not supplied by Wipac

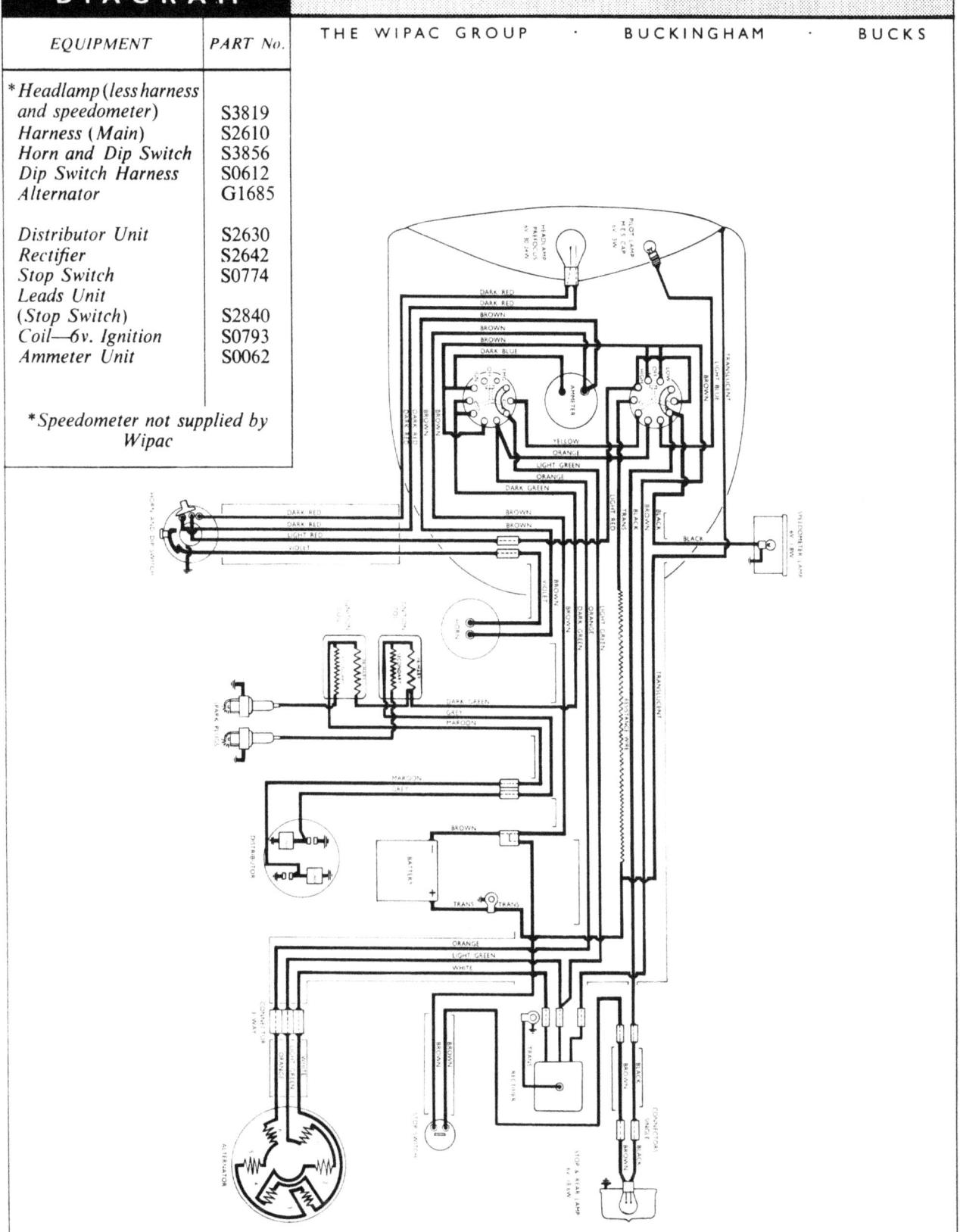

REF. WD/84/814/1

NORTON ELECTRA 400 c.c. TWIN
(12 VOLT SELF STARTER)
MODELS PRODUCED FROM FEB. 1963

THE WIPAC GROUP · BUCKINGHAM · BUCKS

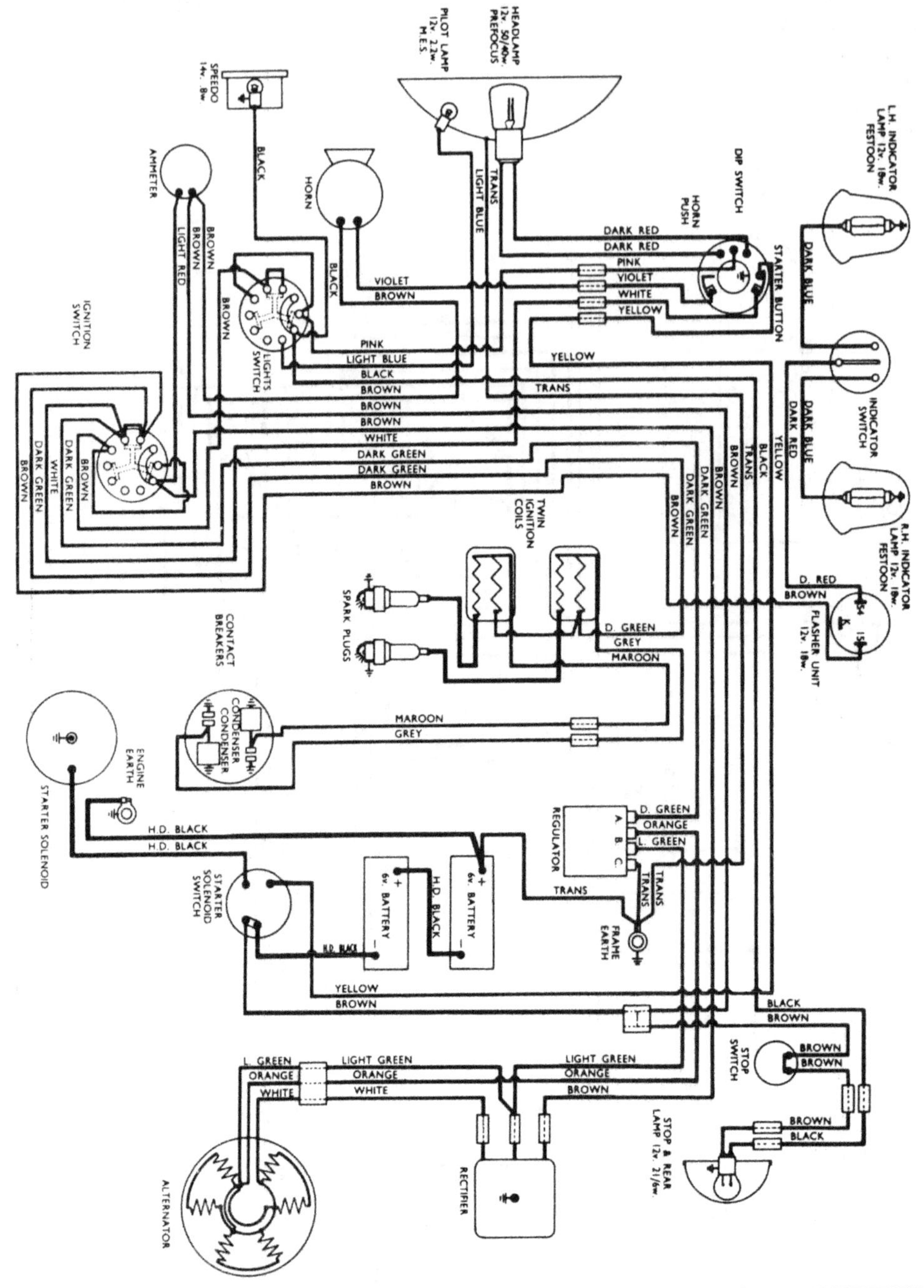

UNIT FOR SPARES	PART No.	UNIT FOR SPARES	PART No.	UNIT FOR SPARES	PART No.
*Headlamp (less harness and speedometer)	†S3428 ††S3799	Alternator Distributor Unit	G1697 S2630	Leads Unit (Stop Switch)	S2840
Harness (Main)	S3429	Rectifier	S2642	Coil—12v. Ignition	S0810
Horn, Starter & Dip Switch	S3859	Stop Switch	S0774	Ammeter Unit	S3162

†Prior to Oct. 1964   ††From Oct. 1964   *Speedometer not supplied by Wipac

REF. WD/48/906/2

WIRING WIPAC DIAGRAM

PIATTI Scooter (A.C. Lighting)
MODELS PRODUCED FROM MAY 1956 to MAY 1958

THE WIPAC GROUP · BUCKINGHAM · BUCKS

UNITS FOR SPARES	PART No.
Ignition—Generator	IG1467
Rear/Park Lamp (Quote bulbs required)	S0213
Switch Unit (Lights)	S0837
Harness (Main)	S0071
Leads Set (Dip Switch)	S0072
Horn & Dip Switch	S1356
Headlamp Front Unit	S0065

WD/10/655/1

WIRING WIPAC DIAGRAM

RALEIGH MOPED RM.8 & RM.9
A.C. LIGHTING
MODELS PRODUCED FROM MAY 1964

THE WIPAC GROUP — BUCKINGHAM — BUCKS

SPARES UNITS	PART No.
Headlamp (complete with harness)	S3688
Harness (Main) (includes S3692)	S3691
Switch Unit (Lights)	S3692
Rear Lamp	S3835

REF. WD/81/989/1

WIRING WIPAC DIAGRAM

TRIUMPH T.10 AUTOMATIC 100 cc. SCOOTER
MODELS PRODUCED FROM APRIL 1965

THE WIPAC GROUP   BUCKINGHAM   BUCKS

SPARES UNITS	PART No.
*Headlamp Unit (less Harness)	S2906
Harness (Main)	S3855
"Tricon" Horn and Dipper Switch	S3858
Leads Set (Dipper Switch)	S3900
Rear/Park Lamp (Quote bulbs required)	S3952
Seat Switch	S3953
Switch (Lights)	S0781
Ignition Generator	IG1741
Leads Set (Rear Lamp)	S3951

*Supplied by Wipac in black only

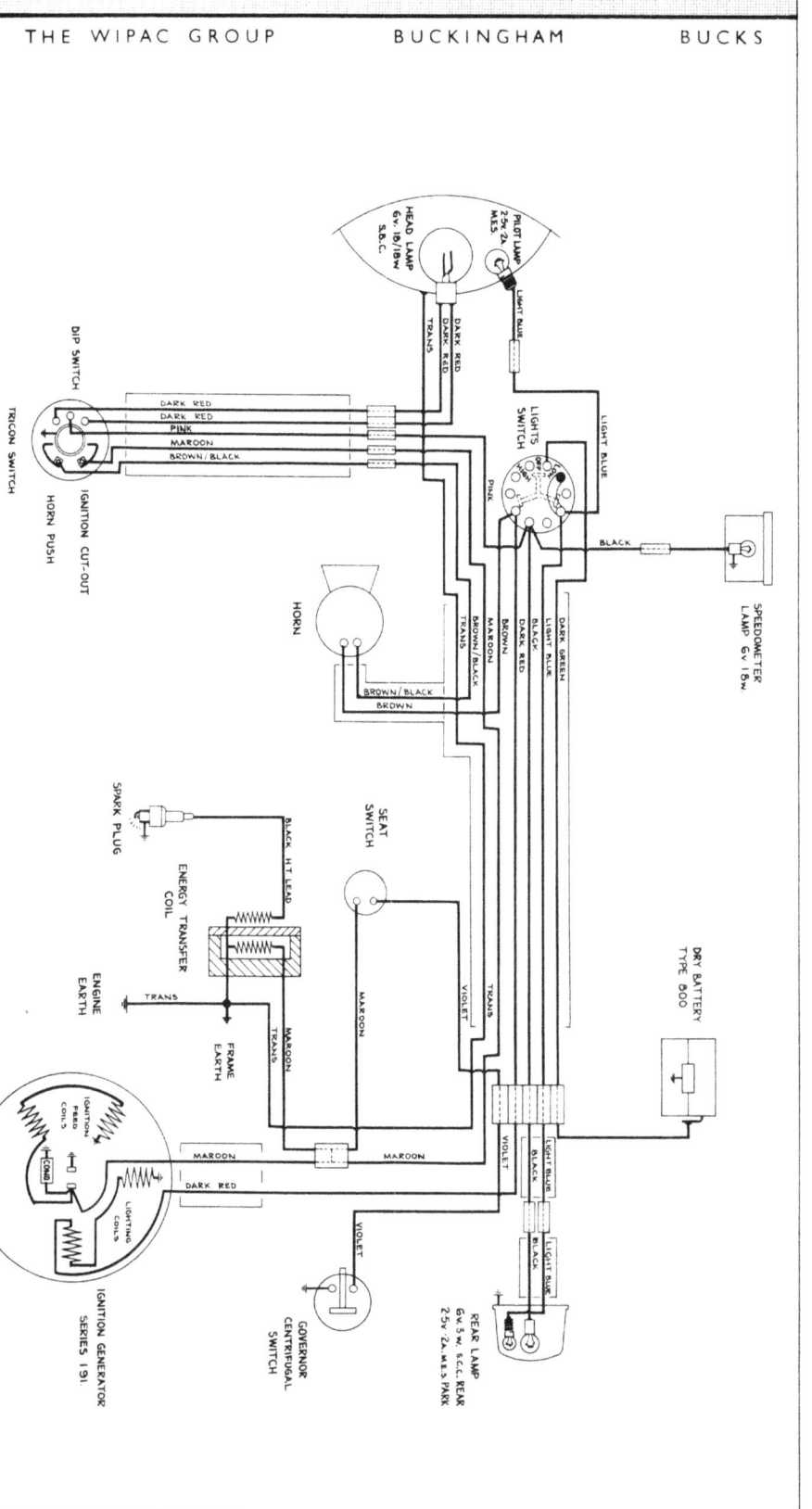

Ref. WD/85/1013

WIRING WIPAC DIAGRAM

TRIUMPH 199 c.c. SUPER CUB T20
Full D.C. Lighting with Coil Ignition
FROM JANUARY 1967

THE WIPAC GROUP BUCKINGHAM BUCKS

SPARES UNITS	PART No.
Alternator Unit	G1781
Headlamp Unit	S4187
Horn & Dip Switch	S3857
Harness (Dip Switch)	S2737
Harness (Main)	S4188
Stop & Rear Lamp (state bulb required)	S3611
Leads Set (Rear Lamp)	S2463
Rectifier Unit	S2642
Stop Switch Unit	S2370
Leads Set (Stop Switch)	S4182
Switch Unit (Lights)	S0781
Switch Unit (Ignition)	S0782
Ignition Coil	S0769

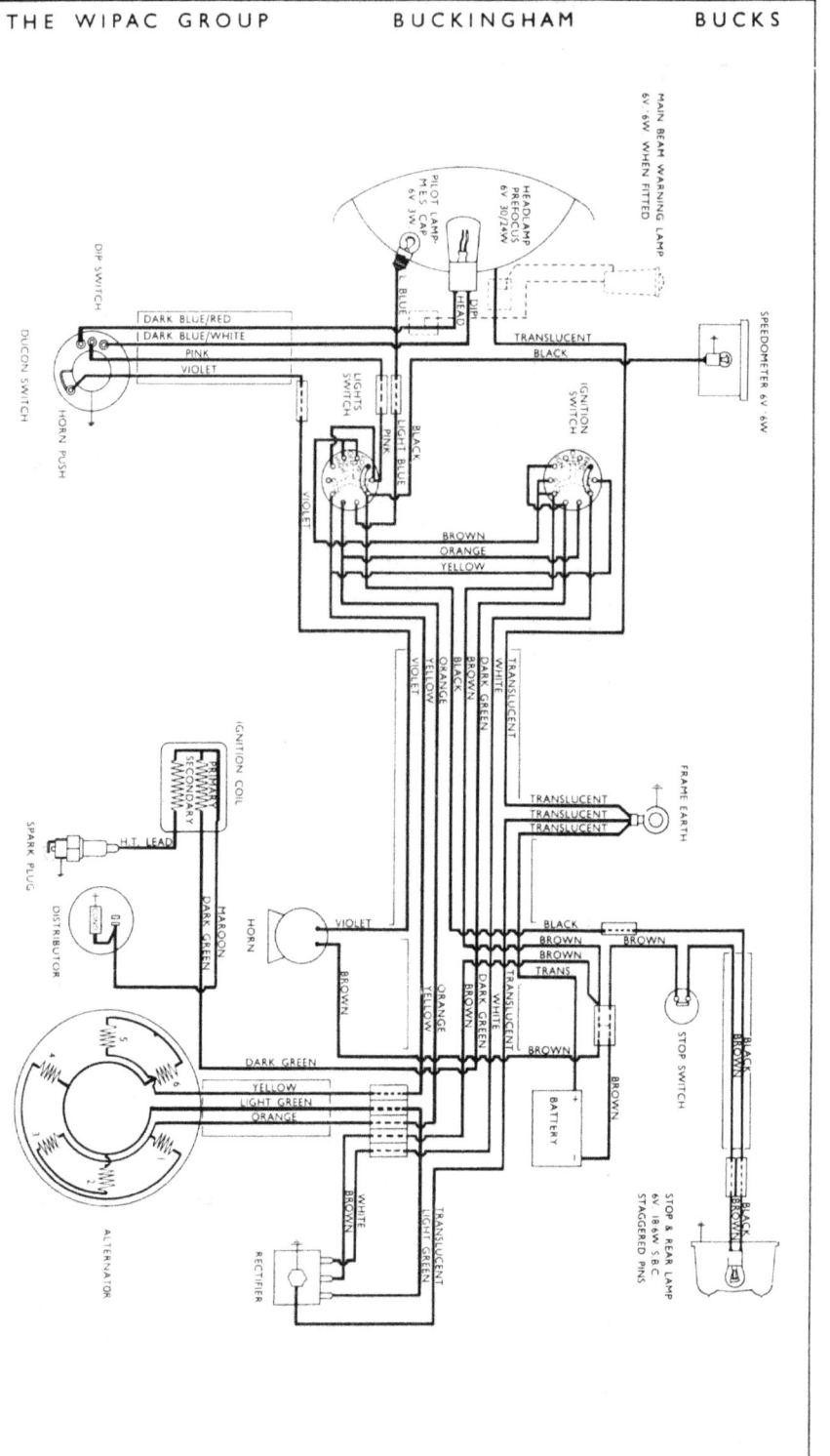

Ref. WD/89/1051

WIRING WIPAC DIAGRAM

TRIUMPH "TINA" 100 cc. SCOOTER
AC LIGHTING
MODELS PRODUCED FROM OCTOBER 1961

THE WIPAC GROUP · BUCKINGHAM · BUCKS

EQUIPMENT	PART No.
*Headlamp Unit (less Harness)	S2906
Harness (Main)	S2878
Horn, Dipper and Cut-Out Switch	S3858
Leads Set (Dipper Switch)	S3900
Rear/Park Lamp (Quote bulbs required)	S3102
Toggle Switch	S2911
Switch (Lights)	S0781
Ignition Generator	IG1649

*Supplied by Wipac in black only

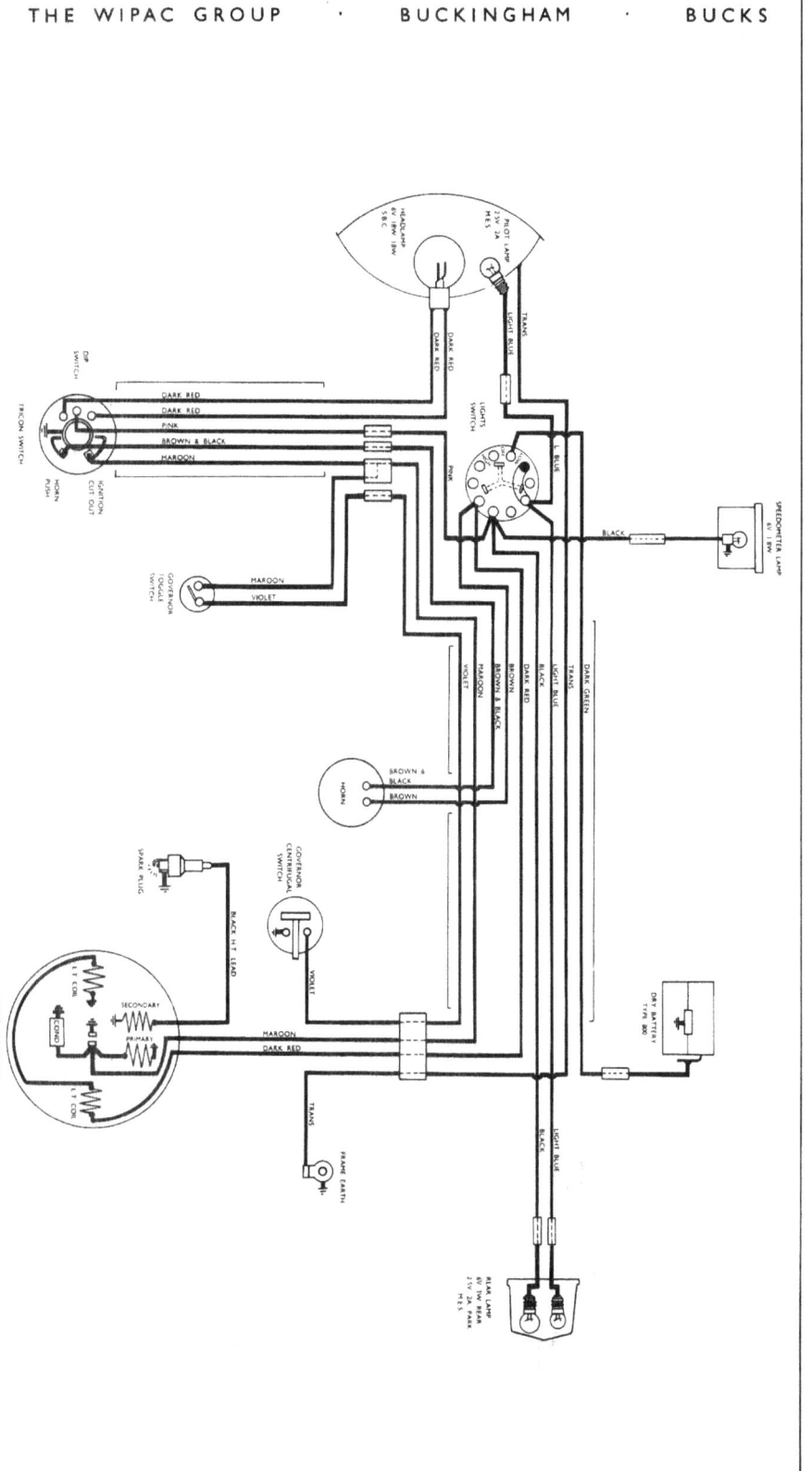

REF. WD/35/830/1

THE FOLLOWING PAGES 159-194 CONTAIN SERVICE BULLETINS AND TECHNICAL DATA SHEETS THAT SUPPLEMENT THE CONTENTS OF THIS MANUAL.

THE READER IS ENCOURAGED TO CHECK BOTH OF THESE SECTIONS CAREFULLY AS THEY MAY CONTAIN INFORMATION PERTAINING TO VARIOUS MODEL UPDATES AND/OR ELECTRONIC EQUIPMENT MODIFICATIONS NOT COVERED ELSEWHERE IN THIS MANUAL.

NOTES

WIPAC SERVICE BULLETIN

6th November, 1950

27-WATT GENIMAG—NON INTERCHANGEABILITY OF FLYWHEELS

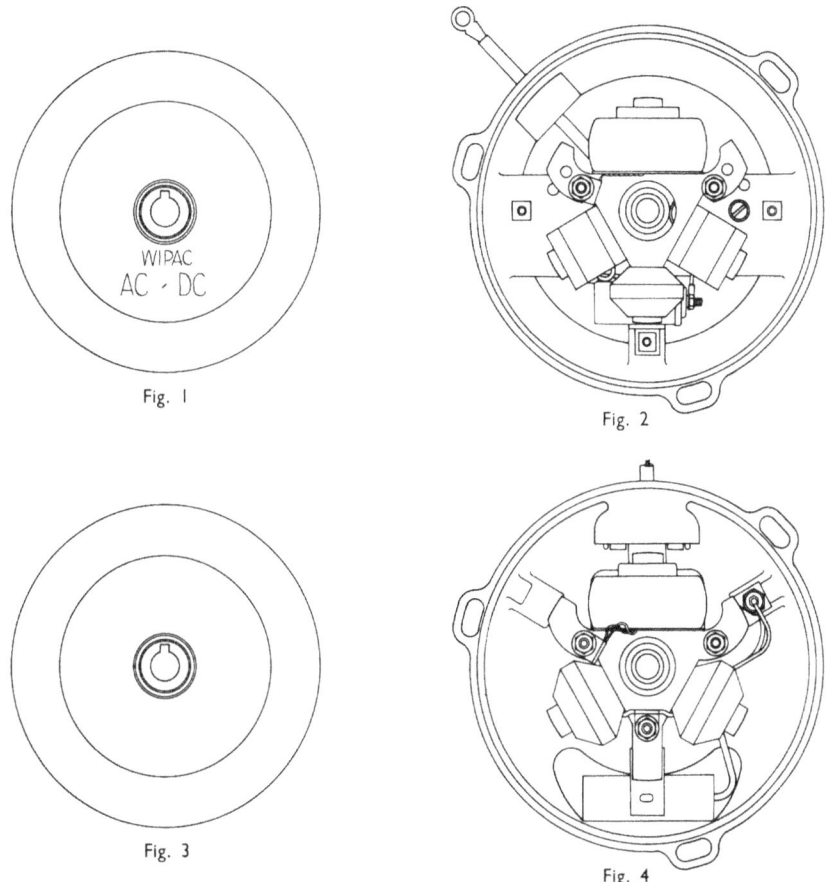

Fig. 1 Fig. 2 Fig. 3 Fig. 4

The 27-watt Genimag (figs. 3 & 4), which was purely an AC unit, has now been superseded by the S55/Mk.8 Ignition Generator (figs. 1 & 2), which unit has been designed to give either AC lighting direct or DC charging through a rectifier.

As the new unit incorporates extra magnets in the Flywheel all users should make careful note of the fact that although similar in appearance the Flywheels of the two units are not interchangeable. The Flywheel of the new S55/Mk.8 Ignition Generator can easily be identified because it is clearly marked ' WIPAC AC/DC ', (Fig. 1).

Great care must be taken to use the correct Flywheel with its appropriate Stator Plate, as if the new type Flywheel (Fig. 1), is used with the old type Stator Plate, (Fig. 4), trouble will be experienced with lamps blowing, and alternatively, if the new type Stator Plate, (Fig. 2), is used with the old type Flywheel, (Fig. 3), insufficient lighting output will be obtained.

SERVICE WIPAC BULLETIN	SUBJECT	STOP SWITCH. FAULTY FITTING ON B.S.A. "BANTAM"		
	Ref. No.	4255	CANCEL	
	AUTHORITY	F.K.M.	INSERT THIS BULLETIN INTO :-	No.2. MANUAL
	DATE OF ISSUE	JUNE 1955		

B.S.A. BANTAM D.D. MACHINES BUILT FROM APRIL TO JULY 1955 INCLUSIVE AND FITTED WITH A WIPAC STOP SWITCH AS STANDARD EQUIPMENT.

ON MACHINES MADE EARLY THIS YEAR, THE STOP SWITCH LOCATED ON THE CHAIN SIDE OF THE LOWER REAR FRAME.

THE CHAIN SOMETIMES STRUCK AND DAMAGED THE SWITCH AND WAS MOVED TO A POSITION IMMEDIATELY OVER THE REAR TUBE.

CERTAIN MACHINES HAVE BEEN ASSEMBLED WITH THE CONTACTS OF THE SWITCH ALMOST TOUCHING THE FASTENING LUG AND HAVE GONE TO EARTH AND BURNED OUT THE WIRING.

REMEDY: FIT SLOT IN SWITCH BRACKET SO THAT THE SWITCH IS AS FAR AWAY FROM THE LUG AS POSSIBLE AND THEN MAKE THE SPRING ADJUSTMENT BY MOVING THE CLIP ON THE BRAKE ROD.

--- oooOooo ---

THE WIPAC GROUP — BLETCHLEY — ENGLAND.
TELEPHONE: BLETCHLEY 3321   TELEGRAMS: WICOMAGSCO BLETCHLEY

SERVICE WIPAC BULLETIN

SUBJECT	OXIDISATION OF CONTACT POINTS		
Ref. No.	2355	CANCELS	1355
AUTHORITY	W.R.F.	INSERT THIS BULLETIN INTO :-	Nos. 1 & 3 MANUALS
DATE OF ISSUE	June 1955		

Most modern magnetos are fitted with tungsten contact points. If magnetos fitted with those points are stored for long periods without use, more particularly under damp or moist conditions, there is a tendency for the contacts to oxidise, with the result that the magneto fails to spark. In order to prevent this happening the contacts of all Wico and Wipac magnetos are treated with a special corrosion resisting material before they leave the works, but if the magneto has been operating prior to storage (say on engine test), it is possible that this protection will be removed. If, therefore, a new magneto fails to spark after storage, corrosion of the contact points will be the probable cause. This is easily overcome by wiping the contacts with a wet rag, making certain at the same time that no fluff from the rag is left between the contacts.

THE WIPAC GROUP — BUCKINGHAM BUCKS — ENGLAND
TELEPHONE: BUCKINGHAM 3031   TELEGRAMS: WICOMAGSCO · BUCKINGHAM

SERVICE WIPAC BULLETIN	SUBJECT	HEADLAMP SWITCH ON:- B.S.A. - 10L, ARIEL COLT LH		
	Ref. No.	3255	CANCELS	
	AUTHORITY	F.K.M.	INSERT THIS BULLETIN INTO :-	NO. 2. MANUAL.
	DATE OF ISSUE	JUNE 1955		

THE FAILURE OF CERTAIN CIRCUITS TO OPERATE PROPERLY MAY BE DUE TO THE HOLLOW METAL CUP LOCATED IN THE SWITCH OPERATING KNOB BEING OUT OF POSITION. THE CUP TENDS TO TURN WHEN THE NUT WHICH HOLDS IT IN POSITION IS TIGHTENED UP, THROWING THE SLOT WHICH LIMITS THE SWITCH TRAVEL OUT OF POSITION.

TO PREVENT MOVEMENT, HOLD THE METAL CUP IN POSITION ON THE FLAT ON THE SWITCH BODY AND APPLY PRESSURE IN AN ANTICLOCKWISE DIRECTION AS THE NUT IS TIGHTENED.

TO TEST, MOVE THE SWITCH KNOB WITH LIGHT FINGER PRESSURE IN BOTH DIRECTIONS IN ALL THREE POSITIONS OF THE SWITCH. THE KNOB SHOULD MOVE BOTH WAYS FOR APPROXIMATELY $\frac{1}{8}"$ BEFORE OPERATING THE SWITCH CONTACTS.

A SPECIAL TUBE SPANNER FOR THIS - PART NUMBER 02100 - IS AVAILABLE, PRICE 5/-D.

THE WIPAC GROUP — BLETCHLEY — ENGLAND
TELEPHONE: BLETCHLEY 320   TELEGRAMS: WICOMAGSCO BLETCHLEY

SERVICE WIPAC BULLETIN

SUBJECT	B.S.A. BANTAM DC. JUNE 1955 FITTING OF STATOR PLATE TYPE IG.1454	
Ref. No.	6255	
AUTHORITY	F.K.M.	NO. 3
DATE OF ISSUE	OCT.1955	MANUAL.

On all B.S.A. D1 and D3 Bantam DC machines manufactured between June 1950 and August 1955, the Ignition Generator was fitted with Stator Plate type IG.1130.

(Identification:- The Headlamp Switch Lever is detachable by means of the fixing screw in the centre).

On all B.S.A. Bantam DC machines manufactured after August 1955, the Ignition Generator is fitted with Stator Plate type IG.1450 or IG.1454.

(Identification:- The Headlamp Switch Lever is non-detachable and has no centre fixing screw).

The Stator Plate IG.1450 or IG.1454 can be fitted to 1950/55 models but in order to limit the charging rate in the "LOW" position the following modifications must be carried out on the Headlamp Switch:-

(1) Remove the YELLOW link between terminals 9 and 11.

(2) After removing this ensure that the LIGHT GREEN wire is securely connected to terminal 9.

THE WIPAC GROUP — BUCKINGHAM — BUCKS
TELEPHONE: BUCKINGHAM 2140   TELEGRAMS: WIPACITY · BUCKINGHAM

SERVICE WIPAC BULLETIN

SUBJECT	SPARK PLUG "WHISKERING"
Ref. No.	SP.21
AUTHORITY	F.K.M.
DATE OF ISSUE	NOV. '55
CANCELS	—
INSERT THIS BULLETIN INTO :-	No. 3 MANUAL (TECHNICAL)

This particular phenomenon is the formation of a fine bridge of conducting material across the plug points which shorts out the plug. It is usually found on plugs in two-stroke engines and is believed to be formed principally from additives in the fuel and lubricating oil. The incidence of "whiskering" has increased considerably since both fuels and oils become adulterated to improve their general performance.

To cure whiskering, or at least diminish the frequency of its occurrence, the following remedies may be employed.

1. Reduce exhaust back pressure, by cleaning out the silencer and pipes.
2. Ensure that the mixture is not too weak.
3. Fit suppressor—5,000 ohms value, or higher, up to 15,000 ohms.
4. Use lubricating oil specially advised for two-strokes.
5. Change grade of petrol used.
6. Fit next harder grade plug.
7. Change shape of plug electrodes as below.

Normal  **Change 1**  **Change 2**

NOTE: Plug electrode arrangements 1 and 2 will give improved starting and tick-over on four-stroke engines as well.

THE WIPAC GROUP — BUCKINGHAM BUCKS — ENGLAND
TELEPHONE: BUCKINGHAM 3031 · TELEGRAMS: WICOMAGSCO · BUCKINGHAM

SUBJECT	B.S.A. Bantam Magneto Series 55 Contact Point Setting			
Ref. No.	125/3	CANCELS		
AUTHORITY	F.K.M.	INSERT THIS BULLETIN INTO	No. 3 Technical Manual	
DATE OF INSERT	1-1-56			

FAULT:

It is sometimes reported that B.S.A. Bantam machines fitted with our series '55' Ignition Generator, will not start nor run unless the contact breaker point setting is about .006" to .008" instead of the correct figure of .015".

CAUSE:

A build up of tolerances on the shaft, the cam and the key in one direction, may result in the points opening before the magnetic flux has been broken, so that no voltage is produced. The action of closing down the gap to about .008" retards this timing relationship and the magneto then fires normally.

REMEDY:

The first remedy to employ is to reverse the small Woodruff Cam Key—that is, put the side which faces to the right, to face to the left. Should this effect no improvement, obtain from us, a special cam, the profile of which is specially ground 5 degrees late.

THE WIPAC GROUP — BUCKINGHAM BUCKS — ENGLAND
TELEPHONE: BUCKINGHAM 3031   TELEGRAMS: WICOMAGSCO · BUCKINGHAM

SERVICE WIPAC BULLETIN	SUBJECT	Magnet Rotors for B.S.A.-C10L and Ariel-Colt		
	Ref. No.	01978	CANCELS	
	AUTHORITY	F.K.M.	INSERT THIS BULLETIN INTO :-	No. 3 Technical Manual
	DATE OF ISSUE	1-6-56		

There is a difference between the Magnet Rotors for machines made before and after August 1955.

The sketch below shows the Keyway positions. Please note that the type on the right of sketch is the 1956 model, which **IS ALSO** suitable for 1953/5 models.

The type shown on left is for 1953/5 models and NOT SUITABLE for 1956. After the date of this Service Sheet, only 1956 style Rotors will be made.

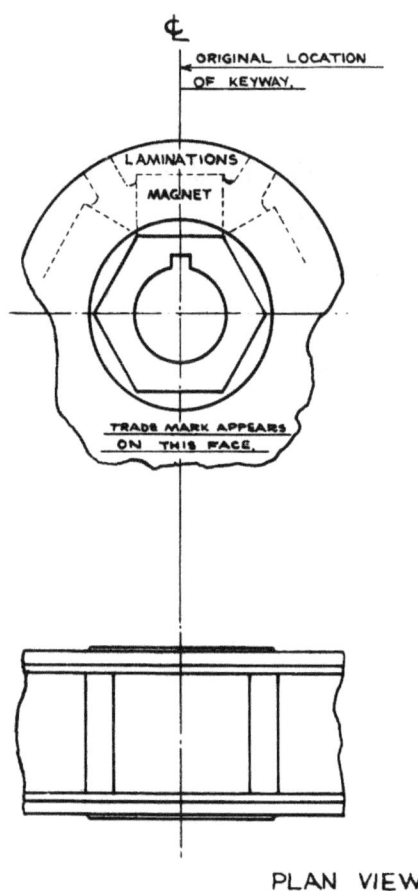 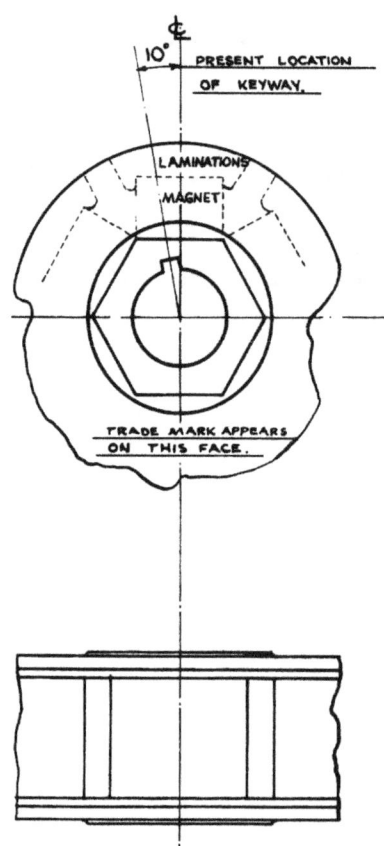

PLAN VIEWS.

THE WIPAC GROUP — BLETCHLEY — ENGLAND
TELEPHONE: BLETCHLEY 3321   TELEGRAMS: WICOMAGSCO BLETCHLEY

SERVICE WIPAC BULLETIN	SUBJECT	SERIES 90 CONTACT BREAKERS
	Ref. No.	257 CANCELS NIL
	AUTHORITY	F.K.M. INSERT THIS BULLETIN INTO:- MANUALS No. 1, 2, and 3
	DATE OF ISSUE	15-2-57

The sketches show that this style of contact breaker has been fitted with rocker arms which differ from each other in the angle and style of the heel or shoe.

Also given below is a list of the models of engine, etc., with the appropriate contact breaker.

For the sake of clarity, only the rocker arm is shown.

No. 1

BRITISH SALMSON	CYCLAID
B.S.A.	DANDY (Before 6.12.56—up to Serial DSE 1307)
B.S.A.	WINGED WHEEL
CYCLEMASTER	CYCLEMASTER
CYCLEMASTER	CYCLEMATE
CYCLEMASTER	PIATTI
J.A.P.	J.A.P. MODEL 0
J.A.P.	J.A.P. MODEL 80
MERCURY	MERCETTE
PLUVIER-LUTERPRO	BERINI
P.P. ENGINEERING CO.	POWER PAK
TEAGLE ENGINEERING	TEAGLE

No. 2

ARIEL	COLT L.H.
B.S.A.	C.10L
FRANCIS BARNETT	CRUISER 80
JAMES	COMMODORE

No. 3

B.S.A.	DANDY (After 6.12.56 from Serial DSE 1308)

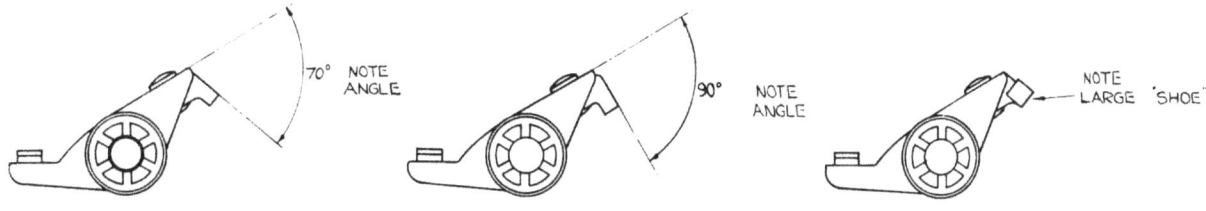

No. 1
Complete Breaker
Part No. 00695

No. 2
Complete Breaker
Part No. 01823

No. 3
Complete Breaker
Part No. S0275

THE WIPAC GROUP — BUCKINGHAM — BUCKS
TELEPHONE: BUCKINGHAM 2140   TELEGRAMS: WIPACITY · BUCKINGHAM

SERVICE WIPAC BULLETIN	SUBJECT	**CONDENSER CHANGE** on Ignition units Series 141 as fitted to **B.S.A., DANDY AND PIATTI SCOOTERS**	
	Ref. No.	1501/258	CANCELS
	AUTHORITY	F.K.M.	INSERT THIS BULLETIN INTO :-
	DATE OF ISSUE	FEB. 1958	No. 3

The original Condenser had the fixing bracket level with the "lead" end of the Condenser barrel. It was fitted in an upright position and so the lead to the contact block was _over_ the core stampings.

In order to give protection to the Condenser lead, it now passes _under_ the core stampings and so requires a Condenser with the bracket attached about two-thirds of the barrel length from the "lead" end, and affixed in the inverted position. See sketches.

Both types of Condenser are under the same part No. S0051.

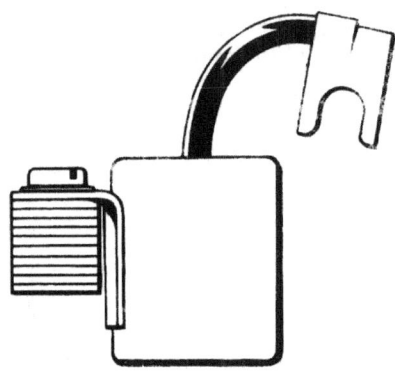   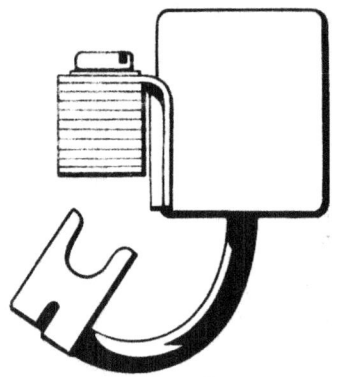

Early Type   *Late Type*

THE WIPAC GROUP — BUCKINGHAM — BUCKS
TELEPHONE: BUCKINGHAM 2140   TELEGRAMS: WIPACITY · BUCKINGHAM

SERVICE WIPAC BULLETIN	SUBJECT	SERIES 90 FLYWHEELS "MAGNETISM"		
	Ref. No.	90/858	CANCELS	NIL
	AUTHORITY	FKM	INSERT THIS BULLETIN INTO :-	MANUALS Nos. 1 & 3
	DATE OF ISSUE	AUGUST 1958		

SERIES 90 FLYWHEELS — MAGNETISM

A number of the above flywheels used on magnetos for lawn mowers etc., are returned to us under complaint as "having lost magnetism".

Where a small flywheel magneto has no LIGHTING coils, only ONE magnet is used, giving two poles magnetised and FOUR "dead".

The lighting models have THREE magnets, giving all six poles magnetised.

A steel rule or screw driver blade test will indicate the difference.

THE WIPAC GROUP — BUCKINGHAM BUCKS — ENGLAND
TELEPHONE: BUCKINGHAM 3031   TELEGRAMS: WICOMAGSCO · BUCKINGHAM

SERVICE WIPAC BULLETIN

SUBJECT	MOTOR CYCLE HEADLAMP SWITCHES		
Ref. No.	HL/659	CANCELS	NIL
AUTHORITY	FKM	INSERT THIS BULLETIN INTO :-	3
DATE OF ISSUE	1.6.59		

The 1959 design switch is an improvement upon earlier types as follows:—

1. Larger and more easily handled operating lever.

2. Stronger and more definite " clicks ".

3. Better contact between pins and sockets by using FLAT instead of ROUND male contact pins.

    Note: Flat pins fit old and new type rubber sockets.

4. One hole simplified fastening in lamp body.

5. The new 1959 switch as a complete unit with operating knob or lever is INTERCHANGEABLE with the earlier types.

It should be noted that whereas in the earlier switches the lever was turned to align with the appropriate letters on the FIXED escutcheon plate—in the later style switch the letters are on the escutcheon plate which ROTATES with the lever. Therefore, the switch lever should be moved so that the appropriate letter FACES STRAIGHT AHEAD.* When the lever itself is straight ahead the switch is OFF.

SWITCH MARKINGS

	Action	Old Type	New Type
3 Position Types	Head	H	H
	Off	Off	*
	Low	L	L
	Ignition	Ign.	I
	Off	Off	*
	Emergency	Emg.	E
	Action	*Old Type*	*New Type*
	Engine Cut-out	C.O.	E
	Off	Off	*
	Low	L	L
4 Position Types	Head	H	H
	Park	P	P
	Off	Off	*
	Low	L	L
	Head	H	H

Note: The 3 and 4 position switches are NOT interchangeable with each other.

THE WIPAC GROUP — BUCKINGHAM — BUCKS
TELEPHONE: BUCKINGHAM 2140   TELEGRAMS: WIPACITY · BUCKINGHAM

SERVICE WIPAC BULLETIN	SUBJECT	CORRECT TIMING FOR AN ALTERNATOR UNIT		
	Ref. No.	AMC 6/59	CANCELS	Nil
	AUTHORITY	E.G.W.	INSERT THIS BULLETIN INTO :-	No. 3 Manual
	DATE OF ISSUE	1.7.59		

Some users of the A.J.S., model 14CS, and Matchless, model G2CS, fitted with A.C. Ignition have experienced difficult starting and, where we have been able to investigate, we found the main cause to be due to the timing of the engine in relation to the magnetic timing of the alternator.

An explanation of the ignition system would, we feel, help the user to make satisfactory adjustments to the machine.

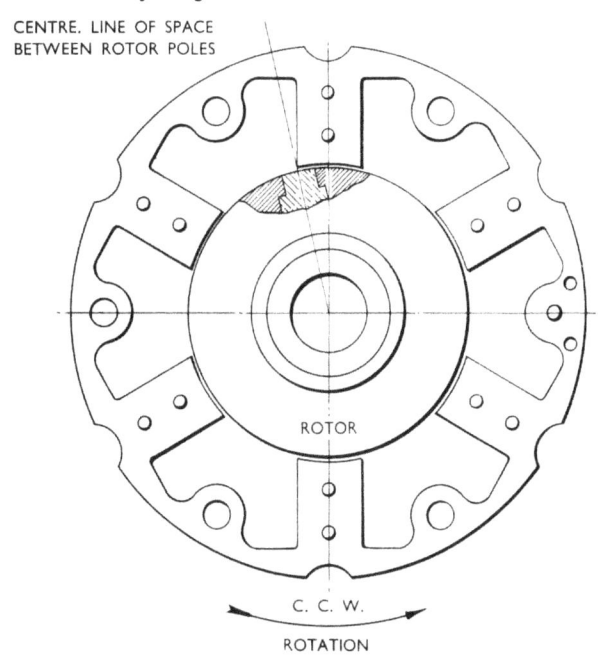

The sketch illustrates the correct position of rotor pole in relation to stator pole when contacts are just opening.

The system uses an alternator which consists of a magnetic six pole rotor rotating inside a six pole stator. On this stator there are four coils, two of which are used for direct A.C. lighting, one coil is for supplying a small charge, via the rectifier, to the battery, the fourth coil supplies the A.C. Ignition Coil.

The energy for the Ignition Coil is produced in peaks, that is the current varies from negative through zero to positive and the contacts of the breaker unit must open at the peak of either positive or negative. As the duration of the peak period is only a few degrees the Engine Manufacturer's timing of 32° B.T.D.C. must be strictly adhered to—this means that the contact breaker setting should be .018" when the points are fully open and just opening when the piston is 32° B.T.D.C. It would be possible to start and run the engine with the contact opening at 28° B.T.D.C., but at 35° B.T.D.C. bad starting and erratic running would be experienced.

THE WIPAC GROUP — BUCKINGHAM — BUCKS
TELEPHONE: BUCKINGHAM 2140   TELEGRAMS: WIPACITY · BUCKINGHAM

SERVICE WIPAC BULLETIN	SUBJECT	RECTIFIER REPLACEMENT		
	Ref. No.	5255T/2	CANCELS	5255 and 5255T
	AUTHORITY	F.B.	INSERT THIS BULLETIN INTO :-	No. 3 Manual
	DATE OF ISSUE	April 1962		

The latest type SQUARE rectifier type W.2 supersedes the well-known "Pancake" type W.1, and besides being a direct replacement for W.1 can also be used to replace types S.1 and S.2.

RECTIFIER DEFINITIONS:

S.1	THIN "FINNED" TYPE, NEGATIVE EARTH. 1st type to be used with WIPAC equipment.
S.2	THICK "FINNED" TYPE. POSITIVE EARTH.
W.1	"PANCAKE" TYPE. POSITIVE EARTH.
W.2	"SQUARE" TYPE. POSITIVE EARTH.

REPLACING S.1 RECTIFIER WITH W.2

(A) Connect both A.C. leads and the D.C. lead according to the colour code as shown in the diagrams.

(B) Reverse the battery leads, *i.e.* connect the positive to earth instead of negative to earth, as W.2 is positive to earth as against the S.1 negative earth.

REPLACING S.2 WITH W.2

Connect A.C. leads and the D.C. lead according to the colour coding.

REPLACING W.1 WITH W.2

Type W.2 is a direct replacement and no difficulty should be experienced. Connect up in accordance with colour coding as previously used with W.1.

CAUTION:

The centre fixing bolt is an earth connection therefore a clean and efficient electrical contact must be maintained to the motorcycle frame at all times.

FOR FULL RECTIFIER TESTING INSTRUCTIONS SEE TECHNICAL DATA SHEET REF. No. T.D.4

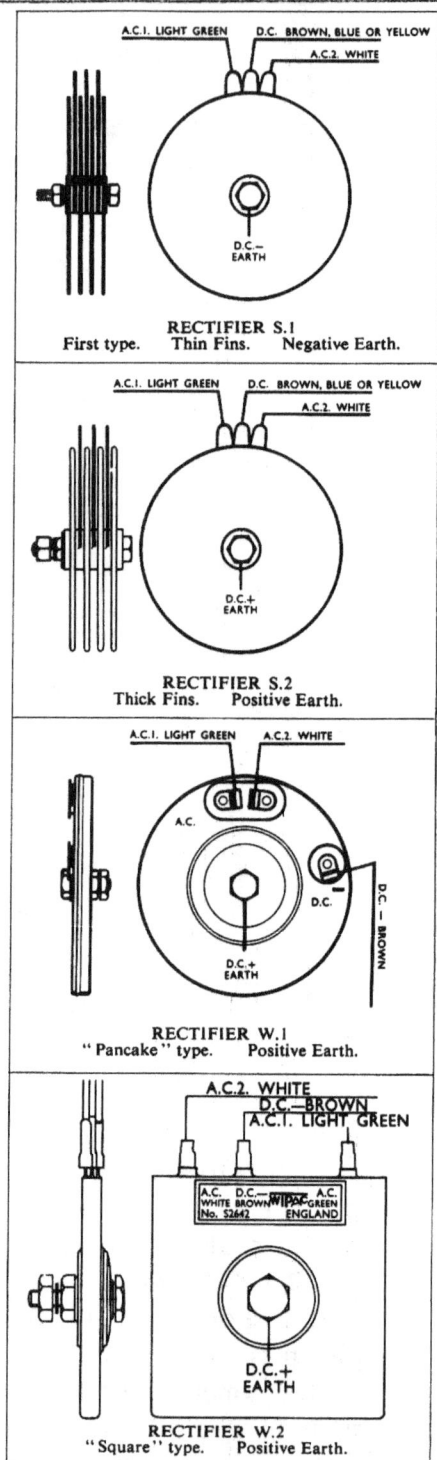

RECTIFIER S.1
First type. Thin Fins. Negative Earth.

RECTIFIER S.2
Thick Fins. Positive Earth.

RECTIFIER W.1
"Pancake" type. Positive Earth.

RECTIFIER W.2
"Square" type. Positive Earth.

THE WIPAC GROUP — BUCKINGHAM BUCKS — ENGLAND
TELEPHONE: BUCKINGHAM 3031   TELEGRAMS: WICOMAGSCO · BUCKINGHAM

SERVICE WIPAC BULLETIN	SUBJECT	**RECTIFIER REPLACEMENT ON FRANCIS & BARNETT CRUISER 80 AND FALCON 87 MODELS.**		
	Ref. No.	R11/62CF	CANCELS	NIL.
	AUTHORITY	FB.	INSERT THIS BULLETIN INTO :-	**No. 3 MANUAL**
	DATE OF ISSUE	JAN. 1963		

Whereas it was previously considered that the fitting of the new square type Rectifier (part number S2642) as a replacement for the original round type (part number S2153) was not a practical proposition due to the size of the captive mounting stud on the Francis & Barnett Cruiser 80 and Falcon 87 Models, subsequent investigation has revealed that by adopting the following procedure the substitution can be easily made.

WARNING

Before attempting to work on the rectifier, it is essential that the battery is disconnected to avoid accidental short circuit.

CRUISER " 80 " MODEL

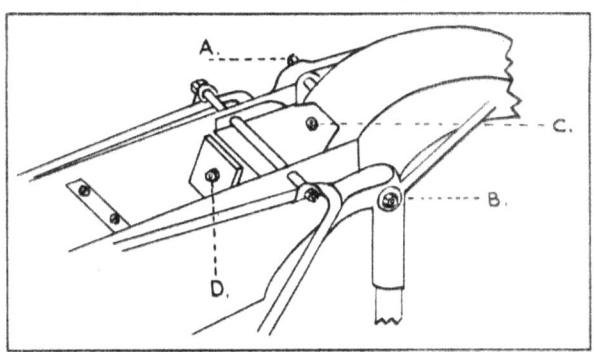

(1) Take off the dual seat in the normal manner to expose the Rectifier. Unplug the brown, green and white leads from the Rectifier sockets and remove Rectifier by unfastening the centre retaining nut ' D '. (See diagram.)

(2) Withdraw the rear suspension securing bolts ' A ' and ' B ' (the nuts are already loosened on removal of dual seat), and $\frac{1}{4}$" nut and bolt ' C '.

The rear mudguard can now be lowered, enabling $\frac{5}{16}$" Rectifier bolt to be removed.

The S2642 square Rectifier can now be bolted in place using the nut, bolt and washer set provided with the replacement unit.

FALCON " 87 " MODEL

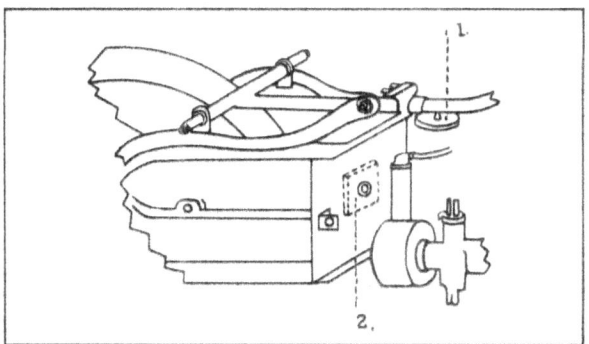

First remove the offside body panels in the normal manner to expose the Rectifier, which can then be disconnected and removed. The later type square Rectifier must now be mounted on the vertical panel to the rear of the carburettor, as illustrated in the diagram, position 2.

This will necessitate drilling a $\frac{1}{4}$" clearance hole 3" from the top of the panel and $5\frac{3}{4}$" from the offside edge. The Rectifier should be bolted into this position using the nut, bolt and washer set provided with the replacement Rectifier, and do not forget to ensure that the earth tag (translucent lead) is secured by the Rectifier fixing bolt.

NOTE

REMEMBER THAT THE RECTIFIER FIXING BOLT IS POSITIVE EARTH RETURN AND IT IS MOST IMPORTANT THAT A CLEAN AND EFFICIENT ELECTRICAL CONTACT BE MAINTAINED TO THE CYCLE FRAME.

THE WIPAC GROUP — BUCKINGHAM BUCKS — ENGLAND
TELEPHONE: BUCKINGHAM 3031   TELEGRAMS: WICOMAGSCO · BUCKINGHAM

SERVICE WIPAC BULLETIN

SUBJECT	ARIEL COLT LH & B.S.A. C10L PRIOR TO SEPTEMBER, 1955. HEADLAMP BODY, SWITCH & HARNESS REPLACEMENT.		
Ref. No.	R3/63/AB	CANCELS	NIL
AUTHORITY	F.B.	INSERT THIS BULLETIN INTO :-	No. 3
DATE OF ISSUE	MARCH 1963		MANUALS

As from the 1st January, 1963, the Headlamp Body and double tier switch with Harness Group as used prior to September, 1955 is obsoleted, and therefore is no longer available.

The current twin switch system is available for replacement purposes.

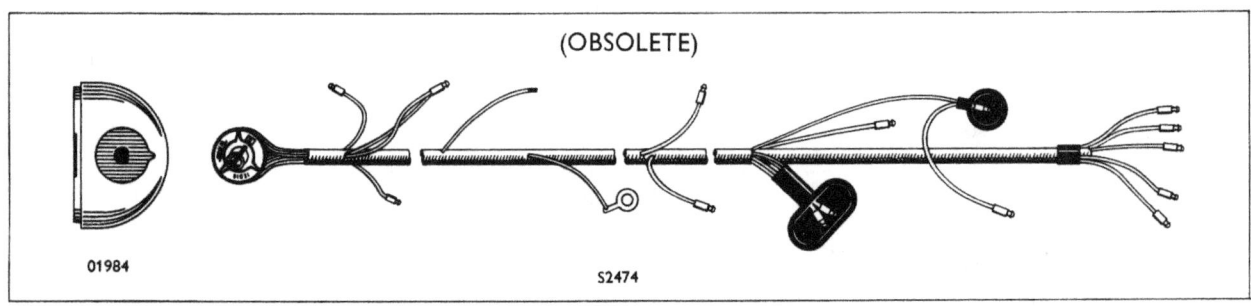

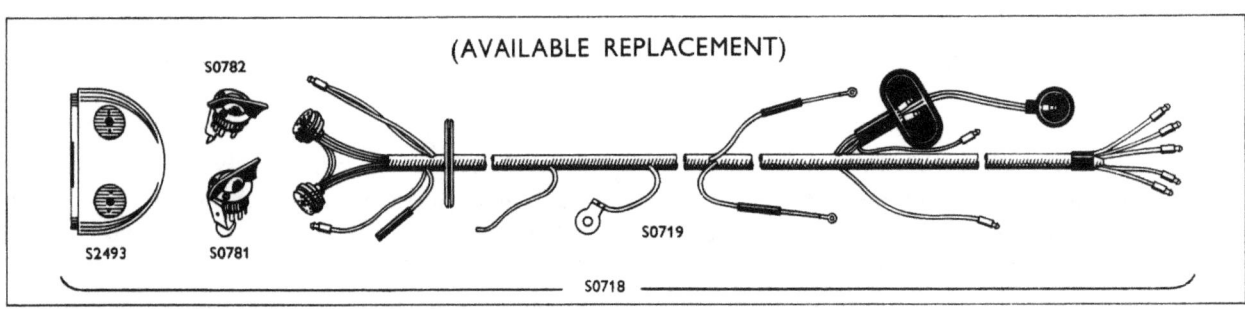

Due to the obsolescence of the original parts, when any one item becomes in need of replacement, for example, Switch and Harness Group (S.2474) it will be necessary to fit the complete Kit S.0718 which consists of :—

        Plug and Harness Group — S.0719
        Ignition Switch — S.0782
        Lighting Switch — S.0781
        Headlamp Body — S.2493

The original rim, reflector and glass set may be used.
For Wiring Diagram, Reference No. WD/49/916 — See Overleaf.

THE WIPAC GROUP — BUCKINGHAM — BUCKS
TELEPHONE: BUCKINGHAM 2140   TELEGRAMS: WIPACITY · BUCKINGHAM

SERVICE WIPAC BULLETIN

SUBJECT	CONTACT BREAKER POINT SETTINGS		
Ref. No.	IGN/160/2	CANCELS	IGN/160
AUTHORITY	F.B.	INSERT THIS BULLETIN INTO :-	No. 3 Manual
DATE OF ISSUE	April 1963		

This table of contact gap settings given below forms a handy reference for most WIPAC equipment. It is MOST IMPORTANT that the gap distances are set as accurately as possible, as even slight variations can seriously affect engine performance.

If the gap is too small, difficulty will be experienced in starting. If too wide, misfiring may occur at the higher engine r.p.m.

Gap	Models
0.012"/0.013"	AJS—Models 8 and 14 Ariel—Colt and Pixie BSA—C10L and Beagle Francis Barnett—Cruiser 80 and 84, Falcon 87 James—Commodore and Captain Matchless—Models G2 and G5 Norton—Jubilee, Navigator and Electra RCA Engines (2 cyl. 350 cc.)
0.015"	British Anzani Unitwin Engine using '73' series Magneto Brockhouse—Corgi BSA Bantam—all Models Caterpillar Starting Engines (CB Magneto) Excelsior—Talisman Twin, Courier and Monarch Scooter Petter PAV4 Industrial Royal Enfield—RE 150 Scott—Autocycle Types 'A' and 'CJ' for Industrial Engines Winconsin V4 Industrial
0.018"	AJS—Model 14CS Trials and Scrambler (to April 1960) BSA—Dandy, Sunbeam Scooter and Winged Wheel EMI—Cyclemaster, Cyclemate Francis Barnett—Trials 83 and Scrambler 82, Plover and Fulmar James—Commando and Cotswold, Flying Cadet, M15 and 150 c.c. Scooter Matchless—G2CS Trials and Scrambler (to April 1960) Piatti Pitcher—Power Pack Pluvier—Berini Triumph—Tina and Tigress
0.020"	FW Series, Industrial Flywheel Magnetos Excelsior Autobyk

NOTE: When adjusting contacts, **NEVER** bend the fixed contact plate or rocker arm to achieve the correct gap. When renewing, ALWAYS replace both fixed and moving contacts.

THE WIPAC GROUP — BUCKINGHAM BUCKS — ENGLAND
TELEPHONE: BUCKINGHAM 3031   TELEGRAMS: WICOMAGSCO · BUCKINGHAM

SERVICE WIPAC BULLETIN

SUBJECT	SERIES 55. IGNITION GENERATOR. STATOR PLATE CASTING SETS.		
Ref. No.	55/357/1	CANCELS	55/357
AUTHORITY	W.R.F.	INSERT THIS BULLETIN INTO :-	MANUAL No. 3
DATE OF ISSUE	SEPT. 1963		

From March 1957 we shall for the purpose of stock simplification supply only one type of STATOR PLATE CASTING SET (Part No. S1225), which has FOUR terminals, as shown in styles B and C below.

Style	Types	Identification and Dates	Style	Types	Identification and Dates
A	FW1005 IG1005 IG1156 IG1133	1 Terminal 2 L.T. Coils Nov. 49 to May 51	E	IG1454 IG1450	3 Terminals 3 L.T. Coils Sep. 55 to date
B	IG1130 (AC) IG1118 IG1179 (AC)	4 Terminals 3 L.T. Coils June 51 to Aug. 55	F	IG1704 (Coil Ignition)	4 Terminals 3 L.T. Coils Oct. 63
C	IG1130 (DC) IG1179 (DC)	4 Terminals 3 L.T. Coils June 51 to Aug. 55			
D	IG1452	2 Terminals 2 L.T. Coils Sep. 55 to date	G	IG1552	4 Terminals 3 L.T. Coils June 59

If required to replace				A.C. or D.C.	Style of Original plate	Action to be taken
B.S.A. BANTAM	...	...	...	FW1005	A.C.	A*	Connect as style A.
B.S.A. BANTAM	...	...	...	IG1005	A.C.	A*	Connect as style A.
BROCKHOUSE CORGI (Mk. 1 & 2)			IG1156	A.C.	A*	Connect as style A.
SCOTT AUTOCYCLE	...	...		IG1133	A.C.	A*	Connect as style A.
B.S.A. BANTAM	...	...	...	IG1130	A.C.	B	Connect as style B. Earth link used.
B.S.A. BANTAM	...	...	...	IG1130	D.C.	C	Connect as style C.
ROYAL ENFIELD R.E.	...	...		IG1118	A.C.	B	Connect as style B. Earth link used.
BROCKHOUSE CORGI (Mk. 4)	...		IG1179	A.C.	B	Connect as style B. Earth link used.
BROCKHOUSE CORGI (Mk. 4)	...		IG1179	D.C.	C	Connect as style C.
B.S.A. BANTAM	...	...	...	IG1452	A.C.	D	Connect as style D, but transfer White wire to terminal 2—Earth.
B.S.A. BANTAM	...	...	...	IG1454 IG1450	D.C.	E	Connect as style C.
B.S.A. BANTAM (D7)	...	...		IG1552	A.C./D.C.	F	Connect as style F.
B.S.A. BANTAM	...	...	...	IG1704	A.C. Lights Coil Ignition	G	Connect as style G.

* These models use the Flywheel with 1 strong and 2 medium magnets. All others use Wheels with 3 strong magnets. A Pull test with screwdriver blade or steel rule will establish the difference.

THE WIPAC GROUP — BUCKINGHAM BUCKS — ENGLAND
TELEPHONE: BUCKINGHAM 3031   TELEGRAMS: WICOMAGSCO · BUCKINGHAM

SERVICE WIPAC BULLETIN	SUBJECT	Adjustment and maintenance of Clear Hooter Alpine and Torino Horns Models HF900 & F725.		
	Ref. No.	1263/CH	CANCELS	Nil
	AUTHORITY	F.B.	INSERT THIS BULLETIN INTO :-	No. 3 Manual
	DATE OF ISSUE	Jan. 1964		

MAINTENANCE & ADJUSTMENT

There are two coils in each horn which operate the diaphragm on the vibrator principle.

MAINTENANCE: Maintenance is restricted to keeping the terminals and the surrounding areas clean.

ADJUSTMENT: The tonal quality and current consumption are accurately adjusted during manufacture. Under normal conditions factory setting, which may be reset by means of a small screw, should not require further attention. In the event of the horn failing to function satisfactorily, the fault may be diagnosed and rectified as follows:—

1. **Loss of Volume of Sound.**

    This condition is due to insufficient current being drawn by the horn.

    Turn the adjusting screw clockwise until the volume of sound is restored to normal. Then turn the screw counter-clockwise as far as possible without loss of sound. Under no circumstances should $3\frac{1}{2}$ amperes be exceeded for 12 volt and $5\frac{1}{2}$ amperes at 6 volt.

2. **Erratic or Intermittent Operation.**

    Erratic or intermittent operation is caused by slight maladjustment of the diaphragm or foreign matter between contact points.

    Turn the adjusting screw clockwise for approximately half a turn. If this fails, turn the screw counter-clockwise until the horn operates at the correct note, which should be within 180 degrees either side of the original setting.

3. **Complete Failure of Sound.**

    In the case of a complete failure of sound, an examination of the connecting cables must be made to ensure that the correct voltage is available at the terminals of the horn.

    (a) If the horn has been losing volume, or some deterioration of tone detected, and then fails, the procedure outlined above in 1—" Loss of Volume of Sound " should be followed.

    (b) If the horn has been functioning satisfactorily and suddenly fails, check the current flowing in the circuit. If this is in excess of $3\frac{1}{2}$ amperes for 12 volt or $5\frac{1}{2}$ amperes for 6 volt, then turning of the screw in a counter-clockwise direction should bring the horn into operation. Conversely, if insufficient current is flowing, then turning the screw clockwise should restore the note.

    The horn may be dismantled for examination of the internal connections and contacts only. Attempts to renew individual coils are neither practical nor economic.

    It is essential that the Horn is fitted to a solid member of the vehicle, and in such a position as the cables from the battery are as short as possible, to eliminate any possible voltage drop.

    When carrying out adjustment for tone, ensure that the horn is mounted either on the vehicle or in such as a vice.

THE WIPAC GROUP — BUCKINGHAM BUCKS — ENGLAND
TELEPHONE: BUCKINGHAM 3031   TELEGRAMS: WICOMAGSCO · BUCKINGHAM

SERVICE WIPAC BULLETIN	SUBJECT	\multicolumn{3}{c}{BATTERY CHARGE RATE B.S.A. MODEL D.7 COIL IGNITION.}
	Ref. No.	R4/65D.7	CANCELS	Nil
	AUTHORITY	F.B.	INSERT THIS BULLETIN INTO :-	NO. 3. MANUAL
	DATE OF ISSUE	MAY 1965		

CASES HAVE BEEN REPORTED WHERE RIDERS HAVE EXPERIENCED DIFFICULTY IN MAINTAINING THEIR BATTERIES IN A CHARGED CONDITION, ESPECIALLY WHEN A GREAT DEAL OF TOWN RIDING AND SLOW RUNNING IS COVERED.

TO OVERCOME THIS CONDITION, AN ALTERNATIVE CONTACT BREAKER CAM HAS BEEN INTRODUCED TO REVISE THE DISTRIBUTION OF GENERATED CURRENT AND PROVIDE A HIGHER CHARGE RATE, PARTICULARLY AT LOW SPEEDS.

IDENTIFICATION.

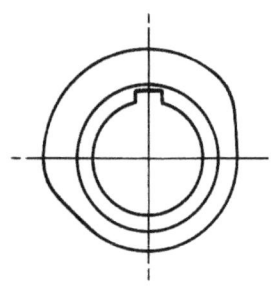   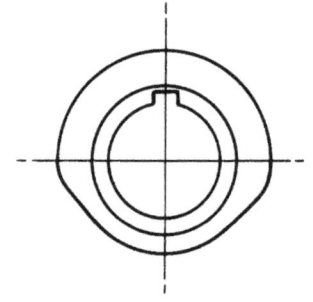

S.1243   S.3794
Original Cam.   New Cam.

THE CAM PART NUMBER S.3794 HAS BEEN FITTED TO ALL D.7 COIL IGNITION BANTAMS SINCE ENGINE NUMBER FD7/5044 AND MUST ONLY BE FITTED TO GENERATORS SPECIFICATION NUMBER IG.1704.

THE WIPAC GROUP — BUCKINGHAM BUCKS — ENGLAND
TELEPHONE: BUCKINGHAM 3031   TELEGRAMS: WICOMAGSCO · BUCKINGHAM

SERVICE WIPAC BULLETIN

SUBJECT	Rectifier Fitting B.S.A. Model D.7 Bantam.		
Ref. No.	C 166./B	CANCELS	Nil
AUTHORITY	F.B.	INSERT THIS BULLETIN INTO :-	No. 3 MANUAL
DATE OF ISSUE	Feb. 1966		

When fitting the small square rectifier, Wipac Part No. S.1044, currently in use on the B.S.A. BANTAM MODEL D.7., it is essential that it is installed with the heat sink section against the frame, otherwise the unit will overheat and its life will be seriously shortened.

When viewing the rectifier, it will be noticed that one side is marked MC.26. <u>The unmarked side is the heat sink.</u> This means that when the rectifier is assembled on the machine, the MC.26 marking will be visible and next to the head of the fixing bolt.

All machines in stock, or recently delivered, should be checked and if necessary the rectifier refitted correctly, otherwise the component can become damaged and the charge to the Battery will fail.

THE WIPAC GROUP — BUCKINGHAM BUCKS — ENGLAND
TELEPHONE: BUCKINGHAM 3031   TELEGRAMS: WICOMAGSCO · BUCKINGHAM

SERVICE WIPAC BULLETIN

SUBJECT	Stop/Tail Lamp Bulb Change. B.S.A. D.7 Bantam - Coil Ignition, Trickle Charge.		
Ref. No.	R. 266/B	CANCELS	NIL
AUTHORITY	F.B.	INSERT THIS BULLETIN INTO :-	No. 3 MANUAL
DATE OF ISSUE	March 66.		

Cases have been reported of prematurely exhausted batteries on the D.7 Coil Ignition Super Bantam, due to heavy use of the Stop Light.

Investigation has shown that this situation arises mainly with Town dwellers and where the machine is used generally for Town work requiring frequent and prolonged use of the rear brake, coupled with very little mileage at usual speeds on the open road.

To overcome this condition, the Stop/Tail lamp has now been fitted with a 6v. 6w/3w. bulb as against the original 6v. 18w/3w. bulb.

THE WIPAC GROUP — BUCKINGHAM BUCKS — ENGLAND
TELEPHONE: BUCKINGHAM 3031   TELEGRAMS: WICOMAGSCO · BUCKINGHAM

B.S.A. SUNBEAM B1
AND
TRIUMPH TIGRESS T.S.1. 175 c.c.
SINGLE CYLINDER TWO-STROKE SCOOTERS
PRODUCED FROM OCT. 58.

ELECTRICAL EQUIPMENT TRICKLE CHARGE SYSTEM

General Description

The ignition and lighting equipment is fed from an ignition generator, the finned magnetic flywheel of which also provides a strong air blast for engine cooling. The generator stator assembly has mounted on its various core legs a high tension transformer coil for ignition, working in conjunction with the condenser and contact breaker points, and two twin coils for lighting and charging. The twin coils are wound with inner and outer elements using the same single core leg in each case.

The two outer coils are connected in series with one end earthed to provide A.C. current for the main headlamp bulb, *so there is no headlight unless the engine is running*. The two inner coils are in series and connected via the rectifier and the switch to the battery and so provide a trickle charge current with the lamp switch in all positions.

Charge rate regulation is achieved by the insertion in the circuit of a series resister in the 'off' and 'low' positions. The resister is cut out in the headlamp position in order to compensate for the dropping of output when the headlamp feed coils are in circuit using the same core legs. The resister is embodied inside the main wiring loom and is, therefore, not visible as a separate unit. Charge current is also provided in the head position and the charge rate values in all switch positions are approximately:—

Lights 'off' position	..	0.5 Amperes
Lights Pilot position	..	Balanced
Lights Head position	..	0.25 Amperes

These figures should be checked at approximately 3,000 r.p.m. and are minimum permissible readings. Charge rates will, of course, vary with engine speed, and the state of charge and condition of the battery, but the above figures will give a fair indication as to the correct functioning of the trickle charge circuit. The trickle charge system provides battery current to operate parking lights, stop lights and a D.C. type horn.

The headlamp has a reflector with an extremely efficient reflecting surface provided by vacuum electronic deposition of aluminium. This reflecting surface should not be touched or cleaned in any way, and will retain its brilliance indefinitely. The bulb is a pre-focus twin filament type giving correct beam, length and spread in head and dip positions.

The main connections in the Wipac system are made by rubber socket connectors to the lights and ignition switches, and also by individual rubber covered bullet type push-in connectors which are handy for wiring checks or the re-installation of new wiring. These connectors are not intended as plugs and sockets for frequent manipulation, and are only used when testing or fault finding, and it is extremely important that they should all be making perfect contact, as should all other connection points throughout the system.

The correct bulb ratings for use in this system are:—

Headlamp	.. ..	6v. 24/24w.
Pilot Lamp	.. ..	6v. 1.8w.
Speedometer Lamp	..	6v. 1.8w.
Rear Lamp	.. ..	6v. 3w.
Stop Lamp	.. ..	Twin 6v. 6w.

TESTING INSTRUCTIONS

Equipment Required

The accurate testing of the equipment can be achieved with the aid of an instrument such as the Wilkson Test Set or, in fact, any other good quality moving coil instrument used in conjunction with a 1 Ohm resistive load. Failing the availability of such an instrument, a fair indication can be obtained by the use of:—

1. A 6v. 36w. bulb with holder and two test wires about 24" long.
2. A well charged 6 volt battery.
3. A 6v. 6w. bulb with holder and two test wires about 24" long.

Charge Rate Testing

The good quality moving coil D.C. Ammeter is connected in series with the battery. This is easily done by disconnecting the brown negative lead from the battery and connecting the instrument in series in the gap. These Ammeter readings should then compare favourably with the figures indicated in the General Description.

Generator Output Testing

1. Before attempting to carry out any test to determine the generator output, it is essential that the red, orange and green generator leads are disconnected from the circuit at the four-way connector situated close by the rectifier.

THE WIPAC GROUP — BUCKINGHAM — BUCKS.
TELEPHONE: BUCKINGHAM 3031   TELEGRAMS: WICOMAGSCO BUCKINGHAM

REF. TD.1/1/2

WIPAC TECHNICAL DATA (CONTINUED)

2. The direct A.C. head lights are supplied between the red wire and earth.

    (a) At 3,000 r.p.m. 6 volts should be obtained on an A.C. volt meter with a 1 Ohm load paralleled across it.

    (b) At 3,000 r.p.m. a good light should be obtained from a 6v. 36w. bulb connected between the red wire and earth.

3. The battery is fed via the rectifier and from the white and orange wires. These wires should at all times be insulated from earth. This may be checked by the use of a simple continuity test circuit made up from the battery and the 6v. 6w. bulb.

    (a) The A.C. output of the charging coils at 3,000 r.p.m. should be 5½ volts on the A.C. volt meter with a 1 Ohm load paralleled across it.

    (b) A reasonably good light should be obtained from a 6v. 36w. bulb connected between the orange and white leads.

Rectifier Testing (Small Full-wave Rectifier—Part No. S.1044)

First, disconnect the rectifier from the circuit by unplugging the white, brown and orange leads from the four-way connector. Next, arrange a simple series circuit with the 6v. 6w. bulb and 6v. battery so that when the circuit is completed the bulb will light. Now break the circuit at any point and connect the NEGATIVE lead to the earth bolt of the rectifier. Then connect the POSITIVE lead to the orange, brown and white leads in turn. A good light should be obtained in each case. This completes the forward flow testing.

The POSITIVE lead should now be connected to the earth bolt, and the NEGATIVE lead connected in turn to the orange, brown and white leads. There should be no light in each case. Any contra indications to the bulb lighting is indicative of a faulty rectifier.

N.B. **THE BATTERY MUST NEVER BE CONNECTED NEGATIVE TO EARTH (TRANSLUCENT LEAD) AS THIS CONDITION WILL INVARIABLY BURN OUT THE RECTIFIER. THE RECTIFIER WILL ALSO SUFFER DAMAGE IF THE ENGINE IS RUN WITHOUT THE BATTERY IN CIRCUIT.**

Premature Bulb Failure

The current feeding the bulbs when the lighting switch is in the headlamp position is A.C. working, **and the bulb loading under these conditions is of the utmost importance.** To ensure that the rearlamps do not blow and consequently overload the headlamp unit, a carry-over type of dip switch is used. This means that during the changeover from head to dip and vice versa both headlamp filaments are lit, thus ensuring that the heavy bulb loading is not transferred to the small tail light bulb, which would result in its failure. Firstly then, check that the dipper switch is functioning correctly, and secondly check that all bulb holder contact spring tensions are satisfactory, as intermittent open circuiting of the bulbs could again lead to circuit overload. Where premature bulb failure does take place, on no account be tempted to use 12 volt bulbs, as this would only aggravate the complaint.

A further point to check is the correct installation of the rectifier and battery. If, whilst the engine is running, the lights are switched on with the rectifier not in circuit or the battery disconnected, then the A.C. voltage will rapidly rise and the bulbs will blow. The A.C. voltage measured on a good quality moving coil meter with the lights switched on should not exceed 8.2 volts at 6,000 r.p.m.

REF. TD.1/2/2

WIPAC TECHNICAL DATA

ALTERNATOR ELECTRICAL EQUIPMENT
(WIPAC SERIES 114)
AS FITTED TO STANDARD ROAD MACHINES
FROM AUGUST 1955

General Description

The lighting and ignition system of Wipac Alternator equipped motor cycles consists of a simple six pole Alternator generating set which supplies current through a metal plate rectifier to the battery, which then feeds the ignition system, lights, horns, etc. The Alternator ring carries six coils which are connected in two sets of three in series. By using one set of three shunted via a resister a certain output is obtained for daylight running. When the pilot or parking lights are switched on the resister is disconnected in order to provide a slightly higher charge rate to compensate for the drain of the smaller bulbs. When the headlights are switched on all six coils are connected with the resister still out of circuit, thus giving maximum output, most of which is absorbed by the headlamp bulb, but still leaving a couple of amperes for maintaining the state of charge of the battery.

The alternating current supplied by the generator is converted to direct current by means of the rectifier which is of the very efficient full wave bridge connected type.

The Wipac Alternator equipment provides an emergency starting system which, when the ignition switch is put into the emergency position connects all the six coils together, and provided the lighting switch is in the 'off' position, gives full output in order to rapidly bring up the voltage of a discharged battery and is effective in obtaining an immediate start under these conditions. *The maximum charging current in the emergency position is very high as there is no drain against it by the lighting system, and the engine should not be run in this position for more than 10—15 minutes.* This type of emergency starting being entirely DC enables the machine to be run through the complete operational range of the engine.

The headlamp has a reflector with an extremely efficient reflecting surface provided by vacuum electronic deposition of aluminium. This reflecting surface should not be touched or cleaned in any way and it will retain its brilliance indefinitely. The bulb is a pre-focus twin filament type giving correct beam length and spread in main and dip positions.

The main connections in the Wipac system are made by rubber socket connectors to the lighting and ignition switches and by individual rubber covered bullet type push-in connectors which are handy for wiring checks or the re-installation of new wiring. These connectors are not intended as plugs and sockets for frequent manipulation and are only used when testing or fault finding, and it is extremely important that they should be making perfect contact as should all other connection points throughout the system.

Fault Finding
Equipment required:—
1. Wilkson Test Set.
2. 6v. 3w. bulb with holder and two test leads about 24" long.
3. A well-charged 6 volt battery.

OR

A. A good quality moving coil AC volt meter to be used in conjunction with a one ohm resistive load.
B. 10-0-10 DC Ammeter.
C. 0-12 DC volt meter.
D. 6v. 3w. Bulb with holder and two test leads about 24" long.
E. A well charged 6 volt battery.

Accurate high grade moving coil instruments must be used, and the one ohm resister must also be accurate otherwise correct readings cannot be obtained.

Low or no charge

1. Before commencing any tests check the voltage of the battery and if completely exhausted substitute one which is known to be capable of accepting a charge.
2. Connect in series with the battery, (easily done by disconnecting the brown negative lead from the double connector), the DC Ammeter and check off the charge rates as detailed below:—

Ignition Switch	Lights Switch	Minimum Charge Rate
Ignition	Off	1.0 a.
Ignition	Low	1.3 a.
Ignition	High	1.0 a.
Emergency	Off	6.0 a.

These figures should be checked at approximately 3,000 r.p.m. and are the *minimum* permissible readings. Charge rates will, of course, vary with engine speed, the state of charge and condition of the battery, but the above figures will give a fair indication as to the correct functioning of the system.

N.B.—*It is essential that the correct wattage bulbs be used throughout the lighting system, as any deviation will seriously upset the charge rates. Their values may be obtained from the appropriate wiring diagram or owners handbook.*

If the meter readings are unsatisfactory then

3. Check the alternator output by disconnecting the white, orange and light green leads from the four-way connector. The maroon lead, where fitted, must be left in place in order to run the engine.

THE WIPAC GROUP — BUCKINGHAM — BUCKS.
TELEPHONE: BUCKINGHAM 3031   TELEGRAMS: WICOMAGSCO BUCKINGHAM

REF. TD.3/1/3

WIPAC TECHNICAL DATA (CONTINUED)

Connect one side of the Wilkson Test Meter (AC volts with one ohm load) or the AC volt meter with the one ohm load paralleled across it, to the white lead, and the other side of the meter to the orange and light green leads in turn. With the engine running at a speed comparable to 30 m.p.h. in top gear, the meter should show a reading of 6.2—6.8 volts between white and light green, likewise white and orange. A low reading on one group of coils would indicate coil failure, and a low reading on both groups of coils will in all probability be due to a low flux density in the six pole rotor. No reading from both groups of coils is indicative of complete alternator failure.

N.B.—THE IMPORTANCE OF THE CORRECT BATTERY CONNECTIONS CANNOT BE OVER-EMPHASIZED. THE BATTERY POSITIVE SHOULD ALWAYS BE CONNECTED TO THE TRANSLUCENT LEAD AND BATTERY NEGATIVE TO THE BROWN LEAD. REVERSAL OF THESE CONNECTIONS WILL INVARIABLY BURN OUT THE RECTIFIER, AND IF THE ENGINE IS RUN UNDER THESE CONDITIONS THE MAGNETIC ROTOR WILL BECOME DEMAGNETISED.

4. Yet another cause of low or no charge rate stemming from the alternator is a short circuit to earth.

In order to check this it is essential to construct a very simple continuity check circuit, viz.: a 6 volt battery introduced in series with the DC volt meter will amply suffice for the purpose. Connect one end of the circuit to the white lead (common to all coils) and the other end to the machine frame earth. If a reading is obtained on the volt meter then one or both groups of coils is earthing out.

It is most desirable to carry out this check with both the stator and rotor left in position on the machine, the reason being that in isolated cases careless handling of the stator may have caused one or more of the soldered coil link connections to have become displaced, thus rubbing on the circumference of the rotor, hence shorting out the coils. Therefore, before condemning the alternator it is essential to check that all connections are well clear of the rotor, gently easing back any which look possible causes of future trouble.

This concludes alternator checks, and if the cause of the trouble has been located, revert to table and recheck the charge rates.

Rectifier Testing

Before attempting to carry out any tests on this unit it is essential that the white, green and brown wires are disconnected from the rectifier at the rectifier plug sockets.

Procedure	Battery Connections	Bulb Connections	Conclusions
Rectifier Check Connect a 6 volt battery in series with a 6v. 3w. bulb across the rectifier terminals (See diagram 1)	Positive—Light Green Positive—White Positive—Brown Positive—Brown	Earthed Earthed Green White	Bulb lights Rectifier O.K. Bulb does not light. Rectifier faulty replace.
Reverse battery connections. (See diagram 1)	Negative—Light Green Negative—White Negative—Brown Negative—Brown	Earthed Earthed Green White	Bulb does not light. Rectifier O.K. Bulb lights Rectifier faulty replace.

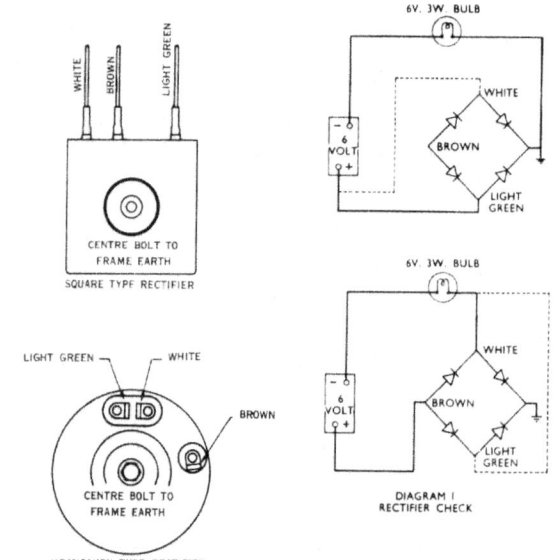

DIAGRAM 1 RECTIFIER CHECK

If it is found necessary to replace this component or to refit a proven good rectifier, ensure that it is rebolted tightly on to a scrupulously clean part of the frame, remembering that the case of the rectifier is DC positive.

The snap connectors should also be a tight fit. Insecurity of any one of the connectors results in arc burning of the terminal, damage internally to the plates and consequential premature rectifier failure.

N.B.—A RAPIDLY FLATTENING BATTERY NECESSITATES AN IMMEDIATE CHECK ON THE RECTIFIER.

Switches

On touring models the two switches are mechanically identical. A faulty switch will invariably give itself away if the procedure outlined below is adopted.

Remove the lamp front and substitute the cable plugs from the ignition switch to the light switch and vice versa. If the switch is faulty then the fault will be transferred from one circuit to the other. Replace the faulty switch with a new one.

Premature Bulb Failure

The premature bulb failure involving all or many of the light bulbs at one time on a full DC battery system is caused by a defective connection in the battery " line ".

REF. TD.3/2/3

WIPAC TECHNICAL DATA (CONTINUED)

This " line starts at—

1. The frame end of the translucent lead from the positive battery terminal and proceeds
2. Positive battery terminal
3. Negative battery terminal
4. Brown wire from battery negative to four-hole connector (bullet terminal)
5. Brown wire from four-hole connector to Ammeter (bullet terminal)
6. Ammeter terminal with brown wire
7. Ammeter terminal with blue wire and
8. Both ends of short insulated link wire in the ignition switch plug which joins blue Ammeter wire to brown wire going to light switch.

It must also be known that should the Ammeter develop an internal open circuit, the bulbs will blow. Also, should the battery have little or no electrolyte, this is partial or complete open circuit with the same results. There is, finally, the remote possibility of one of the actual wires in the battery line being broken. Again bulbs will blow.

No Spark

Check the contact breaker points gap and adjust to the recommended setting where necessary. Check cleanliness of contact faces, these, if in good order should have a light grey frosted appearance. Where fine matter, e.g., oil and grease have been present, the contacts may have a blackened burnt appearance. Should the condition not appear serious, then a light application of fine grade emery cloth will restore them. If in doubt replace the whole breaker group. Check the free action of the breaker arm on the pivot, as any sticking of this arm can cause intermittent difficulty.

N.B.—ON NO ACCOUNT SHOULD THE STAR SHAPED RETAINING WASHER AND THE BREAKER ARM BE REMOVED FROM THE PIVOT AS THE AMOUNT OF END FLOAT IS STRICTLY CONTROLLED, WHICH IS ESSENTIAL TO THE CORRECT FUNCTIONING OF THE CONTACT BREAKERS.

Condensers

Should the capacity be suspect, first check for good contact to earth. Secondly, the condenser may be short circuiting to earth (the battery and bulb is a simple quick test). Third, check by replacement. Visual recognition of a defective condenser or condenser connections is a vivid blue arcing at the contacts.

Circuit Tracing

If the machine is fitted with an Ammeter, switch on the ignition and turn the engine over very slowly, and when the contacts close, a discharge of approximately 3-4 amps should be evident on the Ammeter. Here again, a more accurate measurement can be obtained by putting the DC Ammeter in circuit with the battery.

If the machine is not fitted with an Ammeter then the latter will, of course, be essential. The showing of discharge on the Ammeter is an indication that the current is reaching the contacts by way of the ignition coil primary windings. Should this discharge not show, disconnect the maroon lead from the four-way connector at the alternator and put in series the DC volt meter when a reading should be obtained (one side of the meter being to earth). No reading at this point necessitates a check of the dark green lead to the switch side of the coil.

Remove the terminal from the coil and again connect in the meter as above, where a reading of 6 volts should be obtained providing the battery is well up and the ignition is still switched on. If current is not reaching the coil through the dark green lead, then one must check the ignition plug (black) on the harness.

The wire bridge across two of the terminals inside the plug may be fractured, in which case the engine still starts on either ignition or emergency, but not on both. Provided there is current in the dark green and no current in the maroon lead, then in all probability the primary windings of the ignition coil are defective necessitating coil replacement.

Ignition Coil Check

With the coil out of circuit and the DC volt meter connected up to a battery for continuity check, each end of the circuit across the two terminals should show continuity to prove that the primary winding is intact. Likewise, one lead on to either one of the terminals and the other on to the H.T. Pick-up point will show continuity, but a lower reading on account of the higher resistance in the secondary windings.

Third and last check is to ensure that the coil is not earthing out. To do this leave one lead on one of the terminals and connect the other with the coil case. No readings should show. Similarly with the H.T. Pick-up point.

A defective primary winding may continue to produce a weak spark whereas intermittent performance is invariably caused by a suspect secondary. Should there be any possible doubt about the ignition coil, however, a final check should be made by substitution.

REF. TD.3/3/3

WIPAC TECHNICAL DATA

TESTING RECTIFIERS

TESTING RECTIFIERS

The WIPAC rectifiers illustrated on Service Bulletin 5255T/2 are full-wave bridge-connected types and should be tested for both through flow and reverse flow to determine their correct functioning.

Equipment required:
(1) A good quality moving coil ammeter, Scale 10-0-10.
(2) A well-charged 6-volt BATTERY.
(3) A 6-volt 30-watt BULB.
(4) A 6-volt 0.04-amp BULB.

THROUGH FLOW TEST

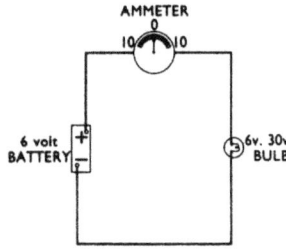

The bulb will light and a reading of approximately 5 amperes will be registered on the meter.

Diagram 'A'

First make up a simple series circuit as shown in diagram 'A'.

To proceed, remove the positive lead from the battery and bridge the gap by connecting the battery positive to the brown (D.C. negative) terminal of the rectifier to be tested, and the ammeter wire to the white and green terminals (A.C. terminals) in turn. In each case the bulb should light and the reading on the ammeter to be in the region of 4.5 amperes. Remove the rectifier and restore the original circuit as diagram 'A'.

Now remove the negative lead from the battery and connect the battery negative to the earth bolt or rectifier case, and connect the bulb lead to each of the A.C. (green and white) terminals in turn. The resultant ammeter readings again should be 4.5 amperes with the bulb alight.

N.B.—The ammeter readings on a brand new rectifier will be approximately 4.5 amperes, but after a period in service the values may fall. Readings above 3 amperes are satisfactory, but below this figure the rectifier should be discarded.

REVERSE FLOW TEST

It is generally assumed that a rectifier is a device which permits a flow of current in one direction but not in the other. The true situation is that a good rectifier will have a reverse flow, but this is very small indeed compared to its forward flow.

WIPAC type rectifiers should not have a reverse flow in excess of 35 milliamps. To check this condition make up a circuit as diagram 'B'.

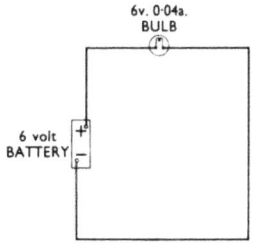

The 6-volt 0.04-amp Bulb has a current consumption of 40 milliamps. When the circuit is completed as shewn the bulb will light.

Diagram 'B'

Proceed by removing the positive lead from the battery and bridge the gap by connecting the battery positive to the rectifier earth bolt or case and the bulb wire to each of the A.C. terminals (green and white) in turn. If the bulb lights in either case the reverse flow is excessive and the rectifier is faulty.

Remove the rectifier and restore the circuit as in diagram 'B'. Disconnect the battery negative and bridge the gap by connecting the battery negative to the D.C. negative (brown) terminal and the bulb lead to each of the A.C. (green and white) terminals in turn. Again, if the bulb lights in either case the unit is defective and the rectifier must be replaced.

THE WIPAC GROUP — BUCKINGHAM — BUCKS.
TELEPHONE: BUCKINGHAM 3031   TELEGRAMS: WICOMAGSCO BUCKINGHAM

WIPAC TECHNICAL DATA

IGNITION GENERATOR AND ALTERNATOR VOLTAGE FIGURES

NOTES: RPM 2/3 and 2/4 refer to the speeds for the readings in Cols. 3 and 4, e.g. RPM 2/3 means from 2,000 to 3,000, RPM 2/4 means from 2,000 to 4,000.

*Disregard fourth (Maroon) wire which is contact breaker feed.

Machine	Details				Col. 1 Readings taken across wire colours.	Col. 2 Value of lamp load or open circuit. See Col. 3	Col. 3 A.C. Volts across lamp load or open circuit. See Col. 2 (Avometer)		Col. 4 A.C. Volts across 1 ohm Resistance. (Wilkson)	
							From	To	From	To
A.J.S. Model 8 & 14		Mk. 4 Alternator	3 wires	RPM 2/3	White/Orange White/Green	Open circ. Open circ.	24·0 24·0	36·0 36·0	6·2 6·2	6·8 6·8
ARIEL Colt LH	Aug. 53 to Aug. 55 Mk. 1 Alternator		4 wires	RPM 2/3	Green/White Orange/Yellow	Open circ. Open circ.	17·0 17·0	26·0 26·0	4·4 6·8	4·8 7·5
ARIEL Colt LH	Sept. 55 to date Mk. 2 Alternator		3 wires	RPM 2/3	White/Orange White/Green	Open circ. Open circ.	18·0 18·0	27·0 27·0	5·7 5·7	6·25 6·25
B.S.A. Bantam	June 50 to July 55 AC/DC IG1130		4 terminals	RPM 2/3	White/Green White/Red	Open circ. Open circ.	14·6 17·0	23·5 25·5	2·8 5·5	3·1 6·1
B.S.A. Bantam	Aug. 55 to date AC IG1452		2 terminals	RPM 2/4	White/Red	28·8 watt	6·3	8·25	5·3	6·4
B.S.A. Bantam	Aug. 55 to date DC IG1454, IG1450		3 terminals	RPM 2/3	White/Green White/Red	Open circ. Open circ.	12·5 13·0	18·25 19·0	4·5 3·5	5·1 4·0
B.S.A. Bantam	Nov. 1958 to date AC/DC IG1552 Trickle Charge		4 terminals	RPM 2/4	Red/Earth White/Orange	28·8 watt Open circ.	5·6 16·5	8·2 32·0	5·3 2·5	7·5 3·4
B.S.A. C.10L	Aug. 53 to Aug. 55 Mk. 1 Alternator		4 wires	RPM 2/3	White/Green Orange/Yellow	Open circ. Open circ.	17·0 17·0	26·0 26·0	4·4 6·8	4·8 7·5
B.S.A. C.10L	Sept. 55 to date Mk. 2 Alternator		3 wires	RPM 2/3	White/Orange White/Green	Open circ. Open circ.	18·0 18·0	27·0 27·0	5·7 5·7	6·25 6·25
B.S.A. Dandy 70	July 56 to date IG1477, IG1493 & IG1501			RPM 2/4	Red/Earth	21 watt	5·2	7·2	3·9	4·6
B.S.A. Sunbeam	AC/DC IG1555			RPM 2/4	Red/Earth Orange/White	28·8 watt Open circ.	5·0 8·8	6·5 17·5	4·9 4·0	6·0 6·0
FRANCIS BARNETT Cruiser 80 & 84	Aug. 56 to date Mk. 4 Alternator		3 wires *	RPM 2/3	White/Orange White/Green	Open circ. Open circ.	24·0 24·0	36·0 36·0	6·2 6·2	6·8 6·8
FRANCIS BARNETT Plover, Fulmar	AC & AC/DC IG1586			RPM 2/4	Red/Earth Orange/White	28·8 watt Open circ.	5·0 8·8	6·5 17·5	4·9 4·0	6·0 6·0
JAMES Commodore 250 Captain 200	Aug. 56 to date Mk. 4 Alternator		3 wires *	RPM 2/3	White/Orange White/Green	Open circ. Open circ.	24·0 24·0	36·0 36·0	6·2 6·2	6·8 6·8
JAMES Flying Cadet, M15 & Pinto	AC & AC/DC IG1586			RPM 2/4	Red/Earth Orange/White	28·8 watt Open circ.	5·0 8·8	6·5 17·5	4·9 4·0	6·0 6·0
JAMES Scooter	AC/DC IG1630			RPM 2/4	Red/Earth Orange/White	28·8 watt Open circ.	5·0 8·8	6·5 17·5	4·9 4·0	6·0 6·0
MATCHLESS Models G2 & G5	Mk. 4 Alternator		3 wires	RPM 2/3	White/Orange White/Green	Open circ. Open circ.	24·0 24·0	36·0 36·0	6·2 6·2	6·8 6·8
NORTON Jubilee & Navigator	Mk. 4 Alternator		3 wires	RPM 2/3	White/Orange White/Green	Open circ. Open circ.	24·0 24·0	36·0 36·0	6·2 6·2	6·8 6·8
PIATTI Scooter	May 56 to date AC IG1467			RPM 2/4	Red/Earth	28·8 watt	5·75	7·8	5·0	6·1
TRIUMPH Tina	AC IG1649			RPM 2/4	Red/Earth	22·8 watt	4·0	5·9	3·75	4·75
TRIUMPH Tigress	AC/DC IG1555			RPM 2/4	Red/Earth Orange/White	28·8 watt Open circ.	5·0 8·8	6·5 17·5	4·9 4·0	6·0 6·0
SERIES 90	7·8 watt			RPM 2/4	Black/Earth	7·8 watt	4·8	7·75	1·75	2·15
SERIES 90	9·0 watt			RPM 2/4	Black/Earth	9·0 watt	4·1	6·0	1·5	1·75
BERINI	9·0 watt			RPM 2/4	Black/Earth	9·0 watt	5·4	7·9	1·9	2·2

THE WIPAC GROUP — BUCKINGHAM — BUCKS.
TELEPHONE: BUCKINGHAM 3031   TELEGRAMS: WICOMAGSCO BUCKINGHAM

Ref. TD5/1/1

WIPAC TECHNICAL DATA

NORTON "ELECTRA" ELECTRICAL SYSTEM

General Description

The lighting and ignition system of the Norton "Electra" consists of a simple 6 pole alternator generating set which supplies current via a metal plate rectifier and relay type voltage regulator to the battery, which then feeds the Ignition system, lights, horns, electric starter, etc. The alternator ring carries six coils, two of which provide a constant charge through the rectifier to the battery under all conditions. When the battery becomes partially discharged the remaining four coils are automatically brought into circuit by the voltage regulator to increase the charge rate. When the battery is restored to a condition of full charge the regulator operates again, disconnecting the additional four coils.

The alternating current supplied by the generator is converted to direct current by means of the rectifier, which is of the very efficient full wave bridge connected type.

The headlamp has a reflector with an extremely efficient reflecting surface provided by a vacuum electronic deposition of aluminium. The reflecting surface should not be touched or cleaned in any way, and will retain its brilliance indefinitely. The bulb is a pre-focus twin filament type (12 volts 40/50 watts) giving correct beam length and spread in head and dip positions.

The main connections in the Wipac system, are made by rubber socket connectors to the Lighting and Ignition switches and by individual rubber covered bullet type push-in connectors which are handy for wiring checks or the re-installation of new wiring. These connectors are not intended as plugs and sockets, for frequent manipulation, and are only used when testing or fault finding, and it is extremely important that they should be making perfect contact, as should all other connections and earthing points throughout the system.

Mounted on the handlebars is a Triconsul type switch which is a combined horn button, dipper switch and starter button. The red button operates the starter and is insulated from earth.

Ignition Switch

The keyed ignition switch is mounted to the right of the headlamp, and although not basically of the locking type, it cannot be operated unless the key is inserted, otherwise the switch knob rotates freely. Although marked Ignition and Emergency the switch may be used in either position for all operational conditions.

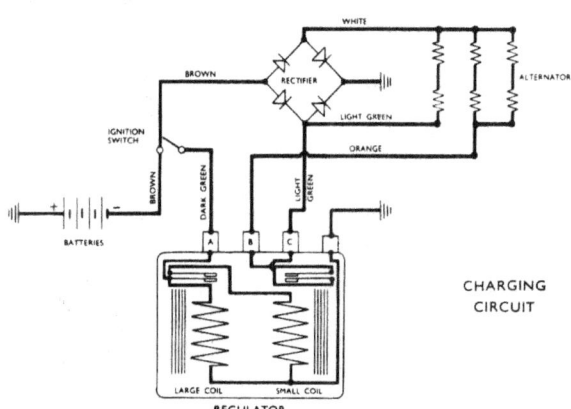

CHARGING CIRCUIT

Voltage Regulator (See Charging Circuit Sketch)

The Voltage Regulator is of the relay type and depending upon the state of charge of the battery, will switch in or out additional generator coils to increase or decrease the charge rate as necessary. The unit has been carefully adjusted at the Factory for optimum performance, and any attempt to alter the settings can only impair its efficiency and invalidate the guarantee.

On removal of the regulator cover two solenoids with their attendant contacts are visible. When the battery is only in a partially charged condition the contact of the larger solenoid (A) remain closed allowing current to flow through the smaller solenoid (C), thereby closing its contacts also. With both contacts closed all six generator coils are in circuit providing maximum charge rate.

When the battery becomes fully charged, sufficient current passes into the coil of solenoid (A) activating the unit and separating its contacts which, in turn, disconnects solenoid (C) and its contacts also open. This condition disconnects four of the generator coils operated by terminal "B", thus reducing the charge rate to prevent damage to the battery by over-charging and "boiling".

Charge Rates:—

Load Condition	Battery Condition	Charge Rates @ 3,000 rpm
No Lights	Regulator in (Battery Low)	7 amps min.
No Lights	Regulator out (Battery charged)	2 amps min.
Pilot Lights	Regulator in (Battery Low)	6 amps min.
Pilot Lights	Regulator out (Battery charged)	Balance min.
Head Lights	Regulator in (Battery Low)	2 amps min.
Head Lights	Regulator out (Battery charged)	–4 amps max.

Alternator Voltage Figures:—

Colour	Loading	2,000 R.P.M.	4,000 R.P.M.
White/Green	O/C	24.0v.	45.0v.
White/Green	1 Ohm	4.5v.	4.75v.
White/Orange	O/C	26.0v.	55.0v.
White/Orange	1 Ohm	7.75v.	9.0v.

The 1 Ohm load should be used in parallel with a good quality moving coil meter to obtain accurate results.

Bulbs:—

Headlamp	12v. 40/50w. Pre-focus
Rear and Stop Lamp	12v. 21/6w.
Pilot Lamp	12v. 2.2w.
Speedometer Bulb	14v. 0.8w.
Flashing Indicators	12v. 18w. Festoon type

The electrical equipment on your Norton "Electra" requires very little maintenance, with the exception of periodically (about once a month) recharging the contact breaker cam wiper felt with a little high melting point grease, and topping up the batteries with distilled water when necessary. However, the following DON'TS should be observed to ensure trouble-free performance:—

DON'T run your bike with the battery disconnected otherwise the voltage regulator will constantly chatter and accelerate wear on the contacts and pivots and the rectifier will overheat. If you switch the lights on all the bulbs will blow.

THE WIPAC GROUP — BUCKINGHAM — BUCKS.
TELEPHONE: BUCKINGHAM 3031   TELEGRAMS: WICOMAGSCO BUCKINGHAM

REF. TD.6/1/2

WIPAC TECHNICAL DATA (CONTINUED)

DON'T connect the battery back to front, i.e. negative to earth instead of positive to earth, otherwise you will burn out the rectifier, and if the engine is run under this condition the magnetic rotor will become de-magnetised.

Rectifier Testing:—

Before attempting to carry out any tests on this unit, it is essential that the white, green and brown wires are disconnected from the rectifier at the rectifier plug sockets.

Procedure	Battery Connections	Bulb Connections	Conclusions
Rectifier Check Connect a 6 volt battery in series with a 6v. 3w. bulb across the rectifier terminals (See diagram 2)	Positive—Light Green Positive—White Positive—Brown Positive—Brown	Earthed Earthed Green White	Bulb lights Rectifier O.K. Bulb does not light. Rectifier faulty replace.
Reverse battery connections. (See diagram 2)	Negative—Light Green Negative—White Negative—Brown Negative—Brown	Earthed Earthed Green White	Bulb does not light. Rectifier O.K. Bulb lights Rectifier faulty replace.

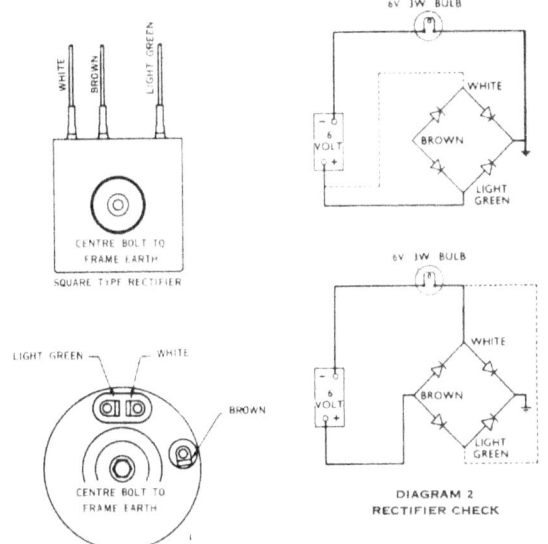

If it is found necessary to replace this component, or to refit a proven good rectifier, ensure that it is rebolted tightly on to a scrupulously clean part of the frame, remembering that the case of the rectifier is DC positive.

The snap connectors should also be a tight fit. Insecurity of any one of the connectors results in arc burning of the terminal, damage internally to the plates and consequential premature rectifier failure.

N.B.—A rapidly Flattening Battery necessitates an immediate check of the Rectifier.

Switches

On touring models the two switches are mechanically identical. A faulty switch will invariably give itself away if the procedure outlined below is adopted.

Remove the lamp front and substitute the cable plugs from the Ignition switch to the light switch and vice versa. If the switch is faulty then the fault will be transferred from one circuit to the other. Replace the faulty switch with a new one.

Premature Bulb Failure

The premature bulb failure involving all or any of the light bulbs at one time on a full DC battery system is caused by a defective connection in the battery " line "

This " line " starts at:—

1. The frame end of the translucent lead from the positive battery terminal and proceeds
2. Positive battery terminal
3. Negative battery terminal
4. Brown wire from Solenoid to four-hole connector (bullet terminal)
5. Brown wire from four-hole connector to Ammeter (bullet terminal)
6. Ammeter terminal with Brown wire.
7. Ammeter terminal with Red wire and
8. Both ends of short insulated link wire in the ignition switch plug which joins Red Ammeter wire to Brown wire going to light switch.

It must also be known that should the ammeter develop an internal open circuit the bulbs will blow. Also, should the battery have little or no electrolyte, this is partial or complete open circuit with the same results. There is, finally, the remote possibility of one of the actual wires in the battery line being broken. Again, bulbs will blow.

Ignition Coil Check

FIRST disconnect the coil entirely.

The tests can be carried out by again using an AVO meter, or a DC Voltmeter connected to the Motor Cycle Battery. Use the AVO on OHMS range.

Continuity can then be checked by taking readings across:
1. The two L.T. terminals to prove that the primary winding is intact
2. Either of the two L.T. terminals and the H.T. pickup.

A lower meter reading is to be expected in condition 2, due to the high resistance of the secondary winding.

Lastly, check for short circuit to earth by taking a reading between the coil case and the H.T. pick-up, similarly between the coil case and L.T. terminals. There should be no deflection of the needle.

A defective primary winding may continue to produce a weak spark whereas intermittent performance is invariably caused by a suspect secondary. Should there be any possible doubt about the ignition coil, however, a final check should be made by substitution.

Condensers

Should the capacity be suspect, first check for good contact to earth. Secondly, the condenser may be short circuiting to earth, (the battery and bulb is a simple quick test.) Third, check by replacement. Visual recognition of a defective condenser or condenser connection is a vivid blue arcing at the contacts.

When an AVO meter is available a further and rather more conclusive check can be made. Use the OHMS X 100 range.

(a) Disconnect the condenser and apply the meter probes, one to the condenser case and one to the lead. The meter needle will nudge forward a few divisions and immediately return to zero.
(b) Remove the probes and wait 15 seconds. Apply probes again and the needle should not move. If it does the condenser is faulty.

SPARE PARTS LIST

Alternator	G.1697
Stator Ring	S.3419
Rotor	S.0734
Breaker Point set	S.3908
Condenser set	S.2767
Ignition coil set	S.0810
Rectifier	S.2642
Headlamp (Less Harness)	S.3428
Main Harness	S.3429
Reflector and Glass set	S.2612
Rim	S.2617
Ignition Switch	S.3297
Ignition Key Group	S.3335
Lighting Switch	S.0781
Main Bulb Holder	S.0768
Triconsul Switch	S.3859
Ammeter	S.3162

REF. TD.6/2/2A

WIPAC TECHNICAL DATA

TRIUMPH T.10 AUTOMATIC 100 c.c. SCOOTER

Both the lighting and ignition systems on the Triumph T.10 Automatic are fed from a Series 191 Ignition Generator, Specification Number IG.1741. This consists of two major parts, namely the flywheel and the stator plate assembly.

Flywheel

This unit is equipped with a fan to provide a strong air draught for engine cooling, and cast into the periphery are six magnets which are virtually self keeping so there is no fear of loss of magnetism on removal from the stator. The cam is a permanent fixture onto the flywheel hub which is key located to the engine crankshaft spindle, to ensure its correct timing location.

Stator Plate Group

The stator plate group has mounted on its core limbs, four low tension coils, two of which feed an external ignition coil via a Maroon lead and earth, whilst the remaining two feed the lighting coils through the Dark Red lead and earth. The stator plate also houses the condenser and contact breaker for ignition. The lighting system is purely A/C and as such, there will be no headlight unless the engine is running.

Horn

An A/C type horn is operated from the lighting supply and it will be found that the pitch of the note will vary slightly with engine r.p.m. Some dimming of the lights may be observed when the horn is operated with the main headlights in use.

Headlamp

The headlamp has a parabolic reflector with an extremely efficient reflecting surface provided by the now widely adopted alluminising process.

This surface, although extremely thin, is far more efficient than that produced by the old silvering method, and is not subject to tarnishing. No attempt should be made to clean or even touch the surface, as this would result in irrepairable damage. If left alone, the reflector will retain its brilliance indefinitely. The headlamp bulb is of the twin transverse filament type, which, used in conjunction with the prismatic block lens gives correct beam length and spread in both head and dip positions.

Harness

The main connection to the lighting switch is made by a rubber shrouded multi-socket connector, whilst the other connections are made by individual rubber covered bullet type push in connectors. These connectors are not intended as plugs and sockets for frequent manipulation, and should only be used for circuit testing and the introduction of replacement parts.

Parking Lights (Optional)

The parking lights on this model are operated from a three volt dry battery and provision is made for a special battery container in the Scooter's toolbox. The battery containers are obtainable from the Triumph/B.S.A. Service Organisation. When exhausted, it is important that the battery is renewed, otherwise the container will be irrepairably damaged by corrosion.

Rear Lamp

The rear lamp houses two bulbs, one of which operates from the Generator A/C supply when the headlight is switched on, and the second and smaller bulb is fed from the dry battery and is used for parking only.

Bulbs

The correct ratings for use in this system are:

Headlamp	6v. 18/18w. S.B.C.
Pilot Lamp	2.5v. 0.2 amp. M.E.S.
Rear Lamp	6v. 3w. S.C.C.
Parking Lamp	2.5v. 0.2 amp. M.E.S.
Speedometer Lamp	6v. 1.8w. miniature bayonet.

Engine Governor

As the T.10 is equipped with an Automatic Drive Mechanism, the operation of which is dependent upon engine speed, a safety device is fitted to prevent the rider inadvertently increasing the engine speed sufficiently to engage the drive mechanism during the starting procedure. The governor is basically a pair of contacts which automatically close and earth the magneto contact breaker, hence extinguishing the spark at approximately 1,500 r.p.m. As the r.p.m. falls below this figure, the contacts open and the spark is restored. The governor is selected by a switch which is mounted under the rider's position on the dual seat. During starting procedure, and when the rider's weight is not on the seat, the governor is in circuit and will operate, maintaining a low engine r.p.m. When the rider is seated, the switch is depressed and operated, thus by-passing the engine governor allowing engine speed to rise to operational r.p.m.

Adjusting Engine Governor

It is recommended that the screwed governor contact is adjusted so that it is $\frac{1}{16}$" clear of the contact on the pivoting " L " shaped arm, when the engine is stationary.

THE WIPAC GROUP — BUCKINGHAM — BUCKS.
TELEPHONE: BUCKINGHAM 3031   TELEGRAMS: WICOMAGSCO BUCKINGHAM

REF. TD.7/1/2

WIPAC TECHNICAL DATA (CONTINUED)

ELECTRICAL TESTING INSTRUCTIONS

Equipment Required

Accurate testing of the equipment can be achieved with the aid of an instrument such as the Wilkson Test set, or an AVO meter, or in fact any other good quality moving coil instrument, used in conjunction with a 1 ohm resistive load.

Generator Output Testing—Lighting Output

It is not recommended that the engine be run at 1,500 r.p.m. (Governor Speed) or over, with the rear wheel on the ground, as heavy wear can occur on one part of the drive belt. The machine should be supported by the pillion footrests so that the rear wheel is clear of the ground.

To check the lighting output of the generator, first unplug the dark Red lighting feed lead which issues from the generator, from the five-way connector in the main wiring harness. Now connect the Wilkson Tester with 1 ohm load, A/C volt scale, between the Red lead and earth, and check the output against the figures tabulated below.

TABLE 1

Wilkson or AVO with 1 ohm Load.

R.P.M.	Voltage
1,500	3.0v.
3,000	4.0v.
MAX.	4.5v.—5.0v.

Where an AVO meter is used, the machine's own bulbs may be used as a load, but prior to testing ensure that all bulbs are in good condition and are correctly rated. Do NOT in this case disconnect the Red Generator lead, but connect the AVO on the voltage range between Earth and the Dark Red lead at the five-way connector. Switch on the lights, make sure they are all alight, then check the output with the Table below:

TABLE 2

AVO using Bulbs as Load.

R.P.M.	Voltage
1,500	3.5v.—4.0v.
3,000	5.5v.—6.0v.
MAX.	7.0v.—7.5v.

Ignition Feed Coils

The Ignition Feed coils operate between the Maroon lead issuing from the generator and earth. A useful check in the case of misfiring is to start the machine, and check between the Maroon lead at the four-hole connector and earth. At 3,000 r.p.m. 5 volts will be obtained on the AVO meter. Where a machine will not start, a test can be made by unplugging the Maroon lead from the four-hole connector and checking with the AVO meter between the Maroon lead and earth. At kickover, i.e. 600 r.p.m., the meter will read 1.0 volt.

Condenser Check

Disconnect the condenser lead from the contact breaker. Using the AVO meter, turn the selector switches to the Ohms × 100 range. Using the test prods from the AVO connect one to the condenser lead and the other to the condenser case. The needle on the AVO will move rapidly, and return to infinity immediately. Remove the test meter prods and wait 15 seconds. Re-apply the prods, and the needle should not again move. If it does the condenser requires replacement. Burned or badly pitted contacts or continuous intense blue spark across the contacts when running is indicative of a weak condenser. A very small white spark across the contact breaker points when running is normal.

Premature Bulb Failure

The current feeding the bulbs when the lighting switch is in the headlamp position is A/C working, AND THE BULB LOADING UNDER THESE CONDITIONS IS OF THE UTMOST IMPORTANCE. To ensure that the rear lamp does not blow and consequently overload the headlamp unit, a carry-over type of dip switch is used. This means that during the change over from head to dip and vice versa, both headlamp filaments are lit thus ensuring that the heavy bulb loading is not transferred to the small tail light bulb which would result in its failure. Firstly then, check that the dipper switch is functioning correctly, and secondly check that all bulb holder contact springs are satisfactory as intermittent open circuiting of the bulbs could again lead to circuit overload. Where premature bulb failure does take place, on no account be tempted to use 12 volt bulbs as this would only aggravate the condition.

Replacing Feed Coils

As it is essential that the link wires between the feed coils be sufficiently short as to prevent their fouling the flywheel during service, replacement coils are not supplied pre-connected. After fitting replacement coils to the stator plate, it will be necessary to connect these together in series and in the case of both the lighting and feed coils, one end earthed. An earth tag is provided on the appropriate coils and these should be secured under the cam grease felt support. The coils bearing the earth connection terminals are positioned on the core limbs closest to the cam grease felt.

Connecting Feed Coils

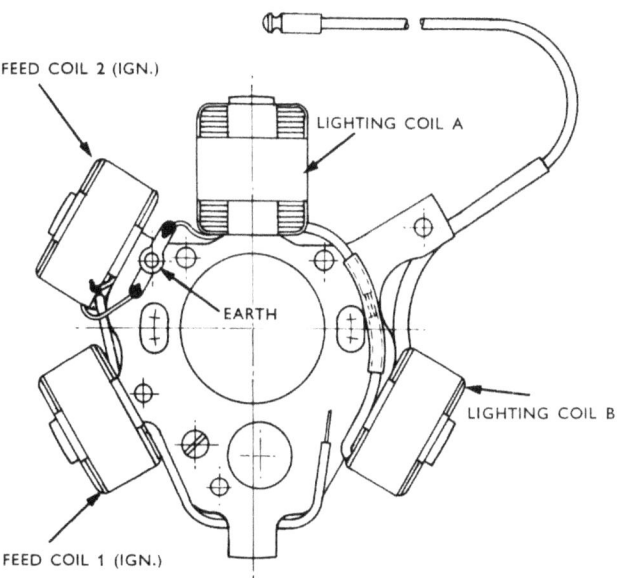

Lighting Feed Coils

Solder inside lead of coil A to outside of coil B and cover solder joint with 1" length of sleeving provided.

Ignition Feed Coils

Solder outside lead of feed coil 1 to outside lead of feed coil 2 and position the joint so that it does not come into contact with earth.

REF. TD.7/2/2

WIPAC TECHNICAL DATA

B.S.A. BANTAM MODELS D.10 and D.14
FULL D.C. LIGHTS AND COIL IGNITION

General Description

The lighting and ignition systems of the Wipac alternator equipped models D.10 and D.14 Bantam consists of a simple six-pole alternator generating set which supplies current through a metal plate rectifier to a battery, which then feeds the ignition system, lights, horns, etc. The alternator ring carries six coils which are connected in three sets of two in series as illustrated in the schematic diagram Figure 1.

The headlamp has a reflector with an extremely efficient reflecting surface provided by the now widely adopted aluminisation process in which a thin film of aluminium is deposited on the reflector under vacuum. This reflecting surface should not be touched or cleaned in any way and it will retain its brilliance indefinitely. The bulb is a pre-focus twin filament type giving correct beam length and spread in main and dip positions.

The main connections in the Wipac system are made by

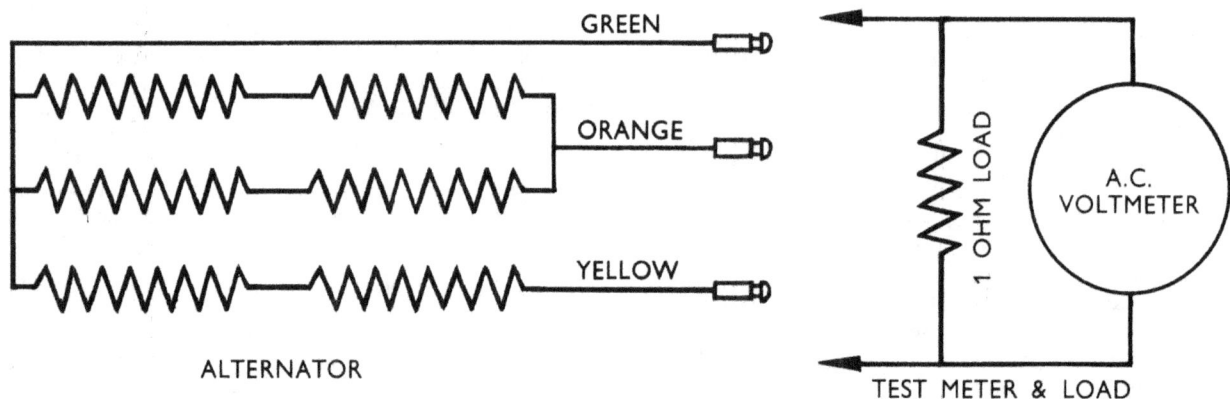

Figure 1.

By using one set of two coils in series, a certain output is obtained for daylight running and when the pilot or parking lights are switched on. When the headlight is brought into circuit, all six coils are connected as three pairs in series parallel as shown in Figure 1, giving maximum output, most of which is absorbed by the head-lamp bulb but still leaving sufficient current for maintaining the state of charge of the battery.

Alternating current supplied by the generator is converted to direct current by means of the rectifier which is of the very efficient full wave bridge connected type.

Wipac alternator equipment provides an emergency starting system which, when the ignition switch is put into the emergency position, connects all the six coils together and, providing the lighting switch is in the 'off' position, gives full output in order to bring up the voltage of a discharged battery and is effective in obtaining an immediate start under these conditions. The maximum charging current in the emergency position is high as there is no drain against it by the lighting system and the engine should not be run in this position for more than 10—15 minutes. This type of emergency starting being entirely DC enables the machine to be run through the complete operational range of the engine.

rubber socket connectors to the lighting and ignition switches and by individual rubber covered bullet type push-in connectors which are handy for wiring checks or the re-installation of new wiring. These connectors are not intended as plugs and sockets for frequent manipulation and are only used when testing or fault finding. It is important that they should be making perfect contact as should all other connection points throughout the system.

Fault Finding

Equipment required:—

1. Wilkson Test Set.
2. 6v. 3w. bulb holder and two test leads about 24" long.
3. A well charged 6v. battery.

OR

A. A good quality moving coil AC volt meter to be used in conjunction with a one ohm resistive load.
B. 10-0-10 DC Ammeter.
C. 0-12 volts DC volt meter.
D. 6v. 3w. Bulb with holder and two test leads about 24" long.
E. A well charged 6v. battery.

THE WIPAC GROUP — BUCKINGHAM — BUCKS.
TELEPHONE: BUCKINGHAM 3031   TELEGRAMS: WICOMAGSCO BUCKINGHAM

REF. TD.8/1/3

WIPAC TECHNICAL DATA (CONTINUED)

Accurate high grade moving coil instruments must be used, and the one ohm resistor must be accurate to obtain correct readings.

No or Low charge

1. Before commencing any tests, check the voltage of the battery and if completely exhausted substitute one which is known to be capable of accepting a charge.
2. Connect in series with the battery, (easily done by disconnecting the brown negative lead from the double connector), the DC Ammeter and check off the charge rates as detailed below:—

Ignition Switch	Lights Switch	Minimum Charge Rates	r.p.m.
Ignition	Off	2.5 a.	3,000
Ignition	Low	.5 a.	3,000
Ignition	High	1.0 a.	3,000
Emergency	Off	4.5 a.	3,000

These figures should be checked at approximately 3,000 r.p.m. and are the minimum permissible readings. Charge rates will, of course, vary with engine speed, the state of charge and condition of the battery but the above figures will give a fair indication as to the correct functioning of the system.

N.B.—*It is essential that the correct wattage bulbs be used throughout the lighting system, as any deviation will seriously upset the charge rates.*

Bulb types:

Headlamp (Main bulb)	6v. 30/24w. British pre-focus
Headlamp (Pilot bulb)	6v. 3w. M.E.S.
Rear-Stop Light bulb	6v. 6/18w. S.B.C. Staggered Pin
Speedometer	6v. 0.6w. B.A.7S Lug Cap.

If the meter readings are unsatisfactory, then:

3. Check the alternator ouptut by disconnecting the yellow, orange and light green leads from the five-way connector, into which the alternator harness is plugged. It will be seen from the appropriate wiring diagram, reference WD/88/1051 and from Figure 1 that the light green lead from the alternator is common to all coils whilst the yellow connects two coils only and the orange the remaining four. Connect one side of the Wilkson test meter (AC volts with one ohm load) or the AC volt meter with one ohm load parallelled across it, to the green lead and the other side of the meter to the yellow and orange leads in turn.

Check with the table below:—

Check Between	R.P.M.	Volts Output
Yellow/Green	2000 — 3000	4 — 4.75
Orange/Green	2000 — 3000	7.5 — 8.5

A low reading on one group of coils would indicate coil failure and the low reading on both groups of coils will, in all probability, be due to a low flux density in the magnetic rotor. No readings from both groups of coils indicates an open circuit in the green supply lead.

Winding resistance between

Lead Colours	Resistance
Yellow/Green	0.25 ohms
Orange/Green	0.4 ohms

N.B.—THE IMPORTANCE OF THE CORRECT BATTERY CONNECTIONS CANNOT BE OVER-EMPHASIZED. THE BATTERY POSITIVE LEAD SHOULD ALWAYS BE CONNECTED TO THE TRANSLUCENT LEAD AND THE BATTERY NEGATIVE TO THE BROWN LEAD. REVERSAL OF THESE CONNECTIONS WILL INVARIABLY BURN OUT THE RECTIFIER, AND IF THE ENGINE IS RUN UNDER THESE CONDITIONS, THE MAGNETIC ROTOR WILL BECOME DEMAGNETISED.

4. A further cause of low or no charge stems from the alternator short circuiting to earth. To check this, it is necessary to construct a simple continuity check circuit, viz.: a 6 volt battery introduced in series with the DC voltmeter will amply suffice. Connect one end of the circuit to the green lead and the other end to the machine frame earth. If a reading is obtained on the voltmeter then the alternator is short circuit to earth. It is desirable to carry out this check with both the stator and rotor in position on the machine, the reason being that in isolated cases careless handling of the stator may have caused one or more of the soldered coil link connections to have become displaced, thus coming into contact with the circumference of the rotor thereby short circuiting all coils. Before condemning the alternator, therefore, it is wise to check that all connections are well clear of the rotor, gently easing back any which look possible causes of future trouble.

Rectifier Testing

Before attempting to carry out tests on this unit, it is essential that the white, green and brown wires are disconnected from the rectifier at the rectifier plug sockets, then check the rectifier as shown in the Figure 2. Should it be found necessary to replace this component or to re-fit a proven good rectifier, ensure that it is rebolted securely on to a scrupulously clean part of the frame, remembering that the case of the rectifier is DC positive. The snap connectors should be clean and tight as poor connections can give rise to rectifier failure owing to overload or arc burning.

Procedure	Battery Connections	Bulb Connections	Conclusions
Rectifier Check Connect a 6 volt battery in series with a 6v. 3w. bulb across the rectifier terminals	Positive—Light Green Positive—White Positive—Brown Positive—Brown	Earthed Earthed Green White	Bulb lights Rectifier O.K. Bulb does not light. Rectifier faulty replace.
Reverse battery connections.	Negative—Light Green Negative—White Negative—Brown Negative—Brown	Earthed Earthed Green White	Bulb does not light. Rectifier O.K. Bulb lights Rectifier faulty replace.

REF. TD.8/2/3

WIPAC TECHNICAL DATA (CONTINUED)

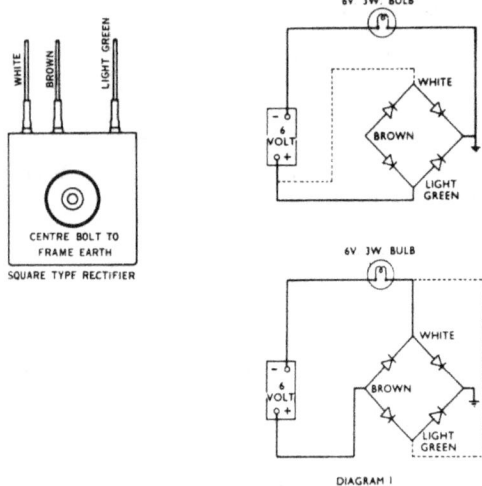

Figure 2.

N.B.—A RAPIDLY FLATTENING BATTERY NECESSITATES AN IMMEDIATE CHECK ON THE RECTIFIER AND ALTERNATOR.

Switches

Both ignition and lighting switches are mechanically identical. A faulty switch will invariably give itself away if the procedure outlined below is adopted.

Remove the lamp front and substitute the cable plugs from the ignition switch to the light switch and vice versa. If the switch is faulty then the fault will be transferred from one circuit to the other. Replace the faulty switch.

Premature Bulb Failure

The premature bulb failure involving all or many of the light bulbs at one time on a full DC battery system is caused by a defective connection in the battery "line"...

The following should be checked:
1. Battery Positive terminal
2. Battery Negative terminal
3. All connections in the four hole connection into which the battery negative lead is fitted.
4. Rectifier earth lead (translucent)
5. Harness frame earth.
6. Both ends of the short link wire in ignition switch joining brown lead from lighting switch to brown lead from main body of harness.
7. Check battery acid level and top up if necessary.

N.B.—IT SHOULD BE KNOWN THAT A BREAK OR POOR CONNECTION IN THE BATTERY LINE CAN CAUSE OVERLOADING TO THE RECTIFIER AND BRING ABOUT ITS EARLY FAILURE.

Contact Breaker

Check the contact breaker points gap and adjust to the recommended setting of 0.12″. Check cleanliness of contact faces, these, if in good order, should have a light grey frosted appearance. Where fine matter, e.g. oil and grease have been present, the contacts may have a blackened burnt appearance.

Should the condition not appear serious, then a light application of fine grade emery cloth will restore them. If in doubt replace the whole breaker group. Check the free action of the breaker arm on the pivot, as any sticking of this arm can cause intermittent difficulty.

N.B.—ON NO ACCOUNT SHOULD THE STAR SHAPED RETAINING WASHER ON THE BREAKER ARM BE REMOVED FROM THE PIVOT AS THE AMOUNT OF END FLOAT IS STRICTLY CONTROLLED, WHICH IS ESSENTIAL TO THE CORRECT FUNCTIONING OF THE CONTACT BREAKERS.

Condensers

Should the capacity be suspect, first check for good contact to earth and security to the contact breaker group. Secondly, a quick check can be made for short circuit to earth; the battery and bulb is a simple and quick test, but first remember to disconnect the condenser from the contact breaker group. Visual recognition of a defective condenser or condenser connections is vivid blue arcing at the contacts when an attempt is made to start the engine or when the engine is actually running.

Where an Avometer is available, a more conclusive check can be made. This is done by firstly, disconnecting the condenser lead from the contact breaker. Select the Avometer to the ohms x 100 range and, using the test prods from the meter, connect one to the condenser lead and the other to the condenser case. The needle on the Avo will move rapidly and return to infinity immediately. Remove the test meter prods and wait 15 seconds. Re-apply the prods and the needle should not again move.

If it does, the condenser requires replacement. It should be noted that a very small white spark across the contact breaker points when running is normal.

Ignition Coil Check

First, completely disconnect the ignition coil from the motorcycle circuit, and connect the DC volt meter across the 6v. battery to produce a continuity check. The meter should register the battery voltage. Now break this circuit at any point and across this break connect the two small screw terminals of the ignition coil. This test will indicate continuity to prove that the primary winding is intact. Likewise, one lead of the test circuit to either one of the primary terminals and the other to the H.T. pick-up will again show continuity but a lower reading due to the higher resistance of the secondary windings.

Third and last check is to ensure that the coil is not earthing out. To do this, leave one lead on one of the primary terminals and connect the other with the coil case. No reading should show. Similarly, with the H.T. pick-up point. Where an ohm meter is available, check the resistances as below:

Primary Resistance   1.3 ohms.
Secondary Resistance   4,500 ohms.

A defective primary winding may continue to produce a weak spark whereas intermittent performances invariably caused by a suspect secondary. Should there be any possible doubt about the ignition coil, however, a final check should be made by substitution.

REF. TD.8/3/3

USE THE TOOL MADE FOR THE JOB

WIPAC SERVICE TOOLS

Part No.	Series	Description and Application	Price £ s. d.
S1715	A 55 & 73	**Fixed Contact Setting Tool**	2 15 0
S2573	CJ1 81	**Condenser Tool** (2 Peg), Late Type	3 6
S2020	CJ1 81	**Condenser Tool,** (3 Peg) Late Type	4 0
S1256	55 & 73	**Flywheel Extractor.** All BSA Bantams, Excelsior Talisman Twin, Courier Monarch, and Brockhouse Corgi.	6 0
S2094	BANTAMAG 90	**Flywheel Extractor** (3 screws) (3BA) Early Type	6 0
S2062	90	**Flywheel Extractor** (4 screws) (2BA) Late Type	6 0
S0075	90	**Flywheel Extractor** (3 screws) (2BA) (Trojan)	6 0
S2359	114	**Ignition & Lighting Switch Main Nut Spanner,** BSA C1OL and Ariel Colt.	6 0
S2572	114	**Auto Advance Plate Extractor Tool,** BSA C10L and Ariel Colt.	6 0
S0222	114 124	**Feeler Gauge** .012", for Contact Breaker Setting. All standard road machines with alternating equipment.	1 6
S0073	141	**Flywheel Extractor.** James Flying Cadet, Scooter and M15. Francis and Barnett Plover 86, Fulmar 88. Triumph Tigress 175 cc. BSA Sunbeam 175 cc., Piatti Scooter, Triumph Tina.	6 0
S0282	150	**Flywheel Extractor.** Berini Moped, BSA Beagle, Ariel Pixie.	6 0
S0502	150	**Flywheel Extractor** (Kelston) Long Shaft.	6 0

THE WIPAC GROUP — BUCKINGHAM — BUCKS.
TELEPHONE: BUCKINGHAM 3031   TELEGRAMS: WICOMAGSCO BUCKINGHAM

VELOCEPRESS MANUALS – MOTORCYCLE BY MAKE

AJS 1932-1948 SINGLES & TWINS 250cc THRU 1000cc (BOOK OF)
AJS 1945-1960 SINGLES 350cc & 500cc MODELS 16 & 18 (BOOK OF)
AJS 1955-1965 SINGLES 350cc & 500cc (BOOK OF)
AJS 1957-1966 FACTORY WSM - ALL SINGLES & TWINS
ARIEL UP TO 1932 (BOOK OF)
ARIEL 1932-1939 PREWAR MODELS (BOOK OF)
ARIEL 1933-1951 (WORKSHOP MANUAL)
ARIEL 1939-1960 4 STROKE SINGLES (BOOK OF)
ARIEL 1958-1964 LEADER & ARROW (BOOK OF)
BMW R26 R27 (1956-1967) FACTORY WORKSHOP MANUAL
BMW R50 R50S R60 R69S (1955-1969) FACTORY WORKSHOP MANUAL
BRIDGESTONE 90 SERIES FACTORY WSM & PARTS CATALOGUE
BRIDGESTONE 175 SERIES FACTORY WSM & PARTS CATALOGUE
BRIDGESTONE 350 SERIES FACTORY WSM & PARTS CATALOGUES
BSA SERVICE SHEETS MASTER CATALOGUE ALL MODELS 1945-1967
BSA BANTAM D1 TO D7 1948-1966 FACTORY SERVICE SHEETS MANUAL
BSA BANTAM ALL MODELS FROM 1948 ONWARDS (BOOK OF)
BSA BANTAM D14 FACTORY WORKSHOP & INSTRUCTION MANUAL
BSA DANDY FACTORY WORKSHOP MANUAL (COMPILATION)
BSA SINGLES & V-TWINS UP TO 1927 (BOOK OF)
BSA SINGLES & V-TWINS UP TO 1930 (BOOK OF)
BSA SINGLES & V-TWINS UP TO 1935 (BOOK OF)
BSA SINGLES & V-TWINS 1936-1939 (BOOK OF)
BSA C10, C11 & C12 1945-1958 FACTORY SERVICE SHEETS MANUAL
BSA OHV & SV SINGLES 250-600cc 1945-1959 (BOOK OF)
BSA C15 & B40 1958-1967 FACTORY SERVICE SHEETS MANUAL
BSA OHV & SV SINGLES 250cc (ONLY) 1954-1970 (BOOK OF)
BSA B31, B32, B33 & B34 1945-60 FACTORY SERVICE SHEETS MANUAL
BSA OHV SINGLES 350 & 500cc 1955-1967 (BOOK OF)
BSA M20, M21 & M33 1945-1963 FACTORY SERVICE SHEETS MANUAL
BSA TWINS A7 & A10 1948-1962 FACTORY SERVICE SHEETS MANUAL
BSA TWINS A7 & A10 1948-1962 (BOOK OF)
BSA TWINS A50 & A65 1962-1965 FACTORY WORKSHOP MANUAL
BSA TWINS A50 & A65 1962-1969 (SECOND BOOK OF)
DOUGLAS 1929-1939 PREWAR ALL MODELS (BOOK OF)
DOUGLAS 1948-1957 POSTWAR ALL MODELS FACTORY SHOP MANUAL
DUCATI 160cc, 250cc & 350cc OHC MODELS FACTORY MANUAL
HONDA 50 ALL MODELS UP TO 1970 INC MONKEY & TRAIL (BOOK OF)
HONDA 90 ALL MODELS UP TO 1966 (BOOK OF)
HONDA 50-65-70-90cc OHC SINGLES 1959-1983 FACTORY WSM
HONDA 125-150cc TWINS C/CS/CB/CA FACTORY WORKSHOP MANUAL
HONDA 125-160-175-200cc TWINS 1964-1980 (WORKSHOP MANUAL)
HONDA 250-305 TWINS C/CS/CB 1959-1967 FACTORY WSM
HOHDA 250-350 TWINS CB/CL/SL 1968-1973 FACTORY WSM
HONDA 450 CB/CL 1965-1974 K0 TO K7 WORKSHOP MANUAL
HONDA C100 SUPER CUB FACTORY WORKSHOP MANUAL
HONDA C110 SPORT CUB 1962-1969 FACTORY WORKSHOP MANUAL
HONDA TWINS & SINGLES 50cc THRU 305cc 1960-1966 (BOOK OF)
HONDA TWINS ALL MODELS 125cc THRU 450cc UP TO 1968 (BOOK OF)
INDIAN PONYBIKE, BOY RACER & PAPOOSE ILL PARTS LIST & SALES LIT
J.A.P. ENGINES 1927-1952 & MOTORCYCLES 1934-1952 (BOOK OF)
MATCHLESS 1931-1939 ALL MODELS 250cc THRU 990cc (BOOK OF)
MATCHLESS 1945-1956 350 & 500cc SINGLES (BOOK OF)
MATCHLESS 1955-1966 350 & 500cc SINGLES (BOOK OF)
MATCHLESS 1957-1966 FACTORY WSM - ALL SINGLES & TWINS
NEW IMPERIAL ALL SV & OHV FROM 1935 ONWARDS (BOOK OF)
NORTON 1932-1939 PREWAR MODELS (BOOK OF)
NORTON 1932-1947 (BOOK OF)
NORTON 1938-1956 (BOOK OF)
NORTON 1955-1963 MODELS 19, 50 & ES2 (BOOK OF)
NORTON 1955-1965 DOMINATOR TWINS (BOOK OF)
NORTON 1960-1970 TWIN CYLINDER FACTORY WORKSHOP MANUAL
NORTON 1970-1975 COMMANDO FACTORY WORKSHOP MANUAL
NORTON 1975-1978 MK 3 COMMANDO FACTORY WORKSHOP MANUAL
PANTHER 1932-1958 LIGHTWEIGHT MODELS 250 & 350cc (BOOK OF)
PANTHER 1938-1966 HEAVYWEIGHT MODELS 600 & 650cc (BOOK OF)
RALEIGH MOTORCYCLES 1919-1933 (BOOK OF)
ROYAL ENFIELD 1934-1946 SINGLES & V TWINS (BOOK OF)
ROYAL ENFIELD 1937-1953 SINGLES & V TWINS (BOOK OF)
ROYAL ENFIELD 1946-1962 SINGLES (BOOK OF)
ROYAL ENFIELD 1958-1966 250cc & 350cc SINGLES (SECOND BOOK OF)
ROYAL ENFIELD 736cc INTERCEPTOR FACTORY WORKSHOP MANUAL
RUDGE 1933-1939 (BOOK OF)
SUNBEAM 1928-1939 (BOOK OF)
SUNBEAM 1946-1957 S7 & S8 (BOOK OF)
SUZUKI 50cc & 80cc UP TO 1966 (BOOK OF)
SUZUKI T10 1963-1967 FACTORY WORKSHOP MANUAL
SUZUKI T20 & T200 1965-1969 FACTORY WORKSHOP MANUAL
SUZUKI TWINS 1962 ONWARDS 125-500cc WORKSHOP MANUAL
TRIUMPH 1935-1939 PREWAR MODELS (BOOK OF)
TRIUMPH 1935-1949 (BOOK OF)
TRIUMPH 1937-1951 (WORKSHOP MANUAL)
TRIUMPH 1945-1955 FACTORY WORKSHOP MANUAL
TRIUMPH 1945-1958 TWINS (BOOK OF)
TRIUMPH 1956-1969 TWINS (BOOK OF)
VELOCETTE 1925-1970 ALL SINGLES & TWINS (BOOK OF)
VILLIERS ENGINE UP TO 1959 INC. 3 WHEELERS (BOOK OF)
VILLIERS ENGINE UP TO 1969 (BOOK OF)
VINCENT 1935-1955 (WORKSHOP MANUAL)
YAMAHA 1961-1967 YA5 & YA6 (WORKSHOP MANUAL & ILL PARTS LIST)
YAMAHA 1971-1972 JT1& JT2 (WORKSHOP MANUAL & ILL PARTS LIST)

VELOCEPRESS TECHNICAL BOOKS – MOTORCYCLE

1930'S BRITISH MOTORCYCLE CARBS & ELEC COMPONENTS (BOOK OF)
1930'S BRITISH MOTORCYCLE ENGINES (OVERHAUL & MAINTENANCE)
1930'S BRITISH MOTORCYCLE GEARBOXES & CLUTCHES (BOOK OF)
CATALOG OF BRITISH MOTORCYCLES (1951 MODELS)
LUCAS ELECTRONICS BRITISH M/CYCLES REPAIR & PARTS (1950-1977)
MOTORCYCLE ENGINEERING (P.E. Irving)
MOTORCYCLE ROAD TESTS 1949-1953 (Motor Cycle Magazine UK)
SPEED AND HOW TO OBTAIN IT (Motor Cycle Magazine UK)
TUNING FOR SPEED (P.E. Irving)
WIPAC (COMBO) MANUAL NUMBER 3 + M/CYCLE & SCOOTER MANUAL

VELOCEPRESS MANUALS – SCOOTERS BY MAKE

BSA SUNBEAM SCOOTER WORKSHOP MANUAL 1959-1965
BSA SUNBEAM SCOOTER 1959-1965 (BOOK OF)
LAMBRETTA 1947-1957 ALL 125 & 150cc MODELS (BOOK OF)
LAMBRETTA 1957-1970 LI & TV MODELS (SECOND BOOK OF)
NSU PRIMA 1956-1964 ALL MODELS (BOOK OF)
TRIUMPH TIGRESS SCOOTER WORKSHOP MANUAL 1959-1965
TRIUMPH TIGRESS SCOOTER (BOOK OF)
VESPA 1951-1961 (BOOK OF)
VESPA 1955-1963 125 & 150cc & GS MODELS (SECOND BOOK OF)
VESPA 1955-1968 GS & SS (BOOK OF)
VESPA 1963-1972 90, 125 & 150cc (THIRD BOOK OF)

VELOCEPRESS MANUALS – MOPEDS & MOTORIZED BICYCLES

CYCLEMOTOR (BOOK OF)
NSU QUICKLY 1953-1963 ALL MODELS (BOOK OF)
PUCH MAXI N & S MAINTENANCE & REPAIR (3 MANUAL COMPILATION)
RALEIGH MOPEDS 1960-1969 (BOOK OF)

VELOCEPRESS MANUALS - THREE WHEELER'S

BOND MINICAR THREE WHEELER 1948-1967 (BOOK OF)
BMW ISETTA FACTORY WORKSHOP MANUAL
BSA THREE WHEELER (BOOK OF)
RELIANT REGAL THREE WHEELER 1952-1973 (BOOK OF)
VINTAGE MORGAN THREE WHEELER (BOOK OF)

VELOCEPRESS MANUALS – AUTOMOBILE BY MAKE

ALFA ROMEO GIULIA WORKSHOP MANUAL 1300 TO 2000cc 1962-1975
ALFA ROMEO GIULIA TECH MANUAL CARBURETED CARS FROM 1962
ALFA ROMEO GIULIA TECH MANUAL FUEL INJECTED CARS FROM 1969
ALFA ROMEO GIULIETTA & GIULIA 750 & 101 SERIES 1955-1965 WSM
AUSTIN-HEALEY SPRITE & MG MIDGET WORKSHOP MANUAL 1958-1971
BMW 600 LIMOUSINE FACTORY WORKSHOP MANUAL
BMW 600 LIMOUSINE OWNERS HAND BOOK & SERVICE MANUAL
BMW 2000 & 2002 1966-1976 WORKSHOP MANUAL
CORVAIR 1960-1969 WORKSHOP MANUAL
CORVETTE V8 1955-1962 WORKSHOP MANUAL
FIAT 500 FACTORY WORKSHOP MANUAL 1957-1973
FIAT 600, 600D & MULTIPLA FACTORY WORKSHOP MANUAL 1955-1969
JAGUAR E-TYPE 3.8 & 4.2 SERIES 1 & 2 WORKSHOP MANUAL
JAGUAR MK 7, 8, 9 & XK120, 140, 150 WORKSHOP MANUAL 1948-1961
METROPOLITAN FACTORY WORKSHOP MANUAL
MGA & MGB OWNERS HANDBOOK & WORKSHOP MANUAL
MG MIDGET TC, TD, TF & TF1500 WORKSHOP MANUAL
PORSCHE 356 1948-1965 WORKSHOP MANUAL
PORSCHE 911 2.0, 2.2, 2.4 LITRE 1964-1973 WORKSHOP MANUAL
PORSCHE 911 2.7, 3.0, 3.2 LITRE 1973-1989 WORKSHOP MANUAL
PORSCHE 912 WORKSHOP MANUAL
TRIUMPH TR2, TR3, TR4 1953-1965 WORKSHOP MANUAL
VOLKSWAGEN TRANSPORTER, TRUCKS & WAGONS 1950-1979 WSM
VOLVO 1944-1968 ALL MODELS WORKSHOP MANUAL

VELOCEPRESS TECHNICAL BOOKS - AUTOMOBILE

FERRARI 250/GT SERVICE AND MAINTENANCE
FERRARI GUIDE TO PERFORMANCE
FERRARI OWNER'S HANDBOOK
FERRARI TUNING TIPS & MAINTENANCE TECHNIQUES
HOW TO BUILD A FIBERGLASS CAR
HOW TO BUILD A RACING CAR
HOW TO RESTORE THE MODEL 'A' FORD
MASERATI OWNER'S HANDBOOK
OBERT'S FIAT GUIDE
PERFORMANCE TUNING THE SUNBEAM TIGER
SOUPING THE VOLKSWAGEN
SOLEX CARBURETORS (EMPHASIS ON UK & EU AUTOMOBILES)
SU CARBURETORS (EMPHASIS ON UK AUTOMOBILES)
WEBER CARBURETORS (EMPHASIS ON ALFA & FIAT)

VELOCEPRESS BOOKS & GUIDES - AUTOMOBILE

ABARTH BUYERS GUIDE
COMPLETE CATALOG OF JAPANESE MOTOR VEHICLES
FERRARI 308 SERIES BUYER'S AND OWNER'S GUIDE
FERRARI BERLINETTA LUSSO
FERRARI BROCHURES AND SALES LITERATURE 1946-1967
FERRARI BROCHURES AND SALES LITERATURE 1968-1989
FERRARI SERIAL NUMBERS PART I - ODD NUMBERS TO 21399
FERRARI SERIAL NUMBERS PART II - EVEN NUMBERS TO 1050
FERRARI SPYDER CALIFORNIA
HENRY'S FABULOUS MODEL "A" FORD
MASERATI BROCHURES AND SALES LITERATURE

VELOCEPRESS BOOKS – RACING

CARRERA PANAMERICANA - MEXICAN ROAD RACE (BOOK OF)
DIALED IN - THE JAN OPPERMAN STORY
IF HEMINGWAY HAD WRITTEN A RACING NOVEL
VEDA ORR'S NEW REVISED HOT ROD PICTORIAL

AUTOBOOKS WORKSHOP MANUALS & BROOKLANDS ROAD TEST PORTFOLIOS

FOR A COMPLETE LISTING OF THE AUTOBOOKS & BROOKLANDS TITLES THAT WE CURRENTLY HAVE AVAILABLE, PLEASE VISIT OUR WEBSITE.

www.VelocePress.com

www.ingramcontent.com/pod-product-compliance
Lightning Source LLC
Chambersburg PA
CBHW060252240426
43673CB00047B/1910